John Robinson and the English Separatist Tradition

National Association of Baptist Professors of Religion

JOURNAL

   Perspectives in Religious Studies
   Editor: Watson Mills
             Mercer University

SERIES

   Special Studies Series
   Editor: Watson Mills
             Mercer University

   Dissertation Series
   Editor: Charles Talbert
             Wake Forest University

   Bibliographic Series
   Editor: E. Glenn Hinson
             Southern Baptist Theological Seminary

JOHN ROBINSON
AND THE
ENGLISH SEPARATIST TRADITION

NABPR Dissertation Series, Number 1

by
Timothy George

MERCER UNIVERSITY PRESS, Macon, Georgia 31207

ISBN 0-86554-043-8

All books published by Mercer University Press are produced
on acid-free paper that exceeds the minimum standards set by the
National Historical Publications and Records Commission.

Library of Congress Cataloging in Publication Data

George, Timothy.
    John Robinson and the English separatist tradition.

    (NABPR dissertation series ; no. 1)
    Originally presented as the author's thesis (D. D.)—Harvard
Divinity School.
    Bibliography: p. 249
    Includes index.
    1. Robinson, John, 1575?-1625.   2. Theology,
Doctrinal—England—History—17th century.
3. Separatists—History—17th century.   4. Theology,
Puritan—England—History—17th century.
I. Title.   II. Series.
BX9339.R55G46   1982   285'.9'0924   82-14201
ISBN 0-86554-043-8

TABLE OF CONTENTS

PREFACE

Until very recently John Robinson has been the object of what might well be called "affectionate obscurity." Celebrated as the pastor of the Pilgrims and the precursor of a host of modern-sounding -isms, he is invariably thought of in connection with the (perhaps apocryphal) quotation: "The Lord hath yet more truth and light to break forth out of His Holy Word." Yet, despite this acclaim, Robinson has been seldom read and only inadequately studied. In the fifty years following the appearance of the Burgess and Powicke biographies (1920), and the attendant flurry of interest generated by the Pilgrim Fathers' Tercentenary Celebration, no full-length study and only a couple of articles worthy of note have been devoted to the man whose "undying spirit" and "broadly tolerant mind" are extolled on the memorial plaque inside the great Pieterskerk in Leiden. This study was undertaken with the belief that a careful reading of Robinson's works would yield a more accurate assessment of his significance as a leading exponent of English Separatism.

In part, the neglect of Robinson can be attributed to the fact that his writings lie buried in rare book rooms of select libraries, save for the edition collected by Robert Ashton in 1851 at the behest of the Congregational Union of England and Wales. While the Ashton edition has served its readers well, the time is long overdue for a modern critical edition of Robinson's works, chronologically arranged and including his writings which have since come to light. The facsimile reprint of Robinson's *Justification* (1977) is a welcome addition to The English Experience series published by Walter Johnson, Inc. In this study, I have used the first edition seventeenth-century imprints, where available, and have preserved the original spelling and punctuation.

The purpose of this study is to examine in the writings of Robinson that interpretation of the gospel and doctrine of the Church which characterized the early Separatist experience. The underlying thesis is that the Separatist phenomenon was not merely the most radicalized form of Puritan protest against the Church of England, but also a distinctive quest for a new sense of Christian community at odds on crucial points with both Anglican and Puritan models. This is not to deny

that Separatists were also Puritans in the larger sense, nor that there were
wide areas of agreement and, in the case of Robinson, even a measure of
Christian fellowship between the Separatists and their brethren who
remained loyal to, if not enthusiastic about, the national Church. However, as Richard Condon has written, "A nuance in an ideological difference is a wide chasm."[1] The Separatists themselves felt that the *differentia*
which gave them a distinctive identity within the ever-widening spectrum
of late Elizabethan-early Jacobean nonconformity were worth defending
in large tomes, and worth as well the forfeit of their careers, families, and
sometimes their lives. I have felt that they are at least worth talking about.

Robinson is a particularly interesting figure by which to gauge Separatist churchmanship and theology. His life (1575-1625) spanned the
crucial years of the Elizabethan Puritan movement, and early Stuart
attempts to deal with religious radicalism. He and King James died in the
same year. As a second-generation Separatist, Robinson inherited an
already well-defined concept of the church. The tension between this
sectarian ecclesiology on the one hand and a high predestinarian theology
on the other is the controlling dynamic in his thought. If it seems that I
have given an inordinate amount of attention to Robinson's theology,
especially to his doctrine of election, this is because that aspect of his
thought has been almost completely ignored in previous studies, and also
because his ecclesiology can only be fully understood when placed in the
context of soteriology.

This study was originally presented as a doctoral dissertation to the
faculty of Harvard Divinity School. I am pleased to acknowledge the
courtesies offered me at the research libraries I used while pursuing this
study: the Treasure Room of the Boston Public Library; the Congregational Library, Boston; the Pilgrim Hall Library, Plymouth, Mass.; the
British Museum and Dr. Williams' Library, London; the Bodleian
Library, Oxford; the Cambridge University Library; the Norfolk and
Norwich Record Office; the Pilgrim Fathers' Document Center, Leiden;
and last, but not least, the Widener, Houghton, and Andover Harvard
Libraries of Harvard.

To my teachers and friends I owe much more than a prefatory
acknowledgment can express: to Professor William J. Wright who first
awakened my interest in the Reformation; to Professors Donald S.
Klinefelter and Donald Weisbaker who taught me to think critically; to
Professor Peter J. Gomes who first directed my attention to John Robinson in his seminar on Tudor Puritanism; to Professors John E. Booty and

---

[1]Quoted, J. Sears McGee, *The Godly Man in Stuart England* (New Haven, 1976), 1.

Wallace T. MacCaffrey who offered valuable suggestions when this study was in its early stages; to Professor Heiko A. Oberman who has stimulated my interest in the doctrine of election and provided friendly and knowledgeable counsel; and, especially, to my mentor and thesis advisor, Professor George Huntston Williams who supervised this study with great kindness and concern and who has been a continuing inspiration during the entire course of my theological education.

I would also like to mention Dr. Stephen Brachlow who kindly provided me a copy of his unpublished Oxford dissertation, "Puritan Theology and Radical Churchmen in Pre-Revolutionary England, with special reference to Henry Jacob and John Robinson, and Principal B. R. White of Regent's Park College, who received me cordially and showed more than a passing interest in my work during a brief stay at Oxford.

To the congregation of the Metropolitan Baptist Church, Cambridge, Mass., which permitted me to serve as associate minister while pursuing advanced studies, and to the Southern Baptist Theological Seminary, Louisville, Ky., which made possible my study in England and allowed me to complete this thesis before assuming teaching responsibilities, I am deeply grateful.

Finally, the completion of this study would not have been possible without the able assistance of Denise Wyse George who typed both the original and revised manuscripts amidst her other responsibilities as wife, mother, and author. In this and in many other ways, she has supported this endeavor with extraordinary patience and grace.

Timothy George
Louisville, Kentucky
Advent, 1981

For Denise . . .
sine qua non

CHAPTER 1

INTRODUCTION:
THE STRUGGLE FOR
THE SEPARATIST PAST

In the year 1644, almost 20 years after the death of John Robinson his *A Just and Necessarie Apologie of Certain Christians no lesse contumeliously then commonlie called Brownists or Barowists* was republished in London, as the title page indicates, "for the speciall and common good of our own Countrimen." This edition of Robinson's *Apologie* followed the reissuance of his *magnum opus, A Justification of Separation from the Church of England* (1639), and two shorter pieces, *The Peoples Plea for the Exercise of Prophesie* (1641), and *New Essayes or Observations Divine and Moral* (1642).[1] Robinson's writings and those of other celebrated "Brownists" such as Henry Ainsworth[2] held an obvious appeal for those strict Separatists who not only refused intercommunion with the parish churches but also even declined to enter their church buildings because of the "idolatrous" services performed there.[3]

In the pre-Revolutionary years, however, the Separatist alternative, both in its rigid and moderate expressions, remained unacceptable to most Puritans committed as they were to the principle of a national Church uniformly reformed in liturgy and polity. Rather it was the

---

[1]T. G. Crippen, "Early Nonconformist Bibliography," *Transactions*, Congregational Historical Society, 1 (1901-1904), 106-07.

[2]Ainsworth's *Counterpoyson* was reprinted in 1642 followed by *A Seasonable Discourse* in 1644.

[3]David Brown, *Two Conferences between Some of those that are called Separatists and Independents concerning their different Tenets* (London, 1650): "That they made them Idols Temples, God branded them, and to this day, that brand is not taken off them, but remaineth still upon them: The blood of Christ hath not cleansed them, the brand is still upon them, as well as upon the Idols themselves to this day: Therefore as the Saints are to keep themselves from Idols, so are they to keep themselves from worshipping in Idols Temples, because the brand is upon them." Cf. Thomas Edwards, *Gangraena* (London, 1646), 79-80.

appearance of a new and complex pattern of Nonconformity, evidenced by the gathering of fully developed and completely autonomous congregations, which presaged the sectarian resurgence of the 1640s and threatened to unravel the well-laid plans of the Presbyterian divines in the Westminster Assembly. To gain a measure of respectability, and to fend off the inevitable charges of schism and sedition, the new "Congregational men" were careful to dissociate themselves from the older Separatist tradition. In a masterful but guarded statement of Independent principles, the five "Dissenting Brethren" of the Westminster Assembly[4] defined their position as a carefully chosen *via media*:

> . . . we believe the truth to lie and consist in a middle way betwixt that which is falsely charged on us, Brownism; and that which is the contention of these times, the authoritative Presbyterial Government in all the subordinations and proceedings of it.[5]

However, the Independents, for all their disclaimers, were indeed advocating and implementing a theory of church government of which the only relevant body of practice was that of the Separatists. Their opponents were quick to seize on the similarity between the two positions, and to revive the specter of Brownism which, so they argued, would surely open the floodgate to a host of other heresies. In support of this theory Presbyterian polemicist Thomas Edwards brought forth the case of Clement Wrighter:

> There is one Clement Wrighter in London, but anciently belonging to Worcester, sometimes a professor of religion, and judged to have been godly, who is now an arch heretic and fearful apostate, an old wolf, and a subtle man. . . . This man about 7 or 8 years ago, fell off from the communion of our churches, to Independency and Brownism, and was much taken with Mr. Robinson's books, as that of the Justification of Separation; from that he fell to Anabaptism and Arminianism, and to mortalism, holding the soul mortal. . . . After that he fell to be a Seeker, and is now an Antiscripturist, a Questionist and Sceptic, and I fear an Atheist.[6]

The Independents were thus forced to come to grips with the charge of Brownism, and to do so in historical terms. This implied a detailed reconstruction of Separatist history and a restatement of the relationship of Congregationalism to Separatism. The ensuing debate, almost denom-

---

[4]The five "Dissenting Brethren" were Thomas Goodwin, Philip Nye, Sidrach Simpson, Jeremiah Burroughes, and William Bridges. All of the brethren while exiled in Holland had held communion with the English churches in Arnheim and Rotterdam. See Berndt Gustafsson, *The Five Dissenting Brethren: A Study on the Dutch Background of their Independentism* (Lund, 1955).

[5]Thomas Goodwin et al., *An Apologeticall Narration* (London, 1643), 24.

[6]Edwards, *Gangraena,* op. cit., 81-82.

inational in tone, engaged two of the leading churchmen of the
seventeenth-century, Congregationalist John Cotton of New England
and Presbyterian Robert Baillie of Scotland.[7]

Baillie's chief task was to show that the Independents were, in fact,
children of their parents, the Brownists, and that Brownism was but "a
native branch of Anabaptism."[8] Against the claim "that Brownism had
sprung from the tenets of the old Unconformists," Baillie pronounced
Cartwright and his followers "very free from the unhappinesse of procreating this Bastard: That ill-fac'd childe will father itself; the Lineaments of Anabaptism are clear and distinct in the face of Brownism."[9]
The disputatious history of the Brownist sects was proof enough that
congregational polity was an unstable and unworkable church order.[10]
Further, through Master Robinson and his Plymouth offspring the error
of Independency had been transplanted to New England, and thence back
to Old England where it "hath been the fountain of many evils already."[11]

The Independents could not well allow such a challenge to pass
unanswered, and Cotton's rejoinder, *The Way of Congregational
Churches Cleared* (1648), attempted a point-by-point refutation. After
rehearsing the highlights of Separatist history and questioning the factual
basis of Baillie's account,[12] Cotton denied any genetic relationship

---

[7]Cotton was the most eminent Puritan divine of New England, a close friend of the
Dissenting Brethren, and a proven advocate of the Congregational way. Baillie was a
professor of divinity at Glasgow and one of the five Scottish commissioners who were
members of the Westminster Assembly. See article in *Dictionary of National Biography*,
1, 892-94 [hereafter, *D.N.B.*] and two recent studies: Larzer Ziff, *The Career of John
Cotton* (Princeton, N.J., 1962), 170-203, and F. N. McCoy, *Robert Baillie and the Second
Scots Reformation* (London, 1974), 94-138.

[8]Robert Baillie, *A Dissuasive from the Errours of the Time* (London, 1645), 13.

[9]Ibid., 12.

[10]Ibid., 214: "Our Argument is backed by experience, as well as by reason; The first
Independent Church we reade of, was that company which Mr. Browne brought over
from England to Middleborough; how long did it stand before it was destroyed by
Independency? when once Anabaptistick novelties, and other mischiefes fell among them,
there was no remedy to prevent the companies dissolution. When Mr. Barrow and his
fellowes, assaied at London to erect their Congregation, the successe was no better; their
ship scarce well set out was quickly split upon the Rocks, was soone dissipate and
vanished. When Johnstoun and Ainsworth would make the third assay, and try if that tree
which neither in England nor Zealand could take roote, might thrive in Holland at
Amsterdam, where plants of all sorts are so cherished, that few of the most maligne qualite
doe miscarry, yet so singular a malignity is innate in that seede of Independency, that in
that very ground, where all weedes grow ranke, it did wither."

[11]Ibid., 17.

[12]For example, Cotton denies any "correspondency" between German Anabaptism
and English Brownism; he points to a Separatist congregation in 1567 "many years before

between his Congregationalism and that of the Brownists: "That the
Separatists were our fathers, we have justly denied it ... seeing they neither
begat us to God, nor to the church, nor to their schism."[13] Far from
imitating the Separatist practice of Leyden or Plymouth, the New England way was inspired by godly divines such as Robert Parker, Paul
Baynes, and William Ames.[14] Indeed, "the way of Independency hath
been bred in the womb of the New Testament of the immortal seed of the
word of truth, and received in the times of purest primitive antiquity,
many hundreds of years before Mr. Robinson was born."[15]

In the same year that Cotton's *Way* appeared, Governor William
Bradford of Plymouth was writing a dialogue between "Som Younge men
borne in New England and sundery Ancient men that came out of holland
and old England."[16] This document, almost catechetical in form, was
evidently intended to communicate the fundamentals of the Separatist
position to youthful inquirers removed by an ocean and a full generation
from the Leyden of John Robinson. Informed by the exchange between
Baillie and Cotton, it offered an interpretation of Separatist history at
odds with both of those recently published accounts. It contained, for
example, the rudiments of a Separatist martyrology[17] and a panegyrical

Bolton," whom Baillie had designated the first Separatist; he claims that Barrow was
executed at Tyburn, not Tower-hill, and without the acquiesence of Queen Elizabeth.
John Cotton, *The Way of Congregational Churches Cleared*, edited by Larzer Ziff in
John Cotton on the Churches of New England (Cambridge, Mass., 1968), 176-80.

[13]Ibid., 189.

[14]Cotton's account of the origins of "non-separating Congregationalism" was revived
by Champlain Burrage, *The Early English Dissenters in the Light of Recent Research*
(New York, 1912) [hereafter *Early English Dissenters*] and given classic exposition by
Perry Miller, *Orthodoxy in Massachusetts* (Cambridge, Mass., 1933). Francis Higginson,
in a famous statement, distinguished the New England way from the Separatist program:
"We will not say, as the separatists were wont to say at their leaving of England, Farewel
Babylon! farewel Rome! but we will say, farewel dear England! farewel the Church of God
in England, and all the christian friends there! We do not go to New England as separatists
from the Church of England; though we cannot but separate from the corruptions in it:
but we go to practice the postive part of church reformation, and propagate the gospel in
America." Cotton Mather, *Magnalia Christi Americana* (Hartford, Conn., 1820), 1, 328.

[15]Cotton, op. cit., 184.

[16]*Plymouth Church Records, 1620-1859*, 1 (New York, 1920), 115-41. The Dialogue
was earlier printed in *Chronicles of the Pilgrim Fathers of the Colony of Plymouth*, ed.
Alexander Young (Boston, 1841), 414-58.

[17]In his preface to the *Dialogue* Nathaniel Morton refers to Bradford's "defence of
such as I may without Just offence tearme martires of Jesus," ibid., 114. Perhaps Bradford
recalled the preface to the Separatist Confession of 1596: "Our God (wee trust) will one
day rayse up an other John Foxe, to gather and compile the Actes and Monuments of his
later Martyrs, for the vew of posteritie, tho yet they seem to bee buryed in oblivion, and
sleep in the dust," *The Creeds and Platforms of Congregationalism*, ed. Williston Walker
(Boston, 1893), 52 [hereafter *Creeds and Platforms*].

review of other Separatist notables including Francis Johnson, Ainsworth, and Robinson. Most important it sought to shake off "the Nick Name of Brownests,"[18] and to anchor the Separatist way more firmly in the experience of the English Reformation.

Thus, in defending Barrow and Greenwood, and implicitly themselves, against the charge of following the teaching of an apostate, i.e. Browne, the ancient men assert:

> They Can noe more Justly be Called Brownists then the desiples might have bin Called Judasitts for they did as much abhor Brownes Apostacye and prophane Course and his defection as the disciples and other Christians did Judas Treachery.[19]

To further dispel the notion that Separatism was a recently imported heresy or a novel invention of late Elizabethan origin, the young men are made to ask: "Was that Browne that fell away and Made Apostacye the first Inventor and beginer of this waye?" To which their elders reply:

> Noe verily for as one answares this question very well in a printed book almost forty yeers agoe; that the prophetts apostles and evangelests have in theire Authentick writings layed downe the Ground therof; and upon that Ground is theire building Reared up and surely settled moreover many of the Martires both former and latter have Maintained it as is to be seen in the acts and Monuments of the Church; alsoe in the dayes of Queen Elizabeth there was a Separated Church wherof mr fitts was Pastour; and another before that in the time of Queen Mary of which mr Rough was Pastour or Teacher and Cudbert Simson a deacon whoe exercised amongst themselves as other ordinances soe Church sensures as excommunication, etc: and professed and practised that Cause before mr Browne wrote for it.[20]

Bradford thus claimed for the Separatists a pedigree no less impressive than that which the Presbyterians and Congregationalists claimed for themselves: they were heirs of the church order established by Christ himself, confirmed by the apostles and martyrs, and set forth with clarity in the pages of the New Testament. Moreover, in the dark days of Queen Mary, and again under the harsh regiment of Elizabethan prelates, Separatist congregations had flourished in the midst of persecution. From these clandestine congregations had come the "latter martyrs" referred to earlier in the *Dialogue.*

Four years later, when Bradford composed his *Third Dialogue,* he attempted, with the aid of the Magdeburg Centuriators, to describe in more detail the extent of the darkness which had befallen the Church after

---

[18]*Plymouth Church Records*, 1, 114.

[19]Ibid., 124.

[20]Ibid., 132-33. The "printed book" referred to at the beginning of the answer is Miles Micklebound's *Mr. Henry Barrowe's Platform* (London, 1611), sig. I 7 verso.

the apostolic age, thereby accentuating the importance of the Separatist recovery of the true New Testament pattern. The young men are admonished not to neglect the history of that recovery lest they forfeit the "blessed fruits" of this divine deliverance.

> We have the rather noted these things, that you may see the worth of these things, and not necligently loose what your fathers have obtained with so much hardshipe; but maintaine these priviledges which not man, but the Lord Jesus, the King of the Church, hath purchased for you. You see how when they were lost in the former ages, both what evill and miserie followed therupon, and how longe and with what difficulty it was, before they could in any purity be recovered againe .... It hath cost much blood and sweat in the recoverie; and will doe no lesse care and pains in the keeping of them.[21]

The Bradford *Dialogues*, together with the exchange between Baillie and Cotton, comprise a significant chapter in the historiography of English Separatism. Each writer recalled and recast the Separatist story with an eye to his own partisan objective—Baillie, to discredit the new Nonconformists; Cotton, to demonstrate the non-sectarian character of Congregationalism; Bradford, to defend the provenance and authenticity of the Plymouth way. Here we are at the fountainhead of denominational history with its emphasis on linear developments and genetic connections. With the emergence of institutionally distinct dissenting churches the concern for denominational genealogy increased, and the history of the Separatists' breach with the established church became the usual prolegomenon to the rise of Nonconformity proper. Thus, Daniel Neal, a product of one of the first dissenting academies, undertook his five-volume history of Nonconformity in order "to account for the rise and progress of that separation from the national establishment which subsists to this day."[22] In the nineteenth century this tradition of pious scholarship was sustained by Benjamin Hanbury whose *Historical Memorials* brought to light many relevant documents concerning the Separatists, "our predecessors—our Fathers and Confessors," and by Henry Martyn Dexter whose bibliography of 7,250 items is still a standard critical tool in the field.[23] Even Albert Peel who, with Champlain Burrage, has contributed more to our knowledge of early Dissent than any

[21]William Bradford, *A Dialogue or 3rd Conference*, in *Proceedings of the Massachusetts Historical Society*, 11 (Boston, 1870), 463.

[22]Daniel Neal, *The History of the Puritans, or Protestant Non-Conformists*, 1 (London, 1731), 3.

[23]Benjamin Hanbury, *Historical Memorials Relating to the Independents or Congregationalists*, 1 (London, 1839), preface. Henry Martyn Dexter, *The Congregationalism of the Last Three Hundred Years As Seen in Its Literature* (New York, 1880) [hereafter *Congregationalism*].

other twentieth-century historian, did not entirely abandon that tradition of hagiography and martyrology already evident in Bradford.[24]

More recently, the limitations of denominational history have been recognized, even by those who are among its most able practitioners,[25] and the linear approach to early Separatist history has come under fire from two of the leading historians of English Puritanism. Christopher Hill bluntly evaluates the method which has characterized so much painstaking research: "There seems to me sometimes to be as much fiction and unwarranted assumption—and sheer waste of time—in tracing the genealogy of sects as of individuals."[26] Patrick Collinson, while more appreciative of the gains registered by historians of Separatism, regards the chronological approach as unduly restrictive and argues for new investigations into the "horizontal and lateral relationships" of the early Dissenters.[27] Both of these opinions should give pause to the historian who sets out to review the question of Separatist origins. He must not impose the outlines of later denominational developments onto the early Separatist conventicles, nor must he make too sharp a distinction between Separatist and advanced Puritan for the period when such labels were still imprecise and sometimes interchangeable. He will recognize that Separatism, in its most organized and articulate form, hardly, if ever, achieved the status of a "movement," and that what success it did obtain was usually dissipated by a recurring fratricidal impulse.

However, taking into account questions of context and perspective, there is the further issue of the Separatists' understanding of their own past. Bradford's *Dialogues* offered not merely a factual reconstruction of Separatist history, but a theological interpretation of that history, an

---

[24]Albert Peel, *The Noble Army of Congregational Martyrs* (London, 1951); *The Congregational Two Hundred, 1530-1940* (London, 1948).

[25]See the following articles in *Baptist Quarterly*: E. G. Rupp, "The Importance of Denominational History," 17 (1957-58), 312-19; Christopher Hill, "History and Denominational History," 22 (1967-68), 65-71; B. R. White, "The Task of a Baptist Historian," ibid., 398-408.

[26]Christopher Hill, *Economic Problems of the Church* (London, 1956), xii.

[27]Patrick Collinson, "Towards a Broader Understanding of the Early Dissenting Tradition," in *The Dissenting Tradition: Essays for Leland H. Carlson*, eds. C. Robert Cole and Michael E. Moody (Athens, Ohio, 1975), 3. In this perceptive essay Collinson urges that scholarly attention be transferred "from the separatist to the non-separatist tradition of Dissent." In fact, recent focus on non-separatist figures such as Ames, Henry Jacob, and Thomas Hooker seems to have followed just this course. The only recent monograph on Elizabethan Separatism is B. R. White, *The English Separatist Tradition* (London, 1971) [hereafter, *Separatist Tradition*], a study Collinson assigns to the "established historical school" of Burrage and Peel, ibid., 5.

interpretation which reflected a distinctive sense of mission and calling. The Separatists saw themselves not as observers, but as participants in the cosmic struggle between Christ and Satan, called upon to play a vital role in the "breaking out of the light of the gospel in our honourable nation of England."[28] In their scattered congregations the churches of God had at last recovered their ancient purity and their primitive order, liberty, and beauty. If the tangled history of their disputes and schisms, as exposed by Baillie and Cotton, seemed to belie this ideal, then these disruptions must be explained as the strategems of Satan and the way of separation must be shown to have preceded these latter troubles. For Bradford this implied a re-reading of the seminal events of the English Reformation in order to offer a plausible account of "the very root and rise" of that enterprise which had led them into "those remote parts of the world . . . as stepping-stones unto others for the performing of so great a work."[29]

[28]William Bradford, *Of Plymouth Plantation*, ed. Samuel Eliot Morison (New York, 1952), 3.

[29]Ibid., 25.

CHAPTER 2

THE ENGLISH SEPARATIST TRADITION

"Much of the Separatists history is yet in the darke and in prison, it were good that all were wrought to the light and the free air."[1]

PRE-ELIZABETHAN PRECEDENTS

On December 30, 1547, Henry VIII affixed his signature to his last will and testament commending his soul to "the glorious and blessed Virgin our Lady Sainct Mary, and all the Holy Company of Heaven," and requiring that masses be said for his soul "while the world shall endure."[2] By this act he demonstrated in death, as he had so often in life, that his true religious sentiments were those of a good and orthodox Catholic. But, with his soul committed to celestial safekeeping, Henry proceeded in the royal will to commit his Kingdom to young Edward, whose upbringing had been supervised by the most Protestant of the king's consorts, Katharine Parr, and to a Council of Regency dominated by Edward Seymour, Earl of Hertford, soon to become Duke of Somerset and Protector of the realm.[3] Thus, the stage was set for the official Protestantizing of England, held in check heretofore by the cautious conservatism of Henry and most of his bishops.

The new religious policy of Somerset and Archbishop Cranmer soon found expression in the famous act of the first Edwardian Parliament,

---

[1]Robert Baillie, *The Dissuasive from the Errours of the Time Vindicated* (1655), 13.

[2]"Testamentum Regis Heinrici Octavi," Thomas Rymer, *Foedera* (London, 1713), vol. 15, 110-16. There is some doubt as to whether the will was signed on December 30 or a few hours before Henry's death on January 27, 1548. See Lacey B. Smith, "The last will and testament of Henry VIII: a question of perspective," *Journal of British Studies* 2 (1962), 18-19.

[3]*Acts of the Privy Council of England*, ed. J. R. Dasent. New series, 2 (1547-1550), 34-35.

For the repeal of certain statutes concerning treason, felonies, etc. (I Edward VI, c.12) which effectively repealed the medieval laws against heresy, such as the writ *De haeretico comburendo*, as well as the *Act of Six Articles* (1539).[4] In addition, an act of general pardon was extended to all of those who had been guilty of religious offences in the previous reign.[5] Stephen Gardiner, whose own position had become more untenable with each move away from the Henrician status quo, expressed grave concern in a letter to Cranmer: "The wall of authority, which I accounted established in our last agreement, be once broken, and new water let in at a little gap, the vehemence of novelty will flow further than your Grace would admit."[6] Somerset and Cranmer, determined to proceed "by slow and safe degrees, not hazarding too much at once,"[7] soon came to appreciate the significance of Gardiner's warning as militant Protestant propaganda gave way to overt and violent action.

Much of the advanced Protestant activity was centered in London, but it is in Kent and Essex, at Bocking and Faversham, that we encounter those conventiclers who, in the oft-quoted words of John Strype, "were the first that made separation from the reformed Church of England."[8] Apart from Strype relevant documents concerning this obscure sect, in the form of depositions, have been preserved in the Harleian Collection in the British Museum and printed, along with extracts from the "Privy Council Register," by R. W. Dixon and Burrage.[9] From these we learn that the congregations, which originally met separately, had merged under the threat of persecution and that they numbered more than 60 in their assembly when they were discovered by the authorities and their leaders arrested.[10]

---

[4]W. K. Jordan, *Edward VI: The Young King* (Cambridge, Mass., 1968), 167-81.

[5]*The Statutes of the Realm*, eds. Alex Luders, *et al.*, (London, 1810-1815), vol. 4, 33-35.

[6]*The Letters of Stephen Gardiner*, ed. J. A. Muller (Cambridge, 1933), 299.

[7]Gilbert Burnet, *The history of the reformation of the Church of England*, ed. Nicholas Pocock (Oxford, 1865), vol. 2, 70-71.

[8]Strype, *Ecclesiastical Memorials* (Oxford, 1822), vol. 2, i, 369.

[9]British Museum, MS. Harleian 421, ff. 133-34; R. W. Dixon, *History of the Church of England* (London, 1885), vol. 3, 206-11; *Early English Dissenters*, vol. 2, 1-6.

[10]Ibid., 4. According to Strype the depositions were taken "about 1550." The extracts from the "Privy Council Register" are related to the year 1551. The Register furnishes the details of the arrest which occurred one Sunday at twelve o'clock in Bocking. The group had met at the house of one Upcharde to discuss the proper posture at prayer—whether they should stand or kneel, wear hats or pray bareheaded—when they were discovered. Before the Privy Council one of the conventiclers admitted that he had refused the communion of the Church of England for more than two years.

To place these Kentish sectaries within the larger context of religious dissent in Edwardian England is a task which has defied historical consensus. Apparently Gilbert Burnet was the first to identify the group as Anabaptist, a designation accepted by Strype and recently revived by Irvin Horst.[11] Dixon described them as "the first separatists or dissenters of England,"[12] M. M. Knappen as "halfway Anabaptists,"[13] while Burrage, despairing of precision, suggested that "they were merely Nonconformists of a rather peculiar type."[14] In fact, there is no evidence that they shared either the Melchiorite Christology of English Anabaptists such as Joan Boucher or the anti-Trinitarian views of George van Parris. Their overriding doctrinal concern seems to have been a strident rejection of predestinarian theology, hence Miles Coverdale's reference to them as "freewill men."[15] One of their company, Cole of Faversham, was reported to have said "that the doctryne of predestynation was meter for divelles then for christian men," while another, Henry Harte, claimed that "ther is no man so chosen or predestynate, but that he maye if he will kepe the commandementes and be salvid."[16] Harte managed to avoid arrest when the group was first apprehended, but was imprisoned under Mary in 1554 and detained in the King's Bench. There he continued his advocacy of a free-will theology and engaged his fellow-prisoner, John Bradford, in serious debate over the doctrine of election.[17] Three other "kenttishemen" of the Bocking conventicle, Humphrey Middleton, Nicholas Sheterden, and Cuthbert Sympson would be among the Marian martyrs immortalized by Foxe.[18] Middleton and Sheterden were burned at Canterbury in

---

[11]Irvin B. Horst, *The Radical Brethren: Anabaptism and the English Reformation to 1558* (The Hague, 1972), 134.

[12]Dixon, op. cit., vol. 3, 207.

[13]M. M. Knappen, *Tudor Puritanism: A Chapter in the History of Idealism* (Chicago, 1939), 149.

[14]*Early English Dissenters*, vol. 1, 53.

[15]*The Writings of John Bradford*, ed. A. Townshend (Cambridge, 1848-1853), vol. 2, 170.

[16]*Early English Dissenters*, vol. 2, 1-2.

[17]See O. T. Hargrave, "The Freewillers in the English Reformation." *Church History* 37 (1968), 271-80. Hargrave treats the sectaries of Kent and Essex as precursors of an indigenous English reaction against a high predestinarian theology, a group that "anticipated by almost a half-century the anti-predestinarian writings of the Dutch theologian Jacob Arminius." For two recent reviews of Harte's career, see Horst, op. cit., 122-36, and J. W. Martin, "English Protestant Separatism at its Beginnings: Henry Hart and the Free-Will Men," *Sixteenth Century Journal* 7 (1976), 55-74.

[18]*Actes and Monuments of the English Martyrs by John Foxe*, ed. George Townsend (London, 1837-41), vol. 7, 306-18 [hereafter *Foxe*].

July, 1555, but Sympson, before going to the stake in 1558, served as deacon of the London underground church thereby providing a personal link between the Kentish conventicle and the more famous proto-Separatist congregation.

While the Kentish conventiclers were not accused of Anabaptism, the government under Somerset did take measures to offset the spread of radical ideas, disseminated by the influx of émigrés from the Continent. In January, 1551, a commission headed by Cranmer was authorized to search out all "Anabaptists and Libertines" so that the purity of religion might be preserved.[19] More positively, official sanction was given to a number of refugee congregations of which the most important was the famous Strangers' Church of London organized under the superintendence of Jan Laski.[20] Although intended to counterbalance the influence of Anabaptist activity,[21] Laski, at least, believed that the Strangers' Church was also meant to serve as a model for further reformation of the English Church itself. In the prefatory epistle of the 1555 edition of his *Forma ac Ratio*, dedicated to King Sigismund of Poland, Laski noted that King Edward desired the strangers to observe all things in their churches according to apostolic practice so that the English churches might be inspired to follow suit.[22]

---

[19]Rymer, *Foedera*, vol. 15, 251. Other members of the commission included Hugh Latimer, Miles Coverdale, Nicholas Ridley, and William Cecil.

[20]The standard study of the Strangers' Church remains the three-volume work by Baron F. de Schickler, *Les Eglises du Refuge en Angleterre*, (Paris, 1892). Also see J. Lindeboom, *Austin Friars: History of the Dutch Reformed Church in London, 1550-1950* (The Hague, 1950); Frederick A. Norwood, *Strangers and Exiles: A History of Religious Refugees* (Nashville, 1969); Phillipe Denis, *Les Eglises d'etrangers à Londres jusqu'à la mort de Calvin: de l'Eglise de Jean Lasco à l'etablissement du calvinisme*, Mémoire de licence, Université de Liège (1973).

[21]King Edward noted this motive for the Strangers' Church in his journal: "It was appointed that the Germans should have the Austin Friars for their church to have their service in, for avoiding of all sects of Anabaptists and suchlike," *The Chronicle and Political Papers of King Edward VI*, ed. W. K. Jordan (London, 1966), 37. Martin Micronius, Flemish reformer and first minister of the Dutch congregation, expressed the same concern in a letter to Henry Bullinger: "Master John a lasco arrived in England on the 13th of May. His coming was greatly to the delight of all godly persons. He has determined to remain in London, and establish a German church, of which he is appointed the superintendent. And indeed it is a matter of the first importance that the word of God should be preached here in German, to guard against the heresies which are introduced by our countrymen. There are Arians, Marcionists, Libertines, Danists, and the like monstrosities, in great numbers," *Original Letters Relative to the English Reformation*, ed. Hastings Robinson (Cambridge, 1847), vol. 2, 560 [hereafter *Original Letters*].

[22]"Peregrinis vero hominibus, qui patriis hac alioqui in parte legibus non usque adeo tenerentur, Ecclesiae concederentur, in quibus omnia libere et nulla rituum patriorum

The charter which constituted the superintendent and ministers of the Strangers' Church as *unum corpus corporatum et politicum* and specified the Augustinian friary as their place of worship also granted a measure of autonomy truly remarkable in sixteenth-century England.

> We order, and firmly enjoining, command as well the Mayor, Sheriffs and Aldermen of our City of London, the Bishop of London and his successors, with all other our Archbishops, Bishops, Judges, Officers and Ministers whomsoever, that they permit the aforesaid superintendent and ministers and their successors freely and quietly to practise, enjoy, use and exercise their own the rites, and ceremonies and their own peculiar ecclesiastical discipline, notwithstanding that they do not conform with the rites and ceremonies used in our Kingdom, without impeachment, disturbance or vexation of them or any of them; any statute, act, proclamation, injunction, restriction or use to the contrary thereof, heretofore had, made, published or promulgated, to the contrary notwithstanding.[23]

This document, in effect, granted immunity from the 1549 Act of Uniformity and established the Strangers' Church as an independent ecclesiastical enclave, outside the episcopal chain of command, responsible only to the King and his Council. Nicholas Ridley, as Bishop of London, was openly hostile to the idea[24] and at least one bishop, Goodrick of Ely, attempted to require the strangers in his diocese to communicate in the English parishes upon threat of imprisonment.[25] Laski, by an appeal to

---

habita ratione, iuxta doctrinam duntaxat atque observationem Apostolicam instituerentur; ita enim fore, ut Anglicae quoque Ecclesiae ad puritatem Apostolicam amplectendam unanimi omnium regni ordinum consensu excitarentur," *Joannis a Lasco Opera tam edita quam inedita*, ed. A. Kuyper (Amsterdam, 1866), vol. 2, 10.

[23]"Mandamus et firmiter iniungendum precipimus tam/Maiori Vicecomitibus et Aldermannis Civitatis nostre Londoniensis Episcopo Londiniensi et successoribus suis cum omnibus aliis Archiepiscopis Episcopis Justicarijs Officiarijs et Ministris nostris quibuscumque quod permittant prefatis Superintendenti/et Ministris et sua suos libere et quiete frui gaudere uti et exercere ritus et ceremonias suas proprias et disciplinam ecclesiasticam propriam et peculiarem non obstante quod non conveniant cum ritibus et ceremonijs in Regno nostro/usitatis absque impeticione perturbacione aut inquietacione eorum vel eorum alicuius Aliquo statuto actu proclamacione iniuncione restriccione seu usu incontrarium inde antehac habitis factiseditis seu promulgatio incontrarium non obstantibus Eo," Rymer, *Foedera*, op. cit., "De Fundatione Templi in Civitate London pro Germanis," vol. 15, 243-44.

[24]J. C. Ridley, *Nicholas Ridley: A Biography* (London, 1957), 232-35; Micronius' letter to Bullinger, August 31, 1550: "All this mischief is stirred up against us by the bishops, and especially by the bishop of London, who does us the more harm, in proportion as he seems more actively to support the word of God." *Original Letters*, vol. 2, 569.

[25]Joannes a Lasco, *Opera*, op. cit., vol. 2, 672: "Rursum perturbantur quidam e nostra ecclesia tam in maiore, quam in minore Sudwerk, vir clarissime! et carceres illis intentantur, nisi ad suas paroecias veniant."

Cecil, was able to secure relief from this pressure and protection against further harassment.[26]

The polity of the Strangers' Church, as drawn up by Laski, was based upon the Reformed examples of Geneva and Strasbourg, but in practice it tended toward the principle of a gathered church.[27] For example, membership was not extended to all foreigners in London, but only to those who publicly embraced the confession of faith and committed themselves to a particular congregation. In line with this policy, the Strangers' Church declined to practice the indiscriminate baptism of infants:

> Yet not all strangers join themselves to our churches;—indeed there are many who while they turn away and avoid all churches, will pretend to the English churches that they are joined to us, and to us that they are joined to the English churches; and so do abuse both them and us,—we, lest the English churches and their ministers be deceived by the imposture of such men, and that under the color of our churches, do baptize only the infants of those who have joined themselves to our churches by public confession of their faith and observation of ecclesiastical discipline.[28]

The refusal to baptize the infants of non-members would characterize Separatist sacramental procedure, and at least one Separatist, some eighty years later, recalled the example of Laski's congregations as a precedent for this practice.[29]

Valérand Poullain, superintendent of the Strangers' Church at Glastonbury, drew up his own confession, independently of Laski, and applied an even stricter test for membership.[30] Candidates were required to

---

[26]Ibid., Strype, *Memorials of Archbishop Cranmer*, vol. 1, 341.

[27]Joannes a Lasco, *Opera*, op. cit., vol. 2, 50.

[28]Ibid., vol. 2, 105-06: "Et non omnes interim peregrini nostris sese Ecclesiis adiungant,—imo vero multi sint, qui dum omnes Ecclesias aversantur ac refugiunt, apud Anglicas Ecclesias nobis, apud nos vero Anglicis se Ecclesiis adiunctos esse fingunt, atque ita et Anglicis et nostris pariter Ecclesiis imponunt,—nos, ne Anglicae Ecclesiae earumque Ministri imposturis eorum duntaxat infantes baptizamus, qui sese nostris Ecclesiis per publicam fidei confessionem disciplinaeque Ecclesiasticae obervationem ediunxerunt."

[29]John Ball, *A Tryall of the New-Church Way in New-England and in Old* (London, 1644), 56: "That our practise may not be censured as novell and singular, give us leave to produce a President of the like care observed and approved by publick countenance of State in the dayes of Edward 6 of blessed and famous memory, who in the yeare 1550, granted Johannes Alasco a learned Noble man of Poland under the great Seale of England, libertie to gather a Church of strangers in London, and to order themselves according as they should finde to be most agreeable to the Scriptures."

[30]On the Glastonbury congregation see *State Papers Domestic*, Edward VI, vol. 13, 70; Strype, *Cranmer*, op. cit., vol. 2, 286; Henry J. Cowell, "The French-Walloon Church at Glastonbury, 1550-1553," *The Proceedings of the Huguenot Society of London* 13 (1928), 483-515; Schickler, op. cit., vol. 1, 59-68.

present themselves on Sunday after the sermon, recite from memory the entire confession, and reply to questions from the minister and elders. Poullain further insisted, to the great displeasure of Calvin, that even candidates who had belonged to Reformed congregations elsewhere submit themselves to his confession. For Poullain the confession seems to have functioned much as the covenant in later Separatist congregations, a fact which prompted his biographer to label him "ein Vorläufer des kirchlichen Independentismus."[31]

The Strangers' Church, as reconstituted under Elizabeth, was grafted into the ecclesiastical hierarchy, the office of superintendent being assumed by the Bishop of London.[32] A relationship between the London strangers and the developing Puritan party is suggested by the fact that letters of Theodore Beza were "very frequently" forwarded through the French congregation.[33] The strangers, however, aware of their precarious status, were more reluctant to befriend those who took the more radical step of separation. On one occasion, having been warned in a letter from the Privy Council not to receive any who "leave and abandon the rites of their native country and join themselves with you," the ministers and elders of the Dutch church promptly promised that they would welcome "no Englishmen who, moved by such principles, seek to separate themselves from their own country customs."[34] While there seems to have been

---

[31]Karl Bauer, *Valérand Poullain*, (Elberfeld, 1927), 150: "In dieser Selbständigkeit der Gemeinde Glastonbury liegt ihre prinzipielle Bedeutung für die Kirchengeschichte. Hier haben wir, lange vor Brown, Smith, und Robinson und ohne täuferische Einflüsse... auf englischen Boden ein Beispiel dessen, was man später als Kongregationalismus und Independentismus zu bezichen pflegte, jene Atomisierung der Kirche, bei der die einzelne Gemeinde ihr Sonderdasein für sich führt und kein Bedürfnis nach einem Zusammenschluss mit anderen Gemeinden zu einen grösseren Bekenntnis—und verfassungsmässig verbunden Ganzen empfindet."

[32]*Actes du Consistoire de l'Eglise Française de Threadneedle Street*, Londres, ed. Elsie Johnston (London, 1937), vol.1, xiv, Huguenot Society, Q. S. 38; Lindeboom, op. cit., 29-34.

[33]Percival Wiburn to Henry Bullinger, February 25, 1567, *Zurich Letters*, ed. Hastings Robinson (Cambridge, 1842), vol. 1, 190 [hereafter, *Zurich Letters*]. See the suggestive article of Patrick Collinson, "The Elizabethan Puritans and the Foreign Reformed Churches in London," *The Proceedings of the Huguenot Society of London* 20 (1963), 528-55.

[34]Letter of Privy Council to Dutch Church, Oct. 22, 1573: "Sive sint qui curiositate ac levitate animi moti, patriae ritus deserere, et vestris se adscribere velint, non recipiendos esse censemus a vobis, ne id contentionem dissensionemque possit creare, tam incommodam nobis, et vobis tam damnosam," *Ecclesiae Londino—Batavae Archivum*, ed. J. H. Hessels (Cambridge, 1889), vol. 2, no. 127, 456-59. The reply of Dutch church, dated Nov. 6, 1573, ibid., no. 130, 482-85: "... neque recipiemus Anglos, qui tali animo patrios ritus deserentes nostris volent adscribi. ..." See also Strype, *Annals of the Reformation* (Oxford, 1824), vol. 2, ii, 517-21.

little, if any, cross-fertilization between the foreign churches and early
Separatist efforts, the very existence of quasi-independent congregations,
with their own liturgy and discipline, was itself a source of envy on the
part of some who found the pace of reformation in the established Church
intolerably slow. One such malcontent, a London incumbent suspended
in 1565 for not wearing vestments, wrote with a tinge of xenophobia:

> It semethe ryghtfull that subiects naturall receve soe much favoure as the
> churches of natyonall straungers have here with us. But we can not once be
> harde soe to obtayne. Thys with them: they an eldershippe; we none. They
> frely electe the doctor and pastor; we maye not. They their deacons and
> churche serauntes with dyscyplyn; and wee notte.[35]

At the accession of Mary the foreign congregations were expelled to
the continent where they were soon joined by some of their former hosts,
the English exiles. Among the first to leave England was the Glastonbury
church of Poullain, made up mostly of French weavers. They were
warmly received in the Reformed city of Frankfort along with a conting-
ent of English émigrés led by William Whittingham.[36] Both of these
refugee churches were beset by intra-congregational disputes involving
questions of liturgy and polity which, in the case of the English, anticipated the early Elizabethan controversies. A partisan account of these
events, published at Zurich in 1574, entitled *A brieff discours off the
troubles begonne at Franckford*, was widely circulated in Separatist
circles.[37] William Bradford regarded the Frankfort episode as the first
battle in "that bitter war" between those who labored for the right
worship of God and those who defended "the ceremonies and service
book, and other popish and antichristian stuff."[38] More important, when
the Separatists found themselves in exile and their own congregations
torn by internal disputes, "the exiled Church at Frankford" would remind
them that, as Robinson claimed, even "the first and best Churches" were
not exempt from such strife.[39]

---

[35]Thomas Earl's notebook, Cambridge University Library, MS. Mm. 1. 29, f. 2.

[36]*Acts of Privy Council*, (1552-54), 349; Anne Hooper to Bullinger, April 20, 1554,
Original Letters, vol. 1, 3. Poullain's congregation was permitted to use the Church of the
White Ladies (Weissfraudenkirche) which they later shared with the English refugees.

[37]Traditionally ascribed to Whittingham, but see Collinson, "The Authorship of *A
Brieff Discours off the Troubles Begonne at Franckfort,*" *Journal of Ecclesiastical
History* 9 (1958), 188-208.

[38]*Of Plymouth Plantation*, 5.

[39]John Robinson, *A Justification of Separation from the Church of England* (Amsterdam, 1610), 55-56 [hereafter *Justification*). The title of George Johnson's exposé of the
Amsterdam disputes also recalls the Frankfort precedent: *A discours of some troubles in
the banished English Church at Amsterdam* (Amsterdam, 1603).

If the Separatists found in the Marian exiles a precedent for their own flight from persecution, they sensed an even stronger identity between their fledgling congregations and the secret assemblies of those whom Foxe called "the true professors of God's gospel,"[40] those convinced Protestants whose clandestine activities constituted a veritable network of underground dissent. Separatist Robert Harrison, some 25 years after the fact, recalled those perilous times:

> Let us examine our selves and call to minde the yeeres that are past, when the fyrie sworde did hange over our heades in the dayes of Queene Marie, and that by so weake a threede, that we looked everie houre when it should fall upon us, when we being straungers from our own houses, walked from house to house, at suche time as the Owles and Backes looke foorth and flye.... We were as Iewes which by Hamans meanes were solde to bee slaine, and destinate to a day of death. And we were as humble Hester, whiche would make no request but for life onelie.[41]

In historical accounts of the Marian persecution the martyrs of rank and influence—Cranmer, Latimer, Ridley, Hooper, Bradford—have received most of the attention. This is understandable in that they also occupy center stage in the narrative of Foxe, the chief source for these events. But the Separatists were more interested in the less notable martyrs, those of the rank and file, whose escapes, hazards, ruses, and imprisonments they recognized in their own experience.

Secret assemblies of Marian Protestants seemed to flourish in London and nearby communities,[42] although they were also known in Suffolk[43] and Kent[44] and as far away as Lancashire[45] and Wales.[46] In 1555, the Council issued a special letter to all bishops urging them "to be very vigorous in searching for the gospellers,"[47] and in the following year new commissions were established "for a diligent search and discovery of heretics."[48] The evidence which survives, mostly depositions and court records, suggests a widespread though diffuse pattern of resistance,

[40]*Foxe*, vol. 8, 417.

[41]*The Writings of Robert Harrison and Robert Browne*, eds. Albert Peel and Leland H. Carlson (London, 1953), 74.

[42]The arrest of conventiclers in the following Essex County districts is recorded by *Foxe*, vol. 8: Hockley, 107; Billericay, 118; Colchester, 303-10; Much Bentley, 382; Islington, 468.

[43]Ibid., 556.

[44]Ibid., 487.

[45]Strype, *Ecclesiastical Memorials*, vol. 3, ii, 149.

[46]*Foxe,* op. cit., vol. 8, 29.

[47]Strype, *Ecclesiastical Memorials*, vol. 3, i, 402.

[48]Ibid., 476.

strongest in and around London but represented throughout the realm.

These underground congregations were sustained by the ministry of itinerant preachers such as Thomas Whittle who, expelled from Essex, "went abroad where he might, now here and there, as occasion was ministered, preaching and sowing the gospel of Christ."[49] William Ramsey, a roving "apostle" who managed to stay one step ahead of his pursuivants, later addressed a letter, on the model of St. Paul, to his friends in the town of South Molton, an Epistle to the "Moltonians," in which he recalled his ministry among them and other congregations dispersed throughout north Devon. "Early and late, privately and openly, as cause required and occasion served,"[50] he had labored in the dark days of Queen Mary. Not all of the gospellers were as fortunate as Ramsey in escaping detection. George Eagles, a former tailor, known variously as "Trudge," "Trudgeover," and "Trudge over the world," because of his "immoderate and unreasonable going abroad,"[51] finally came to the attention of the Council who offered a reward of 20 pounds for his capture. Although he and his company "concealed themselves a great while in the northern parts of Essex, in privy closets and barns, in holes and thickets, in fields and woods,"[52] he was eventually taken near Colchester and executed as a traitor because he had allegedly prayed at one of his meetings for God to change the Queen's heart or else take her away.[53]

Many of the travelling preachers were men of little if any education. John Clement was a wheelwright from Surrey; Thomas Wats a linen draper in Essex; John Careless, a weaver of Coventry; Richard Yeoman, a seller of "laces, pins, and points, and such like things."[54] Rawlins White,

---

[49]Foxe, vol. 7, 718.

[50]British Museum, MS. Lansdowne 377, ff. 8 verso-28 recto. Quoted, Patrick Collinson, The Elizabethan Puritan Movement (Berkeley, 1967), 21 [hereafter Elizabethan Puritan Movement].

[51]Foxe, vol. 8, 393.

[52]Strype, Ecclesiastical Memorials, vol. 3, ii, 43-44.

[53]"At the sessions at Chelmsford, he had indicted of treason, because he had assembled companies together contrary to the laws of the realm; it being enacted not long before, to avoid sedition, that if men should flock together above six, it was made treason. In fine, he was cast, condemned, and cruelly hanged, drawn, and quartered, as a traitor. And as though he were one of the worst sort of rebels, his four quarters were set up in four several great places, namely Colchester, Harwich, St. Osith's, and Chelmsford." Ibid., 44. Christina Garrett identifies Trudgeover as an agent of the exiles, and a disseminator of anti-Marian pamphlets: The Marian Exiles: A Study in the Origins of Elizabethan Puritanism (London, 1938), 35, n. 2, 50. See also Acts of the Privy Council (1556-58), 18, 129-30, 142.

[54]Foxe, vol. 8, 487.

an illiterate fisherman from Cardiff in Wales, sent his son to school to learn to read English, and "every night after supper, summer and winter, would have the boy to read a piece of the holy Scripture, and now and then of some other good book."[55] Within a short while White had learned enough to instruct his neighbors, and with his son by his side, "in some private place or other he would call his trusty friends together and with earnest prayer and great lamentation pass away the time . . . so that by his virtuous instructions, being without any blemish of error, he converted a great number."[56]

The largest and most famous of the underground congregations was the one gathered in London, the one, it will be remembered, referred to in Bradford's *Dialogue* as a "separated church" with its own use of excommunication. George Withers, writing to Frederick III, elector Palatine, some eight years into Elizabeth's reign recalled this Marian congregation:

> Although the church seemed at first to be entirely overthrown, and the godly were dispersed in every quarter, yet a congregation of some importance collected itself at London, chose its ministers by common consent, appointed deacons, and, in the midst of enemies more sharp-sighted than Argus and more cruel than Nero, the church of God was again restored entire, and, in a word, complete in all its parts. And though it was often dispersed by the attacks of its enemies, and a very great number of its members perished at the stake, it nevertheless grew and increased every day.[57]

Written in the heat of the Vestiarian Controversy, Wither's emphasis on the "completeness" of the London congregation may have been a bit of an exaggeration, intended as a contrast to the Elizabethan church—"now lying prostrate, and on the very brink of destruction."[58] Nonetheless, the evidence tends to support the essential accuracy of his description. The continuity of the meetings is noted by Strype: "There was a congregation of godly men at London, in the very mouth of danger, who met together for religious worship all the Queen's reign, from the beginning to the very end of it."[59] The number of communicants is spoken of as 40, 100, and toward the end of the reign, 200.[60] From a deposition of an informant we learn of their various meeting places in the secret and obscure corners of London: "The meeting sometimes is at Wapping, at one Church's house, hard by the water side; sometimes at a widow's house at Ratcliffe . . .

---

[55]Ibid., vol. 7, 29.

[56]Ibid.

[57]*Zurich Letters*, vol. 2, 160.

[58]Ibid., 157.

[59]Strype, *Ecclesiastical Memorials*, vol. 3, ii, 147.

[60]Ibid., 148; *Foxe*, vol. 8, 559.

sometimes at St. Katharine's, at a shoemaker's house, a Dutchman called Frog . . . sometimes at Battle-bridge, at a dyer's house, betwixt two butchers there.[61] On other occasions they are said to have met "in a ship called Jesus ship," "in a cooper's house in Pudding-lane," and "at the Black-friars."[62]

The strength of the congregation was due in no small part to an outstanding succession of ministers: Edward Scambler, Thomas Foule, Thomas Rose, John Rough, Augustus Bernher, and Thomas Bentham.[63] Two of these, Scambler and Bentham, would survive the Marian reign to become Elizabethan bishops, while Bernher would be remembered as the associate and literary executor of Latimer. Rose, like Trudgeover, was found guilty of treason for praying that the Lord soon convert the Queen, "or remove her yoke from the necks of the godly,"[64] but managed to escape to the Continent.

Concerning John Rough, considerably more is known. Before assuming the leadership of the London congregation he had been the subject of a rather checkered career. A native of Scotland he was instrumental in the conversion of John Knox, served as chaplain to the Earl of Arran, held a benefice at Hull, and at Mary's accession, fled to Friesland where he supported himself by knitting. According to Foxe, it was a lack of yarn which prompted his return to England where, perchance, he heard of the London congregation to which he joined himself and was soon elected their minister.[65] Garrett, however, believes that he was an agent of the exiles, sent over to replace Trudgeover,[66] a conjecture given some plausibility by one of the charges at his examination before Bishop Bonner.[67]

---

[61]Ibid., 459.

[62]Ibid., 558.

[63]Ibid., 559, 584. On Scambler and Bentham, see F. O. White, *Lives of the Elizabethan Bishops* (London, 1898), 138-41, 158-60; on Bernher, see D. M. Loades, *The Oxford Martyrs* (London, 1970), 171-72, 225. White, *Separatist Tradition*, 10, does not include Rose among the ministers but Machyn records his arrest in his diary: "The furst day of January where asymbulle of men and women in Bowe chyrche-yerde at nyght of a xxx and aboyffh, and ther thay had the Englys serves and prayers and a lectorne, and thay wher taken by the shreyffes, and Thomas Rosse the menyster, and thay wher cared to the contors and odur plases, and ser Thomas Rosse to the Towre." *The Diary of Henry Machyn*, ed. John G. Nichols (London, 1848), 79.

[64]*Original Letters*, vol. 2, 773; *Foxe*, vol. 8, 581-90.

[65]Ibid., 444.

[66]Garrett, op. cit., 274; White, *Separatist Tradition*, 11-14.

[67]*Foxe*, vol. 7, 446: "Item, Thou dost know, and hast been conversant with all or a great part of such Englishmen as have fled out of this realm for religion . . . and hast succoured, maintained, and holpen them, and hast been a conveyer of their seditious letters and books into this realm."

The relationship of the exiles to the London congregation is further confirmed by the fact that Bentham, Rough's successor, had been active in the exiled communities at Frankfort and Geneva and had served as preacher to the exiles at Basel.[68]

Rough's ministry was cut short when the assembly, meeting under the camouflage of seeing a play, was betrayed. Machyn recorded the event in his diary:

> The xij day of December, being Sunday, there met certain persons that were Gospellers, and some pretended players, at Yslyngtun, takying serten men, and one Ruffe, a Skott and a frere, for the redying of a lecture, and odur matters; and the communyon was played, and should have byne butt the gard cam to sune, or ever the chief matter was begone.[69]

Taken with Rough was Cuthbert Sympson, one of the Kentish conventiclers imprisoned in Edward's reign, and more recently, a deacon in the underground church. Sympson is referred to as "paymaster to the prisoners in the Marshalsea, Ludgate, Lollards' tower . . . and executor to the prisoners that die, and the collector of the assembly when the reading is done."[70] Sympson also kept a book "containing the names and accounts of the congregation,"[71] which, thanks to a premonitory dream, had been given to Mrs. Rough before the arrest and thus did not fall into the hands of the authorities. Placed in the stocks in Bonner's coalhouse and repeatedly racked, Sympson having not divulged the names of his fellow worshipers, was finally burned on March 28, 1558, three months after Rough.

In the shadowy interval between the death of Mary and the passage of the Act of Supremacy there existed a state of religious uncertainty during which "some Ministers of the Word, impatient of Delay, whilst they chose rather to fore-run than expect Laws, began to sow abroad the Doctrine of Gospel more freely, first in private houses, and then in Churches; and the People, greedy of Novelties, began to flock unto them in great number. . . ."[72] Among these impatient preachers was Thomas Lever, a much-travelled exile, who, upon his return to England found Roman worship still sanctioned by law,

---

[68]Garrett, op. cit., 86-87. See also Bentham's letter to Thomas Lever, Strype, *Ecclesiastical Memorials*, vol. 3, ii, 132-35.

[69]*The Diary of Henry Machyn,* op. cit., 160.

[70]*Foxe*, vol. 8, 459.

[71]Ibid., 454.

[72]William Camden, *The History of the Most Renowned and Victorious Princess Elizabeth Late Queen of England*, ed. Wallace T. MacCaffrey (Chicago, 1970), 15.

and the gospel no where to be met with, except . . . in a congregation that
remained in concealment during the whole time of persecution, and then not
venturing forth beyond such private houses as were open to them, on the
cessation of the persecution, they were permitted by queen Elizabeth in open
private houses, but in no public churches.[73]

Lever was frequently present at these meetings of the congregation where
he witnessed the administration of the Lord's Supper and the reconciliation of backsliding members. But the maintenance of the congregation
under Elizabeth was short-lived, and, with the establishment of Protestant worship, its members were presumably assimilated into the various
parishes of London.[74]

THE RISE OF ELIZABETHAN SEPARATISM

The later Separatist appeal to the Marian underground assemblies
presupposed a radical discontinuity between those congregations and the
Elizabethan state church. Robinson's explanation is typical of the Separatist position:

There was not one congregation separated in Queen Maryes dayes, that so
remayned in Queen Elizabeths. The congregations were dissolved, and the
persons in them bestowed themselves in their severall parishes, where their
livings, and estates lay. The circumcised were mingled with the uncircum-
cised, whence came that monstrous confusion, agaynst which we witnes. And
shew me one of your ministers continuing his charge in Queen Elizabeths
dayes, over the flock to which he ministered (in Queen Maryes dayes) the
persequuted gospell. . . . As then an handfull, or bundle of corn shufled into a
field of weeds, though in it selfe it retayn the same nature, yet cannot make
the field a corn field: so neither could this small hadful of separated people in
Queen Maryes days sanctify the whole field of the idolatrous and prophane
multitude in the land, by their seating themselves among them.[75]

---

[73]Lever to Bullinger, August 8, 1559, *Zurich Letters*, vol. 2, 29; *Separatist Tradition*,
20-21.

[74]On September 22, 1560, a royal proclamation warned against violations of the Act of
Uniformity: "And her Majesty also chargeth and commandeth upon pain of imprisonment, that no ministers, nor other person, make any conventicules or secret congregations, either to read or to preach, or to minister the sacraments, or to use any manner of
divine service; but that they shall resort to open chapels or churches, and there to preach,
teach, minister, or pray, according to the order of the church of England," *The Remains of
Edmund Grindal*, ed. William Nicholson (Cambridge, 1843), 298.

[75]*Justification*, 460-61. A similar view is put forth by Ainsworth in *Counterpoyson*,
op. cit., 134: "And what secret congregations there were in Queen Maries dayes, I know
not: but if they were so secret, as onely they met now and then in private, and ordinarily
went to church openly with Papists, they were not a true church of Christ. And that
constreyned union of Papists and of Protestants at the beginning of Queen Elizabeths
reign, under Archbishops, Bishops, Priests, etc. with most of the same mattins, evensongs,
rites, ceremonies, etc. that before had been imposed; this order can never be warranted by
the testament of Christ, nor such a commixture proved to be a true church."

By this reasoning the Separatists could claim the Marian congregations as precursors of their own withdrawal while rejecting the reconstituted Church of England as a mixed multitude falsely gathered "by the blowing of her majestie's trumpet at her coronation in one day."[76] In fact, most of the Marian Protestants seem to have accommodated themselves to the religious policies of the new queen with relative ease. The Prayer Book of 1559 was, after all, not that different from the one they had used in their secret assemblies,[77] and in London the example of Bentham, underground preacher turned established prelate, must have encouraged others to return to their parish churches. But, from the beginning, there were those who were frustrated by the temporising nature of the Elizabethan Settlement, and who, as their frustration gave way to disillusionment, and disillusionment to despair, called to mind the precedent of the Marian congregations. Among the first Separatists apprehended in London in Elizabeth's reign was a certain Smith, "the auncientest of them," who when asked to describe the origins of his group remembered "that there was a congregation of us in this Citie in Queene Maries dayes."[78]

The recrudescence of Separatist conventicles in the late 1560s followed in the wake of the Vestiarian Controversy, the consequence of the first serious attempt at enforced uniformity in the new reign. What, in the halcyon days of 1559, seemed to some of the bishops a small matter— "that comical dress . . . these ridiculous trifles"[79]—had, by 1566, with the appearance of Matthew Parker's *Advertisements*, escalated into a crisis of significant proportion.[80] Far from being harmless *adiaphora*, necessary for order's sake, the garments in question, the square cap, gown, tippet, and surplice, were branded by the advanced reformers as idolothytes, "worse then lowsye: for they are sibbed to ye sarke of Hercules,

---

[76] *The Writings of John Greenwood, 1587-1590*, ed. Leland H. Carlson (London, 1962), 129-30.

[77] Before his martyrdom Rough admitted that he "did allow the service used in the latter time of king Edward's reign," and that he "did teach and set forth the said English service," *Foxe*, vol. 8, 446.

[78] *A parte of a register, contayninge sundrie memorable matters, written by divers godly and learned in our time, which stande for, and desire the reformation of our Church* (Middleburg, 1593), 25 [hereafter *A parte of a register*].

[79] John Jewel to Peter Martyr, November 6, 1559, *Zurich Letters*, vol. 1, 52.

[80] The *Advertisements* are printed in *Documentary Annals of the Reformed Church of England*, ed. Edward Cardwell (Oxford, 1844), vol. 1, 321-31. On the Vestiarian Controversy, see Knappen, op. cit., 187-216; Dixon, op. cit., vol. 6, 44-152; J. H. Primus, *The Vestments Controversy* (Kampen, 1960).

that made hym his owne bowells a sunder."[81] Refusing to subscribe to Parker's requirements, one-third of the London clergy were suspended and deprived of their livings, "of which number," Parker admitted to Cecil, "were the best, and some preachers."[82]

The expelled ministers, especially the preachers, found their way into a variety of semi-ecclesiastical positions ranging from unbeneficed curacies to salaried lectureships and private chaplaincies. In London the parish of Holy Trinity, Minories, formerly occupied by the Sisters of St. Clare, boasted a series of radical curates and lecturers, some of them deprived incumbents, whose connection with the institutional church was tenuous at best.[83] The religious exercises of these preachers and their hearers came to the attention of the chronicler John Stowe who, writing in 1567, noted that "there were many congregations of the Anabaptists in London, who cawlyd themselvs Puritans or Unspottyd Lambs of the Lord. They kept theyr churche in the Mynorys with out Algate."[84] Stowe's equation of the Minories church with "many congregations of the Anabaptysts" suggests a close association between the Minories and the illegal Separatist conventicles which sprang up in and around London between 1567 and 1570.[85]

---

[81][Anthony Gilby], *A Pleasaunt Dialogue, Betweene a Souldior of Barwicke, and an English Chaplaine* (London, 1581), sig. K4 verso.

[82]Parker to Cecil, March 26, 1566: "I must signify to your honor what this day we have done in the examination of the London ministers. Sixty-one promised conformity; nine or ten were absent; thirty-seven denied, of which number were the best, and some preachers." *The Correspondence of Matthew Parker*, eds., J. Bruce and T. T. Perowne (Cambridge, 1853), 269 [hereafter *Parker Correspondence*].

[83]The Minories was one of the privileged "liberties" of London which claimed exemption from both the civil jurisdiction of the city and the ecclesiastical authority of the Bishop of London. The parishioners, acting as patron, chose the curate themselves thereby avoiding the normal procedures of episcopal presentation and induction. The standard study is E. M. Tomlinson, *A History of the Minories* (London, 1907), but see the recent articles by H. Gareth Owen: "The Liberty of the Minories: a study in Elizabethan religious radicalism," *East London Papers*, 8 (1965); "A Nursery of Elizabethan Nonconformity, 1567-72," *Journal of Ecclesiastical History* 17 (1966), 65-76.

[84]*Three Fifteen-century Chronicles with Historical Memoranda by John Stowe*, ed. J. Gairdner, Camden Society Publications, New Series, 28 (London, 1880), 143.

[85]Some historians have been misled by Stowe's use of the term "Anabaptists." Cf. Victoria County History of London, ed. W. Page (London, 1909), vol. 1, 313. Apparently Anabaptism, which had a mild revival in the next decade, was at a low ebb in England in the mid-1560s. Writing in the same year as Stowe, John Jewel asserted: "Your Anabaptistes, and Zuenkfeldians, wee knowe not. They finde Harbour emongste you in Austria, Slesia, Morauria, and in sutche other Countries and Cities, where the Gospel of Christe is suppressed: but they have no Acquaintance withe us." *A Defence of the Apologie of the Churche of Englande* (London, 1567), 30. On the general state of Anabaptism in Elizabethan England, see Duncan B. Heriot, "Anabaptism in England during the 16th and 17th

These transient conventicles, like the Marian congregation a decade earlier, met in private houses and obscure spots throughout the city. Stowe reports that "they assomblyd in a shype or lyghtar in Seynt Katheryns Poole, then in a chopers house, ny Wolle Key in Thames strete . . . then afterward in Pudynge Lane in a mynisters hows in a blynd ally . . . then at Westmynstar . . . and in a goldsmythis house nere to the Savoy. . . . On Estar day at Hogston in my Lord of Londons mans house to the nombar of 120, and on Lowe Sonday in a carpentars hous in Aldarman bury."[86]

Among the first of these congregations was the one gathered by John Browne, sometime preacher at the Minories, and protégé of the powerful Duchess of Suffolk.[87] In late 1567 Browne was arrested along with the "choper" in whose house the church was then meeting. At some point, apparently after his release, certain members decided to withdraw from Browne's group and form their own assembly, an event which greatly weakened the already depleted congregation. A letter from Browne to these "deare Brethren," some of them former officers in his church, has survived:

> Seeing you are no small occasions yourself of the dissolving or breaking up of this little vineyeard or Church of God, for through your ensample the weake are driven backe, the reste are kept in a stay, the godly are grieved, and the enemies rejoice and say that you have a Church alone by your selves, and Fitz hath another by himself etc. So that thei account 4 or 5 Churches divided one from another, so that one of them either cannot or will not joyne one with another.[88]

The demise of Browne's "litle vineyeard" and the proliferation of mutually exclusive conventicles, competing with and isolated from each other, indicate the sporadic and fragmented character of these early dissenting groups and foreshadow the fissiparous tendency of later Separatist developments. Browne, for a while, returned to his more settled position as

---

Centuries," *Transactions*, Congregational Historical Society, 12 (1933-36), 256-71, 312-20; George H. Williams, *The Radical Reformation* (Philadelphia, 1962), 778-90.

[86]*Three Fifteen-century Chronicles,* op. cit., 143.

[87]This Browne and his followers called by Stowe "Brownings" are not to be confused with the more famous Robert Browne and the Brownists. Cf. Dexter, *Congregationalism*, 64. John Browne's relationship to the Duchess of Suffolk and to early Separatist-Puritan circles is discussed in Albert Peel, *The First Congregational Churches: New Light on Separatist Congregations in London, 1567-81* (Cambridge, 1920), 24-30. On Browne's activities in the Minories, see Tomlinson, op. cit., 279.

[88]*The Seconde Parte of a Register being a Calendar of Manuscripts under that title intended for publication by the Puritans about 1593, and now in Dr. Williams's Library, London,* ed. Albert Peel (Cambridge, 1915), vol. 1, 60 [hereafter *The Seconde Parte of a Register*].

chaplain of the Duchess, but surfaced again in the early 1570s as a colleague of the radical Puritan ministers led by John Field and Thomas Wilcox.[89]

Edmund Grindal, as Bishop of London, was charged with the responsibility of dealing with those who abandoned their parish churches to set up separate congregations. His correspondence reveals a mounting concern with sectarian activity in his diocese. In August, 1566, when the initial reaction to the deprivations seemed to be subsiding, Grindal, hopeful that the worst was over, informed Bullinger of the impact of the furor about "things of no importance":

> Many of the more learned clergy seemed to be on the point of forsaking their ministry. Many of the people also had it in contemplation to withdraw from us, and set up private meetings; but however most of them, through the mercy of the Lord, have now returned to a better mind.[90]

Almost two years later, in another letter to Bullinger, Grindal reviewed the situation with more concern:

> Our controversy concerning the habits . . . had cooled down for a time, but broke out again last winter; and this by the means of some who are more zealous than they are either learned or gifted with pious discretion. Some London citizens of the lowest order, together with four or five ministers, remarkable neither for their judgment nor learning, have openly separated from us; and sometimes in private houses, sometimes in the fields, and occasionally even in ships, they have held their meetings and administered the sacraments. Besides this, they have ordained ministers, elders, and deacons, after their own way, and have even excommunicated some who had seceded from their church.[91]

One of the ministers referred to by Grindal was probably Master Patterson who has left a record of an interview, "the talk," he had with the Bishop in September, 1567. Suspended for preaching without a license and for calling the Bishop "a traitor and antichrist," Patterson appealed to an authority higher than Grindal or the Archbishop:

> The Archbishop of archbishops hath not suspended me from preaching, but continueth his commandments to me still . . . and hath also given me a congregation. . . .[92]

---

[89]Browne visited Field and Wilcox then they were in prison in 1573, and was required by Parker to appear before the Ecclesiastical Commission "to answer such matter as he is to be charged withal." *Parker Correspondence*, 390. See also Strype, *The life and acts of Matthew Parkerzk (Oxford, 1821), vol. 2, 68.*

[90]*Zurich Letters*, I, 168.

[91]Ibid., 201-02.

[92]Dixon, op. cit., vol. 6, 178; *State Papers Domestic, Elizabeth*, 44, 20 (*Calendar*, 300). Patterson, like Browne, had ties with both the Minories and the Duchess of Suffolk; cf. Tomlinson, op. cit., 279. On June 28, 1567, the Lord Mayor of London issued a precept directing the constables and other ward officers to assist the church wardens to "appre-

As to the location of his church Pattenson offers not a hint—"my cure is wheresoever I do meet with a congregation that are willing to hear the word of God preached at my mouth."[93] Nothing more is known of Pattenson's activities, but in 1580 his name was included on a list of Separatist martyrs, "godlye and zealous christians" who had "stoode faste to Chrystes institution and holye religion to the death."[94]

In June, 1567, the sheriff uncovered one of the largest of the London Separatist groups, a congregation of nearly 100 worshipers who had rented the Plumbers' Hall under the pretext of holding a wedding. About twenty of their leaders were arrested, seven of whom appeared before Grindal and his Ecclesiastical Commission.[95] After the event the Separatists wrote an *ex parte* account of this encounter—"The true report of our Examination and conference (as neare as wee can call to remembrance)"—which was included in the Puritan anthology, *A parte of a register*, printed surreptiously in 1593.[96] This document, though evidently biased and flawed in its reconstruction of historical detail, provides invaluable insight into the motivation of early Elizabethan Separatism.[97]

---

hend take and commit to warde all and everye such misordered persone . . . as shall Attempt to preche not having redie to be shewed forth good and sufficient lycence," London C. C. Record Office, Journals, 19 f. 48 recto, quoted, H. G. Owen, "London Parish Clergy in the Reign of Elizabeth I," unpub. London Ph.D. thesis (1957), 177.

[93]Dixon, loc. cit.

[94]*The Seconde Parte of a Register*, vol. 1, 149.

[95]Besides Grindal the principal inquisitors include his chaplain, Master Watts, the Lord Mayor of London, Roger Martin, and the Dean of Westminster, Gabriel Goodman. The Lord Mayor, reluctant to discuss matters theological, offers practical advice: "I can not talke learnedly with you in celestiall matters, but I have a mother witte...." The seven Separatists were John Smith, William Nyxson, William White, James Ireland, Robert Hawkins, Thomas Bowelande, and Richard Morecraft.

[96]*A parte of a register*, 23-37; reprinted in *The Remains of Edmund Grindal*, ed. William Nicholson (Cambridge, 1843), 201-16 and in *Puritanism in Tudor England*, ed. H. C. Porter (Colombia, S.C., 1971), 80-94. On the Plumbers' Hall congregation see Neal, op. cit., vol. 1, 252-53, 263-67; *Early English Dissenters*, vol. 1, 80-82; *Separatist Tradition*, 23-25. The most recent discussion of this episode is Patrick Collinson, *Archbishop Grindal, 1519-1583: The Struggle for a Reformed Church* (Berkeley, 1979), 177-83. He interprets Grindal's dealings with these dissidents as fundamentally pastoral rather than punitive.

[97]It has been supposed that the Separatists did not regain their liberty until April, 1569. However, the names of all but two of those examined on June 20, 1567, are included in a list of persons found worshiping in a goldsmith's house within the parish of St. Martin's-in-the-Fields on March 4, 1568. See F. J. Powicke, "Lists of the Early Separatists," *Transactions*, Congregational Historical Society, 1 (1901-04), 141-43; Strype, *The Life and Acts of Edmund Grindal* (Oxford, 1821), 200-01; *The Remains of Edmund Grindal*, op. cit., 216.

In replying to Grindal's charge that, by severing themselves from the society of other Christians, they were rejecting not only the present ecclesiastical establishment but "the whole state of the church reformed in King Edward's days," the Separatists likened themselves to the Marian martyrs:

> It may be shewed in the booke of the Monuments of the Church, that many which were burned in Qu. Ma. time, died for standing against poperie, as we nowe doe.[98]

The Separatist appropriation of Foxe's history has been emphasized by recent historians and, indeed, the account of this examination reads like a transcript of one of the Marian trials given by Foxe.[99] However, some members of the group had personal ties with the London "privy church." For example, the eldest among their number cited as a precedent for their secession, a congregation "of us" which used to meet privately in London in Queen Mary's days. For these Separatists the cast of characters had changed—Elizabeth had replaced Mary; Parker, Pole; and Grindal, Bonner—but their situation was precisely analogous to that of the "privy churches" in the previous reign. Even the questions their inquisitors posed recalled those the Marian Protestants had faced:

> Deane: But who will you have to be judge of the word of God? Hawkins: Why that was the sayinge of the papistes in Queene Maries time. I have hearde it, when the trueth was defended by the worde of God, then they would saye, Who shall judge of the worde of God? The Catholike Church must be judge.[100]

More condemnatory yet, the Elizabethan church still numbered among its ministers some who had openly supported the Roman cause:

> I knowe one that in Queene Maries time, did persecute Gods Saintes, and brought them forth to B. Boner, and nowe he is Minister alowed of you, and never made recantation.[101]

Here, in essence, is Robinson's critique of the Elizabethan Settlement: the Church of England is a mixed multitude, a mingled meslin of good corn and weeds, its ministry tainted both in appearance ("the idolatrous gear") and appointment ("the popish prelacy") by its proximity to Rome.

Already with the Plumbers' Hall men we encounter the two dominant motifs of both the Puritan and Separatist positions to be refined and

---

[98]*A parte of a register*, 32.

[99]These Separatists probably used the 1563 edition of Foxe's book. See William Haller, *The Elect Nation: The Meaning and Relevance of Foxe's Book of Martyrs* (New York, 1963), 118-24; *Elizabethan Puritan Movement*, 89; *Separatist Tradition*, 160.

[100]*A parte of a register*, 35.

[101]Ibid., 26.

re-emphasized in varying degrees during the next half-century: the claim to find in Scripture a warrant and mandate of immediate and specific reforms, and the emphasis upon discipline as an indispensable mark of a rightly reformed church. These dissenters, like their conforming brethren, showed great deference toward the example of the "best reformed Churches." They were well read in John Calvin and Philip Melanchthon, and Grindal's attempt to use a letter from Beza against their position was disallowed by Hawkins: "Wee knowe the letter well ynough: for we have it in our houses, it maketh nothinge against us."[102] What if Bullinger had allowed that vestments could be lawfully used as the Bishop claimed? "I can shew you Bullinger against Bullinger in this thing," boasted Smith.[103] But clearly the overriding appeal of these men was to the authority of Scripture. Throughout the examination the inquisitors sought to isolate the sectaries from the theological consensus of the day: "All the learned men in Europe are against you. . . . Will you be judged by the learned in Geneva? they are against you. . . . All the learned are against you!"[104] To which the Separatists replied with single-minded persistence—"We wil be tryed by the worde of God . . . we wil be judged by the worde of God. . . . We holde nothing that is not warraunted by the worde of God . . . if you can reproove . . . anie thing we holde by the word of God, we will yeelde to you, and doe open penaunce at Paules Crosse, if not, we will stande to it. . . ."[105] Grindal, anticipating Whitgift's elaboration, argued that order in the realm required the magisterial regulation of "things indifferent," things neither prescribed nor prohibited by Scripture. The prisoners, undaunted by the logic of Grindal's theory, demanded a text: "Prove that, saide one, where finde you that saide another?"[106]

One of the clear imperatives of Scripture, so the Separatists believed, was the implementation of discipline:

> And agayne, Christ commaundeth Discipline in the 18. of Matthew, and it was put in practise of the Apostles: But in the Church of Englande, there is none but the Popes discipline.[107]

"The Popes discipline"—an epithet for the system of church courts,

---

102Ibid., 30.

103Ibid., 29.

104Ibid., 29, 35.

105Ibid., 35, 29, 34, 23.

106Ibid., 28.

107Ibid., 35.

ecclesiastical commissions, and canon law retained by the Elizabethan church—was faulty on two accounts. First, it was used by the bishops with the aid of the civil magistrates ("They make the Maior and the Aldermen their servauntes and butchers," complained Nyxson)[108] primarily for the maintenance of order, not for the recovery of the offender and the edification of the church; secondly, it was imposed from without by officers not responsible to the congregation in which the offence had occurred. To deny the Scriptural pattern of discipline was nothing less than to divest Christ of his kingly office:

> You preach Christ to be Priest and Prophets, but you preache him not to be King, neither will you suffer him to raigne with the scepter of his worde in his church alone.[109]

The lack of Scriptural discipline, then, was no trifling matter, nor "extern thing," but a situation fraught with serious theological implications concerning the basic premise of Christian faith, i.e. the doctrine of Christ. The role of discipline in the theological rationale of later Separatism will bear further investigation, but it is significant, at this early stage in the development of the Separatist tradition, to find already two of the formative elements in that discussion: an appeal to the Dominical words of Matthew 18 and an invocation of the *triplex munus Christi*, with the royal office discharged in the exercise of discipline.

Historians of the Free Church denominations have given no little attention to the question of whether and to what extent these Separatist conventicles embodied the principles of congregational ecclesiology. Dexter, for example, regarded the Separatism of 1567-1571 as too episodic and sporadic to warrant the name "Congregational," and Powicke, speaking of the Plumbers' Hall company, denied that "it was 'separatist' in the sense of Independent."[110] On the other hand, Dale claimed that the Richard Fitz church, an offshoot of the Plumbers' Hall group, was the "first regularly constituted English Congregational Church," a claim criticized by Burrage, but supported, with additional evidence, by Peel.[111]

---

[108]Ibid., 33.

[109]Ibid., 26.

[110]Dexter, *Congregationalism*, 114-15; Powicke, "Lists of the Early Separatists," *op. cit*, 141.

[111]Dale, *History of English Congregationalism,* op. cit., 95; *Early English Dissenters*, vol. 1, 90-03; Peel, "The First Congregational Churches," op. cit., 38-46. The Fitz congregation was later cited by anti-Brownist polemicists such as George Gifford and Richard Bernard as the proto-type of the Separatist churches of their day. John Bolton who recanted and then publicly committed suicide at Paul's Cross was apparently a deacon in this church. Ainsworth, *Counterpoyson,* op. cit., 39. There are three surviving

Collinson, recognizing the fluidity of the religious situation in the years preceding the Admonition Controversy, argues against an over-enthusiastic pursuit of denominational genealogy which "may well distort the blurred image that we have of these sects, which in its very indistinctness possesses a certain validity."[112]

To be sure, there is little evidence that these early sectarians possessed either a well-defined program of reform or a highly developed doctrine of the church. Their road to separation had been gradual: they had never assembled together in houses, so they told Grindal, as long as they had had "the worde freely preached, and the Sacramentes administered without the idolatrous geare."[113] Once separated, they did not abandon in theory the concept of a territorial church, nor did they attack the episcopal office itself. Liturgically, they ordered their worship according to a prayer book, a practice repudiated by later Separatists, though it was not the officially sanctioned Prayer Book of 1559 but the "purer" Genevan one. For a while they continued to welcome the ministrations of non-separating Puritans such as Lever and Sampson and the venerable Coverdale. But the experience of separation, reinforced by persecution and imprisonment, intensified the sectarian impulse already latent in the refusal to accept the "popish garments." The clandestine but frequent meetings—"every saboth day in houses, and on the fourth day in the weke we meet"[114]—fostered a sense of personal loyalty and "congregational" identity which increased in proportion to the feeling of alienation from the institutional church. Our preachers, our discipline, our houses, our doings! Your laws, your courts, your ministers, your copes and your surplices, your doings![115] For these men there could be no compromise

---

documents related to the Fitz congregation, printed in full in *Early English Dissenters*, vol. 2, 13-18; cf. State Papers Domestic, Elizabeth, Addenda, vol. 20, 107 (ii). The first of these is a brief statement signed by Fitz, entitled "The order of the privye churche in London"; the third, a petition to Queen Elizabeth signed by 27 members of the congregation, written after Fitz had died in prison. The second document is similar in form to an early Separatist covenant, although the word is not used. It is on the basis of this document that the Fitz church is said to have anticipated Robert Browne. However, the Fitz "covenant" appears to have been modelled on an earlier anonymous treatise circulated in Separatist circles. See *The Seconde Parte of a register*, vol. 1, 55-61.

[112]*Elizabethan Puritan Movement*, 91. Collinson, however, goes too far in claiming that these sects "had taken no steps to elect their own officers or otherwise to set up an independent sectarian organization," ibid., 89. See Grindal to Bullinger, June 11, 1568, *Zurich Letters*, vol. 1, 202.

[113]*A parte of a register*, 24-25.

[114]Burrage, op. cit., vol. 2, 17.

[115]*Elizabethan Puritan Movement*, 89.

with the "traditioners" and the "cold gospellers." They were willing to be accounted the Queen's enemies, to be called "heretickes, seysmatikes, rebells, puritanes," rather than return to their parish churches.[116] As one of their number described the alternative:

> I have now joyned my self to the Church of Christ wherein I have yielded my selfe to the discipline of Gods Word as I promised at my Baptisme, which if I should now again forsake and joyne my self with the traditioners, I should then forsake the union wherein I am knyt with the body of Christ and joyne myselfe to the discipline of Antichrist.[117]

In a sense, the Separatists, few in number and condemned by the intellectual leaders of the Puritan party, posed only a very minor threat to the Established Church. This, in part, accounts for the relative leniency with which Grindal dealt with them. Yet the persistence of their separation and their refusal to submit to episcopal jurisdiction was fraught with revolutionary implications, regarding not only the nature of the Church but also the relationship of Church and state. Nothing less than the royal supremacy and the status of the Queen as Supreme Governor of the Church was at stake. Nor did Grindal fail to discern this, asking pointedly: "Have not we a godly Prince? answere, is she evill?" To which one of Separatists replied ambiguously, "The fruites doe shewe."[118] In these sputtering beginnings of English Separatism there was slowly evolving a concept of the Church—local, visible, disciplined—subject to the Prince only in so far as the Prince was subject to the authority of the Word of God. An undated and anonymous letter sent by "a certaine brother, a mynister from Geneva," exhorted the Separatists to go forward with the work they had begun:

> Seeing that God hath given you the priviledge to build and to choose mynisters, elders, and deacons, and to refuse a false uniformitie, it is not a sufficient discharge to remaine in open and manifest impurity and deformation, because the magistrats stay you.[119]

Because the magistrates stay you! Here, in strikingly similar language, but some twelve years before Robert Browne took up his pen, is a call for "reformation without tarying for anie."

---

[116] *The Seconde Parte of a Register*, vol. 1, 58.

[117] Ibid., 56.

[118] *A parte of a register*, 33.

[119] *The Seconde Parte of a Register*, 62.

"IT IS NOT YNOUGH TO BE WISHERS AND WOULDERS":
BROWNE, HARRISON, AND THE NORWICH COMPANY

The sporadic and circumstantial separation of the London conventiclers would be recalled by later Separatist apologists as a significant
episode in the history of Dissent. Its more immediate impact on the
course of events was less impressive; it was too short-lived and too
ill-organized to provide more than a premonition of things to come. Its
more able leaders soon drew back from the drastic step of separation and
cast in their lots with those advanced Puritans such as John Field and
Thomas Wilcox who were careful to distinguish protest within from
secession without:

> Wee make no separation from the Church of England, acknowledging it,
> notwithstanding the manifold deformities wherewith it is spotted (all of
> which we earnestly wish, desire, and pray, might be removed) to be the
> church of God.[120]

The Puritan protest of the early 1570s, however, went far beyond
reaction to the enforcement of conformity in vestments and ceremonies.
To the old arguments against "popish abuses still remaining" was added a
new and potent weapon in the Puritan arsenal: the assertion of divine-
right presbyterianism and an all-out attack on the episcopal office itself.
This position was given classic exposition by Thomas Cartwright in a
series of lectures on the first two chapters of Acts delivered at Cambridge
University in the spring of 1570. In these lectures Cartwright called for the
abolition of the titles and offices of archbishops, archdeacons, bishops,
deans, chancellors—all of them *nomina suspecta*."[121] Shortly after those
lectures were delivered Grindal, recently translated from London to the
see of York, wrote to Cecil, Chancellor of the university, of "one Cartwright, B.D., and Reader of my Lady Margaret's Divinity Lecture," who,
so he was informed, was daily inveighing "against the extern policy and
distinction of states in the ecclesiastical government of this realm."[122]
Further, "the youth of the University" were flocking to his lectures in
great numbers and were "therefore in danger to be poisoned by him with

---

[120]"The copie of a Letter, with a confession of Faith, written by two faithfull servants
of God, unto an Honorable, and vertuous Ladie," *A parte of a register*, 529.

[121]*The Remains of Edmund Grindal*, 323.

[122]Ibid.

love of contention and liking of novelties."[123]

Among the young scholars who listened to Cartwright in 1570 were two students of Corpus Christi, Robert Harrison and Robert Browne, whose association a decade later would furnish the Separatist cause with its most able and articulate leadership to that date.[124] Little is known about their university careers. Browne later included himself and Harrison in a list of those who "had lived and studied in Cambridge," and "were there knowne and counted forward in religion."[125] Upon leaving the

---

[123]Ibid., 324. Collinson, *Elizabethan Puritan Movement*, 113, plays down the significance of Cartwright's lectures, pointing out that earlier William Turner had arrived at similar conclusions from the same text. However, his attribution to Cartwright of "a somewhat unheroic tendency to withdraw from the scene of conflict" (ibid., 112) seems unfair. Cartwright, after all, was ejected from his chair, expelled from the university, and deported from the country! On Cartwright's role in the early presbyterian movement, see A. F. Scott Pearson, *Thomas Cartwright and Elizabeth Puritanism* (Cambridge, 1925), 1-57; H. C. Porter, *Reformation and Reaction in Tudor Cambridge* (Cambridge, 1958), 163, 174-78, 208-16 [hereafter *Reformation and Reaction*]; D. J. McGinn, *The Admonition Controversy* (New Brunswick, 1949), 28-65.

[124]Browne, who spent no more than five or six years out of a lifetime of eighty-three as a Separatist, yet who bequeathed his name to the movement, has not fared well in the annals of Dissenting historians. John Waddington's jibe is typical: "No educated Congregationalist can feel flattered by the ecclesiastical genealogy that takes its rise from Robert Browne," *Congregational History* (London, 1869), vol. 1, vi. An attempt to redress the neglect and distortion of Browne was begun by Dexter, *Congregationalism*, vol. 1, 61-128, and continued by Burrage, *The True Story of Robert Browne* (London, 1906) and Powicke, *Robert Browne* (London, 1910). The resumé of D. C. Smith's unpublished Ph.D. dissertation at Edinburgh University appeared as "Robert Browne, Independent," *Church History* 6 (1937), 289-349. Two recent dissertations have dealt with aspects of Browne's life and thought: B. R. White, "The Development of the Doctrine of the Church among the English Separatists with especial reference to Robert Browne and John Smyth," unpublished Ph.D. thesis, Oxford University (1960); Alwyn Ray Fraser, "The Magistrate and the Church in the thought of the Elizabethan Separatists," unpublished M. Litt. thesis, Cambridge University (1971).

[125]*A True and Short Declaration, Both of the Gathering and Ioyning together of Certaine Persons: and also of the Lamentable Breach and Division which fell amongst them*, in *The Writings of Robert Harrison and Robert Browne*, op. cit., 397. [Citations will be to the Peel-Carlson edition but will use the original title of the work cited.] Harrison, a native of Norfolk, had matriculated as a pensioner at St. John's, but transferred to Corpus Christi in 1564 and there proceeded B.A. (1567) and M.A. (1572). Browne was admitted to Corpus in 1570 and proceeded B.A. in 1572—"being placed 18th in the list," [Robert] *Masters' History of Corpus Christi College and the Blessed Mary in the University of Cambridge with Additional matters and a Continuation to the present time by John Lamb* (London, 1831), 460. It is significant that Harrison and Browne were at Corpus during the tenure of Thomas Aldrich, a "troublous precision" who signed petitions on behalf of Cartwright and referred to his former patron and predecessor as Master of the college, Matthew Parker, as "the Pope of Lambeth Palace and of Bene't College," ibid., 125; *Parker Correspondence*, 429. On the Aldrich affair see Porter, *Reformation and Reaction*, 149-55.

university both Browne and Harrison took up the occupation of school-masters rather than seeking careers within the church. Browne taught for three years until "he thought that fruict of his labour was toe much uncertaine";[126] Harrison for a briefer time because of his clash with the Bishop of Norwich.[127]

We next find Browne in the company of Richard Greenham, rector of Dry Drayton near Cambridge, who attracted to his household a number of young reformers, all disaffected with the slow pace of religious change. At this time Browne was still ambiguously related to the established church and advocated a position roughly equivalent to that later adopted by the non-separating congregationalists:

> Thus was he setled not to seeke anie approveing or authorising off the bishopes. But because he knewe the trouble that would followe, iff he so precedded, he sought meanes off quietnes so much as was lawfull; and for dealing with the bishopes, he was off this iudgement, that men maie nowe deale with them, as before thei might with the pharises: that is, so far as we nether sinne against God, nor geve offence unto men.[128]

In other words, Browne was in the Church of England, but not of it. Earlier the advanced Puritans had found a manifesto in the *Admonition to the Parliament* with its slogan—"in every congregation a lawful and godly seignorie"—and the implied threat—"a true platforme of a church reformed . . . or els"![129] But soon reaction set in and Parker's new campaign for subscription did much to dampen the promise of 1572. By the end of the decade the abuses listed by Field and Wilcox not only remained but had multiplied: "unlearned and readying" ministers, created by the bishops "60, 80, or a 100 at a clap, and . . . [sent] abroad into the country lyke masterles men"; the prayer book, "culled and picked out of that popish dunghil . . . full of all abominations"; the bishops themselves—"blind busserdes, Wicked fellowes, and idol shepherdes."[130]

---

[126]*A True and Short Declaration*, 398.

[127]Harrison was appointed to the school at Aylsham, a village near Norwich, on the promise that he would be neither the "author nor mayntaynor of any faction here," *Liber Joannie Parkhursti*, Cambridge University MS. Ee. 2. 34, f. 127 verso. Soon after his appointment, however, Harrison was insisting on the omission of the sign of the cross at baptism. Because of this, and perhaps other acts of nonconformity, he was dismissed from his position as we learn from a letter of Parkhurst to Parker, 29 January 1573/74: "I have clenely Dischardged Harrison from the schole at Aylesham," ibid., f. 145 verso.

[128]*A True and Short Declaration*, 403.

[129]*Puritan Manifestoes: A Study of the Origin of the Puritan Revolt*, eds. W. H. Frere and C. E. Douglas (London, 1954), 16, 8 [hereafter *Puritan Manifestoes*].

[130]Ibid., 24, 10, 21; *A True and Short Declaration*, 400.

From prison Field observed with alarm: "The wound groweth desperate."[131] For Browne and others the wound had become intolerable.

Browne's first public break with the church came in 1578 when, after accepting a call to preach at St. Bene't's church in Cambridge, he refused to secure the required license from the bishop. His brother, however, on his own initiative, applied to Archbishop Grindal for a license for him, and on June 6, and June 7, 1579, respectively, he was granted dimissory letters and a license to preach.[132] Browne disposed of both of these documents in a contemptuous manner:

> Howe be it the bishopes seales were gotten him by his brother, Which he both refused beffore the officers, and being written for him would not paie for them, and also being afterward paied for by his brother, he lost one, and burnt an other in the fier, and an other being sent to him to Cambridge, he kept it by him, till in his trouble it was delivered to a Iustisse off peace, and so from him, as is supposed, to the bishop off Norwich.[133]

The justice of the peace was probably Sir Robert Jermyn, a magistrate at Bury St. Edmunds, where Browne was apprehended but dealt with leniently, thanks to his family connection with Lord Burghley.[134] In a letter to Burghley, Jermyn stated that he had "formerly examined both the man and the matter," referred to his "affection towards his [Browne's] weldoing," and expressed the hope that Burghley could prevent Browne from "going to farr," and that he would succeed "in makying hym of a man very hable so very fytt, to yeald the Church his profitable service."[135]

By 1581 Browne had clearly gone too far. He was now in Norwich lodging with Harrison who held the position of Master of the Great Hospital. There "they often had talcke together, of the lamentable abuses, disorders, and sinnes which nowe raigne everie Where."[136] These conversations, held within the shadow of Norwich Cathedral, led to the decision to separate since, as Browne argued, "God wil receave none to commun-

[131]*The Seconde Parte of a Register*, vol. 1, 89.

[132]These are addressed to "Roberto Browne in artibus Bacchalaureo" and are printed in full in Latin in Burrage, op. cit., 5-7. Our knowledge of Browne's call to St. Bene't's derives from Thomas Fuller, *The Church History of Britain* (London, 1842; original edition 1655), vol. 3, 62-66. St. Bene't's, the oldest parish church in Cambridge, was attached to Corpus Christi, and in 1578 became the chapel for the college.

[133]*A True and Short Declaration*, 404.

[134]Sir William Cecil, Lord Burghley, was a distant kinsman, a fact which worked to Browne's advantage on more than this one occasion. See Burleigh to Freke, 21 April 1581, in Fuller, op. cit., 62-63; F. I. Cater, "Robert Browne's Ancestors and Descendants," *Transactions*, Congregational Historical Society 2 (1905).

[135]British Museum, MS. Lansdowne 33, no. 67, f. 167.

[136]*A True and Short Declaration*, 407.

ion and covenant With him, Which as yet are at one with the Wicked."[137] At first Harrison was reluctant to break his ties with the forward preachers of Norwich of whom he "made great accountes . . . and said that much good was done by them."[138] But "he came on more and more"[139] and before long was firmly convinced that it was the duty of God's people to "remove themselves"[140]: "I demand of them [those preachers who remained within the church] if there be any patcher of haulter w^t the Lord, or if thei may yoke an oxe or an asse together in the L. tillage. . . . It is not ynough to be wishers and woulders, as manie be at this daye. . . ."[141] The decisive break came on "a day appointed" when the two leaders gathered with their followers, and

> gave their consent, to ioine them selves to the Lord, in one covenant and felloweshipp together, and to keep and seek agrement under his lawes and government: and therefore did utterlie flee and avoide such like disorders and wickednes. . . .[142]

Norwich was particularly ripe for this resurgence of Separatism for Bishop Freke, unlike his predecessor Parkhurst, had suspended many of the forward preachers in his diocese, including John More, the famous "Apostle of Norwich," and had alienated much of his constituency.[143] Some of these, deprived of their customary ministrations, responded to the appeal of Browne and Harrison. Harrison later defended the secret meetings of the "companie" and described the process which led to the

---

[137]Ibid., 412.

[138]Ibid., 411. In 1580 both Harrison and Browne had appended their names, along with 173 others, to a document entitled "The Supplication of Norwich men to the Queenes Matie," *A Seconde Parte of a Register*, vol. 1, 157-60, which called upon the Queen to establish "that holie Eldership." B. R. White has shown that perhaps as late as 1581 Browne still interpreted "Tell it to the church" in a presbyterian rather than a congregational sense, "A Puritan Work by Robert Browne," *Baptist Quarterly* 18 (1959-60), 109-17.

[139]Ibid., 407.

[140]*A Little Treatise uppon the firste Verse of the 122. Psalm*, 120.

[141]*A Treatise of the Church and the Kingdome of Christ*, 31-32; *A Little Treatise*, 91.

[142]*A True and Short Declaration*, 422. It is likely that the covenant was taken in the first months of 1581 for on April 19 of that year Bishop Freke complained to Burghley of "one Robert Browne a miniester" who had delivered "unto ye people corrupt and contentious doctryne," and had seduced "ye vulgar sort of the people" who were "assembling them selves together to the number of an hundred at a tyme in privat howses and conventicles to heare him. . . ." British Museum, MS. Landsdowne 33, no. 13, f. 38.

[143]On Freke's episcopate see Collinson, "The Puritan Classical Movement in the Reign of Elizabeth I," unpublished Ph.D. thesis, University of London (1957), chapter nine; A. Hassell Smith, *County and Court* (Oxford, 1974), 201-28. On More see article by William A. S. Hewins in *D.N.B.*, vol. 13, 872-73.

covenant-taking as a gradual withdrawal spurred by pressure from the ecclesiastical authorities:

> You charge us that we pswade the people to be rather in houses and corners then to be where there is the publique face of the Church ... for or mynister preached first and we heard him in a Church of lime and stone, from thence we were driven into the Churchyard, from thence into a house adioyning upon the Church-yard, from whence ... to prison. ... We have sought no corners, but were driven from open places into corners.[144]

At this time Norwich was also the center of a thriving community of "strangers," mostly of Dutch origin, which had its own place of worship and was regulated by its own consistory. All of the strangers in Norwich were required to renounce the standard Anabaptist tenets, but as late as 1575 "sondrye straungers borne in the Lowe countryes," were found to "maynteyne the most horrible and dampnable error of the anabaptistes."[145] That some of these Norwich Anabaptists may have influenced Browne, or even have joined with his company, is an intriguing possibility for which, however, conclusive evidence is lacking.[146]

The pressure on the Separatist company continued unabated, and sometime between March 25, 1582, when Harrison resigned his Mastership of the Great Hospital, and August, 1582, when Browne's tract, *A treatise of reformation without tarying for anie* was published in Middelburgh, the decision was made to seek refuge in the Netherlands.[147] We

---

[144] *A Treatise of the Church*, 60, 67.

[145] Transcript from the "Stranger's Book" printed by Stephen S. Slaughter, "The Dutch Church in Norwich," *Transactions*, Congregational Historical Society 12 (1933), 92. See also D. L. Rickwood, "The Origin and Decline of the Stranger Community of Norwich (with Special Reference to the Dutch Congregation), 1565-1700," unpublished M.A. thesis, University of East Anglia (1967).

[146] Thomas Fuller, op. cit., vol. 3, 62, offers the only evidence for Browne's proselyting among the Dutch residents of Norwich: "Brown, beginning with the Dutch, soon proceeding to infect his own countrymen." Anabaptist influence on the early Brownist churches has been strongly suggested by some scholars: J. De Hoop Scheffer, *History of the Free Churchmen* (Ithaca, N.Y., n.d.), 8; Irvin B. Horst, "England," *Mennonite Encyclopedia*, vol. 2, 220; William R. Estep, *The Anabaptist Story* (Nashville, 1963), 207-15; and strongly denied by others: Burrage, *Early English Dissenters*, vol. 1, 68; White, *Separatist Tradition*, xii. The only evidence I have discovered which has not been noted in earlier research is a statement in David Calderwood's "The Historie of the Kirk in Scotland," in which he, quoting from a lost account of Browne's appearance before the session of the kirk of Edinburgh, reported that "he [Browne] affirmed, as the manuscript bereth that the soules died." British Museum, MS. Harleian 4736, vol. 3, p. 1305. Mortalism is generally regarded as an Anabaptist trait, as is the belief in the celestial flesh of Christ for Dutch Anabaptists. Cf. Williams, *The Radical Reformation*, 104-06, 580-92.

[147] Harrison resigned as Master of the Great Hospital on Lady Day (March 25), 1582. Norfolk and Norwich Record Office, "Great Hospital Account Rolls," 1581/82.

learn of Browne's activities in Middelburgh from a letter of one Richard
Godard, an officer of the English Company of Merchant Adventurers,
who informed Walsingham that Browne was exercising, "a ministry in a
corner, deluding certain of her Majesty's subjects that to follow him have
left their ordinary calling in England." To his knowledge the company
consisted of "some thirty or fourty persons, which ar in poore estate, and
for the moste parte visited with sicknes, not well agreinge with the aire in
those parts." He was further informed that a certain William Pagett,
"sometime a brewers clerk in London," had been selling Browne's books
to the English merchants, and these writings he was forwarding to Walsingham and Burghley for their perusal.[148]

The potential impact of Separatist writings was not lost on the authorities in England, and on June 30, 1583, a proclamation declared the works
of Browne and Harrison to be "seditious, scismaticall and erronious
printed Bookes and libelles, tending to the depraving of the Ecclesiastical
government established within this Realme."[149] In the same month two of
Browne's disciples who had remained in England, Elias Thacker and
John Copping, were brought before the assizes held at Bury St. Edmunds
for "dispersing Brownes bookes and harrisons bookes." When they
refused to renounce their deeds but "commended all thinges in the said
bookes to be good and godlye," they were sentenced to be hanged.[150] At
their execution some forty copies of the books in question were burned.

Meanwhile in Middelburgh physical sickness was compounded by
spiritual dissension as the company which in England had pledged "to
hould together" now fell prey to internal wrangling and schism. The
disputes which led to the demise of the group are difficult to reconstruct,
but they involved issues over which later Separatists were to argue with
equal vehemence: the role of the women in the congregation (Browne was
accused of condemning Harrison's wife, "Sister Allens," as a reprobate),
the question of whether the exiles could in good conscience return to
England, and the proper function of the pastoral office. Before the breach
was complete Harrison described Browne as "leaninge to Antichristian
pride, and bitternes," and later complained "that Caine dealt not so ill

[148]Godard to Walsingham, August 22, 1582, Public Record Office S.P. 83/16/117

[149]British Museum, MS. G. 6463, f. 225. Notes from what appears to be an official
examination of Harrison's *A Little Treatise* are found in British Museum, MS. Additional
29546, ff. 113-116 verso.

[150]Sir Christopher Wray to Burghley, July 6, 1583, British Museum, MS. Lansdowne
38, no. 64, ff. 162-63. On Thacker and Copping see Peel, *Noble Army of Congregational
Martyrs,* op. cit., 30-32.

with his brother Abel, as he hath dealt with me."[151] For his part Browne, having been censured by the majority of the company, expelled them from his chamber which was their accustomed meeting place.[152] In the end, according to Browne's report, "he himselfe was threatened to be thurst out of his chamber."[153] With a handful of devoted followers—true "Brownists"—"Trouble-church" Browne, as he was soon to be dubbed by a Puritan opponent, sailed for Scotland whence, following an unpleasant encounter with the presbyterian kirk of Edinburgh, he returned to England, recanted his Separatism, and made a permanent, if tenuous, peace with the church he had renounced some five years before.[154] Harrison, true to the end to his Separatist convictions, continued to lead the depleted company at Middelburg until his untimely death around 1585.[155]

Browne's meteoric career as a Separatist and his subsequent rapprochement with the established Church insured that his legacy would be a dubious one. In his own lifetime he was shunned as an apostate and "a slidebacke" by other Separatists, whereas Puritans regarded him as a dissembler who "cunningly counterfeitheth conformity."[156] Nonetheless, the writings of Browne, and to a lesser extent those of Harrison, contained the basic principles of Separatist ecclesiology. Later Separatists, even when they sought to dissociate themselves from his name and to disengage him from their tradition, were developing and defending a doctrine of the church to which the ill-famed Browne had given formative

---

[151]*A Little Treatise, 93;* Stephen Bredwell, *The Rasing of the Foundations of Brownisme* (London, 1588), sig. A 2 verso [hereafter *The Rasing*].

[152]*A True and Short Declaration*, 426: "The meeting beinge in R. B. chamber, he cae in agaie and tould the, that he was unwillinge the should vees their meetings in his chamber after that manner." See also Audley Danett to Walsingham, September 2, 1583, Public Record Office S P 83/17/3: [the meetings] "ar kepte in Brownes house which he hath hired in the towne."

[153]*A True and Short Declaration*, 429.

[154]On Browne's visit to Scotland, see Calderwood, op. cit., 1305-07. James I in his *Basilikon Doron* (London, 1603), listed Browne with Penry and other "brainsick and headie preachers" who "at sundrie times came to Scotland, to sowe their popple amonst us," sigs. A 4 verso—A 5 recto. Browne's subscription, made on October 7, 1585, is printed in Bredwell, *The Rasing*, 127, 134, 137, 140.

[155]Bredwell, in 1588, wrote of Harrison as if he were dead: "Onely I will produce a testimonie or two of master Harrisons, who in his life time was bewitched by Browne," *The Rasing*, sig. A 2 verso.

[156]Ibid., sig. A 3 recto, sig. A 1 verso.

expression.[157] At least three elements in Browne's thought on this subject were assumed into the standard Separatist position as it was hammered out amidst numerous controversies over the next thirty years: the church as a covenanted community, gathered and separate from the parish assemblies, and entered into by voluntary consent.

Browne's chief contribution to Separatist ecclesiology was to place his church-ideal in the context of a covenant relationship. The church he defined as "a companie or number of beleeuers, which by a willing couenaunt made with their God, are vnder the gouernement of God and Christ, and keepe his Lawes in one holie communion."[158] On a larger scale Browne applied the covenant-concept to all levels and associations within society: civil magistrate and commonwealth, husband and wife, parents and children, masters and servants, teachers and scholars—"there must be a due couenaunt betweene them."[159] Each of these covenant relationships implied the assumption of mutual obligations, the neglect of which would place the covenant in jeopardy. The conditional nature of the covenant also extended to the agreement God had made with his church. He had promised to be our God "*if* we forsake not his gouernement," and "to be the God of our seede, *while* we are his people."[160] Browne's conviction that the Church of England had forsaken its covenant responsibilities, and was therefore in a state of apostasy, precipitated his act of

---

[157]The most succinct summary of Browne's theology is B. R. White, *Separatist Tradition*, 44-66. I am indebted to White's book and to his unpublished dissertation on Browne, although he tends to undervalue Browne's importance for later Separatism.

[158]*A Booke which sheweth the life and manners of all true Christians, and howe vnlike they are vnto Turkes and Papistes and Heathen folke*, 227, cf. 253.

[159]Ibid., 342. On the covenant of marriage Browne sounds distinctively modern: "Marriage is a lawfull ioyning and fellowship of the husband and wife, as of two in one fleshe, by partaking the vse of eche others love, bodie, and giftes, in one communion of dueties.... They must be meete foe eche others liking in behauiour and personage," ibid., 382-83.

[160]Ibid., 254. (My italics.) The conditional character of the divine covenant had been emphasized by William Tyndale, although the source and meaning of his interpretation is debatable. Cf. W. A. Clebsch, *England's Earliest Protestants, 1520-1535* (New Haven, 1964), 181-204; J. G. Moller, "The beginnings of Puritan covenant theology, *Journal of Ecclesiastical History* 14 (1963), 46-67; Michael McGiffert, "William Tyndale's Conception of Covenant," ibid. 32 (1981), 167-84. John F. H. New traces Browne's mutualist understanding of the covenant back to Tyndale, and sees it as a trait which distinguished Separatists from other Puritans, *Anglican and Puritan* (Stanford, 1964), 94-95. Richard L. Greaves shows the fallacy of New's generalization, and offers a more plausible interpretation of Separatist covenant theology, "The Origins and Early Development of English Covenant Thought," *The Historian* 31 (1968), 21-35.

separation and his call for a renewal of the covenant by "the worthiest, Were thei neuer so feuve."[161]

Nonetheless, in spite of his emphasis upon the conditionality of the covenant relationship, Browne did not alter the basic framework of predestinarian theology which he had learned at Cambridge. In his only effort to place his ecclesiology within a larger theological context, *A Booke which Sheweth the life and manners of all true Christians,* Browne devotes the first 34 points to a discussion of the nature of God and the plan of salvation. After setting forth the doctrine of the Trinity and the attributes of God in accordance with orthodox terminology, Browne reviews the three ways in which God has provided the means of salvation: first, in His secret counsel; then, in His readiness to help us; and, in the actual show of that help.[162] God's counsel is further described as the coincidence of foreknowledge and preordination: "He foreseeth & purposeth what helpe we shall haue."[163] Out of God's counsel flow His gratuitous election and predestination which Browne defines as

> his full consent or counsaile, whereby he is setled to saue those whom he hath chosen, and after that manner which pleaseth and liketh him.[164]

Thus the covenant by which the outward Church is gathered presupposes the prevenient calling of the elect, the "inwarde working of the holy Ghost in our hartes," and at the same time offers assurance of the same through the communal seals of baptism and the Lord's Supper.[165] Browne does not go beyond these formulary expressions on predestination and so leaves unexplored the more thorny implications of the doctrine of election such as divine responsibility for the Fall, the role of reprobation in

---

[161]*A True and Short Declaration,* 404.

[162]*A Booke which sheweth,* 240.

[163]Ibid., 242.

[164]Ibid., 251. Cf. Harrison's description of the remnant "saued by the Election of grace, of them selues no more worthie then the rest: but by the Lorde called of purpose, and redeemed from out of the worlde," *Three Formes of Catechismes,* 137.

[165]*A Booke which sheweth,* 256-61, 278-85. Cf. Stephen Mayor, *The Lord's Supper in Early English Dissent* (London, 1972), 29-38. In an earlier "talke" on "matters of the church and Kingdom of God," Browne and Harrison had discussed the inviolability of divine election: "And faith may be wholie Wanting for a time, till the Lord do call vs, and drawe vs vnto him: but the spirit is geuen to the elect euen while thei are infantes. And this spirit, though for a time it maie be hidden and couered, yet can it not cleane be put out and quenshed. Therfore by it we are said to be sealed off God. . . . Wherebie is ment that that spirit shall neuer wholi cease to worck litle or much toward our saluation. Noe more can it be that faith being once thorovvelie wrought, should wholie faile. . . . For though thei sinne neuer so greuouslie, yet iff thei be elect, thei haue alvvaise some conscience of their welfare in Christ, or forevvarning of some grace vvhich is tovvardes them." *A True and Short Declaration,* 409.

the counsel of God, the relation of the visible to the invisible Church, and the possibility of the forfeiture of saving faith. Later Separatists such as Robinson would wrestle with these and related problems in their attempt to affirm both the ecclesiology of the covenanted, disciplined congregation and the doctrine of absolute predestination.[166]

For Browne the basic ecclesiastical unit was not the parish, but the congregation—a congregation which elected its own officers, disciplined its own members, and administered the sacraments only to its committed initiates. Browne's rejection of the parishes as not only unreformed but unreformable ("O ye my messengers, take ye no charge of such Parishes, for they be not Zion")[167] set him apart from the most advanced of his Puritan contemporaries who were determined to work against the system from within the system. In addition, it raised serious questions concerning Browne's loyalty to the civil authority in an age when the parish was the basic administrative as well as religious unit of society. *A treatise of reformation without tarying for anie* was written to counter these charges, but in spite of Browne's protestations of loyalty and his affirmation of "the ciuill sworde," his circumscription of the magisterial role in religion posed a radical challenge to the theory of the royal supremacy. The modern magistrates, unlike the kings of ancient Israel, possess no *ius reformandi*: "they haue no ecclesiastical authoritie at all . . . they [may] doo nothing concerning the Church, but onelie ciuillie. . . ."[168] By the same token, they must not be permitted to impede reformation for "the welfare of the Church must be more regarded and sought, then the welfare of whole Kingdomes and Countries. . . ."[169]

Embedded in the protest against magisterial reformation was a thorough disdain of compulsion in matters religious: "the Lord's people is of the willing sorte."[170] G. F. Nuttall has identified the "principle of free-

---

[166]By stressing Browne's mutualist understanding of the Church covenant relationship, while overlooking his comments on predestination, some scholars, e.g. Fraser, op. cit., 266, have concluded that Browne anticipated the Arminian modification of Calvin's doctrine of election. Browne's statement that through Christ's death "the meanes is offered to all men for to be saued," *A Booke which sheweth*, 247, is cited as support for this view. However, this quotation proves no more than that Browne accepted the universal sufficiency of the atonement in good agreement with most strict Calvinists.

[167]*A Treatise upon the 23. of Matthewe*, 206.

[168]*A Treatise of reformation without tarying for anie*, 155, 164. "For both Iehoshua the high Prieste, and Zerubbabel the Prince, were figures of the high priesthoode and princedome of Christe, and also had an ecclesiastical gouernement ouer the Church, *which our Magistrates haue not.*" Ibid. (My italics.)

[169]Ibid., 159.

[170]Ibid., 162.

dom" as one of four basic ingredients in nascent Congregationalism.[171] While Browne hardly anticipated the developments of the seventeenth century, and had only an inchoate theory of toleration, his emphasis on the voluntary church and the unforced conscience went beyond the thinking of any other English religious leader of his time. While the Queen and bishops sought to govern the church through the enforcement of uniformity, and while the Puritans looked for reformation through legislative enactment, Browne insisted that the kingdom of God came not "by battell, by horses and by horssemen, that is, by ciuill power and pompe of Magistrates: by their Proclamations and Parliamentes. . . . The inwarde obedience, with newnes of life, that is the Lordes kingdome."[172]

"IN SUNDRIE MOST NOYSOME AND VILE PRISONS": BARROW, GREENWOOD, AND THE LONDON SEPARATISTS

Browne's return to the Church of England, as already noted, was met with extreme scepticism by those who saw him as a "slipperie shifter" who had feigned conformity for the sake of liberty, but whose true sentiments were still those of a confirmed Separatist.[173] Stephen Bredwell, a moderate Puritan, anxious to place as much distance as possible between his party and the Separatists, published in 1588 a collection of tracts entitled *The Rasing of the foundations of Brownisme* in which he claimed that Browne, after his subscription, "yet still seduceth, and carieth away from the ordinary assemblies, so many as he can."[174] Among these was a "seelie woman" in the parish of Olaves in Silverstreet whom Browne had so "confirmed in her sottish separation," that she had publicly renounced her excommunication from the church, and "boasted of Bro. spreading of his writings . . . to a hundreth miles distance from London."[175] Further, he was known to have preached one Sunday in a private house "not farre from Ludgate." On this occasion he was "soundly resisted" by "one M. W." who persuaded some of those present to return to church for the next sermon, leaving "Browne with the rest that liked better to tarrie."[176] While

---

[171]G. F. Nuttall, *Visible Saints: the Congregational Way, 1640-1660* (Oxford, 1957), 101-30. On Browne's theory of toleration W. K. Jordan, *The Development of Religious Toleration in England* (London, 1932), vol. 1, 263-75.

[172]*A Treatise of reformation without tarying for anie*, 156-57.

[173]Bredwell, *The Rasing*, 138.

[174]Ibid., 126.

[175]Ibid., 139.

[176]Ibid., 139-40. This is an obvious pun on Browne's famous treatise.

it is difficult to judge the effect of Browne's quixotic ministry during these years, it is significant that he found a ready audience among London dissidents.[177] Bredwell, though admitting that he knew more the nature than the number of the sect he opposed, claimed that "their ful swarme and store be (as it is most likely) in London, and the partes neare adioyning."[178]

On October 8, 1587, twenty-one so-called "Brownestes" were arrested and examined for holding a private conventicle in Henry Martin's house in St. Andrew's in the Wardrobe, near St. Paul's. [179] Among those apprehended was at least one survivor from the Separatist circles of the late 1560s: Nicholas Crane, lecturer in the Minories and sometime preacher to the Plumbers' Hall congregation. Another, John Chandler, was a former member of Browne's Middelburg church. One of the women taken in the group, Margaret Maynerd, claimed that "ther is no church in England" and admitted that "she hath not bin at church theis ten yeres."[180] The leader of this conventicle was John Greenwood, a Norfolk

---

[177]Browne justified his surreptitious preaching in a private letter written on Dec. 31, 1588, to his "Louing Vncke," Mr. Flowers: "An Aunswer to Mr. Flowers Letter," 516-29. Browne's final gesture of capitulation to the ecclesiastical authorities came only in 1591 when he was admitted to the orders of deacon and priest and presented with the living of Achurch-cum-Thorpe in the diocese of Peterborough. Here he remained for forty years, though not without vexing parochial and marital problems. See F. I. Cater, "Robert Browne and the Achurch Parish Register," *Transactions,* Congregational Historical Society, 3 (1906), 126; Burrage, *The True Story of Robert Browne,* op. cit., 40-73.

[178]Bredwell, *The Rasing,* sig. G 2 recto. The persistence of underground dissent in the years following the Armada is reflected in the prediction made in early 1591 by an astrologer who called himself "Adam Foulweather": "Out of the old stock of heresie, this spring it is to be feared, will bloom new schismaticall opinions and strange sects, as Brownists, Barowists, and such balductum devises, to the great hinderance to the unitie of the Church and confusion of the true faith." Quoted in John Booty, "Tumult in Cheapside: The Hacket Conspiracy," *Historical Magazine of the Protestant Episcopal Church* 42 (1973), 293.

[179]Public Record Office, S. P., Domestic, Elizabeth, 204 (10), printed in *Early English Dissenters,* vol. 2, 19-24.

[180]*Early English Dissenters,* vol. 2, 20. Maynerd was an aged widow who subsequently died in the Newgate prison. Crane had been active in the Wandsworth presbytery and wrote a tract against subscription, published in *A parte of a register,* 119-24. Michael Watts, *The Dissenters from the Reformation to the French Revolution* (Oxford, 1978), 35, incorrectly identifies another prisoner, Edith Bury, as a member of Richard Fitz's "priuye churche." He has confused Edithe Burry with Edde Burris who, at any rate, belonged to the Plumbers' Hall group. Cf. *Early English Dissenters,* vol. 2, 11. Chandler, who had eight children, was soon joined in prison by his wife Alyce. Following Chandler's death in the Counter Poultry, Alyce was released from prison on bail. See *The Writings of John Greenwood, 1587-1590,* ed. Leland H. Carlson, 308, 315. [Volumes 4-6 of the Elizabethan Nonconformist Texts comprise the works of Greenwood and Barrow, all of them edited by Leland H. Carlson.]

clergyman who, becoming convinced that his ministry "was wholly evill, both in office, entrance, and administration," had left his cure, and aligned himself with the London Separatists during the years 1585-87.[181] Henry Barrow, Greenwood's associate in the leadership of the congregation, had been out of London when the arrests occurred, but some six weeks later, on November 19, while visiting his friends in the Clink, he was also taken as a prisoner. For the next six years Barrow and Greenwood, the "two founding fathers of Separatism," as Leland H. Carlson has called them, were shuffled from prison to prison, Barrow never being released, and Greenwood only for a short time, before their execution on April 6, 1593.

Barrow was a well-connected gentleman of some means, trained in the law at Gray's Inn, and, before his conversion, a frequent visitor at the Court where he was known as "a Great Gamster and a dicer."[182] According to Governor Bradford his conversion occurred one day when he and a friend were walking in London and passed by a church where the preacher was

> att his Sermon very Loud . . . upon which mr Barrow said unto his Consort Lett vs Goe in and heare what this man saith that is thus earnest Tush saith the other whal shall wee goe to hear a man talk &c: But in hee went and sat downe; and the minnester was vehement in Reproueing sin . . . [and] it touched him to the quick . . . soe as God sett it home to his soule and began to worke his Repentance and Conversion thereby.[183]

---

[181] Ibid., 241. Greenwood, who had entered Corpus Christi, Cambridge, some six years after Browne completed his course there, was made a deacon in 1581, and ordained a priest in 1582. He served as a rector in Lincolnshire, 1582-83, and probably held the curacy at Rackheath in Norfolk when he resigned his benefice in 1585. At his examination in May 1588/89, he was asked "Who disgrated yow [from the ministry]?" To which he replied: "I disgraded myself through God's mercy by repentance," Ibid., 22. Cf. the article by C. L. Kingsford in *D.N.B.*, vol. 8, 527-28; C. H. Cooper, *Athenae Cantabrigiensis*, 1586-1609 (London, 1861), vol. 2, 153-54.

[182] *Plymouth Church Records*, vol. 1, 125. Cf. Barrow's statement at his examination in March, 1588/89: "I had sometime frequented the court," *The Writings of Henry Barrow, 1587-1590*, 179, and George Gifford's slur on Barrow's earlier life: "I doo not know, Master Barrow, what your former conversation hath been: but by your speeches a man would judge that you had spent your time . . . in the societies of carding and dicing," *The Writings of John Greenwood and Henry Barrow, 1591-1593*, 161. Barrow matriculated at Clare Hall, Cambridge, in 1566 and there proceeded B.A. in 1570. He became a member of Gray's Inn in 1576. Cf. *The Register of Admissions to Gray's Inn, 1521-1889*, ed. Joseph Foster (London, 1889), 49. The standard study of Barrow remains F. J. Powicke, *Henry Barrow, Separatist and the Exiled Church of Amsterdam* (London, 1900). Also worthy of note is David W. Atkinson, "A Brief Discoverie of the False Church: Henry Barrow's Last Spiritual Statement," *Historical Magazine of the Protestant Episcopal Church* 48 (1979), 265-78.

[183] *Plymouth Church Records*, vol. 1, 127.

The frivolous libertine turned adamant precisian! Barrow's legal mind and his sharp wit made him an able and provocative disputant, to the consternation of Whitgift. On one occasion after repeatedly refusing to take the oath *ex officio mero*, and suggesting that his accusers be so sworn rather than he, Whitgift exploded:

> Where is his keeper? You shalnot prattle here. Away with him: clap him up close, close, let no man come at him: I wil make him tel on other tale, yet I have done with him.[184]

At his fourth examination, when the inquisitors included Burghley and other members of the Privy Council as well as Whitgift and Aylmer, Barrow showed further contempt for the Archbishop:

Lord Chancellor:	What is that man? (pointing to Canterbury).
Barrow:	The Lord gave me the spirit of boldness, so that I answered: He is a monster, a miserable compound, I know not what to make (call) him: he is neither ecclesiastical nor civil, even that second beast spoken of in the Revelation.
Lord Treasurer:	Wher is that place, shew it.
Barrow:	So I turned to the thirteenth chapter and began at the eleventh verse, and read a litle. Then I turned to II Thessalonians 2. But the beast arose for anger, gnashing his teeth, and said: wil you suffer him, my lords? So I was pluckt up by the warden's man from my knees and caried away.[185]

Barrow later admitted that his "unsanctified mouth" had done his cause no good at this hearing, but from his performance at subsequent examinations there is little to suggest that this was anything but a contrite moment of uncharacteristic prudence.[186]

Apart from the example of their courage and steadfastness in the face of persecution, the chief contribution of Barrow and Greenwood to the Separatist tradition lay in their enormous literary activity. A steady stream of letters, pamphlets, treatises, petitions, and transcripts of their examinations flowed from their pens, a feat made all the more impressive by the fact that they were kept, for extended periods, in "close" imprison-

---

[184]*The Writings of Henry Barrow, 1587-1590*, 104. On the oath "ex officio mero" see *Tudor Constitutional Documents*, ed. J. R. Tanner (Cambridge, 1922), 374, 572. This oath required the accused to, in effect, incriminate themselves before they had faced their accusers, or even learned the full extent of charges against them. Refusal to take the oath was tantamount to a sentence of guilt, from which there was no appeal. Richard Greaves has noted that the excessive use of this device was an important factor in welding an alliance between common lawyers and Puritans, *Society and Religion in Elizabethan England* (Minneapolis, 1981), 679-92.

[185]Ibid., 188.

[186]Ibid., 188-89.

ment.[187] Daniel Studley later testified that he had received the original copy of Barrow's "brief" treatise on the false church (it runs to over 400 pages in the modern critical edition!) "shete by shete at Mr. Henry Barrowes study in the Flette."[188] These he smuggled out of the prison and delivered to one James Forester who saw them through the press, perhaps at Dort.[189] The publication of these prison writings elicited equally lengthy responses from both Anglican and Puritan apologists, notably Robert Some and George Gifford, and these in turn stimulated counterattacks from the sequestered Separatists.[190]

From the writings of Barrow and Greenwood emerged the most comprehensive statement of Separatist principles set forth in the sixteenth century. In the earliest of his extant writings Barrow announced "fower principall and weighty causes" of separation, and his later works consist primarily of variations on this fourfold theme.[191] First, the basis of membership in the parish churches was wrong. Barrow's standard was the same as Browne's: "Ther may none be admitted into the church of Christ, but such as enter by publike profession of the true faith."[192] Yet the Church of England included a mixed multitude of whom some were godly, but most were not: "atheistes, papistes, anabaptistes and heretikes

---

[187]Lancelot Andrewes on one occasion made light of Barrow's confinement: "For close emprisonment you are most happie. The solitarie and contemplative life I hold the most blessed life. It is the life I would chuse." To which Barrow replied: "You can speak philosophically but not christianly," *The Writings of John Greenwood, 1587-1590*, 143. Some of the Separatists were subjected to even harsher treatment. One of them, John Purdie, was forced to grind at the "myll" and then cast into the "Litle Ease," a bizarre cell of awkward dimensions in which the prisoner could neither stand, sit, nor lie, but only squat. Cf. John Lingard, *History of England* (London, 1825), vol. 7, 522; *The Writings of Henry Barrow, 1587-1590*, 26-27.

[188]*The Egerton Papers*, ed. J. P. Collier (London, 1840), 175.

[189]In 1592 Robert Stookes, a sometime disciple of Barrow, testified that "the booke intituled a Breiff Dyssection [sic] of the false Church" [was] "prynted at Dort about Christmas last. . .," ibid., 174.

[190]These writings have been catalogued and placed in historical context by Peter Milward, *Religious Controversies of the Elizabethan Age: A Survey of Printed Sources* (Lincoln, Neb., 1977), esp. 96-99, 172-74.

[191]*The Writings of Henry Barrow, 1587-1590*, 54.

[192]Ibid., 280. The covenant of the Barrowist congregation seems to have been simpler in form than that of the Norwich Separatists. William Clerke, "a worker of Capps," said that on becoming a member he merely "made promise to stand with the said Congregacion soe longe as they did stand for the truthe and glory of god." Another member, "Iohn Barns tayler," testified "that at his first entringe into that societie he made noe other vowe, but that he wold followe them soe farr forth as the word of god did warraunt him," *Early English Dissenters*, vol. 2, 33-34.

of al sortes, gluttons, riotours, blasphemers, perjures, covetous, extortioners, thieves, whores, witches, conjurers, et., and who not, that dwelleth within this iland."[193] Barrow's rejection of the all-inclusive nature of the Elizabethan church surfaced in a brief exchange between him and Whitgift during his first examination:

A[rchbishop]:	Of what occupation are you?
B[arrow]:	A Christian.
A[rchbishop]:	So are we all.
B[arrow]:	I deny that.[194]

The second cause of separation was the "false and antichristian ministrie" which had been imposed on the parish congregations. [195] Beyond the usual Puritan criticisms of pluralism, nonresidency, and moral inadequacy, Barrow insisted that the only lawful and "true entrans" into the ministry was "by the holy and free election of the Lorde's holie and free people."[196] The demand for congregational initiative and consent in the calling of a minister challenged both Puritan and Anglican practice. The Puritans had long made ample use of lay patronage in the placing of "godly preachers," and one of these, Thomas Sperin, sought in vain to justify the system to Barrow.

Sperin:	We have the approbation of the congregation also.
Barrow:	You have not. Your curats (as is said) are made ministers *in nubibus*, without anie flocke. Your parsons are nominat by the patron, and made by the bishop.
Sperin:	The patron's choise is the people's choise.
Barrow:	How can you saie the patron's choise is the people's, when they have neither privitie, consent or assent. Be the patron a woman, an infant, an ideote, have he forty benefices and those in all the parts of the lande, such as he hath never

---

[193] *The Writings of Henry Barrow, 1587-90*, 281.

[194] Ibid., 97.

[195] Ibid., 54.

[196] Ibid., 58, 216. Cf. Barrow's further description of the election process: "For Christ hath appointed that every particular church, all the members thereof gathered togither as well learned as other, with one accord should make choice of their ministerie after due proofe according to the rules prescribed," ibid., 236. For a contemporary Puritan critique of the ministry of the Church of England, see "The View of the State of the Churche in Cornewall," where incumbents are listed and their "conversation" characterized, e.g. "Fletcher, a preacher sometimes. A man carelesse of his callinge and suspected of whoredome"; "Dr Kenold, Canon of Christes church. His conversation is most in houndes"; "Geare, a mass man. Much suspected for religion and for women"; "N. Hockin. A verie youth, a dicer, his father bought his benefice deer"; "John Beale. A common gamster, the best Wrastler in Cornewall"; "Phillips. A drunkerd and a quarreler with other bad qualities" in *The Seconde Parte of a Register*, vol. 2, 98-110.

seene or knowen, yet doth he present, and the people must
accept. [197]

Further, ministers were to be supported only by "the loving, free, yet
dutifull contribution of the flock" over which they presided, not by the
various endowments, tithes, glebes, and stipends by which ministers of
the Church of England were regularly maintained.[198]

Thirdly, the "fals manner of worshiping" practiced in the parish
church required that they be forsaken "speedelye without any delay."[199]
The Book of Common Prayer had long been attacked as "repugnante to
the worde of God," but by the 1580s most Puritans were willing to use it,
at least in a modified form.[200] But Barrow would have none of this
compromise. He reserved some of his choisest epithets for this "dombe
idoll": "Dagon's stump," "abhominable sacrifyse," "a peice of swyne's-
flesh," "a collop of that fowle mezeled hogg."[201] The stinted prayers and
"stagelike dyalogue" prescribed in the *Book of Common Prayer* stifled
the free moving of the Spirit and the spontaneous response of the people
that should characterize worship.[202] For Barrow the supreme criterion for

---

[197] *The Writings of John Greenwood, 1587-1590*, 250. Sperin, rector of St. Mary
Magdalen Church on Mildstreet, had come to confer with Barrow at the behest of Bishop
Aylmer, ibid., 178-81.

[198] *The Writings of Henry Barrow, 1587-1590*, 235. The objection to the indiscriminate
collection of tithes was related to the first "cause" of separation: "The tithes and set
stipendes of these parrish priestes [are] the goods of the prophane, most wicked, and
ungodly, even of al their parrish indifferently. . . But this contribution is an action of the
church, a communion and dutie of the sainctes," *The Writings of Henry Barrow, 1590-
1591*, 263.

[199] *The Writings of Henry Barrow, 1587-1590*, 54.

[200] *Puritan Manifestoes*, 20. In 1583 the Puritan classis at Dedham proposed that "the
booke of common praier shuld be considered of how farre a Pastor might read therein,"
"Minute Book of the Dedham Classis, 1582-1589," Roland G. Usher, *The Presbyterian
Movement in the Reign of Queen Elizabeth* (London, 1905), 28. On the various Puritan
prayer-books from Knox's Genevan Service Book of 1556 to the Westminster *Directory*
of 1644, see Horton Davies, *The Worship of the English Puritans* (Glasgow, 1948),
115-61.

[201] *The Writings of Henry Barrow, 1587-1590*, 56; *The Writings of John Greenwood,
1587-1590*, 168.

[202] Ibid. Barrow defined prayer as "a confident demanding which faith maketh thorow
the Holy Ghost. . . for their present wantes, estates, etc. How now? Can any read,
prescript, stinted leitourgie, which was penned many yeares or daies before, be said a
powring forth of the heart unto the Lord?. . . Is not this (if they wil have their written stuffe
to be held and used as praier) to bind the Holy Ghost to the froth and leaven of their
lips. . . . Is it not utterly to quench and extinguish the Spirit of God?" *The Writings of
Henry Barrow, 1587-1590*, 365-66.

worship was the "testament of Christ" which he considered abrogated "wher any thing is aded to it or taken from it."[203] Anticipating the Quakers of the next century he even refused to call the days of the week by their common names of Sunday, Monday, etc. because "we are otherwise taught to cal them in the booke of God."[204] From the lack of pneumatic worship and the addition of extra-Scriptural "inventions," many taken over from Rome, Barrow drew the drastic conclusion that the parish assemblies, even the church buildings, had become "Babilonish synagogues," into which true believers should not even enter, and which, moreover, ought to be utterly defaced and destroyed![205] The Barrowists held their own worship services in various secluded spots around London. In the summer they often "melt together in the feilds a mile or more about London"; in the winter they assembled by five o'clock in the morning in a house previously designated.[206] The service consisted of Scripture exposition, extemporaneous prayer ("one speketh and the reste doe grone, or sob, or sigh, as if they wold wringe out teares"), the collection, and a common meal occasionally followed by a simple administration of the Lord's Supper.[207]

The charismatic character of Barrowist prayer was based upon a sense of the immediacy of the Spirit and a belief that formal liturgy or read prayers was a positive encumbrance to spiritual worship. The sobbing and groaning which characterized extemporaneous prayer was supported by reference both to the words of Jesus: "God is a spirit, and must be worshiped in spirit and truth" (John 4:24), and to the Pauline statement that "the Spirit helpeth our infirmities with groaning and sighing that

---

[203]Ibid., 55.

[204]Ibid., 180. Barrow cited as Scriptural proof for this practice two texts, one from Genesis where it is said that God termed the days first, second, etc., the other from the Revelation [1:10] where "the Holy Ghost" termed the first day of the week, "the Lorde's day."

[205]Citing Numbers 33:52 and Deuteronomy 12:2, Barrow called upon the magistrate to raze and deface "all these synagogues": "So far is it that God will be worshiped in them, that he will not have them so much as reserved, least they defile the land and draw us to idolatrie," ibid., 470-71; cf. Powicke, *Henry Barrow,* op. cit., 129-31. For a similar call for the dismantling of the cathedral churches, see *The Second Parte of a Register*, vol. 2, 211.

[206]*The Writings of John Greenwood, 1587-1590*, 294.

[207]Ibid. For the Lord's Supper "fyve whight loves or more were sett uppon the table and ... the pastor did breake the bread and then delivered yt unto some of them, and the deacons delivered to the rest, some ... sittinge and some standinge aboute the table, and ... the pastor delivered the cupp unto one and he to an other, and soe from one to another till they had all dronken," *The Writings of John Greenwood and Henry Barrow, 1591-1593,* 307.

cannot be expressed" (Rom. 8:26). To interpose stinted prayers in either public worship or private devotion constituted a threefold impediment to this pneumatic process: first, it elevated a man-made devise, i.e. the Prayer Book, above the immediate movings of the Spirit which was idolatry; second, it violated the New Testament examples of prayer, such as the publican's plea: "God be merciful unto me a sinner," (Luke 18:13) and the holy womens' falling down at Christ's feet (Matt. 28:9), which illustrated the fervor of spontaneous petition and praise; third, it eliminated the personal engagement of the suppliant which was of the essence of prayer:

> You would teach men in stead of powring forth their harts, to helpe themselves upon a booke, yea, to fetch their cause of sorrowing and sighing from an other man's writing, even in the time of their begging at God's hand.[208]

For this reason even the Lord's Prayer, a standard part of Puritan worship, was to be eschewed, except as a model for all prayer in general. It could thus be *read* but not *prayed*. Why? Because no one hath "present need to aske al the peticions therin conteyned at one time: neither can comprehend them with feeling and faith."[209] Greenwood traced the distinction between prayer and reading to the difference between the Greek words προσευχή and ἀνάγνωσις, the former denoting a "powring fourth" of vows, petitions, supplications, and the like, the latter, a passive "receaving into the soule" of such things as we read.[210] To substitute reading for praying was to deprive the congregation of an important aspect of the Spirit's ministry and to induce hypocrisy among the members by requiring them to repeat words and assume attitudes which they did not feel.[211]

The fourth cause of separation recalled the earlier Separatist emphasis upon discipline as an essential ingredient in correct church order: "the

---

[208] *The Writings of John Greenwood, 1587-1590*, 18.

[209] Ibid., 23. The Separatists appealed to the ambiguity of the Greek adverb οὕτως in Matt. 6:9 ("thus," "in this manner") to justify their claim that the Lord's Prayer was intended only as a general model. The Lucan version (11:2) is more prescriptive. Cf. ibid., 295 n. 2.

[210] Ibid., 40, 62-67.

[211] Davies, *The Worship of the English Puritans,* op. cit., 105, has related the two different types of prayer, liturgical and free, to two differing conceptions of the Church: "Liturgical prayer does not demand that the minister should know the members of his congregation; whereas free prayer implies a smaller, more compact community all of whom, theoretically, are known to the minister. . . . Liturgical prayer would therefore require a parish as a background, with the wider horizon of the nation; free prayer suggests not Israel but the remnant, i.e., the compact unit of the congregation as a worshipping family."

false and antichristian government wherwith ther churches are ruled."[212] Barrow firmly believed that Christ has "left but one form of government" for the church, and this inviolable form, spelled out in the New Testament, implied complete congregational autonomy both in the election of officers and in the correction of wayward members.[213] "Dothe not sin abound, yea, overflow? How is it then beatten down," asked Barrow.[214] Not by the hierarchy of courts ranging from the High Commission and Court of Faculties to the local commissaries' courts, and neither by the presbyterian system of consistories, classes, and synods. The "new Duch classes" would merely substitute one form on tyranny for another: "their pastors and elders for their parson and questmen, their synodes in stead of their commissaries' courts, their high councils in stead of the High Commission."[215] The least member of the church had as much interest in censure and excommunication as the pastor, and no person or group within the congregation (presbytery) or above the congregation (bishop) might arrogate this prerogative to themselves. The officers of the congregation, differing in function but not in status, were five in number: pastor, teacher, elders, deacons, relievers.[216] These, together with the other members, jointly wielded the "scepter of Christ" through the exercise of congregational self-discipline, thus proving themselves, and not the parish churches, to be "the garden enclosed, the spring shut up, the orchyard of pomgranades with sweete fruites ... the kingdome of Christ: yea his sister, his love, his spouse, his queene, and his bodie."[217]

A false membership, a false ministry, a false worship, a false government! All of these "causes" were interrelated, and together they implied a situation of total apostasy. In this context the possibility of significant

---

[212] *The Writings of Henry Barrow, 1587-1590*, 54.

[213] Ibid., 127.

[214] Ibid., 62.

[215] Ibid., 561. See the article on "courts" in S. L. Ollard and Gordon Crosse, *A Dictionary of English Church History* (London, 1912), 154-61. The "Duch" classes of the Puritans were so called because they seemed to be modelled on those of the Dutch Reformed Church.

[216] *The Writings of Henry Barrow, 1587-1590*, 216-23. The elders were called alternately governors or ancients. The relievers were widows of at least sixty years. H. M. Dexter, *Congregationalism*, 222, claimed that Barrow and Greenwood had founded a Congregationalism that stood "midway between Brownism and Puritanism," and which granted more power to the pastor and elders than to the congregation. He was followed in this judgment by Burrage, *Early English Dissenters*, vol. 1, 129ff., but White, *Separatist Tradition*, 73, rightly contends that the Barrowist polity was strikingly similar, if not indebted, to Browne.

[217] *The Writings of Henry Barrow, 1587-1590*, 215.

reform along the lines suggested by the Separatists appeared quite remote, and Barrow's thought took on an increasingly apocalyptic tenor: "our Samson, Christ Jesus, doth alredy shak not onely the pillers but the foundations of [this ruinous sinagog] . . . he will shortlye show himself with his myghtye angels in flaming fier, rendering vengance. . . . Tack warning, therfor, and come out whilest you may."[218] The Separatists, in a petition of August, 1590, addressed to the Privy Council, warned that their retention "in sundrie most noysome and vile prisons" would result in the pulling down of "God's wrath upon the whole land for the bloud of his servants."[219] At the same time Barrow developed an attitude toward his suffering and imprisonment which might be characterized as a "theology of martyrdom," not unlike that espoused by many of the continental Anabaptists.[220] At a conference with several clergymen held a few days before his execution, Barrow, after acknowledging that Cranmer and others had been martyrs in Queen Mary's days, shook his fetters and exclaimed: "But these holy bands of mine are much worse glorious, than any of theirs."[221] This attitude may also account, in part, for the harsh invective Barrow reserved for the Puritans who remained within the established church. Never one to shirk the duty of "writing my conscience plainly," Barrow felt especially betrayed by the "tolarating prechers" who had compromised with the bishops rather than endure the fire of persecution:

> Christ crucified you all abhorr, you can not abide his crosse, you will not suffer . . . but dayle seek new cavills, distinctions and evasions to hide anie trueth which bringeth danger, or to avoide the crosse of Christ, and therfore you shall not reigne with him.[222]

With Barrow and Greenwood the fine line between advanced Puritan and Separatist, already widened considerably by Browne and Harrison, now became a gaping chasm unbridgeable by even the most schizophrenic of

---

[218]Ibid., 112, 60. Cf. the recent study of Paul Christianson, *Reformers and Babylon: English apocalyptic visions from the reformation to the eve of the civil war* (Toronto, 1978), esp. 47-92.

[219]*The Writings of John Greenwood, 1587-1590*, 290.

[220]Cf. Ethelbert Stauffer, "Anabaptist Theology of Martyrdom," *Mennonite Quarterly Review* 19 (1945), 179-214.

[221]*The Writings of John Greenwood and Henry Barrow, 1591-1593*, 237. Sir George Paule who was present on this occasion commented: "Thus he, in Newgate at that time, in the presence of many, with great insolence, did triumph," *The Life of John Whitgift* (London, 1612), 51.

[222]*The Writings of John Greenwood and Henry Barrow, 1591-1593*, 111; *The Writings of John Greenwood, 1587-1590*, 194.

religious personalities. Those who tried to maintain fellowship with both parties found themselves, as likely as not, excommunicated as "apostates."[223]

The execution of Barrow and Greenwood on April 6, 1593, followed six weeks later by that of their recent convert John Penry, deprived the Separatists of their most able spokesmen, and signaled the conclusion of Whitgift's successful campaign against the Puritan and sectarian movements.[224] The remainder of Barrow's followers, faced with the stark alternative of exile or death, chose the former, and, following the pattern set by Browne, soon relocated in the Netherlands, taking residence in Amsterdam rather than Middelburg, perhaps out of a desire to avoid the difficulties which had beset their predecessors in Zealand.[225] While their stay in the Netherlands would be longer than that of the Norwich company, their congregation would be subject to equally fractious disputes. Francis Johnson and Daniel Studley, two disciples of Barrow, emerged as pastor and elder of the group, and in 1595 they were joined by the learned Henry Ainsworth, who was elected teacher. But the exiled church was distracted by a series of internal conflicts ranging from a debate over the propriety of the pastor's wife's attire, to the sexual misadventures of Studley, to an eventual break between Johnson and Ainsworth which left the congregation permanently divided. The most significant document produced by the Amsterdam church was the *Confession* of 1596, probably co-written by Ainsworth and Johnson. The preface to the *Confession* laments the loss of Barrow and Greenwood, and recites their fourfold

---

[223]Cf., for example, the case of Daniel Bucke: British Museum, MS. Harleian 6849ff. 216 recto-217 recto; *Early English Dissenters*, vol. 1, 127-28, 282 note 2.

[224]Barrow and Greenwood were convicted of felony under *23 Eliz. cap. 2, sec. 4* which enacted that "if any person . . . devise and write . . . any false seditious and slanderous matter to the defamation of the Queen's Majesty," such a person would be punishable by death, G. W. Prothero, *Select Statutes and Other Constitutional Documents Illustrative of the Reigns of Elizabeth and James I* (Oxford, 1894), 77-80. This Act of 1581, like the one under which they had been convicted in 1587 (*23 Eliz. cap. 1, sec. 4*), had been enacted against Catholic recusants. Sir John Neale, *Elizabeth I and her Parliaments, 1584-1601* (New York, 1958), 290-92, suggests that the timing of their executions (they had been twice reprieved) was due to Whitgift's reaction to a Parliamentary defeat. Penry was associated with the Barrowist congregation only during the last two years of his life. He is often linked with the Marprelate tracts, but his role in this controversy is a matter of continuing controversy. Cf. the conflicting views of D. J. McGinn, *John Penry and the Marprelate Controversy* (New Brunswick, N.J., 1966), and L. H. Carlson, "Martin Marprelate: His Identity and His Satire," in *English Satire: Papers Read at a Clark Library Seminar, January 15, 1972* (Los Angelos, 1972). Cf. also Carlson's recent study, *Martin Marprelate, Gentleman* (San Marino, Cal., 1981).

[225]The statute which mandated their exile was passed in April 1593, and entitled "An Act to retain the Queen's subjects in obedience," *The Statutes of the Realm*, vol. 4, part 2, 843-46; cf. also Neale, op. cit., 293-96.

indictment of the Church of England.[226] Through this document, frequently cited by Robinson as "our Confession,"[227] as well as through their own writings, the legacy of Barrow and Greenwood was transmitted to the next generation of Separatists.

---

[226]The *Confession*, reprinted in Walker, *Creeds and Platforms*, 53, attributes the death of the two Separatist leaders to the Queen: "shee . . . having hir finger so deep in the blood of Gods children." The complicity of the Queen was denied by later Separatists such as Governor Bradford, *Plymouth Church Records*, vol. 1, 126-27.

[227]*Of Religious Communion, Private and Publique* (Leyden, 1614), sig. G 4 verso [hereafter *Of Religious Communion*].

CHAPTER 3

JOHN ROBINSON, 1575-1625

"Although wee can see the worke goe but slowlie forwarde in our dayes, yet in
the next generation it may rise more speedily to the glorie of God."[1]

John Robinson was the eldest of three children born to John Robinson, yeoman, and his wife Ann, in the parish of Sturton-le-Steeple in
Nottinghamshire. Although no contemporary biography of Robinson
has survived, and earlier historians were frequently inexact about the
details of his early life, it now seems certain that he was born in the year
1575 or 1576.[2] The careful research of Walter Burgess earlier in this
century established that the Robinsons were a substantial family in the
village of Sturton, highly respected, moderately well-off, with close ties to
John Quippe, vicar of the local parish.[3] Young John may have received

---

[1]Robert Harrison, *A Little Treatise uppon the firste Verse of the 122. Psalm* (1583),
113.

[2]This date is deduced from an entry of matriculation in the registers of the University
of Leyden made on Sept. 5, 1615: "*Coss. permissu* Joannes Robintsonus; Anglus, an.
xxxix. Stud. Theol. alit familiam."

[3]Walter H. Burgess, *John Robinson: The Pastor of the Pilgrims* (New York, 1920),
10-16 [hereafter Burgess, *Robinson*]. Robinson receives honorable mention in all of the
standard Dissenting histories: Neal, *History of the Puritans* (1732), vol. 2, 72-75; Brook,
Lives of the Puritans (1813), vol. 2, 334-44; Hanbury, *Historical Memorials* (1839), vol. 1,
185-212; J. B. Marsden, *The History of the Early Puritans* (London, 1853), 294-98;
George Punchard, *History of Congregationalism* (New York, 1867), vol. 3, 300-44.
Dexter, *Congregationalism*, 359- 410, was the first to attempt a critical biographical
treatment based on a firsthand scrutiny of primary documents. Subsequent biographers
have built, with varying success, upon his research: John Brown, *The Pilgrim Fathers of
New England* (New York, 1896); Ozora S. Davis, *John Robinson: The Pilgrim Pastor*
(Boston, 1903); R. W. Dale, *History of English Congregationalism* (London, 1907); F. J.
Powicke, *John Robinson* (London, 1920). The standard study remains Burgess, in spite of
Robert M. Bartlett's nicely illustrated *The Pilgrim Way* (Philadelphia, 1971). Robinson's
career has also been surveyed in the excellent Ph.D. dissertation by Stephen Brachlow,
"Puritan Theology and Radical Churchmen in Pre-Revolutionary England, with special
reference to Henry Jacob and John Robinson," (Oxford, 1978). Much of Brachlow's
research on Robinson is reflected in his two articles: "More Light on John Robinson and
the Separatist Tradition," *Fides et Historia* 13 (1980), 6-22; "John Robinson and the Lure
of Separatism in Pre-Revolutionary England," *Church History* 50 (1981), 288-301.

some of his earliest instruction from Quippe, although he undoubtedly
spent the standard seven years (ages eight to fifteen) in a nearby grammar
school where a thorough grounding in the "trivial" part of the medieval
cirriculum prepared him for the more demanding disciplines of the
university.[4]

"BEFORE WE CONCEAVED THE LEAST THOUGHT OF SEPARATION": THE YEARS AT CAMBRIDGE

At the beginning of her reign, coincident with the Act of Uniformity,
Queen Elizabeth wrote to Cecil, Chancellor of Cambridge, of her desire
to have the university "put in order, both for augmentation of good
learning and for establishing of such uniformity in the cause of religion . . .
as by the laws of our realm is ordained."[5] In spite of Cecil's policy of
outward conformity, reinforced by royal visitations and revision of the
university statutes, Cambridge developed into the unrivalled academic
center of the Puritan movement. By the 1590s many of the young scholars
who had flocked to Cartwright's lectures were now entrenched in positions of leadership and authority within the university: Laurence Chaderton was Master of Emmanuel, William Whitaker, Master of St. John's,
Roger Goad, Provost of King's. While the nerve-center of the regional
classes remained at London with Travers and Field, questions of doctrine
and procedure were frequently referred to the Cambridge Puritans, and
three "national synods" (1583, 1587, 1589) were held at the university.[6]
As we have noted, a few of the Puritans spawned at Cambridge turned
Separatist, and proved capable leaders for the sectarian cause. Harrison
and Browne were Corpus Christi men, and the three martyrs of 1593 were
also graduates of Cambridge: Barrow of Clare, Greenwood of Corpus

---

[4]On education in Elizabethan grammar schools, see Craig R. Thompson, *Schools in
Tudor England* (Washington, D.C., 1958). Burgess, *Robinson*, 29, surmises that Robin-
son's attendance at a nearby grammar school across the county line, in Gainsborough or
Lincoln, may account for his frequent designation as "Lincolniensis." Cf. article by
Archibald Geikie, *D.N.B.*, vol. 17, 18-22.

[5]*A Collection of Letters, Statutes, and Other Documents . . . Illustrative of the
University of Cambridge during the Reformation*, ed. John Lamb (London, 1838), 275.

[6]In 1583 the Dedham classis commissioned "Mr. D. Chapman, Mr. Stocton and Mr.
Morse to craue the iudgmentes of some godly men in Cambridge tutching the question of
the Sabboth," Usher, *Presbyterian Movement*, op. cit., 30. On the role of Cambridge in
the Puritan movement, see Porter, *Reformation and Reaction*; Mark H. Curtis, *Oxford
and Cambridge in Transition, 1558-1642.* (Oxford, 1959); V. H. H. Green, *Religion at
Oxford and Cambridge* (London, 1964), 79-136.

Christi, and Penry of Peterhouse. The early Separatists, unlike the Puritans, did not cultivate their ties with the university, but included the entire educational system in their sweeping condemnation of the Church of England. Browne, before he had formed the covenanted company at Norwich, preaching unordained and unlicensed in St. Bene't's, inveighed against "that wofull state of Cambrige, whereinto those wicked prelats and doctors of diuinitie haue brought it."[7] Barrow identified the universities with the medieval religious orders and called for their dissolution:

> I hope . . . it apeareth unto all men . . . what kind of fellowships these universitie colleges are, what kind of cages full of vncleane birdes, of foule and hateful spirites, etc. . . . yet is their judgment of the Lord, even the same judgment and end, which are in their sight executed upon their elder brethren and sisters the templars, the monkes, and knightes of their St. Jhon of Jerusalem, the abbies, fririers, nunneries, they had one and the self same popish original with these . . . Therfore Queene Elisabeth hath, and ought by as good right to abolish them, as her progenitor did the abbaies.[8]

Browne and Barrow separated as fully from the universities in which they were trained as they did from the parishes in which they were baptized.

When Robinson came up to Cambridge in 1592 the most recent defector from Puritanism to Separatism was Francis Johnson, a fellow of Christ's, who, with another "yonge precision," Cuthbert Bainbrigg, had preached "certen factiouse sermons" in January, 1589.[9] Both men refused to take the oath *ex officio mero*, and were imprisoned; Johnson refused to recant his sermons, and by the end of the year found himself expelled from the university. Within a few months he had united with the Barrowist congregation of which he would eventually become pastor. The expulsion of Johnson created a minor furor within the university (37 fellows signed a petition on his behalf), but it was only one in a series of events by which Whitgift and the Court of High Commission squelched both the Puritan classical movement and the scattered Separatist conventicles. Around 1591 when presbyterian Cartwright shared the company of the

---

[7] *A True and Short Declaration*, 404.

[8] *The Writings of Henry Barrow, 1587-1590*, 350-51. Ironically such a scheme seems to have been contemplated—briefly—by Henry VIII. Cf. J. B. Mullinger, *The University of Cambridge* (Cambridge, 1884), vol. 2, 75-84. For a comparison of Puritan and Separatist views on the role of education, see Greaves, *Society and Religion*, 356-62.

[9] Cambridge University Registry Guard Books, vol. 6 (1), no. 23. On the Johnson affair see *Cambridge University Transactions during the Puritan Controversies* (London, 1840), vol. 1, 548-58; *Reformation and Reaction*, 155-63. The most recent treatment is Peter Lake, "The Dilemma of the Establishment Puritan: the Cambridge Heads and the case of Francis Johnson and Cuthbert Bainbrigg," *Journal of Ecclesiastical History* 29 (1978), 23-35.

Fleet with congregationalist Barrow, Edmund Chapman, graduate of
Trinity and leader of the Dedham Puritans, wrote to his former tutor of
"the stormy and sharpe seasons and winterlike wether" which had
befallen their cause.[10] The 1590s would prove to be a decade of entrench-
ment for the Puritans, of attrition and exile for the Separatists. In the
meantime another generation of noncomformists, Puritan and Separatist, was in the making. But long before lines of demarcation were
drawn—"before we conceaved the least thought of separation," as Robinson put it[11]—they shared a fellowship of learning and piety as students at
Cambridge.

From the humble status of sizar Robinson rose rapidly through the
academic ranks. Robinson was admitted to Corpus Christi on April 9, 1592 as one of
the "sizartores" and given for his tutor, Thomas Jegon. Thomas Jegon
was the younger brother of John Jegon, Master of the College, a man
portrayed by a contemporary as "short of stature, somewhat corpulent,
and of no very pleasing countenance."[12] The elder Jegon was to serve as
Vice-Chancellor of the university (1596-1599) before becoming Bishop of
Norwich, in which capacity Robinson would have dealings with him a
decade later. Corpus was one of the older foundations at Cambridge,
established in 1352 by the union of the guilds of Corpus Christi and the
Blessed Virgin Mary.[13] Among the most illustrious alumni of the sixteenth century were Matthew Parker, Master and benefactor of the
College, Nicholas Bacon, Lord Keeper of the Great Seal, and Christopher
Marlowe.

From the humble status of sizar Robinson rose rapidly through the
academic ranks. After four years of study devoted primarily to rhetoric,
logic, and philosophy, he proceeded Bachelor of Arts in 1596. In 1599, on
March 28, he was made Master of Arts. However, two years before he had
taken the M.A., he was elected to a vacant fellowship in the college, an
indication of his superior abilities and, perhaps, of his close ties with the
Jegons.[14] As a Fellow of Corpus Robinson promised to be absent no

---

[10]Usher, *Presbyterian Movement, op. cit.,* 78.

[11]*Justification*, 60.

[12]*Master's History of Corpus Christi College,* op. cit. 151.

[13]H. P. Stokes, *Corpus Christi* (London, 1898), 7-17.

[14]Robinson's early inception as Fellow, while unusual, was not contrary to the revised
statutes promulgated by Parker in 1570: "Statuimus et ordinamus quod in electione
sociorum Collegii predicti Magister et socii sive scholares ejusdem Collegii, qui per
scrutinium socios in virtute juramenti eligant simpliciter meliores non habendo respectam
ad aliquam affectionem carnalem, nec instantiam seu requisitionem aliquorum, aut
procurationem, sed quos cognoverint esse honestos, castos, humiles, pacificos, et modes-
tos, graduatos, aut qui in artibus liberalibus responderit, disputaverint, et declamaverint,

more than 65 days during the year, to assume responsibility for the instruction of the younger students, and to preach on a rotating basis with the other Fellows at the adjoining parish of St. Bene't's, the advowson of which the College had acquired in 1578. In accordance with the statutory requirement, Robinson was ordained shortly after entering his fellowship. Thus we find him listed in the college register of 1603 as "Johannes Robinson Nottinghamiensis Artium Mag^r Sacerdos."[15] Robinson retained his fellowship until his departure from the university in 1604 when his plans for marriage mandated his resignation.[16] The "order book" of Corpus yields two additional facts about Robinson's career in the College: in 1599 he was elected "Praelector Graecus," a lectureship denoting proficiency in Greek, and in 1600 he was appointed "Decanus," an administrative post involving oversight of the students.[17]

These meager details gleaned from university records, while indicative of impressive academic accomplishments, hardly convey the importance of the Cambridge years for Robinson's intellectual and religious development. He belonged to what William Haller has called "the spiritual brotherhood," a fraternity of "precise" men which included in the mid-1590s William Ames, Richard Bernard, and John Smyth, and towards the end of the decade a host of younger students, the Cottons, Sibbes', and Wards of the next generation, all of whom shared the distinction of having "come to Cambridge, and that in Mr. Pirkins tyme."[18] William Perkins, whose life dates correspond almost exactly to Elizabeth's reign (1558-1602), was a Fellow of Christ's until 1595, and afterwards lecturer in St. Andrew's Church. In an age of great preachers Perkins was unparalleled in his command of the pulpit. Thomas Fuller reported that he "would pronounce the word *damn* with such an emphasis, as left a doleful echo in his auditors' ears a good while after."[19] But his influence extended

---

quemadmodum statuta Academiae pro eo gradu requirunt, et qui proxima determinatione post electionem suam acualiter procedant. Et qui in temporis progressu studio Theologiae vacent et intendant." *Master's History of Corpus Christi,* op. cit., 280.

[15]Burgess, *Robinson,* 39.

[16]Robinson later recalled this event when, writing against ecclesiastical regulation of marriage, he noted that the Church of England forbids marriage "to fellowes in Colledges," *Justification,* 378.

[17]Burgess, *Robinson,* loc. cit. On the status of Greek studies at Cambridge during Robinson's tenure, see W. T. Costello, *The Scholastic Cirriculum at Early Seventeenth-Century Cambridge* (Cambridge, Mass., 1958), 62-64.

[18]William Haller, *The Rise of Purtianism* (Philadelphia, 1938), 49; "The Diary of Samuel Ward," in *Two Elizabethan Puritan Diaries,* ed. M. M. Knappen (Chicago, 1933), 119.

[19]Thomas Fuller, *The Holy State and Profane State* (London, 1642), 81.

far beyond the circle of eager listeners at Cambridge. His writings were translated into Dutch, French, Irish, Czech, German, and Welsh, not to mention Latin, and were among the first books brought over to the New World.[20]

Perkins, though a friend of Cartwright, repudiated the term "puritan," and deemed the *Book of Common Prayer* to be "profitable and necessary."[21] Even less did he approve of the Separatists—"those Brownists and Sectaries are blind and besotted, who cannot see that the Church of England is a goodly heape of Gods corne."[22] The burden of his preaching and writing was sound doctrine and practical piety; he did not linger long with questions of polity, nor even with the commonplace abuses still prevalent in his day.[23] Still, Robinson drank deeply from Perkins' well, and frequently cited his authority as a man "of great account (and that worthily) with al that fear God, how ever he were against us in our practise."[24] In 1624 Robinson edited Perkins' catechism which (with his own Separatist emendations, to be sure) he commended as "fully containing what every Christian is to believe touching God and himself."[25]

In the epistolary preface to his "Treatise of predestination" (1598) Perkins admitted the motive for his theological work: "that I might clear the truth, that is (as they call it) the Calvinists doctrine, of those reproaches which are cast upon it."[26] The Calvinists' doctrine, however,

---

[20]Among the books brought from Leyden to Plymouth by William Brewster were the collected works of Perkins. Eventually eleven copies of Perkins' treatises ended up in Brewster's library, one of which bears on its title-page the handwritten superscription, "John Robinson's Book." Cf. *The Books of the Pilgrims*, eds. Laurence D. Geller and Peter J. Gomes, (New York, 1975), 31-32. In the same year that the Mayflower sailed—1620—"fower great books" were also donated to the Jamestown colony, "for use of the Collegiates hereafter." One was an English translation of Augustine's *City of God*, "the other three greate Volumes wer the workes of Mr Perkins newlie corrected and amended." *The Records of the Virginia Company of London*, ed. S. M. Kingsbury (Washington, D.C., 1906), vol. 1, 421.

[21]*The Workes of William Perkins*, eds. J. Legatt and C. Legge (London, 1616-1618), vol. 3, 119.

[22]Ibid., 425.

[23]See, for example, this statement which could well have come from the lips of Whitgift: "Till God put into the hearts of parliamentes and princes to look to this great and needful work [of further reform], let us ministers learn our duties: and first, we who are in the universities, are here admonished to looke to ourselues," ibid., 458.

[24]*Justification*, 421.

[25]*The Works of John Robinson*, ed. Robert Ashton (London, 1851), vol. 3, 426 [hereafter *Works*].

[26]Ibid., 605. Cf. Perkins, *Opera Omnia Theologica* (Geneva, 1624), vol. 1, 116: "ut criminationes veritati, id est, doctrinae (ut apellant) Calvinianae iniectas diluam."

which Perkins felt called upon to defend was not exactly the doctrine of Calvin, but an elaboration of that doctrine informed, in method at least, as much by developments in contemporary Continental theology (e.g. Beza, Girolamo Zanchi, Andreas Musculus) as by "Master Calvin of blessed memory."[27] Thus Perkins' first book, the famous *Armilla Aurea*, consisted of 58 chapters and a diagram showing the categories of theology divided and subdivided, Ramus-like, with predestination placed under the general heading of the doctrine of God rather than (as with Calvin) in the context of soteriology.[28] In Perkins' diagram of "the order of the causes" of God's almighty double-willing and double-working of salvation and damnation, there were circles within circles, with the decrees of election and reprobation antecedent to the decrees of creation and the Fall. Calvin himself had spoken of a "double decree," and Luther had argued the same against Erasmus.[29] But recognizing the limits of revelation Calvin had also noted: "Those things which the Lord has laid up in secret, we may not search: those things which he has brought out into the open, we may not neglect."[30] Perkins belonged to those who were not afraid to rush in where Calvin had feared to tread. His supralapsarian position was an extreme statement of the doctrine of predestination, not to be sanctioned even at the Synod of Dort, but in the lecture halls and

---

[27] *The Workes of William Perkins,* op. cit., vol. 2, 616. To Perkins' most famous treatise of Case-divinity, "A Case of Conscience, the greatest that ever was: How a Man may know whether he be the Child of God or No,"(London, 1592), was appended a major treatise by Zanchi on predestination which Perkins had "englished" for this purpose. On Zanchi see Otto Gründler, *Die Gotteslehre Girolami Zanchis*(Neukirchen, 1965). See also William H. Chalker, "Calvin and Some Seventeenth Century English Calvinists," unpublished Ph.D. dissertation, Duke University (1961), 87-139, and R. T. Kendall, *Calvin and English Calvinism to 1649* (Oxford, 1979), 51-76.

[28] *The Armilla*, translated into English under the title *A Golden Chaine, or the Description of Theologie, containing the Order of the Causes of Salvation and Damnation, according to God's Woord*, had run to thirteen editions by the year of Perkins' death. The famous diagram, intended as an "ocular Catechism" for those who could not read (or were slow to understand!) may have been modelled on an earlier version used by Beza in his *Tabula Praedestinationis* (Geneva, 1555). For the provenance and translation of this work see Frédéric Gardy and Alain Dufour, *Bibliographie des oeuvres théologiques, litteraires, historiques et juridiques de Théodore de Bèze* (Geneva, 1960), 47-53.

[29] *Luther and Erasmus: Free Will and Salvation*, eds. Gordon Rupp and Philip S. Watson (Philadelphia, 1969), 169-76, 239-46.

[30] John Calvin, *Institutes of the Christian Religion*, ed. John T. McNeill (Philadelphia, 1960), vol. 2, 925 (3, 21. 4). My translation differs slightly from that of the McNeill edition. Cf. *Joannie Calvini Opera Selecta*, eds., P. Barth and G. Niesel (Munich, 1931)[hereafter *Calvini Opera*], vol. 4, 373: "quae in occulto recondita Dominus reliquit, ne scrutemus: quae in apertum protulit, ne negligamus." [Hereafter citations to the *Institutes* will be to the McNeill edition unless otherwise stated.]

pulpits of Cambridge it was sound divinity—to all but the "new pelagians," as Perkins called them, whose opposition to the "Calvinian gospel" erupted into a major controversy in 1595.[31]

In retrospect there seems to have been a steady undercurrent of proto-Arminian opinion in England from the "Free-Willers" associated with Henry Harte to Antonio de Corro, Spanish reformer and lecturer at Oxford, to the nuanced positions of Richard Hooker and Lancelot Andrewes. At Cambridge this sentiment was best represented by Peter Baro, a native of France who held the singular distinction of having been ordained by Calvin himself and who, since 1574, had been Lady Margaret Professor of Divinity. As early as 1581 he had crossed swords with Laurence Chaderton over the nature and form of true faith, and found himself accused of universalism, Arianism, and popery. But Baro was not one to exacerbate a quarrel, and for a while he managed to avoid further confrontation with the "watchdogs of orthodoxy."[32]

However, William Barrett, the chaplain of Gonville and Caius and a protégé of Baro, had little of his mentor's discretion and none of his tact. In a sermon on April 25, 1595, preached *ad clerum* in Great St. Mary's, Barrett called into question certain corollaries of the doctrine of predestination such as the indefectibility of faith, the certainty of Christian assurance, and the unconditionality of the decree of reprobation.[33] He moreover used this solemn occasion to heap bitter abuse upon Calvin and other divines noted for their high predestinarian theology: Beza, Peter Martyr, Zanchi, and Francis Junius. The offended party, including "a certain little man [*homuncio quidam*] called Perkins," was shocked at the heretical impudence of the young chaplain: "we never heard the like preached in Cambridge, or elsewhere," they wrote to Whitgift.[34] In short order Barrett was summoned before the Heads who forced him to publicly recant his earlier statements, to admit that "the reprobation of the

---

[31] *The Workes of William Perkins,* op. cit., vol. 1, 10. On Perkins' doctrine of predestination see Ian Breward, "The Significance of William Perkins," *Journal of Religious History* 4 (1966), 113-28; Michael T. Malone, "The Doctrine of Predestination in the Thought of William Perkins and Richard Hooker," *Anglican Theological Review* 52 (1970), 103-17.

[32] *Elizabethan Puritan Movement,* 236.

[33] The documents relating to Barrett's sermon and the ensuing controversy are printed in John Strype, *The Life and Acts of John Whitgift* (Oxford, 1822), vol. 3, 317-47. See the recent accounts by Porter, *Reformation and Reaction,* 344-75, and Frederic E. Pamp, "Studies in the Origins of English Arminianism," unpublished Ph.D. dissertation, Harvard University (1950), 129-75.

[34] Strype, *Whitgift,* vol. 2, 236-42.

ungodly was from eternity," and to acknowledge the slandered theologians as "*Ecclesiae nostrae lumina et ornamenta.*"[35] But Barrett would not be so easily subdued. He appealed his case to Whitgift who seemed at first to agree with certain of his points, particularly the distinction between *certitudo* (a pious assurance which could accompany faith) and *securitas* (a presumptive certainty which was unwarranted in any Christian). One might be *certus* of salvation, but not *securus*.[36] Heartened by the Archbishop's initial support Barrett revoked his recantation. On closer examination, however, Whitgift withdrew his support agreeing that Barrett "had erred in divers points . . . some of his opinions being indeed Popish."[37] Before Whitgift's order that Barrett deliver a second recantation could be enforced, he had fled the country. Soon thereafter he converted to the Roman Church, a turn of events which must have pleased the Calvinists almost as much as the Catholics.

One of Whitgift's arguments in urging toleration for Barrett was that his opinions had violated no particular Article of Religion. The Barrett affair, then, provided the occasion for the formulation of the Lambeth Articles of November, 1595. Early on in the controversy Whitgift complained to the Heads of their over-hasty procedure against Barrett about "a matter disputable . . . wherein learned men did and might dissent without impiety."[38] It was an argument with a familiar ring: the old slogan about "things indifferent" writ theologically. As in liturgy and polity there were issues not essential to one's salvation, so too in doctrine there were "matters disputable," and the deep mysteries of election and reprobation were among them. But "these stickling Heads," as Strype called them, were not convinced: "This doctrine [is] not about inferior points of matters in difference, but of the substantial grounds, and chief comfort, and anchor-hold of our salvation."[39] Of course, the Cambridge Calvinists interpreted the Thirty-Nine Articles in the light of their own predestinarian theology. They had moved against Barrett precisely because he had flouted "the doctrine of our Church set down in the book of Articles."[40]

---

[35]Ibid., vol. 3, 318-19.

[36]Ibid., vol. 2, 240.

[37]Ibid., 277.

[38]Ibid., 240.

[39]Ibid., 253, 249.

[40]Ibid., 262. Cf. Perkins' claim that "our owne Churches in England hold, beleeve, and maintaine, and preach the true faith, that is, the ancient doctrine of salvation by Christ, taught and published by the Prophets and Apostles, as the booke of the Articles of faith agreed upon in open Parliament doth fully shew." *The Workes of William Perkins*, vol. 1, 313.

But therein lay the rub. For the Thirty-Nine Articles, especially Article XVII ("*De praedestinatione et electione*"), were subject to a variety of interpretations, not all of them consonant with the theology of Perkins. A full decade before Barrett's sermon had brought the issue to a head, a Puritan petition had asked

> whether the 17th article, speaking of election, be well put downe, that maketh no mention of reprobation, seing Paule speaking of the one, speaketh of the other?[41]

It was one thing for the Heads to assert that their predestinarian theology was not contrary to Article XVII; it was something else for them to claim that it admitted of no construction other than theirs. Whitgift was quick to perceive that the issue involved the royal prerogative in matters ecclesiastical:

> It is a most vain conceit to think, that you have authority in matters of controversy, to judge what is agreeable to the doctrine of the Church of England; what not. The law expressly laying that upon her Majesty, and upon such as she shall by commission appoint to that purpose.[42]

The Lambeth Articles, then, were intended by their framers to give official sanction to certain dogmatic propositions hitherto less precisely defined, to supplement the Thirty-Nine Articles in such a way that the future Baros and Barretts of the Church of England could not hide behind the cautious wording of the earlier formulations. For example, whereas Article XVII was silent on reprobation, and Barrett had equivocated on this point, the Lambeth Articles spoke with clear logic: "God from eternity has predestined some to life, and others he has reprobated to death."[43] Further, they denied the *causa efficiens* of predestination to lie in the foresight of faith, or of any thing that is in the person predestinated but only in the will of God, *sed sola voluntas beneplaciti Dei*. Moreover, one endowed with true faith (*vera, viva, justificans fides*) could be fully assured of his eternal salvation: we may depart (*recidere*) from a grace given, but we may not utterly fall (*excidere*) from it.

The promulgation of the Lambeth Articles by Whitgift represented a victory of sorts for the Calvinist party, but it was neither a total nor a lasting one. In the first place, Queen Elizabeth, at the prompting of Burghley, rejected the Articles and forbade their dissemination or discus-

---

[41]*A Seconde Parte of a Register*, vol. 1, 197.

[42]Strype, *Whitgift*, vol. 2, 252.

[43]The Lambeth Articles are printed in Philip Schaff, *The Creeds of Christendom* (New York, 1877), vol. 3, 523-25 [hereafter *Creeds of Christendom*].

sion.[44] More importantly, the beginnings of a deep-seated and long-term reaction against the uncompromising predestinarianism of the university Calvinists were generated by this controversy. Though Baro was forced to leave the university because of his opposition to the Articles, he left behind a substantial body of sympathizers, chief among whom was John Overall who had succeeded William Whitaker (the framer of the Articles) as Regius Professor of Divinity. Like Baro, Overall attacked the Articles as a novel departure from sound doctrine: "And this is the opinion of Zwingli, Calvin, and the Puritans, unknown to all the ancient Fathers, even to Augustine and his readers."[45] And, like Baro, Overall defended the proposition that since God willed all to be saved, the death of Christ was sufficient to that end. The gospel of universal grace: a point much discussed by Perkins, and a matter to prove eminently "disputable" at Cambridge and beyond.

In 1598, the year before Robinson proceeded M.A., John Jegon, as Vice-Chancellor, wrote to Whitgift:

> For matters of Scholes, may it please your G. to understand that the Questions of Reprobation, and certainty of fayth, have lately bene revived, threatninge some disturbance. . . .[46]

In the same year Perkins published his final word on the subject of predestination in a treatise entitled *De praedestinationis mode et ordine et de amplitudine gratiae divinae*.[47] This work, which adds little to our knowledge of Perkins' position, was bought and read by a Dutch Reformed pastor in Amsterdam, who replied to it with a work of his own:

---

[44]At the Hampton Court Conference of 1604 the Puritans made another unsuccessful attempt to append the Lambeth Articles to the Thirty-Nine Articles. They were, however, incorporated into the Irish Articles of 1615 which provided a connecting link between the Calvinism of the 1590s and that of the Westminster Confession.

[45]Cambridge University, St. John's College MS. H. 15, f. 4: "Et haec est sententia Zwingli, Calvini et Puritanorum, ignota omnibus antiquis Patribus, etiam Augustino et eius lectatoribus."

[46]Cambridge University Library MS. Mm/1/35, Baker 24, f. 382.

[47]Perkins may have written this treatise in response to a letter of Baro to Niels Hemingius, professor at Copenhagen and former pupil of Melanchthon. Baro had asked, "Do the elect believe, or are the believers elect?" He also distinguished three varieties of predestination taught in the Reformed Church: (1) the view of Calvin and Beza, that God had decreed absolutely to elect and to reprobate without any regard to actual or original sin; (2) the view of Zanchi and Bellarminus, that the decrees were consequent to the Fall (the infralapsarian position,) hence sin was a material cause of reprobation, though not of election; (3) the view held by Baro and supported by Hemingius, Melanchthon, and the early Augustine, that God had invited all men to salvation but had predestined only those whom he foreknew from all eternity would believe in Christ. Baro's letter was published in 1613 as *Summa trium de Praedestinatione Sententiarum*.

Examen Modestum Libelli.[48] The pastor was Jacob Harmenszoon, better known, then and now, as Jacobus Arminius. Perkins' treatise and Arminius' response to it constituted a significant link between the Cambridge quarrels of the 1590s and the ever-widening dispute which would take its name from the Amsterdam pastor, soon to be Leyden professor and unwitting founder of a party.

In the larger context of the history of Christian doctrine the stirs at Cambridge were a relatively minor episode in the recurring controversy over the nature and implications of divine grace. But in the history of the Church of England, and in the personal development of John Robinson, the events of the 1590s were a watershed. Hitherto the Puritans had attacked their opponents almost entirely on the grounds of discipline and polity. The doctrine established by law had not been a major area of concern. It was believed, for the most part, to be the doctrine of a rightly Reformed church, an impression reinforced no doubt by the Calvinist inclinations of Grindal and Whitgift himself. However, in the aftermath of the Baro-Barrett affair, and the supression of the Lambeth Articles, the predestinarian theology which had been taken for granted was now very much open to question. Increasingly, the doctrinal content of the Church of England was seen to be seriously deficient at what, with some justification, might be called the most crucial of Reformation insights: the sovereignty of God in the act of salvation. Thus the Puritan effort of the seventeenth-century was motivated by the need for reformation in doctrine as well as reform of discipline.

For twelve years John Robinson lived, moved, and had his being in the Cambridge of William Perkins and Peter Baro. While we cannot reconstruct his participation in the debates (Burgess suggests that he disputed with Overall in 1600, but there is no evidence for this[49]), we would be surprised if the cumulative impact of the articles and sermons, the points and propositions had no significant effect on his mature thought. In fact, the doctrine of election was Robinson's primary theological preoccupation; in this regard he was a true disciple of Perkins. All of the thorny questions debated at Cambridge, questions concerning the nature of God, the extent of human depravity, the scope of the atonement, the possibility of the forfeiture of grace, the order of the divine

---

[48]This is translated as "Modest Examination of Perkins's Pamphlet" in *The Writings of Arminius*, ed. James Nichols (Buffalo, N.Y., 1853), vol. 3, 252-484. A. W. Harrison in *Arminianism* (London, 1937), 21, erroneously states that Perkins may have attracted the attention of Arminius through John Robinson who republished this catechism in 1592. As noted earlier it was in 1624 that Robinson edited Perkins' catechism.

[49]Burgess, *Robinson*, 53.

decrees, and, above all, the relation of election, predestination, and free will, were pre-echoes of later disputes in which Robinson would play a substantial part. In Separatist historiography Robinson's role in the Arminian controversy has been overshadowed by his reputation as a defender of Separatism and pastor of the Pilgrims. One of the aims of this study is to show that his concern for election is directly related to his motive for separation. In one of his earliest writings as a Separatist Robinson confronted Joseph Hall, later Bishop of Norwich and delegate to the Synod of Dort, with "the error of universal grace, and consequently of free-will, that groweth on apace amonst you: what do you else but put in for a part with God in conversion?"[50] He had listened well at Cambridge.

"FOR SYON'S SAKE HE MUST SPEAKE": THE MINISTRY AT NORWICH

On April 5, 1603, four days after Queen Elizabeth had died, James VI began his progress from Edinburgh to London. To many of his subjects, especially those of the Puritan persuasion, the new king, fresh from the rightly reformed kingdom of Scotland, offered the promise of renewed reform, perhaps even a fresh settlement of religion. While they wept for their deceased Deborah, they hailed their new sovereign with eager expectancy:

> The unlookt for death of our Eliza Queene
> England in sable weed hath justly mournde,
> Whose soule with God in highest blisse is seene,
> Whose earth to heaven, whose death to life is turned.
>   Cease now to weepe, for our Eliza dwels
>   With glorious Saints, in glory that excels.
> Learne now thy time to turne, learne to reioyce,
> Prayse God with heart, with shout let heavens ring,
> In change thou couldst have never better choyce,
> Then God hath made in sending James thy King.
>   Live James, foule Rome and Antichrist confound
>   Gods blessed love let sway in Britan ground.[51]

Four months later, on August 5, with the King's accession still much in the air, John Robinson, described as "a tall blackman" from Cambridge, mounted the pulpit in the parish church of St. Andrew's in

---

[50] *Works*, vol. 3, 411.

[51] *Northerne poems congratulating the kings maiesties entrance to the crowne* (London, 1604), 39.

Norwich to deliver the afternoon sermon.[52] He took for his text Psalm 118:24, "This is the daie which the Lord have made: lett us reioice and be glad in it," a propitious choice for the third anniversary of King James' deliverance from the Gowrie Plot. With the mayor and aldermen of the city present, along with "a great multitude of people," Robinson exhorted the congregation to give thanks for the happy estate and peace of the commonwealth in the time of Queen Elizabeth, for God's favor in preserving King James from the treason of Gowrie, and "for sending hym to raigne over us, by whose raigne there is great hope of the contynuaunce of peace and the gospell to be preached." So far an exemplary sermon. But then, reported Michael Peade, public notary who was present for the occasion,

> he shewed unto the people that for their synnes God would take awaie their prince and king from them if they did not tourne to the Lord and repent them: and shewed examples out of the scriptures of God's punishment and judgment that waie, and then reckoned upp the synnes in this land and negligence of Magistrates not punishing the same as they ought to be, and so begann and cryed out against unlearned ministers calling them dombe dogges and their unlawfull calling: then against comon lawyers. . . .

It was a serious matter to characterize the calling of ministers, even unlearned ones, as "unlawfull," and the remark about the "negligence of Magistrates" was bound to raise eyebrows in some quarters. As the afternoon wore on the preacher from Cambridge waxed bolder turning his attention to the corrupt system of ecclesiastical courts.

> Then he used theis speches; that for Syon's sake he must speake and for Syon's sake he would not holde his tonge, and so reckoned the abuses in the Commission Courtes, Consistories and Comissarie Courtes and the great contempt and indignitie offered unto the ministers and preachers of the gospell, good men and learned men, in the said Comission and Consistorie Courtes and have had no redresse; and enveighed against the use of the censure of excommunicacion, which the Judges of those Courts would pronounce in light causes; (and gave an example) as one should be called by a citacion in causa subtractionis decimarum before a Comissarie and, if the partie appeare not att the daie, he should be excommunicated and so caste out of the Church, an intollerable abuse of such a fearfull censure; and in Consistories and Comissarie Corts if one had comitted adulterie or fornication or such like, the partie appearing confesse his falt, the sayd Judges make

---

[52] *The Registrum Vagum of Anthony Harison*, ed. Thomas F. Barton, Norfolk Record Society (1963), vol. 1, 34-36. This document is labelled "Dr. Robinson's Sermon at Norwich." This is the only contemporary reference I have seen to Robinson as doctor, and it is incorrect. Robinson had not proceeded B.D. when he resigned his fellowship; the D.D. usually required three years of residence past the B.D. In addition, many Puritans objected to the academic doctorate believing the doctoral office to belong exclusively to a local congregation. On Cartwright's criticism of divinity degrees, see Greaves, *Religion and Society,* 358-59.

a sporte att you and inioyne their penaunce in a white shete and a white round etc and there they bring them into the church as one should be brought uppon a stage etc.; instead which the Judges should praie and wepe over them for their fall and offences so comitted they laugh and flout att you which is a great abuse in the Church: and so contynewed in that vehement humor, hoping that ere it be long their thoughts should be reformed and in that sort concluded his sermon.

Toward the end of his sermon Robinson, "speakinge verie vehemently," according to another witness, "sayd that these thinges were intollerable and according to the wordes of hys text sayd yt was high tyme to cry 'Lord now hillp,' when enormityes are growen to this height." It was a stunning performance, and Robinson was soon represented to Bishop Jegon as being "somewhat factious."[53] In order to clear himself Robinson appeared before his old Master from Corpus Christi, and "in some sorte clered hym self" of the charges. Still, Jegon, recently translated to the see of Norwich, and desiring to avoid the appearance of countenancing any form of nonconformity, required Robinson to furnish him with two letters of recommendation before he would license him to preach in his diocese. One of these was written by Sir Arthur Heveningham who commended Robinson as a man "of a verie honeste conversation and zealous in settinge forthe the true worde of God."[54] The other was signed by Thomas Newhouse, William Fleming, and Robinson himself. It testified to "his abilytye and sufficiencye (by the blessing of God) to do good in his Churche and in the place wherunto he shalbe called."[55] Having satisfied himself as to the intentions of his former associate, Jegon issued the required license, and shortly thereafter Robinson was appointed as a minister in the parish of St. Andrew's.[56]

---

[53]Ibid., 157.

[54]Ibid., 158. As the deputy lieutenant for Norfolk Heveningham had close ties with the Privy Council. He had also served as sheriff. Cf. A. H. Smith, *County and Court,* op. cit., 126-33; 147-48.

[55]Ibid., 159. This letter is dated November 25, 1603.

[56]The call to St. Andrew's would have come sometime between late November, 1603, when Jegon received the letters of recommendation and February 10, 1603/04, when Robinson resigned his fellowship at Corpus Christi. Until the beginning of this century most writers followed Neal, op. cit., 72, in assigning Robinson to a benefice "about Yarmouth." At that time Champlain Burrage discovered in the Bodleian Library an anonymous manuscript (MS. Jones 30) which purported to be "An Answ[er] to Mr. Robinson." In fact, the manuscript includes selections from a now-lost treatise of Robinson (probably his earliest writing as a Separatist) as well as the answers of the Puritan respondent, identified by Burrage as John Burgess. The manuscript was first published as *New Facts concerning John Robinson, Pastor of the Pilgrim Fathers* (Oxford, 1910), and reprinted as *An Answer to John Robinson of Leyden by a Puritan Friend* (Cambridge, Mass., 1920), Harvard Theological Studies, vol. 9. [The latter edition is cited here.] In "An

St. Andrew's had a venerable history of dissent going back to the days of the Marian martyrs when Elizabeth Cooper, a pewterer's wife of the parish, was burned in the Lollards' Pit "for embracing the reformed faith."[57] During the first decades of Elizabeth's reign St. Andrew's developed into a thriving center of the Norwich "prophesyings," while Bishop Parkhurst looked the other way. But if Parkhurst "winked at schismatics and anabaptists," as Burghley complained to Archbishop Parker in 1561, his successor, Edmund Freke did not.[58] In the upheaval of 1576 when "19 or 20 godlie Exercises of preching and Catechizing [were] putt downe in this Cittie," and John More, the senior minister at St. Andrew's deprived, the congregation refused to accept the new incumbent calling him "turnecote" and saying "that the Byshop who had commanded hym thither had no more authorytye then a comon mynister."[59] In 1597, seven years before Robinson took up his charge in the parish, the curate Richard Lathe was cited by the apparitor for not reading the injunctions quarterly and for irregularity in the churching of women.[60]

The tradition of nonconformity at St. Andrew's was reinforced by the relatively independent status of the church in selecting its own ministers. At the Dissolution the advowson of the parish had come into the hands of the Crown, but in 1552 Edward VI granted the advowson to William Mingay and William Necton "to be held of the King by fealty only, and not *in capite*."[61] For the years 1557-58 Mingay and Necton presented two curates for the parish, thus giving rise to the practice which would prevail during Robinson's tenure and beyond. In 1561, according to the Parish Book, the two patrons conveyed the advowson to the parish itself for the

---

advertisement of the answerer servinge for introduction," Robinson is identified as "sometimes a preacher in Norwich," and mention is made of "his seperation from that churche or parish of St Andrewes in Norwich of which he had lately beene a minister," ibid., 2. Further on in the manuscript Robinson admits that he was indeed a minister at St. Andrew's, but "neuer anie member, having my house standying (which is the infallible determinacion of members) within another parish, and my children baptized there," ibid., 5.

[57]Coleman and Rye Libraries of Local History, Norwich, MS N726.5: "Notes on the Church of Saint Andrew, Norwich, by F. R. Beechens" (n.p., 1883) [hereafter Beechens].

[58]Conyers Read, *Mr. Secretary Cecil and Queen Elizabeth* (London, 1955), 261.

[59]*The Seconde Parte of a Register*, vol. 1, 145; A. H. Smith *County and Court,* op. cit., 211.

[60]*Bishop Redman's Visitation, 1597*, ed. J. F. Williams, Norfolk Record Society (1946), 29. The 14th Injunction of 1559 required that "all parsons, vicars and clerks, shall once every quarter of the year read these injunctions openly and deliberately before all their parishioners, at one time or at two several times in one day," ibid., 18.

[61]Beechens, op. cit.

amount of £ 13.6.8.[62] Technically, then, St. Andrew's was a donative in
the hands of feoffees who served as trustees for the parish, upon whose
presentation the Bishop would license. This procedure, not uncommon in
the diocese of Norwich, was later a point of controversy between Robinson and a Puritan friend who displayed an intimate knowledge of St.
Andrew's. Robinson asserted that

> the waye by which the ministers of St. Andrewes enter is not the playne waye
> of the Lord but the crooked path of a Lord Bishop's ordinacion and approba-
> cyon and of a patron's presentacyon, yea whether the people will or noe.[63]

To which his respondent replied:

> I marvayle howe a man professing sinceritye, as you doe, could force his
> conscyence so farre as to saie, that the ministery of St Andrewes came not in
> by the Lord's plaine waye of election, seyng you knowe the minister therof is
> freelye chosen by the congregacyon not by the patron nor by the Bishop.[64]

Robinson conceded that St. Andrew's enjoyed this special privilege, but
in other respects it was not unlike the other parish churches: it lacked the
power of excommunication and its members could not dismiss their
ministers ("vnsadle their riders") without episcopal approval. In short, St.
Andrew's was not "that heauenlie Ierusalem, which Christe hath enfran-
chised."[65] Looking back on his years in Norwich through Separatist
lenses, Robinson may have felt that St. Andrew's was "not so gathered
out of the world, nor separated and sanctefied" as his friend alleged, but
in 1604 it was the most forward parish in Norfolk and a suitable cure for a
man of Robinson's disposition and ability.[66]

The incumbent and co-minister with Robinson was Thomas Newhouse, himself recently come from Cambridge where he had been (with
Perkins) a Fellow at Christ's.[67] Newhouse followed an outstanding suc-

---

[62]Ibid., Cf. Francis Blomefield, *An Essay towards a Topographical History of the
County of Norfolk* (London, 1806), vol. 4, 300.

[63]*An Answer to John Robinson*, 73.

[64]Ibid., 73-74. On the lay control of presentation see "The Conditions of the Archdeaconry of Norwich in 1603," *Original Papers of the Norfolk and Norwich Archeological
Society* (1888), vol. 10, 1-49.

[65]*An Answer to John Robinson*, 77, 74.

[66]Ibid., 17. According to the visitation returns of 1603, St. Andrew's was the second
largest parish in the Archdeaconry of Norwich, with 240 registered communicants,
Norfolk Archaeology 10 (1888), 178.

[67]At Christ's Newhouse was the tutor of Samuel Ward and the object of his frequent
anger as we learn from Ward's diary: May 12, 1595, "Thy anger against Mr. Newhouse for
his long prayers"; July 31, 1596, "My anger att Mr. Sharp and Mr. Newhouse for calling
me in jest Kyte"; Aug. 12, 1596, "Also my anger att Mr. Newhouse att supper for saying he
had eaten all the bread," *Two Puritan Diaries*, op. cit., 103, 114.

cession of ministers, mostly Cambridge men, among whom were the
famous John More, George Gardiner, later Dean of Norwich and chaplain in ordinary to Queen Elizabeth, and Robert Hill of St. John's,
known for his "book of Divinity" printed at Cambridge while he was
minister in Norwich.[68] Robinson would have shared the preaching
responsibilities of the parish with Newhouse, taking one of the Sunday
sermons and perhaps an additional lecture during the week.[69] One
member of their congregation, Thomas Lane, mayor of the city in 1603,
recalled their joint ministry when, by his will, he bequeathed 40 shillings
each to "Thomas Newhouse and Mr. Robinson, preachers of God."[70] So
successful were their efforts that "divers convenient seates" were erected
so that space could be made for the large numbers attending the sermons,
"which before that tyme wanted seates."[71]

The years 1604-1606 would prove decisive both in the career of
Robinson and in the fortunes of Puritanism. The mood of partly fearing,
partly hoping, evident already in Robinson's celebrated sermon of 1603,
tilted decidedly in favor of the former as the outlines of the King's
ecclesiastical policy became increasingly clear: "I feare daily," wrote
Richard Rogers from Essex in 1604.[72] Shortly after his arrival in London,
the King was presented with an unsigned petition, claiming to represent
the views "of more than a thousand of your Majesty's subiects and
Ministers," and calling for the "reformation of certaine ceremonies and
abuses in the Churche."[73] The petition urged the King to convene a
"Conference among the Learned" to further discuss the removal of
abuses, and to become directly involved in the process of reform:

---

[68]Beechens, op. cit.

[69]By 1614 a third minister was associated with St. Andrew's: "Mr. Greaves was
appointed lecturer every Monday morning at 7 o'clock, Mr. Heylet every Thursday
morning at 7 o'clock; and the parish minister's lecture was every Friday morning at 7:
o'clock." Blomefield, op. cit., 302. Greaves, like Newhouse, had been a Fellow at Christ's,
Two Puritan Diaries, op. cit., 110, note 30.

[70]Public Record Office B 11/109. The Lane will, proved in the Prerogative Court of
Canterbury, provides one of the few references to Robinson for this period of his life. Lane
died in January, 1606-07. Cf. Basil Cozens-Hardy and E. A. Kent, *The Mayors of
Norwich, 1403-1835* (Norwich, 1938), 67.

[71]*The Registrum Vagum of Anthony Harison,* op. cit., 279-80.

[72]*Two Puritan Diaries,* op. cit., 31.

[73]*A History of the Conferences and other Proceedings connected with the Book of
Common Prayer, 1558-1690*, ed. Edward Cardwell (Oxford, 1840), 130. The Millenary
Petition is found, with slightly varying texts, in several British Museum manuscripts:
MSS. Additional 28571, f. 175; 8978, f. 107; MS. Egerton 2877, f. 174 b.

God, wee truste, hathe appointed your highness our phisitian to heale those
diseases, and wee saye with Mordecai to Esther, Who knoweth whether you
are come to the Kingdome for such a tyme.[74]

James, too, thought of his accession in eschatological terms, as he made
clear in his first oration before the House of Lords: "And now in the end
and fulnesse of time [hath not God united these two kingdomes] in my
Person . . . whereby it is now become like a litle World within it selfe."[75]
But he conceived of his relationship to his subjects in metaphors more
exalted than that of physician to patient: "I am the Husband, and all my
whole Isle is my lawfull Wife; I am the Head, and it is my Body; I am the
Shepherd, and it is my Flocke."[76] It was a conception of divine right that
boded ill for the aims of the petitioners.

Though the demands of the Millenary Petition were moderate, and its
tone mild if not timid, Whitgift, and more especially Richard Bancroft
who would shortly succeed him to the primacy, saw in the request for "the
discipline" to be administered according to Christ's "owne institution," a
return to the classis-presbyterianism of the 1580s, and the imposition of a
Geneva-type polity on the Church of England. Consequently, the famous
encounter at Hampton Court (the "Conference" asked for in the petition,
and granted by the King) marked the beginning of a new and vigorous
campaign for conformity rather than the hoped-for reformation envisaged by the Puritans.[77] The basis for Bancroft's counter-offensive was the
set of Ecclesiastical Constitutions and Canons, hammered out in the
Convocation of the Province of Canterbury and given royal sanction by

---

[74]Cardwell, *A History of the Conferences*, loc. cit.

[75]*The Kings Maiesties Speech, as it was delivered by him in the upper house of the
Parliament to the Lords Spirituall and Temporall on Munday the 19. day of March 1603*
(London, 1604). Reprinted in *The Political Works of James I*, ed. Charles H. McIlwain
(Cambridge, Mass., 1918), 272.

[76]Ibid.

[77]The traditional source for the Hampton Court Conference is William Barlow's
semi-official account, *The Summe and Substance of the Conference* (London, 1604).
Mark H. Curtis, "Hampton Court Conference and Its Aftermath," *History* 46 (1961),
1-16, has argued for a reassessment of the Conference which relies less on Barlow's
portrayal of the King as an implacable foe of the Puritans ("I shall make them conforme
themselues, or I will harrie them out of the land"), but sees him instead as a third party at
the Conference, aligned neither with the bishops nor the Puritans. In any event, the
modest gains registered by the Puritans were more than negated through the efforts of
Bancroft. Though opposed to the Conference from the beginning because it seemed to
give the Puritans equal status with the bishops (and so told the King, according to Barlow:
"*Schismatici contra episcopos non sunt audiendi*"), Bancroft was able to turn the Conference to his advantage by discriminate enforcement of its agreements, and by effective
control of propaganda concerning the Conference, of which Barlow's tract is the best
example.

King James in the spring of 1604. These canons, 141 in number, represented a fundamental revision of the canon law and the codification of the numerous statues, injunctions, articles, and episcopal orders inherited from the pre-Reformation church and developed, rather haphazardly, over the course of the last four reigns.[78]

While many of the canons were appropriated intact from existing formulations, at least 44 were new and many of these reflected the exigencies of 1604.[79] For example, the first twelve canons defined the criteria for membership in the Church of England, and mandated excommunication for those who impugned the King's authority in causes ecclesiastical or who affirmed the worship, doctrine, or government of the Church by law established to be *"impias, antichristianas, aut superstitiosas."*[80] Three of these canons (9-11), anticipating noncompliance on the part of some ministers, explicitly forbade the formation of a "new brotherhood" or secret conventicles.[81]

Along with the canons certain regulations concerning preaching were issued which forbade, among other things, afternoon sermons of the type Robinson had delivered at St. Andrew's in 1603. Preachers were to limit themselves to a simple exposition of the catechism, funeral sermons only excepted.[82] In addition, it was decreed that

> Noe preacher, of what type soever, under the degree of a bishop, or a deane, at the least . . . presume to preach in any popular audience the deepe points of predestination, election, reprobation, or of the universality, efficacity, resistability or irresistability of God's grace.[83]

---

[78]On the Canons of 1604 see Stuart B. Babbage, *Puritanism and Richard Bancroft* (London, 1962), 74-123; Roland G. Usher, *The Reconstruction of the English Church* (New York, 1910), vol. 1, 359-402. The canons are printed in Edward Cardwell, *Synodalia* (Oxford, 1842), vol. 1, 164-329. For an assessment of the medieval and Tudor legislation, cf. the Report of the Archbishop's Commission on Canon Law, *The Canon Law of the Church of England* (London, 1947), 47-59.

[79]Cf. Usher, *Reconstruction,* op. cit., 386-89, for a comparison of the Canons of 1604 with the Injunctions of 1559, the Advertisements of 1564, and the Canons of 1571.

[80]Cardwell, *Synodalia,* op. cit., 168.

[81]Ibid., 169-70: "Quicunque inposterum a sanctorum communione, qualiter in ecclesia Anglicana existet ex apostolorum regulis approbata, seipos segregabunt, et novo fraternitatis cujusdam foedere consociati, christianos omnes, quotquot doctrinae, disciplinae, ritibus, ac ceremoniis ecclesiae Anglicanae se conformes exhibent, prophanes ducent, et indignos quibuscum in christiana professione communicent, excommunicentur. Quicunque inposterum affirmabit, and tuebitur, ullos conventus, coetus, aut congregationes subditorum indigenarum infra hoc regnum existere, praeter eos, qui ex hujus regni legibus tenentur, et approbantur, qui verarum, et legitimarum ecclesiarum nomen possint sibi jure vendicare, excommunicetur."

[82]Babbage, op. cit., 94.

[83]Ibid.

A counsel of moderation, it would seem, intended to contain the bitter controversies which had so recently convulsed Cambridge. But the flames had smoldered too long to be quenched so quickly. The issue was revived at Hampton Court where Overall, a veteran of the Cambridge disputes, asserted that "the Elect might often fall from grace and faithe . . . and if they do not repent they shall perish," to which even the King took exception.[84] With the nonpredestinarian Bancroft at the helm of the Church, and with the Lambeth Articles again rebuffed, to some it might seem that the Church of England was now seriously compromised in its doctrine of grace.

On July 16, 1604, the King issued a Proclamation in which he declared his intention to enforce strictly the recently-issued canons. In particular, he warned the beneficed clergy to conform by November 30, "or else dispose of themselves and their families some other ways."[85] The loss of family income was a serious threat and a grim prospect for Robinson whose wife Bridget gave birth to at least two children during their Norwich years.[86] The task of enforcement began in earnest in 1605, and it is likely that Robinson was suspended *ab officio* at some point during this year. The immediate cause and circumstances of his suspension are difficult to reconstruct. An anonymous Puritan in the "Answer to Mr. Robinson" referred to their deprivations:

> for you and I and others because we could not obserue all other thinges required, were put from preaching as from a specyall parte of our ministerye.[87]

Joseph Hall, on the authority of certain "witnesses," presented a somewhat fuller account in *A Common Apology of the Church of England against the Unjust Challenges of the Over-Just Sect, commonly called Brownists*, which appeared in 1610:

---

[84]Usher, *Reconstruction,* op. cit., 336, 344. "But his Majesty there interposed and saide, the electe indeed might fall, but neuer finally, so that they perish, for they shall rise agayn by repentance. . . ." ibid.

[85]J. R. Tanner, *Constitutional Documents of the Reign of James I* (Cambridge, 1930), 71.

[86]Cf. the reference to "children" baptized at Norwich, cited on page 72, note 56. The parish register of St. Andrew's records the death of a young child in 1605: "Anne Robynson buryed the xxi of June," Norfolk and Norwich Record Office, MS. PD 165/1 (5), f. 13. In December, 1604, a petition of "sundrie Gentlemen, Justices of Peace in Lancashire," was presented to the King on behalf of "the poore wyues and Children of these faythfull Preachers [who are] likely to Fall into greate extremitie and Beggery." *State Papers Domestic, James I*, 14, vol. 10 A, no. 61.

And touching ceremonies, you refused them formerly, but not long; and when you did refuse them, you knew not wherefore; for immediately before your suspension you acknowledged them to be things indifferent; and for matter of scandal by them, you had not informed yourself, by your own confession, of a whole quarter of a year after. . . . But, refusing them, you submitted to the prelates' spiritual jurisdiction. . . . Now upon more grace, refusing the prelacy, you have branded the ceremonies. So you did before your separation.[88]

During these months of partly refusing, partly conforming, Robinson was beset by inward spiritual turmoil, being drawn more and more toward the alternative of separation, but careful to take "the most adviced deliberations" he possibly could: "humblying my self before [the Lord, and] with men, for whose advice I spared neyther cost nor paines, but sought out in everye place the most sincere and iudicious in the land for resolucyon to the contrarye. . . ."[89] Robinson later recalled that the high esteem in which he held certain godly persons had forestalled his early interest in Separatism,

blushing in my selfe to have a thought of pressing one hayr bredth before them in this thing, behynde whom I knew my slefe to come so many miles in all other things; yea and even of late tymes, when I had entered into a more serious consideration of these things and (according to the measures of grace received) searched the scriptures, whether they were so or no, and by searching found much light of truth, yet was the same so dimmed and overclouded with the contradictions of these men and others of the like note, that had not the truth been in my heart as a burning fyre shut up in my bones, [I] had never broken those bonds of flesh and blood, wherein I was so streytly tyed.[90]

After he had been suspended, but before he had taken the final step of separation, Robinson sought employment as the Master of the Great Hospital at Norwich, the position held some 25 years earlier by Robert Harrison.[91] Hall referred to Robinson's unsuccessful application to this post in an *ad hominem* aside at the conclusion of his treatise:

---

[87]*An Answer to John Robinson*, 55.

[88]*The Works of Joseph Hall*, ed. Philip Wynter (Oxford, 1863), vol. 9, 91-92.

[89]*An Answer to John Robinson*, 3.

[90]*Justification*, 48-49.

[91]The mastership was a municipal office vested in the mayor and aldermen, although it involved preaching responsibilities and required induction by the Bishop. Cf. Bromefield, op. cit., vol. 4, 400. Even before he had been appointed to the cure at St. Andrew's, Robinson had received money for preaching at the Hospital: "Item to Mr. John Robynson for preachinge iiii sermons xxxs & to Mr Mayor, Shreve & certain other persons of the saide Bishops guifte xs in all—xls," Norfolk and Norwich Record Office, "Great Hospital Account Rolls," 1601/02.

> Neither doubt we to say, that the mastership of the hospital at Norwich, or a
> lease from the city (sued for with repulse), might have procured that this
> separation from the communion, government, and worship of the Church of
> England should not have been made by John Robinson.[92]

Also, while still in Norwich, Robinson seems to have gathered around
him a little band of loyal supporters, mostly former parishioners at St.
Andrew's, whom he led in exercises of prayer and devotion. Writing in
1608 Henry Ainsworth described these clandestine services:

> Witnes the late practice in Norwich, where certeyn citizens were excommuni-
> cated for resorting vnto and praying with Mr. Rob, a man worthily rever-
> enced of all the city for the graces of God in him . . . and to whom the cure and
> charge of their sowles was ere while committed.[93]

The first indication that Robinson had established contact with noncon-
forming circles in his native district comes from late spring of 1605. The
occasion was a return to his home village of Sturton and a sermon
preached there on Whitsunday. Despite his impending (or recent) deprivation Robinson must have been something of a local celebrity, and his
sermon drew an audience from several parishes. Seven of those present
were subsequently cited before the archdeacon's court where two of them,
John Denman and his wife, of East Retford, admitted "that they were
absent from theire owne parishe church uppon the laste Saboath daye
and there [at Sturton] did here Mr Robinson a strainger preache who

---

[92] *The Works of Joseph Hall,* op. cit., vol. 9, 116. Cf. John Bastwick's oft-quoted
statement that Robinson had told him "that if hee might in England have injoyed but the
liberty of his ministry there, with an immunity but from the very ceremonies, and that they
had not forced him to a subscription to them, and impressed upon him the observation of
them, that hee had never separated from it or left that church." *The utter routing of the
whole army of all the independents and sectaries* (London, 1646), 117. This may have been
true when Robinson was still in the process of transition from advanced Puritan to
Separatist; it was certainly not true of the Robinson of 1610 who penned the massive
Justification, nor of the "mature" Robinson who allowed a limited fellowship, but not
communion with the godly of the Church of England. Bastwick, it is well to remember,
wrote as a polemicist of the 1640s, at a time when the campaign to "rehabilitate" Robinson
was well under way.

[93] Ainsworth, *Counterpoyson,* op. cit., 246. Such a meeting would have been in direct
violation of Canon 73: "Statuimus et ordinamus, ut nulli deinceps presbyteri, sive verbi
divini ministri, vel alii quicunque in privatis ullis aedibus, vel alio quovis loco seorsim
conveniant, consilium capturi de quovis re, aut ratione per ipsos vel ipsorum suasu ac
consilio per alios ineunda, quae ad doctrinae in ecclesia Anglicana stabilitae, vel libri
publicae liturgiae praejudicium, aut derogationem ullatenus spectare possit." Cardwell,
Synodalia, vol. 1, 206. Robinson may have had this group of disaffected members in mind
when, writing about St. Andrew's, he referred to "the persecutions raised even amongst
them selues against such as professe the feare of God in anye sinceritye," *An Answer to
John Robinson,* 17.

[94] Ronald A. Marchant, *The Puritans and the Church Courts in the Diocese of York,
1560-1642* (London, 1960), 152. Marchant's research has added significantly to our
knowledge of the origins of Jacobean Separatism in Nottinghamshire. Cf. ibid., 137-66.

whether he was licensed sufficientlie or not theie knowe not."[94]

Neither Robinson's role in the Norwich "conventicle," if we may call it that, nor his sermon at Sturton, indicated that he had yet "renounced our Ministery received from the Bishops," and cast in his lot with the Separatists.[95] They were, however, significant episodes in the interval between deprivation and separation. Robinson continued to exercise his exceptional gifts as a preacher, even though he was suspended, and increasingly the locus of his ministry was a company of closely-knit followers, committed to one another, but alienated from the conforming majority. At the same time, he became restless in his irresolution, traveling from place to place "where I hoped most to find satisfaction to my troubled heart."[96] The culmination to this period of wavering and indecision seems to have occurred on a particular Sunday when he returned to the familiar scenes of his student years at Cambridge. In the morning he attended a sermon delivered by Laurence Chaderton, Master of Emmanuel, on the text "Tell it to the Church" (Matt. 18:17) in which Chaderton interpreted "church" to mean "the whole Church and not some part only."[97] In the afternoon he went to hear Paul Baynes, that "holy Baynes" who succeeded Perkins at St. Andrew's Church, whose sermon consisted of four points based on Eph. 5:7-11: "(1) That the [servants of God] are light and the [wicked] darkness between which God hath separated. (2) That the godly hereby are endangered to be leavened with the other's wickedness. (3) That the wicked one hereby hardened in receiving such approbation from the godly. (4) That others are thereby offended, and occasioned to think them all alike, and as birds of a feather which so flock together."[98] Neither Chaderton or Baynes had intended his sermon to serve as a clarion call for separation; both were moderate Puritans in the tradition of Perkins, still hopeful of better things from the still young reign of King James. But Robinson had heard more than the preachers had preached. In a private conference with Baynes following his sermon, Robinson demanded whether "these very reasons make not as effectually and much more, against the spiritual communion of God's people . . . with the apparently

---

[95]*Justification*, 383.

[96]*A Manumission to a Manuduction* (Leyden, 1615), 20.

[97]Ibid. Outside of Perkins Chaderton probably had a greater influence on Robinson than any other of his teachers at Cambridge. Chaderton's famous treatise, *A fruitful sermon upon the 3.4.5.6.7 and 8 verses of the 12. Chapiter of Romans*, originally published in 1584, was reprinted by the Pilgrim Press at Leyden in 1618, and frequently cited in Robinson's works. On Chaderton's career see W. Dillingham, *Life of Laurence Chaderton* (Cambridge, 1884).

[98]*A Manumission to a Manuduction*, loc. cit.

wicked, to whom they are as light to darkness."[99] Robinson left Cambridge, perhaps for the last time, apparently convinced, at last, of the course he must take.[100]

"HERE AND THERE UP AND DOWN WITHOUT SURE FOOTING . . . IN THIS PRESENT EVIL WORLD": SCROOBY, AMSTERDAM, AND LEYDEN

When Robinson was in his first year at Cambridge, and Barrow and Greenwood were awaiting execution in the Fleet, Francis Bacon offered the following assessment of the Separatist movement:

> And as for those which we call Brownists, being, when they were at the most, a very small number of very silly and base people, here and there in corners dispersed, they are now, thanks be to God, by the good remedies that have been used, suppressed and worn out.[101]

In the same year Sir Walter Raleigh, before the House of Commons, gave a widely varying estimate of sectarian strength. The Brownists, he considered, were "worthy to be rooted out of any commonwealth." But there were practical problems with banishment: "If two thousand or three thousand Brownists meet at the Sea, . . . at whose charge shall they be transported, or whither will you send them? I am sorry for it. I am afraid there be ten thousand or twelve thousand of them in England."[102] Both Bacon and Raleigh were ill-formed about the actual number of Separatists, but Raleigh more so than Bacon. During the last decade of Elizabeth's reign Separatism, though not extinguished, was at its lowest ebb.

Francis Johnson remained in the Clink until 1597 when, with his brother George, he attempted to establish a Separatist colony in Canada

---

[99] Ibid.

[100] It would be helpful could we assign a precise date or even the correct year to this incident. In 1604 Baynes was suspended from his regular preaching duties and removed from Christ's as a "factious exorbitant" person. Cf. Baynes, *Diocesans Tryall* (n.p., 1621), preface. This would suggest an early date for the Robinson visit, but it is possible that Baynes may have preached at his old post in an unofficial capacity on subsequent occasions. Like Luther's *Durchbruch* and Wesley's Aldersgate experience, Robinson's insight at Cambridge was an integrating moment at the end of a long process of struggle and doubt. According to William Ames Robinson admitted, to a certain "acquaintance," that he had been "amongst some company of the seperation before his comming to Camb. . . . exercising amonst them," *A Second Manuduction* (n.p., 1615), 29. Still, he had come to Cambridge with a "troubled heart" and the two preachers he heard were the unwitting instruments of his new-found resolve.

[101] *The Works of Francis Bacon* (London, 1803), vol. 3, 60.

[102] Simonds D'Ewes, *The Journals of all the Parliaments during the Reign of Queen Elizabeth* . . . (London, 1682), 517. Cf. J. E. Neale, *Elizabeth I and her Parliaments, 1584-1601,* op. cit., 288-89.

by which they hoped to demonstrate the compatibility of religious dissent and political loyalty: "wee may not onlie worshippe god as wee are in conscience perswaded by his Word, but also doe vnto her Maiestie and our Country great good service, and in tyme also greatlie annoy that bloodie and persecuting Spaniard about the Baye of Mexico."[103] This seems to have been the first instance of Separatist designs on America.[104] Following this abortive experiment Johnson rejoined the remnant of Barrow's old congregation which by then was settled in Amsterdam. Apart from Amsterdam, there were a few Separatist conventicles which flourished in certain outlying areas controlled by the Crown or frequented by English merchants. An example of the former was Ireland whence Henry Ainsworth came in 1596, "most Reddy and pregnant in the Scriptures," to assume the office of teacher at Amsterdam.[105] And, by 1599, the Brownists had infiltrated the Barbary merchant company in Morocco, where the Muslim potentate, Ahmed IV, better known to the English as "Mully Hammet," permitted both Catholics and Protestants of all persuasions to worship within his jurisdiction, though he "neither approove[d] the one nor the other."[106] Within England proper, however, Separatism, in terms of organized congregations, was effectively suppressed until the first decade of the seventeenth century.

The recrudescence of Separatist activity "in the North parts," i.e. where the counties of Yorkshire, Lincolnshire, and Nottinghamshire converge, followed directly upon the Puritan failure at Hampton Court and the promulgation of the Canons of 1604.[107] The campaign for enforcement had begun in 1604 with the deprivations of Richard Clifton of Babworth and Richard Bernard of Worksop. These were followed by the ejections of John Smyth from his lectureship at Lincoln, and Robin-

---

[103]"The humble Petition of her highnes faithfull Subiects falsly called Brownistes," printed in *Early English Dissenters*, vol. 2, 125-26.

[104]In 1605 the thought also occurred to Joseph Hall when on his map of the "Other World," he identified a large section of the North American coastline as "Doxia," land of opinionated sectaries, which was translated into English as "Sectarioua," *The discovery of a new world*, ed. Huntingdon Brown (Cambridge, Mass., 1937), 24. On the misadventure of the Johnson brothers, see David B. Quinn, "The First Pilgrims," *William and Mary Quarterly* 23 (1966), 359-90. Cf. A. L. Rowse, *The Elizabethans and America* (New York, 1959), 164-66.

[105]*Plymouth Church Records*, vol. 1, 136. Cf. the Separatist petition addressed to "Mr. Wood a Scottish preacher in Ireland, *anno* 1594," *Mr. Henry Barrowes platform, Which may serve, as a preparative to purge away prelatisme* . . . (n.p., 1611), sig. D 2 recto.

[106]Peter Fairlambe, *The Recantation of a Brownist* (London, 1606), sig. G 3 recto - G 4 verso.

[107]*Of Plymouth Plantation*, 8.

son from his curacy at Norwich. In 1606 these four, together with two prominent Puritans, Arthur Hildersham and John "Decalogue" Dod, and a number of others, gathered at the house of Lady Bowes at Coventry to discuss what course of action they might take in the wake of the widespread deprivations.[108] It was a virtual summit meeting of the local clergy, and the overriding topic of discussion was "about withdrawing from true Churches, Ministers, and Worship corrupted."[109] Smyth, like Robinson, had gone through a period of indecision on the question of separation: "I doubted 9 months I acknowledg."[110] But at the conference he praised God for the resolution of his doubts, and sought to persuade his colleagues that the Church of England was beyond hope of reform, and that they should join him in separating from her. The majority at the conference, led by Hildersham, rejected Smyth's call for radical action, but Robinson agreed with him as did Bernard at the time.

These three, seemingly united in their resolve to separate from the Church of England at the Coventry conference, would soon separate from one another, each to pursue a distinctive path of reformation. Bernard, after a brief experiment with separation, returned to the Church of England, and, with the zeal of a new convert, attacked his erstwhile associates in separation.[111] Smyth, on the other hand, would go further than any English Separatist before him, eventually making a three-fold separation from the Church of England: from its polity, in erecting a separate congregation; from its liturgy, in rejecting set prayers, public reading of the Scriptures, and especially his baptism; and from its doctrine, in repudiating both original sin and predestination. Robinson would emerge as the defender of separation against both Bernard's retrenched conformity and Smyth's re-modeled anabaptism. The tension,

---

[108]The actual number of deprived minitters has been matter of some debate, ranging from 50 according to the Laudian historian Peter Heylyn, to 400, the estimate given by Brook, *Lives of the Puritans,* op. cit., vol. 1, 64. Babbage, op. cit., 217, places the number at 90. However, his accounting included, for example, neither Robinson nor Smyth.

[109]*The Works of John Smyth,* ed. W. T. Whitley (Cambridge, 1915), vol. 2, 534 [hereafter *Smyth*]. None of Robinson's biographers has placed him at this conference, but in the preface to his *Justification,* addressed to Bernard, he referred to it: "But a speach of your own uttered to my self (ever to be remebred with fear and trembling) can not I forget, when after the conference passing betwixt Mr H and me, you uttered these wordes, Wel, I wil returne home, & preach as I have done, and I must say as Naaman did, the Lord be mercifull unto me in this thing: and thereupon you further promised . . . that you would never deale against this cause, nor with-hold any fro it." *Justification,* 10.

[110]*Smyth,* loc, cit.

[111]Cf. Smyth's reference to Bernard's "covenant made with one hundreth people, a thing of such note & observation as that the whole country ringeth of it: but alas againe you have revolted from all this truth." Ibid., 331 Cf. *Justification,* 94.

embodied in these two opponents, between a high Calvinist theology and a sectarian ecclesiology is the controlling dynamic in Robinson's thought, and his resolution of it, his chief contribution to the theology of English Separatism.

The story of how various "professors . . . whose hearts the Lord had touched" gathered themselves into congregations at Gainsborough and Scrooby has often been told, but never better than by William Bradford who, as a young man of seventeen, was an eyewitness of the event. He later described how the Separatists professors who came from "sundry towns and villages" in the lower Trent valley "became two distinct bodies or churches," one associated with Smyth, the other with Robinson.[112] But while geography, in part, prompted this initial division, differences in temperament and policy between the two leaders may also have been a factor. The issue of fellowship with nonseparating Christians had already surfaced, and Robinson later recalled that he had "refused to ioyn [with Smyth] because I would use my liberty in this point [of private communion] & for which I was by some of the people with him excepted against, when I was chosen into office in this Church."[113] This passage, especially the last phrase, which, the context makes clear, refers to "the while we abode in Engl[and]," would suggest that Robinson was formally inducted into office while the group was still in Scrooby, a point much debated in Separatist historiography.[114]

Shortly after the Coventry conference at the home of Lady Bowes the congregation which gathered around Robinson in the Scrooby Manor observed the Separatist ritual of covenant-taking. John Murton, a disciple of Smyth, who later wrote against Robinson's predestinarian theology, recalled this event:

> Do we not know the beginnings of [Robinson's] Church? that there was first one stood vp and made a couenant, and then another, and these two ioyned together, and so a third, and these became a Church, say they, etc.[115]

---

[112]*Of Plymouth Plantation*, 9. Whitely, *Smyth*, lxviii-lxix, places the division after the migration to Holland on the dubious grounds of Hall's attempt to link Robinson with Smyth in such phrases as: "Your partner, yea your guide; M. Smith and his shaddow; M. Smyth whom you followed; Master Smyth your oracle and generall."

[113]*Of Religious Communion*, sig. G 4 recto.

[114]Ibid. The argument for a later induction is based on an over-weighty interpretation of the word "afterwards" in *Of Plymouth Plantation*, 10: "And also that famous and worthy man Mr. John Robinson, who afterwards was their pastor for many years." Burrage holds that Robinson became pastor for the first time in Leyden, but Dexter and Burgess opt for the earlier period.

[115]John Murton, *A Description of what God hath predestined concerning man* (n.p. 1620), 4. W. Walker, *Creeds and Platforms*, 82, incorrectly places the Scrooby covenant-

Bradford's account includes a paraphrase of the covenant which was similar in form to that of the Barrowist congregation:

> the Lord's free people joined themselves (by a covenant of the Lord) into a church estate, in the fellowship of the gospel, to walk in all His ways made known, or to be made known unto them, according to their best endeavors, whatsoever it should cost them, . . .[116]

The manor house in which they met was administered by William Brewster, graduate of Peterborough and former aide to William Davison, diplomat and Principal Secretary to the Privy Council.[117] Though not chosen as ruling elder until they were settled in Leyden, Brewster, from the beginning, placed the wide range of his past experiences in the service of the struggling company. Also active in the leadership of the Scrooby church was Richard Clifton, deprived from his cure at Babworth, "a Graue and fatherly old man . . . haueing a Great white bread."[118] Clifton followed the Separatists to Amsterdam where he detached himself from the Scrooby congregation and became teacher of the Ancient Church.

For about one year after the covenant ceremony, the Scrooby group continued to meet "every Sabbath in one place or another."[119] During this time Robinson continued the somewhat brazen practice of preaching in the churches he had repudiated, thereby attracting lay converts from the ranks of disaffected Puritans.[120] This unauthorized preaching and the success of the Separatists' activity came to the attention of Toby Matthew, recently elevated to the primacy of York, who on September 10, 1607, delivered a sermon "Contra Brownists" at Bawtry, a village which bordered Scrooby on the north.[121] The Archbishop thereupon initiated a series of actions designed to eradicate the pockets of Separatism within

---

taking in 1602. This date was first suggested by Nathaniel Morton in his *New Englands Memorial* (1669). Cf. Harold Worthley, "The Lay Offices of the Particular Churches of Massachusetts, 1620-1755: An Investigation of Theory and Practice," unpublished Th.D. dissertation, Harvard University (1970), 31-35.

[116]*Of Plymouth Plantation*, 9.

[117]The standard work on Brewster is Ashbel Steele, *Chief of the Pilgrims, or the Life and Time of William Brewster* (Philadelphia, 1857). Davison had signed the order for the execution of Mary, Queen of Scots which precipitated his fall from favor, and occasioned Brewster's return to the manor and post-mastership of Scrooby.

[118]*Plymouth Church Records*, vol. 1, 139. On Clifton see the article by Thompson Cooper, *D.N.B.*, vol. 3, 543-44.

[119]*Of Plymouth Plantation*, 10.

[120]In 1607 the churchwardens of South Leverton and of Treswell were cited before the commissary, Thomas Petty, for permitting Robinson to preach in their churches, Marchant, op. cit., 156.

[121]Ibid., 159.

the diocese of York. His plan was to prosecute the lay patrons whose connivance and support had enabled the Separatists to flourish. Brewster and Richard Jackson of Scrooby were summoned to court at Southwell and fined £20 apiece; when they failed to appear a warrant for their arrest was issued.[122] Thomas Helwys of Broxtowe Hall, near Nottingham, was similarly cited, and his wife Joan was imprisoned for three months in York Castle along with Gervase Neville, a member of Smyth's church, whose appearance before the High Commissioners recalled Barrow's earlier examinations: he refused to answer under oath, and railed against the "Antichristian Hierarchie" of the Archbishop.[123] Faced with the unhappy alternative of imprisonment or banishment, the Scrooby church chose the latter and, following the exodus of Smyth's band, they "resolved to get over into Holland as they could."[124] For a while Robinson stayed behind, "to help the weakest," a precedent to be followed some twelve years later when they would embark on another, more adventurous, migration.

When Robinson's company arrived in Amsterdam, "the Fair of all the Sects, where all the Pedlars of Religions haue leaue to vend their Toyes," as a contemporary satirist described it, there were already three English churches in the city: Smyth's group, the Ancient Church led by Johnson and Ainsworth, and the recently-founded Begynhof Church, a presbyterian congregation of English merchants pastored by John Paget.[125] The "toubles" of the older Separatist church had been noised abroad by George Johnson's vivid description of his sister-in-law's immodest apparel. Though duly "admonished" by George, she continued to wear "whalebones in the bodies of peticotes . . . foure or five gould Rings at once . . . excess of lace . . . tucked aprons, like round house . . . [and]the painted Hipocritical brest, shewing as if there were some special workes, and in truth nothing but a shadow." She had moreover, "laide in bedd on the Lordes day till 9 a clock, and hindered the exercise of the worde, she being not sick, nor having any iust cause to lie so long."[126] George

---

[122]Marchant, ibid., 164, suggests that the fines were not collected but see Joseph Hunter, *Collections concerning the Founders of New Plymouth* (Boston, 1880), 131.

[123]Dexter and Dexter, *The England and Holland of the Pilgrims,* op. cit., 392-93.

[124]Bradford, loc. cit.

[125]Dexter and Dexter, op. cit., 419. On the origins of the Begynhof Church, see Alice C. Carter, *The English Reformed Church in Amsterdam* (Amsterdam, 1964), 15-25. In 1618 Paget published *An Arrow against the Separatism of the Brownists* in which he portrayed, with a certain relish, the misfortunes of the Separatist sects.

[126]George Johnson, *A discourse of some troubles and excommunications in the banished English Church at Amsterdam,* op. cit., 135-36. At his brother's excommunication

demanded that such behavior be censured by the congregation, but in the
end it was George who was censured and excommunicated, along with his
elderly father who had come over from England to pacify his quareling
sons. More recently, Thomas White, a Separatist from "the West parts of
England," had left the church amid a blaze of controversy in which the
elder, Daniel Studley, was implicated in a number sordid sexual misdeeds
including, if we are to believe the accusations upheld in court, exhibitionism, incest, and child abuse.[127] At the time of Robinson's arrival still
another dispute was brewing, between the "Franciscans" and the "Ains-
worthians," which would shortly lead to schism. It is understandable,
then, that Robinson would try to keep his distance from the Ancient
Church; and in February, 1609, "Jan Robar[thsen]" was in Leyden
petitioning the burgomasters on behalf of "one hundred persons or
thereabouts . . . of the Christian Reformed Religion," for the right "to
come to live in this City."[128]

While still in Amsterdam Robinson received a letter from Joseph
Hall, rector of Halsted in Essex, popular preacher at Court, and later
Bishop of Norwich, deploring his separation as a form of spiritual matri-
cide: "You could not do a greater injury to your mother, than to flee from
her."[129] Apparently, Hall perceived the Separatists as Puritans in a hurry
whose chief ground for departing was scrupulosity over ceremonies. It
was the valor of Christian teachers to oppose abuses, not to run away
from them. "It has been a thousand times better to swallow a ceremony,
than to rend a church."[130] Robinson's reply, which Hall called "a stom-

---

Francis told the congregation that George "had a crackt brain," ibid., 184. Cf. M. E.
Moody, "A Critical Edition of George Johnson's *A Discourse of Some Troubles and
Excommunications in the Banished English Church at Amsterdam*, 1603," unpublished
Ph.D. dissertation, Claremont (1979).

[127]Francis Johnson, *An Inquiry and Answer of Thomas White* (Amsterdam, 1606), 52.
Cf. Studley's rather weak defense against these charges in Richard Clifton, *An Advertisement concerning a Book lately published by Christopher Lawne* (Amsterdam, 1612),
115-25.

[128]Burgess, *Robinson*, 100. George F. Willison, *Saints and Strangers* (New York,
1945), 70, assumes that there was an organic union of the Scrooby Separatists with the
Ancient Church. This is not borne out by Paget, *An Arrow*, op. cit., 58, who, addressing
Ainsworth, says: "By such a reason as this you might prove that Mr. Robinson and his
company separated from you at his first coming into this land, because they gathered a
new Church apart from you in the same citie, you being here a Church before them."

[129]*Works*, vol. 3, 401. Robinson's reply to Hall's letter is not extant, but it was printed
by Hall in his counter-reply, *A Common Apology,* op. cit. Hall, three years Robinson's
senior, had been at Emmanuel when Robinson was at Corpus. Cf. T. F. Kinloch, *The Life
and Works of Joseph Hall* (London, 1951), 143-48.

[130]*Works*, vol. 3, 403-04.

achful pamphlet," answered the charge of unnaturalness in rejecting "our 'mother, the Church of England'; she is our 'mother,' so may she be, and yet not the Lord's wife!"[131] Further, what more had the Separatists done in departing from the Church of England than their opponents had in abandoning their "mother's mother, the Church of Rome?" And were not "Luther, Zuinglius, Cranmer, Latimer, and the rest begot to the Lord in the womb of the Romish Church?"[132] The reason for separation was not the abuses themselves, but rather the inability to apply the scriptural method of correction: "This power and presence of Christ you want; holding all by homage, or rather by villanage, under the prelates."[133] At the same time Robinson was careful to claim that they had made no willful separation from the kingdom of England. The Church of England, or "State-Ecclesiastical," they accounted Babylon,

> but for the commonwealth and kingdom, as we honour it above all the states in the world, so would we thankfully embrace the meanest corner in it, at the extremest conditions of any people in the kingdom.[134]

While far from presenting a full-orbed defense of Separatism, Robinson's response to Hall was a noteworthy entry in the growing body of controversial literature to which Johnson, Ainsworth, and Smyth had already contributed. It was also the first intellectual exchange between a spokesman of Separatism and a Jacobean Anglican of stature.

The Scrooby Separatists, together with a few recruits from the Ancient Church, arrived in Leyden in late spring, 1609, hoping for better prospects in their struggle with "the grim and grisly face of poverty," and for relief from the fractious disputes of the past year. They were admitted to Leyden on the condition that "that behaved themselves honestly," a reference perhaps to the goings-on in Amsterdam.[135] Soon after their admission to Leyden the magistrates received a letter from Ralph Winwood, Ambassador of King James at The Hague, which protested the

---

131 Hall, *Works*, op. cit., 2; *Works*, vol. 3, 407.

132 Ibid., 408.

133 Ibid., 417.

134 Ibid.

135 In addition to the Studley affair, the Amsterdam magistrates were called upon in the wake of the Ainsworth-Johnson schism to settle a dispute over the ownership of the meeting house. *Of Plymouth Plantation*, 16. D. Plooij, *The Pilgrim Fathers from a Dutch Point of View* (New York, 1932), 44-45. On the Leyden years see *Dexter and Dexter,* op. cit., 472-590; J. G. de Hoop Scheffer, *History of the Free Churchmen . . . in the Dutch Republic* (Ithaca, N.Y., 1923); A. Eekhof, *Three Unknown Documents concerning the Pilgrim Fathers in Holland* (The Hague, 1920); J. W. Verburgt, *Leyden and the Pilgrim Fathers* (Leyden, 1970).

action of the city in allowing the disaffected Englishmen to settle there. The response of the city authorities, a masterpiece of diplomacy, claimed that the petition of the "memorialists" had been granted, "*wy oyt hebben geweten ofte alsnoch weten, dat de supplianten uyt Engelandt gebannen ofte van de secte der Bruynisten syn souden.*"[136] Technically, of course, the Separatists had not been banished from England; they had not even acquired the necessary permission to leave! And, by the seventeenth century, "Brownists" was a *nomen horrible* none of the Separatists were willing to claim.

The move to Leyden placed Robinson in the mainstream of Dutch intellectual life. As a member of the famous university, founded in 1575, he participated in the familiar debates over grace and free will which consumed all of Holland in the years preceding the Synod of Dort. On several occasions he was persuaded by Polyander, the leading theologian of the city, to dispute publicly with Episcopius, leader of the Arminian party. At the same time Robinson developed friendly relations with the other English-speaking church in the city, the Leyden counterpart to the Begynhof Church in Amsterdam.[137] Though he disagreed with the polity and practices of this *gereformeerde gemeente*, he held its ministers, Robert Dury and later Hugh Goodyear, in high esteem. Upon Robinson's death in 1625 some of his depleted company, which had not made their way to Plymouth, united with Goodyear's church, including, for a while, his widow Bridget.[138]

Within his own congregation, which grew to the sizable number of 300 at its height, Robinson exerted a forceful but moderate leadership which earned the respect of his flock and the admiration of "frinds and strangers" alike.[139] By all accounts he was a model pastor, "very profitta-ble in his minnestry and Comfortable to his people." Bradford put it

---

[136]Plooij, op. cit., 45.

[137]On this church see Keith L. Sprunger, "Other Pilgrims in Leiden: Hugh Goodyear and the English Reformed Church," *Church History* 41 (1972), 46-60, and two articles by Alice C. Carter: "The Ministry to the English Churches in the Netherlands in the Seventeenth Century," *Bulletin of the Institute of Historical Research* 33 (1960), 166-74; "John Robinson and the Dutch Reformed Church," in *Studies in Church History*, ed. G. J. Cuming (Leiden, 1966), vol. 3, 232-41. During the sojourn of the Pilgrims, Leyden was the home of still another refugee church, that of the Walloons who had fled from Belgium which was still in the hands of the Spanish. Cf. Bradford's reference to those "of the French church in that city," *Of Plymouth Plantation*, 20.

[138]Jan Hoornbeek, *Summa Controversarium Religionis* (Rheims, 1658), 741: "Sed post obitum eius, oborta in coetu contentione et schismate super communione cum Ecclesiâ Anglicanâ in auditione verbi, D. Robinsoni vidua, liberi, reliquique propinqui et amici in communionem ecclesiae nostri recepti fuerunt."

[139]*Plymouth Church Records*, vol. 1, 139.

simply: "His love was great towards them, and his care was always bent for their best good, both for soul and body."[140] At his death they felt they had suffered "such a loss as they saw could not be repaired; for it was as hard for them to find such another leader and feeder in all respects as for the Taborites to find another Ziska."[141] Robinson's pastoral reputation and the harmony which prevailed at the "Church of the Green Door" during his tenure—in striking contrast to Separatist squabbling elsewhere—contributed, no doubt, to his popularity and credibility as an apologist for the Separatist way.[142]

The decision to move from Holland to America implied that Robinson would be separated from a large segment of his congregation, although this separation was intended to be temporary, for Robinson promised John Carver, the leader of the expedition, not to "foreslow my bodily Comeing att the first opportunetie."[143] But Robinson did not make it to America, and consequently the scene of departure and his celebrated "Farewell Address" have assumed a poignancy in Separatist historiography which they might not otherwise have had. When the time for departure had come Robinson proclaimed "a day of sollemne humilliation" on which he delivered a lengthy sermon (his text was Ezra 8:21: "theire att the River by Ahaua I proclaimed a fast, that wee might humble ourselves before our God and seek of him a Right way for vs and our children") and led the congregation in "powering out prayers to the lord."[144] The next day there followed the tearful scene at Delftshaven when "theire Reuerend Pastour [fell] downe on his knees and they all with him with watery Cheekes Comended them with most feruent prayers to the Lord." Having bidden farewell to their home of twelve years, their friends, and some their families, on a receding tide—"the tide which stayes for noe man," Bradford noted—they set sail for "those vast unpeopled Countryes of America."[145]

---

[140]Ibid., 138-39; *Of Plymouth Plantation*, 18.

[141]Ibid., 18-19. The Taborites, a party of separatist Hussites who fought pitched battles with the less rigoristic Utraquists in the fifteenth century, were a popular example of pre-Reformation dissenters to English Nonconformists.

[142]In 1611 Robinson and several members of his company purchased a piece of property on the Kloksteg known as "De Groene Port." Here, within the shadow of the great Pieterskerk, Robinson and a number of his congregation lived and gathered frequently for worship. Cf. Bradford's statement that Robinson lectured "thrice a week" to his congregation, ibid., 21.

[143]*Plymouth Church Records*, vol. 1, 45.

[144]Ibid., 43.

[145]Ibid., 44, 27. Though one of the most familiar panels of western civilization, depictions of the Pilgrims' departure are frequently inexact. Cf. the recent account of

> But they kne[w] they were pilgrimes and looked not much on these thinges, but lifted vp theire eyes to heaven; theire dearest Country and quieted their speritts.[146]

Robinson continued to advise the Plymouth settlers on doctrinal and practical matters until his death, and in the "Desarts of dismal Circumstances," as Cotton Mather would later characterize their unsettled condition, they remembered his example and his teachings: "That we have been here and there up and down without sure footing is our portion in this present evil world."[147]

We may well question the authenticity of the "Farewell Address" in the form in which it has been transmitted to us:

> In the next place, for the wholesome counsel Mr. Robinson gave that part of the Church whereof he was Pastor, at their departure from him to begin the great work of Plantation in New England. Amongst other wholesome instructions and exhortations, he used these expressions, or to the same purpose: We are now, ere long, to part asunder; and the Lord knoweth whether ever he should live to see our faces again. But whether the Lord had appointed it or not; he charged us, before God and his blessed angels, to follow him no further than he followed Christ; and if God should reveal anything to us by any other Instrument of his, to be as ready to receive it, as ever we were to receive any truth by his Ministry. For he was very confident the Lord had more truth and light yet to break forth out of his holy word.[148]

Clare Cross who has Robinson leading the Pilgrims from Amsterdam to New England in 1618!—a triad of mistakes. For the founding of Plymouth Colony see Ruth A. McIntyre, *Debts Hopeful and Desperate: Financing the Plymouth Colony* (Plimoth Plantation, 1963), esp. 14-34; George D. Langdon, Jr., *Pilgrim Colony: A History of New Plymouth* (New Haven, 1966); Francis Dillon, *A Place for Habitation, The Pilgrim Fathers and Their Quest* (London, 1973).

[146]According to Samuel E. Morison it was this passage which gave rise to the term "Pilgrim Fathers." Cf. *Of Plymouth Plantation*, 47, note 4. However, the preface to the *Confession* of 1596, adopted by Robinson's congregation, had already used the word to describe the experience of the whole Separatist diaspora: "Wee are but strangers & pylgrims, warring against manie and mightie adversaries," *Creeds and Platforms*, 58. The term "Pilgrim Fathers" first occurs in an ode written for the Boston celebration of Forefathers' Day in 1799. See Albert Matthews, "The Term Pilgrim Fathers," Colonial Society of Massachusetts, *Publications* 17 (1915), 300-92.

[147]Cotton Mather, *Magnalia Christi Americana*, ed. Kenneth Murdock (Cambridge, Mass. 1977), 130; *Justification*, 62.

[148]This account of Robinson's address was written some twenty-five years after the event by Edward Winslow in *Hypocrisie Vnmasked* (London, 1646), 97-98, a work intended to minimize the differences between the Plymouth church and the "mainline" Puritans. Cotton Mather, op. cit., 144-45, rendered the speech in the familiar first person in 1702, and was followed in this by Neal, *History of the Puritans*, vol. 2, 146-47. Cf. William Wallace Fenn, "John Robinson's Farewell Address," *Harvard Theological Review* 13 (1920), 236-51; the article by Alexander Gordon, *D.N.B.*, vol. 17, 22.

Yet the sentiment, if not the words, is that of Robinson. In his reply to
Hall's "censorious epistle" Robinson asked, "If God have caused a further
truth, like a light in a dark place, to shine in our hearts, should we still
have mingled that light with darkness?"[149] However, more often than not,
the "more truth and light" quotation, lifted out of the context of Robinson's thought, has become a *Stichwort* for a variety of tendencies, claiming to find in the Pilgrim pastor a precocious enthusiast. In particular,
some, with a vested interest in maintaining the mythological status of the
Pilgrim Fathers' have sought to detach Robinson from the Separatist
tradition which preceded him, and have assigned him a spiritual pedigree
more worthy of a founder of American civilization. Others, in search of a
denominational progenitor of a progressive bent, have minimized, or
even denied, Robinson's indebtedness to Calvinist theology.[150] On the
one hand, this has led to an uncritical adulation of Robinson as the
advocate of liberalism, individualism, religious toleration, democracy,
etc.; on the other, it has resulted in a serious distortion of his theology.
The next two chapters, then, will attempt a fresh examination of two
aspects in Robinson's thought: the theological rationale for separation,
and his exposition of the doctrine of election.

---

[149] *Works*, vol. 3, 407.

[150] Daniel Plooij, op. cit., 35, for example, extolls Robinson as a champion of conscience in the tradition of Socrates, Jesus, and Martin Luther—"one man standing before
the whole world of ecclesiastical and imperial power," while Christopher Hill, *Society and
Puritanism in Pre-Revolutionary England* (New York, 1964), 252, has Robinson anticipating Rousseau's view of representative government. Recent Unitarian and Congregationalist historians have been equally anxious to rescue Robinson from the taint of
Calvinism. See Charles C. Forman, "John Robinson: Exponent of the Middle Way,"
Proceedings of the Unitarian Historical Society 17 (1973-75), 22-23, and especially Robert
Bartlett, *The Pilgrim Way,* op. cit., 174: "It puzzles one to find that Robinson, a liberal of
his time, can still be counted in the fold of the Calvinists. How could he be a traditional
follower of the iron-handed Genevan when his writings, his nature, and spirit were so
much more humane? He certainly was no disciple of the man Calvin, the adamantine
brain. . . ." A significant exception to this stereotypical view is registered, ironically, by the
Marxist historians, Charles and Katherine George, *The Protestant Mind of the English
Reformation, 1570-1640* (Princeton, N.J., 1961), 46, who regard Robinson as "the major
intellectual among the separatists, [sharing] as most of the other separatists do not, the
orthodox Calvinist theology of the English Church."

CHAPTER 4

THE JUSTIFICATION OF SEPARATION

"The Brownists make discipline (and that too of their own devising) such an essential argument of the visible church, as they think where that is not, the magistrate there be tyrants, the ministers false prophets, no Church of God is, anti-Christianity doth reign."[1]

"SION . . . ON THE TOP OF EVERY HIL": THE CHURCH VISIBLE

The Reformation Context of Separatist Ecclesiology

The fundamental impulse of Separatist ecclesiology, as defended by John Robinson in *A Justification of the Separation from the Church of England*, issued from a peculiar correlation of the two principal concerns of Reformation theology, the subjects, respectively, of the third and fourth books of Calvin's *Institutes*: the basis of saving faith and the locus of the true Church.[2] Luther's quest for a gracious God found resolution in

---

[1]Thomas Rogers, *The Faith, Doctrine, and Religion professed and protected in England* (1607), 98.

[2]A quarto volume of nearly 500 pages, *A Justification* is Robinson's longest work, and the most comprehensive exposition of the Separatist position issued in the seventeenth century. Richard Bernard's tentative espousal of Separatism and his prompt recoil into the ranks of the conformists generated a bitter dispute between him and the Nottinghamshire Separatists who had emigrated to Holland, taking with them certain recruits from Bernard's parish at Worksop. Bernard responded with a "hue and crie," published as *Christian Advertisements and Counsels of Peace* (London, 1608), sig. A 7 verso. This, in turn, elicited two replies from the Separatists: Ainsworth's *Counterpoyson* (Amsterdam, 1608) and Smyth's *Parallels, Censvres, Observations . . .* (Amsterdam, 1609). While Robinson was in the process of preparing his own response, Bernard's counter-reply to Ainsworth and Smyth, *Plaine Euidences: the Church of England is Apostolicall, the seperation Schismaticall* (London, 1610), came into his hands. In writing *A Justification*, therefore, Robinson was able to respond to Bernard's latest contribution to the controversy, "in all the particulars which are of weight," *Justification*, 476. No attempt is here

the doctrine of justification by faith alone, the article by which the Church stands or falls (*articulus stantis vel cadentis ecclesiae*). The gospel, then, for Luther was constitutive of the Church; it was, as Werner Elert has said, "the real organizing principle of the church."[3] The gospel begat the believers, gathered them into fellowship (*Gemeinschaft*) around pulpit and table, and united them into a supraindividual communion (*Gemeinsamkeit*).[4] *Ubi evangelium, ibi ecclesia*: where the gospel is, there is the Church.

The contour of the Church, however, in its historical reality as opposed to its spiritual nature, as it was organized, for example, in Saxony or Nuremberg, proved difficult to define with precision. Forced by John Eck at Leipzig to declare himself a "Hussite," Luther also adopted the Wyclif-Hus conception of the Church as "the whole number of the predestined" (*praedestinatorum universitas*), though he later traced this definition to its proper source in Augustine.[5] The invisible Church (*ecclesia invisibilis*), or to use Luther's preferred term, the hidden Church, (*ecclesia latens*), transcended the categories of time and space in that it derived from the eternal election of God: it was a Church "not limited to any place, person, or time."[6] But Luther was a reformer as well as a theologian, and he was compelled by the exigencies of the Reformation to consider the Church in its earthly aspect, to define it—however approximately—as visible and recognizable. To do this Luther spoke of the marks (*notae*) or tokens (*tesserae*) of the Church by which a mere aggregate of individuals might be distinguished from a *congregatio sanc-*

---

made to retrace the tedious course of the discussion. Robinson himself felt that "the readyest way [would be] to reduce things to some heads, and so to prosequute them in order," but he was determined to follow Bernard "step by step, notwithstanding all his vnorderly wandrings and excursions." Ibid., 122-23.

[3]Werner Elert, *The Structure of Lutheranism* (St. Louis, 1962), 259. [Originally published in German as *Morphologie des Luthertums* (Munich, 1931).]

[4]On Luther's provisional concept of the Church as a "gathered *ecclesiola* and his influence on the subsequent congregationalist tradition in Lutheranism," see George H. Williams, " 'Congregationalist' Luther and the Free Churches," *Lutheran Quarterly* 18 (1967), 283-95. On Luther's ecclesiology generally see the valuable article of Karl Holl, "Die Entstehung von Luthers Kirchenbegriff," *Gesammelte Aufsätze zur Kirchengeshichte*, (Tübingen, 1923), vol. 1, 245-78, and Ernst Rietschel, *Das Problem des unsichtbar-sichtbaren Kirche bei Luther*, Schriften des Vereins für Reformationsgeschichte 50 (1932). More recent treatments are found in Gordon Rupp, *The Righteousness of God* (London, 1953), 310-43; John Headley, *Luther's View of Church History* (New Haven, 1963), 29-41; Paul Althaus, *The Theology of Martin Luther* (Philadelphia, 1966), 287-342; Scott H. Hendrix, *Ecclesia in via* (Leiden, 1974).

[5]*Luthers Werke, Kritische Gesamtausgabe* (Weimar, 1883-   ), vol. 2, 287-35. [Hereafter *WA*.]

[6] *WA*, vol. 7, 684, 20: "nit an yrgend eyne statt, person odder zeytt gehafftet."

torum. For Luther the sole, uninterrupted, infallible mark was and remained the gospel, but the gospel in a particular sense—as it manifested itself in the Word rightly preached and the sacraments rightly administered.[7]

Luther's insistence on the necessity of the marks permitted him, and Melanchthon after him, to ward off the charge that he had dissolved the Church into a *Platonicam civitatem*, a docetic construct removed from the order of earthly reality.[8] Nonetheless, two elements in Luther's description of the visible Church militated against a rigorous application of the principle of discernibility. First, not only did the visible Church include "many hypocrites and sinners" along with the godly, but no attempt should be made "in this life" to distinguish one from the other.[9] To do so would be to anticipate the Last Judgment, and to preclude the mysterious (and indiscernible) working of the Spirit through Word and sacrament. In this sense Luther's church was truly a *Volkskirche*: "May the merciful God preserve me from the Christian church in which everybody is a saint!"[10] Secondly, the visible Church, even in its most concrete and "notable" form, remained only a mask, its reality as communion or fellowship perceptible by faith alone. Thus in 1542, writing to Amsdorf of his recently acquired office as Bishop of Magdeburg, Luther stressed the hiddenness of the visible Church:

> For it is necessary for the Church to appear in the world. But it cannot appear except in a mask, a veil, a shell, or some such covering. . . . And such a mask is a married man, a politician, a domestic person, John, Peter, Luther, Amsdorf, etc. Yet none of these is the Church, which is neither Jew nor Greek, male nor female, but Christ alone.[11]

---

[7]Cf. Article 7 of the *Confessio Augustana*: "Est autem Ecclesia congregatio Sanctorum, in qua Evangelium recte docetur et recte administrantur Sacramenta." *Creeds of Christendom*, vol. 3, 11-12. An early formulation of the "tokens" is found in Luther's response to Sylvester Prierias (1521): "Quo ergo signo agnoscam Ecclesiam? oportet enim aliquod visibile signum dari, quo congregemur in unum ad audiendum verbum dei. Respondeo: Signum necessarium est, quod et habemus, Baptisma scilicet, panem, et omnium potissimum Euangelium: tria haec sunt Christianorum symbola, tesserae et caracteres." *WA*, vol. 7, 720, 32-36.

[8]Cf. Melanchthon's "Apology of the Augsburg Confession," in *The Book of Concord*, ed. T. G. Tappert (St. Louis, 1959), 171. For a contemporary Catholic reinstatement of this criticism, see Yves Congar, *Vraie et Fausse Réforme dans l'Eglise* (Paris, 1950).

[9]*Creeds of Christendom*, vol. 3, 12.

[10]*WA*, vol. 46, 583, 11. "Der barmhertzige Gott behute mich ja für der Christlichen Kirchen, darin eitel Heiligen find"!

[11]*WA*, Briefwechsel, vol. 9, 610, 47-53. "Oportet enim Ecclesiam in mundo apparere. Sed apparere non potest, nisi in larua, persona, testa, putamine and vestitu aliquo. . . . At tales laruae sunt Maritus, politicus, domesticus, Iohannes, Petrus, Lutherus, Amsdorffius, ect., cum nihil horum sit Ecclesia, quae nec est Iudeus nec Graecus, nec masculus nec femina, Sed vnus Christus etc."

Always wary of the temptation to collapse faith into sight, to equate institutional form with spiritual reality, Luther avoided what might be called an "ecclesiology of glory" by stressing the "givenness" of the gathered community, the source of its life in Christ, rather than its outward, empirical manifestation.

If Luther's predominant concern was with the Christological and evangelical center of the Church, later reformers took up the difficult task of determining with some precision its circumference.[12] Calvin, in particular, faced by a resurgent Catholicism on the one hand and a proliferating sectarianism on the other, developed a more formal theory of the relation of the invisible Church to the Church as an external institution recognizable as "true" by certain distinguishing marks. Calvin, no less than Luther, was convinced that the ultimate foundation of the Church lay in God's secret election. Thus, the Church was inviolable, based on God's unfailing predestination, so that "even if the whole fabric of the world were overthrown, the Church could neither totter nor fall."[13] It included not only saints presently living, but all of the elect from the beginning of the world. Yet the Church in this sense was truly "beyond our ken" (*incognitam*); we must leave to God alone the knowledge of His Church which we cannot see with the eyes nor touch with the hands.

Properly speaking it is this invisible Church of which confession is made in the Apostles' Creed. But in the *Institutes*, at the beginning of Book IV, Calvin conceded that the third article of the Creed could be applied "in some measure" (*aliquatenus*) to the *ecclesia externa* as well. It was a significant concession, and the balance of Book IV was given over to a discussion of the sense in which we might "believe" (as opposed to the weaker "believe in" [*Inst.* 4,1,3]) the visible Church. Calvin related the necessity for the visible Church to the universal human incapacity to perceive God apart from "external helps" (*externa subsidia*).[14] Shut up in

---

[12]This image was first used by Gordon Rupp, op. cit., 310. A recent elaboration is P. D. L. Avis, " 'The True Church' in Reformation Theology," *Scottish Journal of Theology* 30 (1977), 319-45, and *The Church in the Theology of the Reformers* (Atlanta, 1981), 13-63. In his comparative study of Reformation views of the Church, Avis offers a sound interpretation of the mainline reformers, but he has misunderstood Separatist ecclesiology, particularly the Separatist doctrine of the marks of the Church.

[13]*Institutes* 4,1.3. *Calvini Opera*, vol. 5, 6: "etiamsi tota orbis machina labefacteur, corruere ipsa et concidere nequeat." On Calvin's ecclesiology see Otto Weber, "L'unité de l'église chez Calvin," *Revue de theologie et de philosophie* 9 (1959), 153-65; Geddes MacGregor, *Corpus Christi* (Philadelphia, 1959); Alexandre Ganoczy, *Calvin, théologien de église et du ministère* (Paris, 1964); Benjamin Milner, *Calvin's Doctrine of the Church* (Leiden, 1970).

[14]*Institutes,* 4,1,1.

the prison house of flesh, and encumbered with ignorance, sloth, and fickleness of disposition, fallen man is able to perceive only the faintest vestiges of God in nature, and even these issue only in idolatry and self-condemnation. The visible Church, then, is an illustration of the principle of accommodation (*attemperatio*). Just as in the Scriptures God has adapted his message to our meager minds, as a nurse might condescend to babble (*balbutit*) with an infant, so in providing outward means of grace in a visible Church, he has accommodated himself to our limited capacity.[15] To describe the way in which the Church functions as an external aid to faith, Calvin applied to it the dual metaphors, well-worn by Patristic and medieval usage, of *Mater et Magistra*. As "mother" the visible Church conceives, bears, nourishes, and sustains the believers during their earthly pilgrimage. As "teacher" the visible Church instructs its members in "heavenly doctrine" (*caelestis doctrina*), and so leads them into the state of spiritual adulthood. To break the unity of the visible Church, therefore, was to become "a traitor and apostate from Christianity"; it was an act of sacrilegious disloyalty, deserving the "whole thunderbolt of God's wrath."[16]

With so much at stake, it became all the more crucial to ascertain what were the "marks of the true church" (*notae verae ecclesiae*), lest one be lulled into complacency by a corrupt church (Rome), or fall into capricious separation from a true church (Anabaptists). Calvin is clear about the function of the *notae*:

> For, in order that the title "church" may not deceive us, every congregation that claims the name "church" must be tested by this standard as by a touchstone.[17]

By so directly associating the *notae* with the act of testing and verification, Calvin has surpassed Luther's concept of the marks as mere indicators of the visible Church. They have become in some sense causative, constitutive of the visible Church. In the Reformed Confessions the *notae* are thus distinguished from the traditional Nicene attributes (*una, catholica, apostolica, sancta*) precisely because they are not merely descriptive, but dynamic: they call into question the unity, catholicity, apostolicity, and holiness of every congregation which claims to be a church, and so subject it to an outward, empirical examination.[18] In this way "the face of

---

[15] Ibid.

[16] *Inst.*, 4,1.10.

[17] *Inst.*, 4,1,11: "Nam ne sub Ecclesiae titulo impostura nobis fiat, ad illam probationem, ceu ad Lydium lapidem, exigenda est omnis congregatio quae Ecclesiae titulo obtendit." *Calvini Opera*, vol. 5, 15.

[18] Cf. Heinrich Heppe, *Reformed Dogmatics*, ed. Ernst Bizer (London, 1950), 657-94.

the church" emerges into visibility before our eyes (*Inst.* 4,1.9). Significantly, Calvin did not follow Bucer, as did the Reformed tradition generally, and the Separatists *par excellence*, in elevating ecclesiastical discipline to the technical status of a *nota*.[19] For Calvin, as for Luther, the more certain (*certioribus*) marks remained the Word purely preached and the sacraments duly administered. However, he did not for that reason disparage the importance of discipline for the well-being of the Church. If the saving doctrine of Christ was the soul of the Church, then discipline served as its sinews (*pro nervis*), through which the members of the body were held together, each in its own place.[20] Discipline, then, pertained to the constitution and organization, if not to the definition, of the external Church. It belonged to the arena of visibility insofar as it too was a criterion of testing, both individually in self-examination and self-mortification, and corporately in the public procedures of admonition, censure, and excommunication.

Calvin's concern for the order and form of the visible Church derived from his emphasis upon sanctification as both the process and goal of the Christian life. Luther, in his mature doctrine of justification, broke decisively with the medieval tradition (in its radical Augustinian as well as its neo-Pelagian strands) in refusing to equate God's act of "making righteous" (*Gerechtmachung*) with the infusion of sanctifying grace. Justification, as the imputation of alien righteousness, retains its forensic character as *extra nos*: even faith, the subjective corollary of the divine pronouncement, is effected "without our cooperation" (*sine nobis*); it is something done to us rather than by us.[21] For Luther sanctification retains its cultic connotation of "set apart," or "consecrated," and, as such, it too is an alien possession.[22] Such a radical disjunction between

---

[19]However, Calvin, in the first edition of the *Institutes* (1536) approached Bucer's view by including "example of life" among the "certain sure notes": "Quanquam autem fidei certitudine agnosci a nobis electi non possunt, quando tamen scriptura certas quasdam notas nobis describit, ut antea dictum est, quibus, electos et filios Dei a reprobis et extraneis distinguamus, quatenus a nobis vult agnosci, debent quodam caritatio indicio pro electis ac ecclesiae membris haberi omnes, qui et fidei confessione et vitae exemplo et sacramentorum participatione eundem nobiscum Deum ac Christum profitentur." *Calvini Opera*, vol. 1, 89. On Bucer, see Avis, *Church in Theology of Reformers*, 48-50.

[20]*Inst.* 4,12.1: "Proinde quemadmodum salvifica Christi doctrina anima est Ecclesiae, ita illic disciplina pro nervis est: qua fit ut membra corporis, suo quodque loco inter se cohaereant." *Calvini Opera*, vol. 5, 212.

[21]*WA* x (1), 291, 26. Cf. *WA*, vol. 42, 452, 23.

[22]Cf. Ian D. Kingston Siggins, *Martin Luther's Doctrine of Christ* (New Haven, 1970), 154: "Sanctification for Luther normally does not mean the process of moral purification or improvement in virtue."

justification and sanctification prevented a doctrine of "works" from creeping in through the back door, but at the same time it opened the windows to antinomian and quietistic tendencies which precipitated several major modifications of Luther's doctrine within Lutheranism itself.[23] These, in turn, provoked the strident reaction of Lutheran orthodoxy in which justification and union with Christ are even more sharply divided.[24]

In contrast to the unilateral accentuation of justification in the Lutheran Confessions, Calvin gave precedence to sanctification in his systematic arrangement of the "benefits of Christ." The two are connected as distinct but interrelated "moments" in the appropriation of the work of Christ. Together they comprise a twofold grace (*duplicem gratiam*) or double cleansing (*double lavement*), so that "actual holiness of life, so to speak, is not separated from free imputation of righteousness."[25] Sanctification is a gradual process, begun in regeneration, continued throughout life, and consummated at the Second Advent when the elect will fully realize their goal of conformity to Christ. In this life the locus of sanctification is the visible Church in which the elect participate in the benefits of Christ not as isolated individuals, but as members of a body in which "all the blessings which God bestows upon them are mutually communicated to each other."[26] In this way the visible Church becomes a "holy community," an agent of sanctification in the larger society where every aspect of life is to be brought within the orbit of Christian purposes and Christian regulations.[27]

The theory of Calvin provided the basic orientation for Separatist ecclesiology, although certain distinctive features of Separatist thought and practice were similar to, if not influenced by, developments among

---

[23]George Major and Justus Menius claimed that no one could be justified without good works. Andreas Osiander held that justification implied an inherent holiness received by the infusion of Christ's "essential" righteousness. A later reaction, motivated by similar concerns, was that of Pietism.

[24]Cf. Article 4 of the Formula of Concord in *Creeds of Christendom*, vol. 3, 121-26.

[25]*Inst.* 3,11.1; *Corpus Reformatorum*, eds. G. Baum, E. Cunitz, and E. Reuss (Brunswick, 1853-1897) 50, 437. *Inst.* 3,3.1: "Neque tamen a gratuita iustitiae imputatione separetur realis (ut ita loquar) vitae sanctitas" (*Calvini Opera*, vol. 4, 55).

[26]*Inst.* 4,1.3: "Quasi dictum esset hac lege aggregari sanctos in societatem Christi, ut quaecunque in eos beneficia Deus confert, inter se mutuo communicent." *Calvini Opera*, vol. 5, 5.

[27]Ernst Troeltsch, *The Social Teaching of the Christian Churches* (Chicago, 1931), vol. 2, 596-602, argues on the basis of the Weber thesis that Calvin's doctrine of the church implied an "activist" social theory in contrast to the "acquiescent" stance of Lutheranism. Cf. the more recent study of David Little, *Religion, Order, and Law: A Study in Pre-Revolutionary England* (New York, 1969).

the continental Anabaptists. Although Robinson was determined to follow Calvin no further than he had followed Christ, and criticized the Calvinists of his day who "stick where he left them," at least three elements in his reformulation of the Separatist position derive from the complex of ideas held in tension in Calvin's doctrine of the Church.[28] 1) The visible/invisible, outward/inward polarity is preserved to emphasize *both* the ultimate foundation of salvation in God's eternal decree *and* the manifestation of Christ's sovereignty in the form and constitution of the external Church. 2) The *notae*-concept, expanded and formalized to include discipline, functions as a litmus test to draw an even more circumscribed perimeter around the visible Church. 3) Within the "Lord's walled orchard" the demands of corporate sanctification require a vigorous fellowship of mutual edification and participation which distinguishes the true visible Church from all other "bodies" as a unique kind of communal order sustained by the Spirit of life.

Separatism: Donatism Writ English?

English Separatists of the sixteenth and seventeenth centuries were the objects of a twofold and somewhat contradictory characterization. On the one hand, "the manifold strange and dangerous innovations" of their position led contemporary Puritan and Anglican observers to associate them with sectarian trends recently imported from the Continent, especially Anabaptism and Familism.[29] At the same time, they were identified with a variety of ancient and often obscure heretics: Luciferians, Novatians, Audians, Petrobrusians, Cathari. "Can our way both be a novelty & new devise, and yet agree so well with the ancient schismatiques condemned in former ages?" asked Robinson.[30] By far the most common and incriminating label attached to the Separatists was that of

---

[28] Burgess, *Robinson*, 240. Cf. Barrow's opinion of Calvin: "I gladly acknowledg him a painful and profitable instrument, in the thinges he saw, and times he served in, yet not without so newly escaped out of the smoky fornace of poperie, he could not so sodeinly see or attaine unto the perfect beawtie of Sion." *The Writings of Henry Barrow, 1587-1590*, 287.

[29] Richard Hooker, *Of the Laws of Ecclesiastical Polity* ([The Folger Library Edition] Cambridge, Mass., 1977), vol. 1, 36. Cf. Robert Harrison's complaint: "For we help one anothers wantes as we are able, and you say behold Anabaptists and men of the family of loue," *The Writings of Robert Harrison and Robert Browne*, 65.

[30] *Justification*, 42. Cf. Richard Bernard, *Christian Advertisements*, 24-26.

"Donatists."[31] Thus in 1590 George Gifford attacked Barrow and Greenwood in *A Plaine Declaration that our Brownists be full Donatists,* and in 1605 Oliver Ormerod presented the following dialogue between The Puritan and The Protestant:

> The Puritane: Doe we agree with the Donatists? The Protestant: Yes, the Donatists deuided themselves from the congregations of other men, and had their priuate conuenticles: so haue you. . . . But let vs come to our Brownists, which are indeede the very brood of the Donatists.

The Protestant thereupon lists thirty ways in which the Brownists approach the Donatist error, and so "separate themselues from us."[32]

The Separatist arguments against the Church of England, and the call for others to join in their flight from Babylon, implied an ecclesiastical exclusiveness which seemed to subordinate God's gratuitous justification to one's status in a particular church order. Stirrings of inward piety would not suffice so long as one remained in spiritual subjection to "yᵉ popes bastardes," for

> Christe dwelleth not, where he ruleth not. His Churche and Kingdome in this worlde is outwarde and visible, and except he gouerne visiblie, euen by his outwarde ordinances: It is vayne for vs to say, He ruleth in our hartes.[33]

As the Donatists of old had denied the efficacy of Catholic sacraments, so the Separatists argued the same against the parish assemblies—"there sacraments ar but dead synes/& pretended sacraments . . . the true sacraments aptayne vnto the aparant church."[34] Browne, who declared the government of the church to be "all in all," went so far as to claim that we are "baptised into the gouernement of Christ in his Church."[35] Stephen Bredwell saw the emergence of a new legalism in Browne's ecclesiology since it required "the couenant to bee helde by woorkes, [which] is the high way to Popery." Moreover, to claim that "obedience and holy life are causes of our iustification . . . and not tokens or fruites only," was to

---

[31]As a historical movement the Donatists were a schismatic body in the African Church who refused to accept episcopal consecration by a traditor, and thus denied the *ex opere operato* character of the sacraments. They were effectively challenged by Augustine, and were destroyed as an organized church by the Arab invasions of the eighth century. Donatism as a rigoristic tendency persisted and re-appeared in various forms. Its defining characteristic may be described as a passion for the holiness of the church at the expense of its unity. In this sense it was attributed to the Separatists.

[32]Oliver Ormerod, *The Picture of a Puritane* (London, 1605), sigs. O 1 verso - O 3 recto.

[33]*The Writings of Robert Browne and Robert Harrison*, 32, 110.

[34]Ibid., 40.

[35]Ibid., 160, 214.

subvert the gospel of grace and forfeit even "the name of a Christian."[36]

When Robinson entered the lists as a Separatist exponent he was at once confronted with the assumption that his position entailed a confusion of the visible and "Catholike" churches:

> But it is a small thing with you & your partie oftentymes to confound the Catholike Church, which consistes onelie of the first borne whose names are written in heauen, & the particular visible Churches, wherein maie be electe and reprobate, vesselles of honor & dishonor, & so to abuse your selues.[37]

Modern historians of Congregationalism, for the most part, have accepted the judgment of the Separatists' opponents in relating their motive for separation to a desire to correlate the visible Church with the invisible, and thus to base church membership on the secret counsel of God. Perry Miller speculates that by the process of rigorous examination and supervision, the covenanted brethren could become "practically certain" of the election of prospective members, and thus "make in [the visible church] the acquaintance of their future neighbors in heaven."[38] More recently, John von Rohr has argued that the Separatist emphasis upon church order as one of the *fundamenta* of the Christian faith led them to affirm that "outside the church—that is, outside the congregationally organized and governed church—there is no salvation."[39] However, both of these interpretations ignore the carefully drawn distinction between visible and invisible Church made by the Separatists themselves, a distinction more pronounced in Robinson's writings than in earlier Separatist literature due to his highly developed doctrine of predestination. [40]

---

[36] *The Rasing*, 44, 41.

[37] *An Answer to John Robinson*, 75.

[38] Perry Miller, *Orthodoxy in Massachusetts, 1630-1650* (Cambridge, Mass., 1933), 57. Yet Edmund Morgan, *Visible Saints: The History of a Puritan Idea* (Ithaca, N.Y., 1963), 65, has shown that the test for election, so important in the development of the New England way, was not applied by the Separatist churches in Holland, nor by the Plymouth church in the 1620s.

[39] John von Rohr, "*Extra Ecclesiam Nulla Salus*: An Early Congregational Version," *Church History* 36 (1967), 107-21. Von Rohr also includes a number of non-separating congregationalists (Jacob, Ames, Bradshaw) in his survey of ecclesiastical exclusivists, though he hardly mentions the visible/invisible distinction which is common to all of this literature. John F. H. New, *Anglican and Puritan*, 95, also writes of "the quasi-Donatist nature of Separatism's theology." He, too, has failed to see that the *conditional* covenant theology of the Separatists applied only to the visible Church, never to the invisible Church which was constituted by God's *unconditional* election.

[40] Stephen Brachlow, "Robinson and the Lure of Separatism," 297, has attempted to justify Miller's argument by lifting out of context the following quotation from Robinson: "There is indeed, but one Church of Christ . . . all that are of the visible Church are also of

Robinson shared with the non-separating Puritans a similarity of background and experience which included the all-important moment of conversion. His acceptance of Separatism involved not a repudiation of those "former graces," but, as he saw it, the maturation of a spiritual process begun and nurtured for many years within the very church he had now come to regard as false:

> We do with all thankfulnes to our God acknowledg, and with much comfort remember those lively feelings of Gods love, & former graces wrought in vs, & that one special grace amogst the rest by which we have been enabled to drawe our selves into visible Covenant, and holy communion. Yea with such comfort and assurance do we call to mynde the Lords work of old this way in us, as we doubt not but our salvation was sealed up vnto our consciences by most infallible marks and testimonyes (which could not deceave) before we conceaved the least thought of separation, and so we hope it is with many others in the Church of Engl. yea and of Rome too.[41]

Election, then, cut through a broad spectrum of confessional and ecclesiastical structures, and extended even to the manifestly false Church of Rome! Bernard suggested that the existence of elect infants within Rome entitled it to be called, in some sense, a true visible Church. Robinson denied this explaining that

> they are not necessarily eyther the true visible Church, or of it, because they are Christs . . . for God hath his in Babylon, which are visible Citizens, of that visible City of fornication, (though the Lords in respect of election, and the beginnings of personal sanctification).[42]

Moreover, the sovereignty of God could so overrule the ecclesiological aberrations of man that the "most accursed" means might be used to bring forth praiseworthy results. Robinson speculated that "if some Iesuite, or other, sent by the Pope into America amongst the Pagans and Infidels, should there perswade any to beleeve & confesse one God, and his sonne Iesus Christ made man for the redemption of the World," this would be cause for rejoicing, though not for embracing the Jesuits'

---

the invisible, and all of the invisible of the visible Church, which are indeed not two, but one Church." The context, however, makes it clear that this suspension of the visible/invisible distinction refers only to an ideal situation. One can speak about it only in "the right disposition of things by the revealed will of God." The fact that there are "many of the visible Church, which are not of the invisible, and so answerably, many of the invisible Church, which never come into the visible," is "not according to the revealed will of God, in his word; but by mans default, and sin" (*Justification*, 313). The whole passage in question is precisely an attempt to distinguish the visible/invisible Church, not an effort to blur the distinction.

[41]*Justification*, 60.

[42]Ibid., 282.

ministry.[43] The presence of "hundreds and thousands" of elect saints within the Church of England led Robinson to hope that, within less than 100 years, there would be "a very plenteous harvest" of true believers who would forsake the false spiritual estate established by law and join themselves into particular congregations.[44] Robinson thus addressed the reluctant saints in England: "We pray for the perfecting of Gods work in you, and that as we think many of you his people in Babylon, so you may come out of her."[45]

If there were elect saints outside the perimeter of the true visible Church, then there were hypocrites within. Again, the visible or external Church which is "by men discernable," is distinguished from the internal, the invisible, "which onely the Lord knoweth."

> For we doubt not but the purest Ch: vpo earth may consist of good and bad in Gods ey, of such as are truely faithfull, and sanctified, & of such as have onely for a tyme put on the outside and vizard of sanctity, which the Lord will in due tyme pluck of, though in the mean while mans dim sight cannot pearce through it. [46]

The presence of "seeming saynts" within the visible Church occurred because the Separatists, no more than the monarchs of England, were able to make windows into men's souls. Since faith and repentance were inward graces, known only to God, the criterion for church membership was reduced to an outward profession of faith, and "other outward appearances," by which the Church, "probably, & in the judgement of charity, (which is not causelesly suspitious), deem him faithfull, and holy in deed, as in shew he pretendeth."[47] There were, then, sheep without, and wolves within; and Robinson consistently refused to correlate the irrevocable decrees of election and reprobation with ecclesiastical alignments where probability and judgments of charity were necessary criteria of admittance: "And straung it is . . . to make it all one, to be saved & to be of the visible Church; & to be condemned, & to be out of it."[48]

---

[43]Ibid., 65-66.

[44]Ibid., 259, 62. Cf. 64: "Whilst we withdraw our selves from them, we do in no sort condemn their persons, (which stand or fall to the Lord)."

[45]Ibid., 78.

[46]Ibid., 112.

[47]Ibid., 113, 271.

[48]*Of Religious Communion*, 95. Barrow, in refuting the charge of Donatism, had expressed an opinion similar to Robinson's. "Yet doe wee not herebie restraine the infinite power of God from saving or calinge his elect even by the doctrine of the false church . . . but God hath manie thousandes deare elect there, yea, even in the popish churches, whom he in his due tyme by his appointed meanes wil cal." *The Writings of Henry Barrow,*

Unlike the continental Anabaptists, but in good agreement with the earlier Separatist tradition (e.g. the *Confession* of 1596), Robinson retained a high doctrine of predestination. God's "invisible justification," based upon his sovereign election, was prior to, and, indeed, the presupposition of, the true *visible* Church. Yet Robinson never allowed his concern for the latter to obscure his commitment to the former. Our exposition of the lineaments of Robinson's doctrine of election must await chapter five. At this juncture, however, it is important to realize that his expressed motive for separating from the Church of England related not to a quest for soteriological exclusivism, but rather to a concern for corporate sanctification through obedience to Christ.

Edification: The Motive for Separation

For all of his stress upon the reality of the invisible, supramundane Church, and his allowance for the mysterious outworking of election, it is adherence to that other anchor of Calvin's ecclesiology, the principle of discernibility, which most acutely distinguished Robinson from his Puritan interlocutor, and gave to Separatism its most distinctive emphasis. While the visible church was not the exclusive ark of salvation, it remained nonetheless "the onely ordinary beaten way" to heaven. Unto it alone pertained the promises of the outward covenant, the valid seals of that covenant, and the benefits of the Christian ministry. Robinson thus spoke of it, in exalted metaphor, as "heaven upon earth":[49]

> If ever I saw the beauty of Sion, & the glory of the Lord filling his tabernacle,
> it hath been in the manifestation of the divers graces of God in the Church, in
> that heavenly harmony, and comely order, wherein by the grace of God we
> are set and walk.[50]

In the *ordo salutis*, then, church order belonged not to the "invisible justification" of the individual believer, but to the outward, empirical process of sanctification defined in communal terms as the dynamic interaction and mutual edification of the Lord's free people.[51] In a later writing, and in an obviously irenical context, Robinson expressed the motive for separation thus: "Our faith is not negative; nor [that] which

---

1590-1591, 275. Barrow, however, did not employ the visible/invisible distinction which he believed to be an unscriptural formulation concocted to account for corruption in the Church. Cf. F. J. Powicke, *Henry Barrow*, op. cit., xxiii.

[49]*Justification*, 122.

[50]Ibid., 212.

[51]Ibid., 312.

consists in the condemning of others, and wiping their names out of the bead-roll of churches, but in the edifying of ourselves."[52]

Yet the very act of separation implied a severe and radical judgment on the validity of the Church of England, if not on the ultimate destiny of its members. It meant not only the rejection of the national Church, but also the severance of fellowship with all of those who remained within it, even though some of them, as a later writer put it, were admittedly "sound in the vitals of Christian religion."[53] As Robinson explained to Bernard: "We [cannot] acknowledge any of you for brethren in that visible comunion of Saincts which is the Church, notwithstanding the loving and respective remembrance wherein we haue very many amongst you severally considered for your personal graces."[54] To do so would be to acknowledge the entire fraternity to whom the "forward" were conjoined—brother Priest, brother half Priest, brother dumb Priest, brother Atheist, brother Epicure, brother witch, brother conjurer, even brother recusant Papist. Not until Bernard had disclaimed "the fatherhood of the Prelates, [and] the brotherhood of the vnhallowed multitude," could Robinson welcome him into "our fathers house" and "make all spiritual melody with you in the Lord."[55]

Negatively, the policy of exclusion was based on the conception of sin as contagious and transferable. To remain in fellowship with the parish assemblies was no static act of disobedience; it was to participate in and be corrupted by the manifest evil which flourished there:

> But being taught by the Apostle . . . that a little leven leveneth the whol lump, we cannot be ignorant how sour the English Assemblies must needs be: neither may we be justly blamed though we dare not dip in their meal, least we be soured by their leven. [56]

Since the parish assembly was not permitted to "meddle with the reproving" of an offender in their midst, but had recourse only to the external machinery of the ecclesiastical courts, then those who remained within the Church became just as guilty, "by connivency," as the offending member, in the same way that Achan's trespass was imputed to all of Israel: "When a man doth not consider or observe his brother as he ought,

---

[52] *Works*, vol. 3, 63.

[53] Samuel Clarke, *The lives of sundry eminent persons in this later age* (London, 1683), 170.

[54] *Justification*, 104.

[55] Ibid., 105.

[56] Ibid., 16.

nor watch over him in the holy communion of saynts wherein he is set . . . then [he] may be guilty of the sin of an other, yea though he be utterly ignorant of it."[57] But in the Church of England, the lack of fraternal discipline corresponded to the prevailing philosophy, "that every man shall answer for himself, and every tub stand vpon his own bottom." Where brotherly admonition was attempted at all, it was regarded as a "precise curiosity of busyheaded people," not as a vital function of the spiritual community.[58]

However, it was not sufficient merely to reject the false church in England and withdraw into a state of spiritual lethargy. "Men are not to come out of Babylon, and there to stand stil, & remember the Lord a farr of." As "lively stones" they must "couple themselves together by voluntary profession & covenant" into a "spirituall building, the Lords Temple," and thus they "may find Sion the Lords mountain prepared on the top of every hil."[59] The true Church, then, emerges into visibility as the organic union of "gathered" saints, knit together by the bond of the Spirit into a communion whose "supream end" is "sanctity and holiness to the glory of God."[60]

In describing the internal dynamic of the true visible Church Robinson had recourse to the rich and nuanced imagery suggested by the Pauline concept of edification.[61] The word οἰκοδομή, is used by Saint Paul, that "penman of the Holy Ghost," as Robinson called him, in a twofold sense.[62] It refers, in the first place, to his particular apostolic and missionary responsibility in the founding and "building up" of specific churches (II Cor. 10:8; 12:19; Rom. 15:20). More commonly, however, it is used to describe the process of mutual service and mutual obligation by which "the whole body, bonded and knit together by every constituent

---

[57]Ibid., 245.

[58]Ibid., 252.

[59]Ibid., 127.

[60]Ibid., 109.

[61]The present discussion relies particularly on the excellent study of John S. Coolidge, *The Pauline Renaissance in England: Puritanism and the Bible* (London, 1970), esp. 23-54. Coolidge traces the emergence of the distinctively Puritan (i.e. Pauline exegesis of edification to the debate over *adiaphora* in the Vestiarian Controversy, and discovers "the whole mystery of Elizabethan Puritanism" (p. 27) in this concept. While he concedes that "the vision of the living Church, planted and visible in England, passes to the Separatists and to those who come to be called Congregationalists or Independents,"(p. 60) and finds rudiments of it in Browne, he does not pursue the theme in later Separatist writers.

[62]*Justification*, 139. Cf. the articles by Otto Michel in *Theological Dictionary of the New Testament*, eds. Gerhard Friedrich (Grand Rapids, Mich., 1967), vol. 5, 136-48. [Originally published in German as *Theologisches Wörterbuch zum Neuen Testament*.]

joint . . . grows through the due activity of each part, and builds itself up"
(Eph. 4:16, NEB). The root-idea of "building" is thus transformed in Paul
by its association with two organic metaphors, one horticultural, the
other physiological. In the former, the spiritual task of the community is
described as "planting," and "watering," which issues in an "increase"
given by God. "You are God's garden, God's building," Paul told the
Corinthians (I Cor. 3:6-9).[63] Again, the mixed metaphor of planting and
building is used to describe, doxologically, the ultimate purpose of the
Church:

> May Christ dwell (κατοικῆσαι) in your hearts in love. With deep roots and
> firm foundations (ἐρριζωμένοι καὶ τεθεμελιωμένοι; *cf.* the Vulgate: *radicati
> et fundati*), may you be strong to grasp, with all God's people, what is the
> breadth and length and height and depth of the love of Christ . . . So may you
> attain to fullness of being, the fullness of God himself (Eph. 3:17-19, NEB).

To describe the furtherance of life and growth within the Christian
community, Paul incorporates the metaphors of building and planting
into the more pervasive *leitmotif* of his ecclesiology—his concept of the
Church as the "body of Christ" (I Cor. 12:27; Rom. 12:5). While the more
complex imagery of the Church as a cosmic body, in contrast with Christ
its celestial head, is probably a deutero-Pauline extrapolation, the twofold thrust of the σῶμα-image is present already in I Corinthians.[64] First,
it points to the transcendent and eschatological character of the Christian
community by defining its existence as *participation* in the risen, exalted
Messiah. We are brought into the body by baptism, and sustained therein
by the eucharistic fellowship and the discriminate dispersement of *charis-
mata*. The *ecclesia* is thus distinguished from the surrounding world, the
"outsiders" (I Cor. 5:12), by its origins in the life of Christ, and by the
integrity of that life within its ranks. Secondly, the analogy to the human
body implies an organic network of mutual dependence in which each
member is vitally related to the other. God has so "tempered the body
together" (συνεκέρασεν τὸ σῶμα), that even the weaker, inferior
members are essential to its well-being (I Cor. 12:24). Together they are
"fitly framed together" and "builded together" for a habitation of God
which "groweth unto an holy temple in the Lord" (Eph. 2:21-22, KJV).
The emphasis is upon the harmony of form and mutual interrelationship

---

[63]"θεοῦ γεώριον θεοῦ οἰκοδομή ἔστε."

[64]On the Pauline conception of the Church as body, see the article by Eduard
Schweizer in *Theological Dictionary of the New Testament*, op. cit., vol. 7, 1024-1094;
John A. T. Robinson, *The Body* (London, 1952); Ernst Käsemann, *Perspectives on Paul*
(Philadelphia, 1969), 102-21.

of the individual members as they participate in the upbuilding of the community. Edification, then, as the fulfillment of the prophetic utterance ascribed to Christ by the Gospel of Matthew (16:18), "Upon this rock I will build (οἰκοδομήσω) my Church," refers not only to the act of incorporation and participation by which the Church is constituted, but also to the process of integration and growth by which the Church sustains its life amid "the weak and beggarly elements" (Gal. 4:9) of this world.[65]

When applied to the Separatist ideal of the visible Church, the principle of edification underscored the *conditionality* of the *outward* covenant and the necessity for constant vigilance. While the "invisible, internall, and effectuall" calling of God, based upon election, was unconditional and irrevocable, the continuance of a visible Church in outward covenant depended upon the maintenance of discipline within:

> If [a Church] depart from the Lord by any transgression, and therein remayn irrepentant, after due conviction, and will not be reclaymed, it manifests vnto vs, that God also hath left it, and that, as the Church by her sin hath separated from, and broken covenant with God, so God by leaving her in hardnes of hart without repentance, hath on his part broken, and dissolved the covenant also.[66]

The visible Church was always *ecclesia in via*: in the process of being "built up" or torn down, of growing toward holiness or of relapsing into decay. As a living organism the Church must ever guard against "corruptions essentiall" which "eat out the very heart of a thing." Robinson reacted against the Puritan proclivity to tolerate corruptions within the Church of England: "What is death but the corruption of the man? as *generatio & corruptio* are opposed. And what is rottennes but the corruption of the body?"[67]

The issue of "things indifferent," well worn by several generations of querulous debate, surfaced again in the polemical exchange between the conforming Puritans and their brethren on the other side of the Separatist divide. The retention of "popish ceremonies" in the Church of England, and their imposition upon the parish clergy by the Canons of 1604, had

---

[65]In this connection edification is the supreme criterion for the exercise of spiritual gifts within the Church (I Cor. 14:26), and the overriding consideration in the matter of an "offended" brother (I Cor. 8:13). Thus the libertine slogan, "All things are lawful," must give way to the higher principle, "But all things edify not" (I Cor. 10:23). Cf. Günther Bornkamm, "The Edification of the Congregation as the Body of Christ," *Early Christian Experience* (New York, 1969), 161-69.

[66]*Justification*, 248.

[67]Ibid., 67.

been a source of Robinson's initial nonconformity. In his response to Bernard, Robinson focussed on three of these ceremonies—the cross in baptism, kneeling at communion, and the wearing of the surplice. These three were of particular interest because they corresponded to the two traditional *notae*, the Word and the sacraments, on the basis of which its apologists had argued the Church of England to be a true visible Church.[68] Both Puritans and Separatists objected to these ceremonies, and on much the same grounds: they were inducements to idolatry. William Bradshaw, a non-separating congregationalist, inveighed against the posture of kneeling for the reception of the sacramental elements: "If the Apostle banished Love feasts from the Lords Supper, because of the abuse, and brought the Church to the simplicitie of the first institution, Is it not a tempting sinne to retaine the Idolatrous kneeling of Papistes, and reject the exemplary sitting of our Master Christ?"[69] The phrase "tempting sinne" was suggestive of a wider range of concern than the mere scrupulosity of an individual conscience might suggest. The act of kneeling was no neutral gesture, or "extern thing," but the intrusion of a ritual which not only transgressed the scriptural example, but also harked back to the sacramental exhibitionism of Rome. It became, then, not an instrument of edification, but a means of stumbling, an occasion for offense. In his answer to Hall's "Censorious Epistle" Robinson pointed to the detrimental implication of this ceremony:

> "Where," say you, "are those rotten heaps of transubstantiating of bread?" And where, say I, learned you your devout kneeling to or before the bread, but, from that error of transubstantiation? Yea, what less can it *insinuate* than either that or some other the like idolatrous conceit?[70]

The crux of Robinson's objection was not the act of kneeling itself (although his understanding of the scriptural imperative in worship would demand a literal re-enactment of the Last Supper), but the purported meaning it conveyed, a meaning which belied the proper character of the Lord's Supper as the effectual pledge of "our conjunction, and incorporation with Christ, and one with another."[71]

---

[68] Cf. John Jewel, *An Apology of the Church of England*, ed. John E. Booty (Ithaca, N.Y.), 30-36; Richard Hooker, *Works,* op. cit., vol. 1, 193-206.

[69] William Bradshaw, *A Proposition concerning Kneeling in the very act of receiving* (London, 1605), 8-9. Cf. Wilfred W. Biggs "The Controversy concerning Kneeling in the Lord's Supper—after 1604," *Transactions*, Congregational Historical Society 17 (1952), 51-62.

[70] *Works*, vol. 3, 411. (My italics.)

[71] *Justification*, 92.

Those within the Church of England who agreed with Robinson concerning the nature of the ceremonies were presented with three options by the Canons of 1604 and the ensuing campaign for subscription: separation, exile, or conformity. Few chose to follow Robinson into separation, but several, including Bradshaw and Ames, followed his example of self-imposed exile in the Netherlands where they hammered out their distinctive ecclesiology removed—somewhat—from the watchful eyes of the Archbishop's pursuivants. Others, however, chose to swallow their scruples for the sake of their ministries, and remained with the Church of England. These "formerly great advauncers of the cause of reformation," as Robinson dubbed them, whose "zeale rises and falls as the tymes serve," were regarded by the Separatists as deserters of the cause, latter-day Esaus who had exchanged their birthright for a benefice.[72] For their part, the Puritans, forced to ceremonial conformity, and stung by the Separatists' attack, were placed in the awkward position of defending their action by means of the very arguments the prelates had hurled at their spiritual forbears a generation earlier! So kneeling at communion, wearing the surplice, and the like, were, after all "things indifferent." If by "yeelding somewhat" in these matters they could retain their pulpits, then it was an equitable compromise.[73] When confronted with the rhetoric about edification, they resorted to another, more convenient, passage in the Pauline corpus, namely his statement that he became "all things to all men" that he might "by all means save some" (I Cor. 9:22).[74] Robinson referred to the position of the conforming ministers: "They wil advance prayer, viz, their service book; that they may extenuate preaching; comend peace, that they may smother truth . . . and everywhere send men back into themselves, that they may keep them from looking vpon others, and so make them carelesse of such duties towards their brethren, as Gods word bindes them unto."[75] But "bare conversion," the fruit of such preaching, and the alleged seal of such a ministry, did not a true visible Church make. To subordinate the imperatives of life and growth within the Church to such a consideration was to oppose one commandment of the Lord to another. No one should presume "against the Lord in the least ceremony or circumstace," lest the least sin "prove a burden vntollerable," but "to exact obedience in and unto [the ceremo-

---

[72]Ibid., 5.

[73]Richard Bernard, *Christian Advertisements*, 16.

[74]See, for example, the visitation sermon, preached in 1605 by Sebastian Benefield, *A Sermon preached at Wotton Under Edge* (Oxford, 1613). Benefield was later Lady Margaret Professor of Divinity at Oxford, and a notable opponent of the Arminians.

[75]*Justification*, 24.

nies], whether they offend or not, whether they edify or destroy, were intolerable presumption."[76]

Ultimately, the controversy over "things indifferent" centered on the thorny issue the limits of civil authority in matters religious. The term *adiaphora* had been introduced by the Lutheran reformers in connection with the Leipzig Interim, when it was used to designate matters on which concessions might be made to the Catholics for the sake of peace without sacrificing the essentials of Protestant doctrine. In spite of its various adaptations, on the Continent and in England, the concept was never completely detached from this religio-political *Sitz im Leben.*[77] Thus, in response to Cartwright's claim that the absolute standard in the use of things indifferent must be the "profit or hurt of our brethren," Whitgift agreed, "with this priviso, that it is not every man's part in the church to judge and determine what the circumstance of the times and persons maketh profitable or hurtful, but theirs only to whom the government of the Church is committed." To question obedience to magistrates in such indifferent things was, in effect, "to pluck the magistrate his sword out of his hand."[78] Cartwright, when faced with the choice of following the logic of edification or of "tarrying for the magistrate," chose the latter course, and succumbed to Whitgift's judgment: "We must not seditiously & waiwardly shake the throane of Authoritie," he told the Separatists.[79] The Separatists, however, faithful to Cartwright's initial insight ("The foolish Barrowist deriveth his schisme by way of conclusion, as to him it seemeth, directly and plainely out of your principles," Hooker pertinently reminded the Puritans[80]), refused to recognize the category of *adiaphora* in matters pertaining to the life of the Church. Thus when Whitgift urged the oath upon Barrow as a thing indifferent, he was met with the standard response:

---

[76] Ibid., 23, 11. *Works*, vol. 3, 410.

[77] On the significance of adiaphorism in the early English Reformation, see Bernard J. Verkamp, *The Indifferent Mean* (Athens, Ohio, 1977).

[78] *The Works of John Whitgift*, ed. John Ayre (Cambridge, 1852), vol. 2, 1-5.

[79] *Cartwrightiana*, eds. Albert Peel and Leland H. Carlson, (London, 1951), 253. Cf. Cartwright's letter to his Separatist sister-in-law, Anne Stubbe: "For notwithstandinge yf it were my choice to avoide [the ceremonies], I ought out to ioyne wᶜʰ them yet havinge no aucthority, or no strength and power to make good the authority of sepatinge of them, I ought not therefore to cease the seruice of God wᴄʰ is coᵐaunded," ibid., 72.

[80] *The Works of Richard Hooker,* op. cit., vol. 1, 39.

B[arrow]:	And if it be indifferent, as yow say it is, then doe I wel in not using it.
A[rchbishop]:	Nay, you doe not wel in refusing it, for therein yow shew yowr self disobedient to the higher powers set over yow by God.
B[arrow]:	Even now yow said it was a thing indifferent; if it be so, ther is no power can bring me in bondage to my libertie.
A[rchbishop]:	Where finde yow that?
B[arrow]:	In St. Paul, I Corinthians [6:12].[81]

Robinson, in consonance with the earlier Separatist tradition, refused to treat the ceremonies as ordinances devoid of spiritual potential. Everything depended on "the proper ends and uses," and nothing was simply indifferent in the use; it was "either good or evill according to the furtherance or hinderance which it affoardeth to the mayn."[82] If the ceremonies served to enhance the worship of the Church, to make it "the more comely, orderly, and edificative," then they ought to be continually and diligently used, "yea though they were forbidden by the Highest power vpon earth." On the other hand, as was the case with the ceremonies in question, "if they advantage not," they must be forborne at all costs.[83] The process of edification was, by its very nature, autonomous. It served to disengage effectively the Church from any allegiance to civil authority which would impede its upbuilding and constant growth in sanctification which was essential to its nature as a "living temple." The Word of God, Robinson believed, warranted a "clean and an other and different course of obedience in things civil, and in things ecclesiasticall."[84] In respect to the "outward man" the magistrate was charged with the general administration and government of the world. In this capacity he could demand obedience, even to "the civill hurt and hinderance" of his subjects. *But in causes ecclesiasticall not so*"! These matters pertain to the "special administration of the Church, and serve for the edification and building vp of the inward man to life eternall."[85] Within this sphere

there is no King of the Church but Christ, who is the King of Saincts and Saviour of Syon, no Lord but Jesus, who is the onely Lord and Lawgiver of his Church. And all his lawes & statutes tend to the furtherance and advancemet of every one of his subjects in their spiritual estate, & neyther King nor Kezar may or ought to impose any law to the least praejudice of the same, neyther ar they therein (if they should) to be obeyed.[86]

---

[81] *The Writings of Henry Barrow, 1587-1590*, 94.

[82] *Justification*, 26-27.

[83] Ibid., 27.

[84] Ibid., 29.

[85] Ibid., 30.

For minds disposed to compromise, this line of reasoning presented a most unattractive alternative. Cartwright characterized it as "peevish" and made his peace with the authorities.[87] Others laughed at it, and accounted it "a matter scarce worth thinking upon."[88] The Separatists, however, pursuing the idea of edification to its logical end, rejected the traditional notion of an inclusive Christian society, and withdrew into voluntary consociations to build "Sion . . . on the top of every hil." The Separatists concurred with the Puritans in the familiar catalogue of complaints repeated *ad nauseam*, it must have seemed to some, since the Admonition Controversy. But from their reading of the religious situation they drew a conclusion which no Puritan was prepared to accept, namely, that the Church of England, as a national Church, was not, nor indeed could be, truly the Church at all. In a rare outburst of verbal violence, worthy of Barrow or even Müntzer, Robinson denied the Church of England to be the "Temple of God," compiled and built of spiritually "hewn" and "lively stones," of the "cedars, firs, and thyme trees of Lebanon." Instead, it was but

> a confused heap of dead, and defiled, and polluted stones, and of all rubbish of briers and brambles of the wilderness, for the most fitter for burning than for building; we take ourselves rather bound *to show our obedience* in departing from it, than our valor in purging it: and to follow the prophet's counsel in flying out of Babylon, 'as he-goats before the flock.'[89]

To *show* our obedience [to Christ]! Herein lay the forward thrust of the Separatists' self-identification, presumptious for such a "handful," it seemed to Hall, as the true visible Church. [90] But edification not only defined the true Church over against "the outsiders"; it was also the principle of cohesion within the community. Thus, while the Church Visible was recognizable by its constitution and form, it was only by the constant exercise of congregational discipline that the Church maintained its integrity of life and purity of witness. The Church Visible was

---

[86] Ibid.

[87] *Cartwrightiana,* op. cit., 254.

[88] Richard Bernard, *Christian Advertisements*, sig. A 3 recto.

[89] *Works*, vol. 3, 416. (My italics.) The image of the Church as a "building" or "house" persists throughout Robinson's thought. Cf. his admonitory letter to the Pilgrims as they were about to depart for New Plymouth: "As men are Carefull not to haue a New house shaken with any violence before it be well settled and the prtes feirmly knitt soe I beseech you much more Carefull; that the house of God which you are and are to be: be not shaken with vnnecessary Noueltyes or other oppositions att the first settleing therof." *Plymouth Church Records*, vol. 1, 47.

[90] Ibid., 403.

always in the process of becoming, and therefore also ever susceptible to dissolution, to being "dischurched." In this conception the visible Church could never be seen as a mere *repositorium* of doctrine and sacraments, divorced from the phenomena of faith and growth, and so from the Lordship of Christ. Discipline was no appurtenance or accessory which might be dispensed with without serious damage to the life of the Church; it was an essential *nota* by which the Church maintained its vigor in casting off whatever would tend to undermind or debilitate it.

"CAST IN THE APOSTOLICALL AND PRIMITIVE MOULD": THE CHURCH PLANTED

"Not a partial but a perfect rule": The Authority of Scripture

Having traced the motivation for separation to a particular concept derived from the epistles of Saint Paul, we now find it necessary to examine, more generally, Robinson's understanding of scriptural authority, and its relation to the constitution and form of the Church Visible. The Separatist appeal to the scriptural norm was only one manifestation of a much wider cultural transformation effected by the translation and dissemination of the Bible in the sixteenth century. Thomas Hobbes, looking back on this era, wrote in *Behomoth*: "After the Bible was translated . . . every man, nay, every boy and wench, that could read English thought they spoke with God Almighty and understood what he said, when by a certain number of chapters a day they had read the Scriptures once or twice over."[91] It was this unquestioning, if not always uncritical, acceptance of the Bible as "a word from God" which prompted John Bunyan, a Separatist of a later day, to ask: "Have you never a hill Mizar to remember? Have you forgot the close, the milk house, the stable, the barn, and the like, where God did visit your soul? Remember also the Word—the Word, I say, upon which the Lord hath caused you to

---

[91] Thomas Hobbes, *Works*, ed. William Molesworth (London, 1839-1845), vol. 6, 190. Hobbes' comment is corroborated by William Weston, a Jesuit priest who observed a large Puritan gathering of 1588 which was held near his prison cell in the Isle of Ely: "Each of them had his own Bible, and seduously turned the pages and looked up the texts cited by the preachers, discussing the passages among themselves to see whether they had quoted them to the point, and accurately, and in harmony with their tenets. Also they would start arguing among themselves about the meaning of passages from the Scriptures--men, women, boys, girls, rustics, labourers and idiots--and more often than not, it was said, it ended in violence and fisticuffs. [This took place] on a large level stretch of ground within the precincts of the prison. Here over a thousand of them sometimes assembled, their horses and pack animals burdened with a multitude of Bibles." *The Autobiography of an Elizabethan*, ed. P. Caraman (London, 1955), 165.

hope."[92] The Word, to the Pilgrims as to the Elizabethan public generally, meant the Geneva or "Breeches" Bible of 1560 which contained, in addition to the text of Holy Writ in clear, crisp English, a comprehensive chain of references and annotations keyed to the prevailing consensus of Calvinist theology. It was, in effect, a "portable library of Divinity."[93] Like the continental Anabaptists in their *Gespräche* with the mainline Reformers, English Separatists were ever ready, as the Plumbers' Hall conventiclers had told Grindal, to be "judged by the Word." They discovered in it a mirror of their own lives, and of life itself. More importantly, perhaps, it was a call to action: a manual of obedience with a veritable blueprint for restoring "the old glorious beautifull face of Christianity," a task which distinguished the Separatist from Puritan and Anglican alike.[94]

In the first of his *New Essays, or Observations Divine and Morall*, Robinson echoes the opening words of the *Institutes* when he declares that "all our wisdom to happiness consists summarily in the knowledge of God, and of our selues."[95] The two aspects of this *duplex cognitio*, however, are so interrelated that "neither can be without other, in any competent, or profitable measure."[96] In other words, self-knowledge both derives from the knowledge of God, and points again toward contemplation of Him. This at once raises the question of the "knowableness" of God, and here Robinson warns against the temptation to pry into God's essence. Some "ambitious and curious wits" have an insatiable desire to raise themselves up to God's level, or, failing that, to "pull him down to their dwarfish conceptions." But "the essence of God is known onely to himself."[97] What we can know of God are his attributes—His power, wisdom, will, goodness, etc.—insofar (but only insofar) as they are directed toward us, that is as they "concur to the produceing of all, and everie one of his works."[98]

---

[92]John Bunyan, *Grace Abounding to the Chief of Sinners* (London, 1928), 5.

[93]A. E. Peaston, *The Prayer Book Tradition in the Free Churches* (London, 1964), 24.

[94]John Owen, *A Vindication of the Animadversions on Fiat Lux* (London, 1664), 207.

[95]*Observations Divine and Morall for the Furthering of knowledg, and vertue* (Leyden, 1625), 1 [Hereafter *Observations*]. This is a collection of 62 essays, published in the year of Robinson's death, ranging in subject matter from weighty theological topics to more practical concerns such as credit and the education of children. They were reprinted twice in the seventeenth century (1628, 1642). Cf. Works, vol. 1, 1-259 and *Tensions in American Puritanism*, ed. Richard Reinitz (New York, 1970), 65-76.

[96]*Observations*, 1.

[97]Ibid., 2.

[98]Ibid., 14.

For Robinson "knowledge of self" does not carry the modern connotation of personal or psychological introspection. Rather it extends to the whole order of "created goodnesse" which yields a certain objectively clear, though strictly limited, knowledge of God. He thus describes the correspondence of celestial bodies and earthly elements:

> Amongst the works of God most wise . . . it is most admirable, that the Heavenly bodies, the Sun, Moon, and Starres should by their influence, and operation, have such power, and effects upon the bodies here below, as to change, order, and dispose the Ayer, Earth, and Water, with all things framed, and compounded of them as they appear to do, *by Scripture, sence, and experience.*[99]

Situated between the angels and the animals in the "chain of being," man is able to apprehend the attributes of God in His works, "as in a most clear Looking glasse."[100] Though we are not able by this "glimpse of light in the Creatures" to attain to the knowledge of God as Redeemer,

> yet are we both to honor him according to it, and to be provoked by it to further search, and enquire after him, in such means of revelation, as by which he further manifests himself; which are his Word and Gospel of Salvation.[101]

Scripture, then, *along with* "sence and experience" constitute a dual source for the knowledge of God as Creator, while Scripture *alone* reveals God as "mercifull Redeemer . . . in the face of Christ Iesus." When the "lesser glimpse" of the former is compared to the "glorious light" of the latter, it appears as only a small hole in a "dark Dungeon," the existence of which nonetheless exculpates God from the charge of having left Himself without a witness, and renders man, including "the verie wisest of the Heathen," inexcusable.[102]

Robinson defines Holy Scripture as that "Divine Instrument and means, by which we are taught to beleev what we ought, touching God, and our selvs, and all creatures; and how to please God in all things, unto eternall Life."[103] Interestingly, he says relatively little about the mode of inspiration, although it is clear that the Spirit of God is "the Author both of matter, and manner, and writing."[104] He thus maintains the distinction,

---

[99] Ibid., 21, 17. (My italics.) On the English adaptation of this medieval commonplace, see E. M. W. Tillyard, *The Elizabethan World Picture* (New York, n.d.), 87-100.

[100] *Observations*, 19.

[101] Ibid., 20.

[102] Ibid., 20, 4.

[103] Ibid., 53.

[104] Ibid., 55.

later lost in Reformed theology, between the "Word of God" and "Holy Scripture." The Word is prior to its inscripturation in the sense that it refers to the oral transmission of manifold revelations which were only later committed to writing at the "suggestion" of the Holy Spirit. Robinson offers three reasons as to why God chose to have "his Word *become* Scripture": to preserve it from corruption since "things set down in black, and white" are most firm; to facilitate the spread of Christian teachings since books and writings can make entrance "whither the voyce of Teachers cannot come"; to further the unity of Christians in the same truth. It might seem in the light of increasing ecclesiastical diversity, that this last goal had hardly been achieved; but Robinson asks, if churches differ so much while using the same rule, "what would they do, if their rules were different, or uncertain?"[105] The extent of the Word in its written form was identical, Robinson believed, with those books properly called canonical, to the exclusion of the apocryphal writings. God has preserved the canonical writings from "miscarrying" and so has committed them to the custody of the Church as its "publike treasurie."[106]

Before turning to Robinson's use of Scripture in his defense of Separatist polity, it will be helpful to examine briefly his understanding of two problems raised by the Protestant principle of *sola scriptura*: the methodology of scriptural interpretation, and the relationship of Scripture and Tradition. The Separatist tradition from Browne onwards was distinguished by an extreme emphasis upon the perspicuity of Scripture. So clear is Scripture in its essential content that even unlearned believers can

---

[105] Ibid., 54.

[106] Ibid. Though Article 6 of the Thirty-Nine Articles distinguished the canonical Scriptures from "the other bookes" which might be read for "example of lyfe and instruction of manners" (*Creeds of Christendom*, vol. 3, 490-91), the Separatists consistently opposed the close association of non-canonical books with Holy Writ. Cf. the following dialogue from Barrow's fifth examination: "Ther was brought a great Bible in folio, faire bound, which the Archbishop refused, and called for an other, which was held to me by one of his men, and I commaunded to lay my hand upon it. Barrow: To what ende? Canterbury: To sweare. Barrow: I have not learned to sweare by any creatures. Canterbury: This is the word of God—the Bible. Barrow: I began to open the book, and meant indeed to have asked him if the Apocrypha Scripture and notes, which were in it, were the word of God: but Canterbury, belike suspecting some much matter, would not suffer me to look into it; to whom then I answered that that book was not the eternal word of God." *The Writings of Henry Barrow, 1587-1590*, 193-94. In *A Just and Necessary Apology* Robinson professed himself ready to subscribe to all articles of the Belgic Confession except the sixth which permits the public reading of apocryphal writings. These he characterized as "so stuffed with trifles, fables, lies, and superstitions of all sorts, that the middle place between the Old and New Testament, as ill becomes them, as it would do a Turkish slave, and leper, between the two noblest princes of all Europe." *Works*, vol. 3, 10.

readily grasp its meaning. In fact, for Browne, academic training was a hindrance, not a help, in the interpretation of God's Word:

> For ye say ye may not looke on holye Scriptures, nor search out wisdome and knowledge, tyll you haue throughlye learned Aristotle, or spent your seauen yeares at Cambridge, in studying of the sciences. Then shal you handle the Scriptures with your cleane washed handes. . . . You clense your handes with Logike, you say, to handle the Scriptures purelie: nay rather you have swallowed vp such filthye stuffe, and haue cast the vomite thereof vpon the Scriptures.[107]

Robinson also accepts the principle of perspicuity and claims that Scripture "is therefore discernable by its self, as is the Sun by its own beams, and light." However, he insists that the minister of the Word, who is both a "Translator" and an "Interpreter," be equipped with certain skills in his exposition of the sacred text. Chief among these is proficiency in the original languages of Scriptures, for "as the waters are most pure, and sweet in the Foundation; so are all writings (Divine and humain) in the Originall Tongues."[108] Nonetheless, the former *Praelector Graecus* of Corpus Christi College showed no sympathy for the "formalist" sermon with its lavish display of Hebrew and Greek—"the hoctpotch at Paules crosse, or at Saint Maries in Cambridge, [which] must needes be sauced by vaunt of the tongues."[109] Hebrew and Greek were primarily for the study, not the pulpit where a faithful translation, one which agrees with the original "word for word, so far as the idiom, or proprietie of the Language will bear," would better serve to edify the congregation.[110] Robinson belabors this seemingly obvious point, because John Smyth, by a strange inversion of liturgical logic, had re-introduced the use of Hebrew and Greek into the "spiritual worship" of his church at Amsterdam! Translations, Smyth argued, were at best imperfect, "not equipol-

---

[107] *A Treatise upon the 23. of Matthewe*, 181.

[108] *Observations*, 55, 58.

[109] *A Treatise upon the 23. of Matthewe*, 172. Robinson's objection to the use of classical languages in worship was shared by Puritans of all persuasions. Cf. Thomas Hooker's comment: "I have sometime admired at this: why a company of Gentlemen, yeomen, and poore women, that are scarcely able to know their A.B.C. Yet they have a minister to speake Latin, Greeke, and Hebrew, and to use the Fathers, when it is certaine, they know nothing at all. The reason is, because all this stings not, they may sit and sleep in their pinnes, and go to hell hoodwinckt." *The Sovles Preparation for Christ* (London, 1632), 69. Ainsworth, however, by far the most productive exegete among the Separatists, was a Hebraist of international standing: "he had not his better for the hebrew toungve in the universitie [of Leyden] Nor scarce in Europa," *Plymouth Church Records*, vol. 1, 136. Equally worthy of note was Bradford's attempt to master Hebrew near the end of his life. Cf. Isidore S. Meyer, "The Hebrew Preface to Bradford's History of the Plymouth Plantation," *Publications of the American Jewish Society* 38 (1949), 289-305.

[110] *Observations*, 58.

lent to the originalles in a thousand particulars." They were, then, only another form of apocryphal writing, and no part of canonical Scripture.[111] Robinson agreed that translators and translations were subject to error, but, even so, the Scriptures are "the same, whether in the Originall; or other Language, into which they are faithfully translated."[112]

Although the perspecuity of Scripture insured that the meaning of a given text was always accessible, it did not follow that the proper interpretation was necessarily obvious. There were, in fact, "things left more dark in the Scriptures," though this obscurity resulted from our "naturall blyndenes" rather than from any defect in the text.[113] When interpreting these, as well as less doubtful passages, the basic hermeneutical rule is the same: *Scriptura sui ipsius interpres*.[114] This means simply that Scripture is to be interpreted by Scripture: "one place must be expounded by another, the more brief and obscure by the more plain and larg." Robinson cites in support of this comparative technique an axiom of rabbinic exegesis: in gathering the meaning of a text, it is necessary to look "above and below, as the Iews use to speak," that is, at the upper and lower vowel points.[115] In this way the word or phrase in question will be related to "the main drift" and spurious exegesis avoided. In keeping with the mainline Protestant emphasis, Robinson held that Scripture contained but one proper and immediate sense, the literal, which should be followed insofar as it comported with the whole body of Scripture, and did not lead to absurd or blasphemous conclusions. This did not, however, inexorably bind the meaning of a text to the words in which it was expressed. A Scripture might "contain," that is, command, promise, or threaten, any number of things which could be gathered only in inference or consequence. Here Robinson calls to mind the discussion of Jesus and the Saducees about the resurrection, and Christ's appeal to Exodus 3:6, "I am the God of Abraham, and so forth,"

> which words do no way conclude the resurrection of the body (which was the question) by an immediate consequence, and yet the collection was good and necessary.[116]

---

[111]*Smyth*, vol. 1, 280. Smyth, however, did allow for the use of translations in the "preparation" for worship. On the controversy between Smyth and the Ancient Church over this issue, see Ainsworth, *A Defence of the Holy Scriptures* (Amsterdam, 1609), and *Smyth*, vol. 1, 269-320.

[112]*Observations*, loc. cit.

[113]*Justification*, 32.

[114]For this formulation in Luther, see *WA*, vol. 7, 97, 16.

[115]*Observations*, 61.

[116]*Justification*, 32.

So the correct interpretation of a given passage often depended upon a process of evaluation, comparison, deduction, what Robinson called in one place "common sence," and in another, "the discourse of reason soberly used and sanctifyed by the word."[117] Reason, in this sense, is not another authority different from, or in competition with, Scripture. It is rather that "natural light" by which we are able, in some measure, to understand Scripture, and to apply that understanding in obedience.

However, just as the natural knowledge of God can never disclose the content of redemption, so natural reason is insufficient for the understanding of Scripture apart from the supernatural interposition of the Holy Spirit. The act of scriptural revelation is, as it were, bounded by two poles, both of which have as their proper subject, the Holy Spirit. At one end is the process of inspiration by which the canonical writings "were penned by infallible, and immediate direction of the Holy Ghost."[118] At the other end is the moment of illumination wherein the inspired text is authenticated and unveiled by the inward testimony of the Holy Spirit, its real Author.[119]

The principle of interior revelation, however, when wrested from its connection with the outward Word, could lead to the attenuation of Scripture itself. It was precisely this danger which Robinson saw in the spiritualizing hermeneutic of the Smyth and Helwys churches. Stressing the immediacy of God's act in regeneration, understood as a prerequisite to believers' baptism, and the Trinitarian implantation in the baptizand as inferred from the Johannine comma, Smyth came to the conclusion that one so divinely begotten was "aboue the law and scriptures," and became himself the epiphany, or at least the inner reflection, of the Triune God:

> That the new creature which is begotten of God, needeth not the outwoard scriptures creatures or ordinances of the church . . . seeing that he hath three witnesses in himselfe, the father, the word, and the holie ghost: which are better then all scriptures. [120]

---

[117] *Observations*, 56; *Justification,* loc. cit.

[118] *Observation*, 72.

[119] Cf. Calvin's formulation in *Inst.* 1,7,4: "Nam sicuti Deus solus de se idoneus est testis in suo sermone: ita etiam non ante fidem reperiet sermo in humano cordibus quam interiore Spiritus testimonio obsignetur." *Calvini Opera*, vol. 3, 70. Robinson also reacted against a static concept of Scripture which made "the word of God a very charm." Indeed, he insisted that the "word is a morall agent, having in itself no naturall vertue, but working merely by the will of the authour, and supernaturall efficacy of the spirit, which like the winde, bloweth where it listeth." *Justification*, 447.

[120] *Smyth*, vol. 2, 743-44.

In response to this, Robinson more strongly stressed the coinherence of Word and Spirit, claiming that nowhere in Scripture itself is the inward Spirit contrasted with the outward Word. Rather, they are invariably conjoined. Smyth's perfectionism and his disparagement of the outward Word undercut, argued Robinson, the principle of edification in that they removed the need for constant growth as well as the external means by which it is effected:

> For any such perfection in this world, as wherein a man stands not need continually to renue his repentance, and to purg him self of the remnants of sin . . . and to grow in the knowledg, and grace of God by the vse of the Scriptures . . . is the most dangerous delusion.[121]

Until we come to the "face to face" vision in the eschaton, we need "the glasse of the word" as a stimulus to further growth. Nor is this need attenuated by the illumination of the Spirit within, "since the inward grace doth not abolish but establish the outward meanes."[122] A visible Church, in other words, requires a legible and audible Word.

The self-authenticating and self-interpretive character of Scripture precludes Robinson from according any credence to Tradition as a second source of equal authority to the written Word. Here, of course, he is on common ground with Protestantism generally over against the Council of Trent.[123] There is, however, the further question of the extent to which the material sufficiency of Scripture can be corroborated by external witnesses. The main drift of Robinson's answer here is negative as well:

> The custom of the Church is but the custom of men: the sentence of the

---

[121] *Of Religious Communion*, 126.

[122] Ibid., 124.

[123] George H. Tavard, *Holy Writ or Holy Church: the Crisis of the Protestant Reformation* (London, 1959) has argued that the Patristic and medieval synthesis which gave to extrascriptural Tradition "a place next to Holy Writ" (p. 17) was challenged in the late Middle Ages by two opposing trends, one which exalted the Church, in its curial aspect, over Scripture, the other which sharply contrasted Scripture and the Church, and thus "paved the way for a complete denial of the Church" (p. 40). In his refinement and critique of Tavard's thesis, Heiko A. Oberman, *The Harvest of Medieval Theology: Gabriel Biel and Late Medieval Nominalism* (Cambridge, Mass., 1962), 361-93, has distinguished two general notions of Tradition which he has characterized as "Tradition I" and "Tradition II," the former, a single-source theory which locates the interpretation of Scripture in the doctors of the Church, the latter, a two-source theory which allows for an equally-binding, extra-biblical oral tradition handed down through episcopal succession. While both of these terms imply a continuity of the visible Church which Robinson's restitutionist ecclesiology would not permit, he in fact approaches "Tradition I" insofar as he appeals to the teachers of the Church.

Fathers but the opinions of men: the determination of Councils but the judgements of men.[124]

Human consensus, by its very nature, is variable. But "the Authoritie of Gods Word, and testimonie is alwaies the same, as being grounded upon his unchangeable veritie." So complete is the perfection and clarity of God's Word that should a man "finde the Book of Holy Scriptures in the high-way, or hidden under a stone, yet he were bound to learn, receav, beleev, and obey them," though without, or even against, the "approbation of all the men in the World."[125]

Nonetheless, while the thrust of Robinson's argument is against those who would pin their faith upon the "sleeves of the Churches Authoritie and Clergies leaning," he does allow for a certain "lawfull and convenient use" of human testimony in divine things.[126] He contrasts the dangers inherent in either over-reliance or over-abstention in respect to human authorities:

> He that depends too much upon other mens judgment, makes as if the Word of God came not to himself at all: He that neglects it, as if it came to him onely.[127]

In assessing the relative value of those "speciall Instruments" whose commentaries and expositions were worthy of scrutiny, Robinson accords precedence to the Fathers of "that first Age after Christ," whose writings are eminently more profitable than, say, "the subtilties of the schoolmen" who lived when the "Mysterie of Iniquitie had gotten too great both height, and breadth." The chronological measure, however, is not an absolute one. Augustine, for example, is said to have examined more diligently and discerned more exactly the truth about predestination and free will, "then others his Ancients."[128] For all this, Scripture remains the true touchstone by which all other writings and opinions must be tested, though a discriminate use of Tradition is not to be despised as a derivative and ancillary authority. Robinson summarizes the significance of Tradition in four propositions. 1) It is a helpful apologetic devise by which those who trust more in Fathers and councils than in the written word can be "twice overcome" when beaten with their own weapons. 2) It induces moral probability, though not absolute

---

[124]*Observations*, 70.

[125]Ibid., 67, 55-56.

[126]Ibid., 67, 71.

[127]Ibid., 63.

[128]Ibid., 69; *Justification*, 33.

necessity of truth. 3) It helps remove the aspersion of schism by demonstrating the harmony of practice and belief among the churches. 4) It cultivates modesty and diligence by pointing to the "judgment of others" in matters of controversy.[129]

Robinson's Scriptural presuppositions were, by and large, those of Calvin and the Reformed tradition in its English adaptation. William Ames, in his *Medulla theologica*, summarized the essence of scriptural theory for this tradition: "All things necessary to salvation are contained in the Scriptures and also those things necessary for the instruction and edification of the church. Therefore, Scripture is not a partial but a perfect rule of faith and morals."[130] For Robinson the distinction between things necessary to salvation, and things necessary for edification corresponded to the justification/sanctification polarity which he identified in terms of invisible and visible Church. On the one hand Scripture is a transcript of God's promises which are "a kinde of middle thing between his purpose and performance of good unto them, whom he loveth." In this way God hath bound himself to the elect, indeed made Himself a debtor to them, "promise being, as we say, due debt." But while salvation "he promiseth *absolutely* unto his; other good things (ordinarily) *upon* condition."[131] To the Word as the means by which faith is begotten must be joined "the observation of whatsoever Christ hath appointed his Apostles to teach," so that we may

> grow in grace; if not in bulk, yet in firmnesse; as when the body leavs growing in bignesse, it knits better than before. Neither indeed can we be safe from being drawn away from God otherwise, then by continuall drawing nearer unto him. For, our way to Heaven, is up a hill, and we drag a Cart load of our corruptions after us; which, except we keep going, will pull us backward, ere we be aware.[132]

The Word, then, confronts the believer as promise, but also as demand, as a summons to obedience in every detail, implied or expressed. "God is God," said Robinson, "in the smallest things, which he requires."[133]

Church order was certainly no small thing in Robinson's reading of Scripture, but the Separatists were not alone in claiming biblical warrant

[129] *Observations*, 71-72.

[130] William Ames, *The Marrow of Theology*, ed. John D. Eusden (Boston, 1968), 189. While there were many points of contact with the Anglican understanding of Scripture, there were also significant differences. See Egil Grislis, "The Hermeneutical Problem in Richard Hooker," in *Studies in Richard Hooker*, ed. W. Speed Hill (London, 1972), 159-206.

[131] *Observations*, 9-10. (My italics.)

[132] Ibid., 34.

[133] Ibid., 72.

for a particular polity. Presbyterians were experts at it themselves, and by the end of the sixteenth century, episcopacy had its defenders who argued *sola scriptura* as well. The polemical warfare between these "politial" absolutists was essentially a battle over the Word, the texts flying thick and fast, with an occasional Father or Reformer thrown in for good measure. How confusing indeed, we might suppose, if they had not had the same rule!

"A New Old Testament"?: Continuity and Contrast

At the heart of the Puritan-Separatist debate over "tarrying for the magistrate" were two competing, ideal conceptions of true Christianity, one theoretically in consonance with, the other irreconcilably opposed to, the prevailing national mythos. For all their differences over the structure of the Church, and the role of the monarch as Supreme Governor therein, Puritan and Anglican alike shared a common vision of England as the "elect nation" whose history was paradigmatically foreshadowed in the experiences of ancient Israel. Thus the Admonitioners promised Elizabeth that if she would reform the "horrible abuses" which beset the Church, God would "deliver and defend you from all you enemies, either at home or abroad, as he did faithfull Jacob and good Jehosaphat."[134] Through successive reigns this image of a zealous and godly prince, divinely appointed to remove the obstacles to religious progress, was reinforced by apt appeal to the historical books of the Old Testament. John Foxe, one of the chief shapers of this tradition, depicted Edward, "this evangelical Josias," suppressing the remnants of Roman idolatry, restoring the Bible, and relieving the poor.[135] In like manner, Edwin Sandys, in an Accession Day sermon in 1579, compared the observance of the accession of Elizabeth—the English Judith, Deborah, and Hester—to Israel's commemoration of the exodus from Egypt.[136] In an

---

[134]*Puritan Manifestoes*, 18. The concept of Protestant England as the New Israel reinforced the theory of Royal Supremacy, and made appeals to Old Testament parallels more directly relevant. Cf. the view of Nicholas Fuller that "we [are] now the people of God, the Jews being cut off," Faith Thompson, *Magna Carta* (Minneapolis, 1948), 260. See also the perceptive article by Conrad Russell, "Arguments for Religious Unity in England, 1530-1650," *Journal of Ecclesiastical History* 18 (1967), 201-26.

[135]*Foxe*, vol. 5, 698. Cf. William Haller, *The Elect Nation: The Meaning and Relevance of Foxe's Book of Martyrs* (New York, 1963), 110-39. On the Puritan adaptation of this tradition see James C. Spalding, "Restitution as a Normative Factor for Puritan Dissent," *Journal of the American Academy of Religion* 44 (1976), 47-62.

[136]*The Sermons of Edwin Sandys*, ed. John Ayre (Cambridge, 1842), 76.

age of exploration and new discovery, the fusion of religious metaphor and national sentiment contributed to the self-assured assessment of England's place among the nations and her mission to the world:

> There is no doubt but that we of England are his saved people, by the eternal and infallible presence of the Lord predestined to be sent unto these Gentiles in the sea, to those isles and kingdoms, there to preach the peace of the Lord, for are not we only set upon Mount Zion to give light to all the rest of the world? . . . It is only we, therefore, that must be these shining messengers of the Lord, and none but we.[137]

By attempting to establish non-parochial churches on the basis of "the infallible rule of Christs Testament," the Separatists challenged the appeal to Old Testament precedent as a justification for a national or magisterial reformation.[138] Robert Harrison, in an early formulation of Separatist typology, denied that English monarchs were the counterpart of rulers in ancient Israel:

> Yf they aleadg the Kyngs of Juda and Moses and Kings of Isreall for beginning of refformation in the church—we answer that they did in ecclesiasticall or spirituall matters they did it as they wear fygurs of christ and that y[t] they did syvillye in fforsying they did it bye the sevyll sword for they had authoritye in both casses y[t] our Kings and Princes want ffor the fyguratyue maner was ended in Christe.[139]

Christ, not Edward or Elizabeth, is the antitype of the Old Testament magistrates in their capacity as initiators of reform within the Church. To base the form of Church government upon the example of Israel, Robinson said, would require "a new-found land of Canaan," and "a new old

---

[137]Letter of John Davys (1550?-1605), explorer. Quoted, E. D. Marcu, *Sixteenth-Century Nationalism* (London, 1976), 80. Cf. also the even more chauvinistic comment of Job Throckmorton, that "the Lord hath vowed himself to be English," in J. E. Neale, *Queen Elizabeth I and her Parliaments* (London, 1957), vol. 2, 170.

[138]*Justification*, 20. For those seeking a Biblical parallel for the English establishment, the New Testament Church was a far less fruitful model than the Jewish theocracy. The New Testament texts more often referred to in this connection, "Render unto Caesar" (MT. 22:21) and "Be subject unto the higher powers" (Rom. 13:1), are negative exhortations addressed to a persecuted minority rather than calls for allegiance to a godly nation. Thus Whitgift is led to disclaim the status of the earliest Church, "in the time of the cross," as a normative pattern for later church order: "The time was not yet come whereof the prophet said, 'Kings shall be thy nursing-fathers and princes shall be thy nursing-mothers'." *Works*, vol. 1, 390-91.

[139]*A Treatise of the Church*, 41. Separatist typology has been the focus of several recent studies. See esp. Thomas M. Davis, "The Traditions of Puritan Typology," unpublished Ph.D. dissertation, University of Missouri (1968), and Richard Reinitz, "The Separatist Background of Roger Williams' Argument for Religious Toleration," in *Typology and Early American Literature*, ed. Scavan Bercovitch (Amherst, Mass., 1972), 107-37.

testament" for the former has long since been "abrogated and disanulled."[140]

The logic of figurative argument, if applied consistently, would seem to displace the Old Testament with the New as a qualitatively different epoch in the history of salvation. Typology, however, has a connective as well as a disjunctive function, and Robinson stressed, alternately, one over the other in his attempt to place the Separatist church-ideal in the context of soteriology. In respect to the covenant of grace, which derives from God's eternal decision in election and is therefore unconditional, Robinson's fundamental emphasis is upon the *continuity* of Old and New Testaments. The efficacy of Christ's death, the historical radius of this covenant, extends retroactively to the Patriarchs and Prophets in equal measure to those who live in a later dispensation. "There are not two new Covenants, or Testaments established in the blood of Christ but one."[141] The land of Canaan itself, "into which Joshua or Jesus, the type of *our and their true Jesus*, was to bring them," was a sacrament of God's presence, and a pledge of their eternal home in heaven.[142] The content of this covenant God confirmed to Abraham and to his seed by circumcision, and to us by baptism; it is there "the same with ours now for substance; and established in Christ to come, as ours in Christ in the flesh."[143] Abraham is thus contrasted to Moses, the mediator of the Covenant of Law, already implanted in men's hearts by creation, but requiring re-promulgation because it was "almost worn out."[144] The substance of the two covenants, Law and Gospel, Robinson finds running

---

[140]*Justification*, 278, 197.

[141]*Of Religious Communion*, 73. Robinson's emphasis here is essentially that of Calvin who claimed against "that wonderful rascal Servetus and certain madmen of the Anabaptist sect," that "the covenant made with all the patriarchs is so much like ours in substance and reality that the two are actually one and the same (*unum prorsus atque idem sit*): *Inst.* 2,10.2 *Calvini Opera*, vol. 3, 404. On the theological problem of the two covenants in Anabaptist hermeneutics, see George H. Williams, *The Radical Reformation,* op. cit., 815-32, and Alvin J. Beachy, *The Concept of Grace in the Radical Reformation* (Nieuwkoop, 1977), 146-52.

[142]*Of Religious Communion*, 75 (My italics.)

[143]Ibid., 76.

[144]*Observations*, 64. George Selement, "The Covenant Theology of English Separatism and the Separation of Church and State," *Journal of the American Academy of Religion* 41 (1973), 66-74, claims that the Separatists made a radical division "between the Abrahamic covenant, which they asserted no longer applied to Christians, and the covenant of the New Testament" (p. 68). This statement fails to recognize both the two-sided character of Separatist covenant-language (the visible/invisible Church distinction), and the (originally Pauline) contrast between the Mosaic and Abrahamic covenants.

pari passu through both the Old Testament and the New: Moses preached the Gospel to the Israelites in the wilderness, and Christ expounded the Law (especially in the Sermon on the Mount). Yet the ministry of Moses was chiefly legal, and the ministry of Christ chiefly evangelical. This quantitative distribution of Law and Gospel accounts for the popular, though not properly scriptural, designation of an "old" and a "new" testament.

With respect to the constitution of the visible Church, however, the apostolic model is normative, though even here the base line between re-formation and restitution is not drawn simply in terms of Old and New Testaments. The lines of continuity extend to "all the visible Churches gathered and planted by the Lord" from the beginning of the world in that their essential nature is the same—simple, uniform, unmixed.[145] The first of these was a "Church of Angels" in heaven which was in its constitution and collection "good and holy without mixture" though some thereafter fell from their original estate. After that God created a "Church of mankind in Paradise" consisting of two persons, Adam and Eve, "both holy and good." Out of this primeval Church eventually Cain proved himself to be a "degenerate branch," and so was broken off, and driven from the visible presence of God. Robinson traced the lineage of visible churches through Abraham and the Patriarchs down to John the Baptist and Christ himself who came to "repayr the desolations of Sion," and to establish a new order for the visible Church.[146] Since the Lord "hath the same ends and respects in the creating and restoring of his Ch," all true visible churches, have in common certain defining characteristics: they are gathered of good matter not bad, their members enter into union with one another by means of a covenant, and they are able to purge visibly unrighteous members from their midst.

While the covenant of grace cuts across both Testaments, and is never for Robinson absolutely coincident with the visible Church, and while all visible churches conform in their essential nature to the angelic and Paradisaic examples, there is nonetheless a striking and significant contrast between the form of the visible Church in the Mosaic dispensation and that promulgated by Christ and the Apostles. Robinson described the unique arrangement which God made with his ancient people:

> The Lord did chuse the whole nation of the Iewes to be his peculiar people, and took all and every one of them into covenant with himself, gave them the

---

[145] *Justification*, 113.

[146] Ibid., 114-15.

> Land of Canaan for an inheritance, as a type of the kingdome of heaven, erected a polity over them, civil and ecclesiasticall, in the judiciall and ceremonial law, called the old testamet, making the same persons and all of them, though in divers respects the Church, and the comon wealth.[147]

A striking feature of this national covenant was the existence of a "representative church." Communion in the holy things of God required, then as now, that all members participate jointly in the duties of worship, "for the mutuall aedification of the parts." Yet it was clearly impossible for the whole body of the nation, "in its intire, simple, proper, or personall parts, and members," to be gathered into such an assembly. God therefore designated one special place where sacrifices would be offered and services rendered on behalf of the entire nation. Properly speaking, then, there was "that one onely visible Church vpon the face of the earth, tyed to one temple, altar, sacrifice, Preisthood, in one place."[148] The Church of the Jews enjoyed, in a measure not extended to any other visible Church before or since, "that absolute promise of the Lords visible presence."[149] Even in their deepest apostasy the Lord sustained them in outward covenant, by extraordinary means when ordinary failed. This, because it was necessary for the Messiah to be born in a true church, and so fulfill therein the demands of the Law. "*But with vs it is otherwise: the times are altered and the dispensations of them.*"[150] The coming of Christ has set the visible Church on a completely different footing; it is now "reformed, perfited, and otherwise ordered then before."[151]

Robinson described the Church of the new dispensation in terms of a fourfold contrast with that of the old. First, its scope is particular rather than national. Since the Lord "divorced his ancient wife the nation of the Iewes, he never maried, nor will marry, nation more."[152] Now a true visible Church may appear whenever

> two or three faithfull people do arise, separating themselves fro the world into the fellowship of the gospell, and covenant of Abraham.

Such a group is a Church truly gathered, "though never so weak, a house and temple of God rightly founded vpon the doctrine of the Apostles and

---

[147]Ibid., 188.

[148]Ibid., 194, 250.

[149]Ibid., 248.

[150]Ibid., 249-50. (My italics.)

[151]Ibid., 293.

[152]Ibid., 308. Cf. 267: "A national Church since Christs death, and the dissolution of the Iewish Church, is a monstrous compoind, and savours of Iudaism."

[153]Ibid., 221.

Prophets."[153] Secondly, the representative character of the Jewish Church has been altered, so that when the Church is multiplied by "the suddayne, and extraordinary conversion" of more than can easily assemble in one place, then several particular congregations are formed, each of them possessing the full prerogatives of a complete Church. They thus appear "like so many distinct flocks, [which] do ordinarily heard together, and so communicate in the word, prayer, sacraments, and censures."[154] The vestiges of the representative system which are maintained in other churches, such as the College of Cardinals and General Council in Rome or Convocation and episcopal consistories in England, violate the integrity and independence of each autonomous "collection" of saints. Thirdly, no Church of the present dispensation can claim the kind of divinely-sustained stability which was guaranteed in the Mosaic period. Each visible Church must constantly subject itself to the scepter of Christ by the vigorous application of discipline, or else place itself in jeopardy of being "dischurched." All the more important, then, was the fourth contrast which Robinson located in the institution of excommunication as the distinctive ordinance of particular churches in the new dispensation. To be sure, excommunication was "typed out" in the Jewish Church, and that in several respects: first, in the segregation of the ceremonially unclean; and more exactly, in the severity of civil sanctions, banishment and capital punishment, which were applied to obstinate offenders. But both of these practices which pertained to the Law, the former in its ceremonial, the latter in its judicial, aspect, were part of "those worldly and carnal ordinances" which were rendered obsolete by the coming of Christ:

> Now as the judicialls (which were for the government of the Congregation civily) are dead, and do not bind any civil polity, save as they were of comon equity: so are the ceremonialls, (which were for the Ch: polity) deadly: and may not be revived by any Church, save as any of them have new life given by Christ. [155]

---

[154]Ibid., 196.

[155]Ibid., 198. Robinson accepts the common division of the Law into three parts: moral, ceremonial, judicial. The moral law, embodied in the Decalogue, is equally binding in both dispensations, though its accusatory function has been nullified by the death of Christ (cf. *Works*, vol. 3, 46-54). In the former dispensation the ceremonial law was an accessory to the first table, the judicial to the second table, of the Decalogue. The content of both was chiefly figurative and so fulfilled in Christ, although the judicial may still be applied by civil magistrates in situations of "comon equity." Cartwright on this premise advocated the execution of idolators and adulterers, whereas Robinson, moved by a different concern, called for a more humane solution. Cf. *Works of Whitgift*, vol. 1, 270.

By contrast, excommunication, in the new dispensation was an exclusively congregational concern, the means by which a covenanted community maintained its status as a true visible Church.

In the attempt to cull from the New Testament a single true and permanently valid blueprint for church order, no passage figured more prominently than the parable of the tares. Robinson complained that men both learned and unlearned considered the Separatists "beaten all to fritters" with this parable, "as with some thunderbolt."[156] The exegetical skirmish centered on the proper interpretation of the "field" which contained both tares and wheat. The Separatists' opponents, Robinson acknowledged, followed "the most beaten way" in making the field the visible Church, a *corpus permixtum* made up of wicked and righteous alike. This identification, first suggested by Pope Callistus and reemphasized by Cyprian and Augustine, was accepted by Calvin as the standard reading.[157] It seemed, therefore, to counter the Separatist conception of the visible Church, planted anew, with saints for its matter and a covenant for its form. But, Robinson argued, if the field be the Church, since the parable forbids absolutely the rooting out of any tares, then there would be no use of excommunication at all, and notorious offenders would be permitted to remain undisturbed in the Church. Rather, the field is the world as Christ, "who best knew his owne meaning," explained it to be, and the description of tares and wheat growing together, a solemn warning to the civil magistrate not to "weed out" even the most heretical of his subjects lest, unbeknownst to him, he be guilty of persecuting one of the elect. [158] The harvest is the end of the world when the tares are

---

[156]*Works*, vol. 3, 75. This was a favorite sermon text for those who opposed the Separatists. Henoch Clapham, a former Separatist himself, declared: "Nine sermons I publikely and largely delivered in Southwarke by London, vpon the Parable of tares. . . . I choose this Parable before other scriptures, because it is a ground of grounds for direction vnto Churches state and condition: the verie scripture which many peruert to their owne ruine: and yet (*ne male memini*) the first scripture whereby I recouered my standing." *Antidoton: or A Soveraigne Remedie against schisme and heresie* (London, 1600), 10.

[157]Cf. Callistus' view: "Ἀλλὰ καὶ παραθολὴν τῶν ζιζανίων πρὸς τοῦτο ἐφ η λέγεσΘαι: Ἀφετε τὰ ζιζάνια συναύξειν τῷ σίτῳ' τουτέστιν ἐν τῇ Ἐκκλησία τοὺς ἁμαρτάνοντας." Hippolytus, *Philosophumena sive Haeresium Omnium Confutatio*, vol. 9, 12 (Paris, 1860), 444, and Calvin's comment: "So long as the church is on pilgrimage (*peregrinatur*) in the world, the good and the sincere will be mixed in it with the bad and the hypocrites." *Calvin's New Testament Commentaries*, eds. D. W. and T. F. Torrance, vol. 2, 74-75; *Corpus Reformatorum*, vol. 45, 368.

[158]*Justification*, 119. That Robinson's advocacy of toleration could be derived from his doctrine of predestination seems never to have occurred to the pious historians of Dissent, most of whom lauded the former trait while explaining away the latter. Robinson argued against Augustine's interpretation of *compelle intrare*, holding that such a course of compulsion would only produce "Atheists, Hypocrites, and Familists: and being at first

delivered over to "their finall perdition" never to offend the Church again.[159]

We may compare Robinson's exposition of this parable with that of Perkins as a measure of their contrasting conceptions of the visible Church. Perkins agreed with Robinson that God's final "fanning time" will be at the end of the age, when the wicked are definitively separated from the righteous to be "blowne into hell." But on this side of the Last Judgment God's fanning time is twofold. First, when the Word is preached "to a Nation or Congregation" it separates the wheat from the tares somewhat—in affection, in certain "notes" of distinction. More drastic is the second fan of separation at death whereby God gathers the souls of the godly into heaven, and blows the souls of the wicked into hell. Yet even after this, their bodies lie together, "lodged in the same graue of the earth," indicative of their common placement in the "field" of the Church. Perkins applied the parable to his situation: "For us in England, the case stands thus: Our Church doubtlesse is Gods corne fieeld, and we are the corne-heap of God . . . but withall we must confesse, we are full of chaffe, that is, of prophane and wicked Hypocrites."[160]

As we have noted, Robinson also acknowledged the presence of hypocrites in the visible Church, but this occurred "by man's default, and

---

constrained to practise against conscience, loose all conscience afterwards. Bags, and vessels overstrained break, and will never after hold any thing." Moreover, even among most heretical of sects there might be "divers truly, though weakly led" of the elect (*Observations*, 51-52). However, Robinson did not argue, as did the Anabaptists earlier and Roger Williams later, against *all* civil compulsion in matters religious. While a complete survey of Robinson's theory of magistracy is beyond the scope of the present study, the following points may be noted: (1) Robinson assigned to the magistrate certain functions usually performed by the Church, e.g. marriages and funerals. (2) He saw the magistrate as preserver of *both* tables of the Law, with a corresponding right to punish breaches of either (*Justification*, 184). (3) He defended the right of the magistrate to bear the sword holding that Jesus' command to love our enemies and not kill them, to pray for them and not punish them, applied only to the individual Christian: the magistrate could pray and punish at the same time! (*Of Religious Communion*, 128). 4) The magistrate may repress public idolatry and "provoke" his subjects to hear the Word preached, though he is forbidden to enforce compulsory church membership, and his right to execute "bodily vengeance" upon disobedient subjects does not extend to capital punishment for heresy or idolatry (*Justification*, 299, 136). 5) Robinson radically separates the *office* of magistracy from the *person* of the magistrate: "A King, Husband, Father, etc. though an Heathen, Idolater, Atheist, or Excommunicate, is as well, and as much a King, Husband, Father, as if he were the best Christian living" (*Observations*, 48). 6) Robinson accepts no form of resistance theory, but encourages "pacient sufferance" in the face of a tyrannical regiment. For Robinson's views on toleration, see W. K. Jordan, *The Development of Religious Toleration in England,* op. cit., vol. 2, 242-47; on his relationship to Williams, Cyclone Covey, *The Gentle Radical: A Biography of Roger Williams* (New York, 1966), 62-72.

[159]*Justification*, 119.

[160]*The Workes of William Perkins,* op. cit., vol. 2, 425.

sin" and required correction whenever discerned.[161] But in England membership was perforce automatic, and unrelated to the "profession of faith" by which the inward graces residing in the heart are publicly manifested:

> Let a man but hire a house within the precincts of your parish, and he is ioyned member in your Ch: *ipso facto*, though he cannot manifest the least kernel of faith, or repentance, yea though he professe himselfe an atheist, heretick, sorcerer, blasphemer (or that which is worse if worse can be).[162]

Such an arrangement precluded that "voluntary yeelding, or submission unto the Gospel" which was essential in the establishment of a visible Church, and so contradicted the constitution demanded by Christ.[163]

In defying the theology of a national covenant and starting all over, as it were, in the plantation of new churches, the Separatists seemed to their contemporaries to be devoid of all historical consciousness. No one put it more forcefully than Hall:

> What! so true and glorious a light of God, and never seen till now! No worlds, times, churches, patriarchs, prophets, apostles, martyrs, fathers, doctors, Christians ever saw this truth look forth besides you, until you![164]

Indeed, Robinson conceded, the new dispensation had been primarily one of darkness, with "bryars and thornes" present in the Apostolic age and "monstrous errours and corruptions" soon thereafter.[165] The rise of Antichrist had been gradual, beginning "in the seed onely, or as an embrie in the wombe," advanced (though unwittingly) by the old Catholic Fathers, and finally grown to a "perfit man, consisting of the head the Pope, and the body, the Hierarchy ecclesiastical."[166] In keeping with his fluid ecclesiology Robinson does not speak of a general fall of the Church which can be identified with a particular event, e.g. the accession of Constantine. Rather, there are a series of "falls" of particular churches. For example, when the assembly of saints in the city of Rome, broke its covenant with the Lord he "gave her, as an harlot, a bill of divorce and put her away." Accepting the traditional account of Joseph of Arimathea's apostolate in Britain, Robinson notes that there were "at the first true Churches planted in [England], by the preaching of the gospell, and the

---

[161]*Justification*, 313.

[162]Ibid., 90, 270.

[163]Ibid., 303.

[164]Hall, *Works*, vol. 9, 36.

[165]*Justification*, 32.

[166]Ibid., 281, 50.

obedience of fayth."[167] These congregations too soon succumbed "through the seduction of Antichrist" making necessary a "new gathering" after the Romish apostasy which engulfed the whole world.[168]

Yet even in the darkness the Lord had raised up "many witnesses" some of whom were "killed by the beast, some of old and others of late tymes."[169] The Separatists, Robinson believed, were the true spiritual heirs of these martyrs, a righteous remnant whose obedience in restoring the true visible Church signalled the imminent downfall of the still ensconced Antichrist. As the people of God "in old tyme" were called out of Babylon civil to rebuild the temple in Jerusalem, so are the people of God now to build themselves into a lively temple, "leaving Babylon to that destruction and desolation (*yea furthering the same*) to which she is devoted by the Lord."[170] While the overthrow of Antichrist would be accomplished with a single act of eschatological violence, his demise, like his emergence, would be the result of a rather extended process. True religion, Robinson noted, "is not always sown and reaped in one age."[171] Following the schematization of Church history outlined by Foxe, Robinson saw the three centuries prior to the Reformation as a period of preparation with the light of the gospel intermittently breaking through the darkness, especially in the witness of Wyclif and Hus. The Reformers, those "godly guides of separation," had established the precedent for true reformation in departing from the Church of Rome, though they were so recently delivered from Antichristian bondage that many truths they only saw dimly.[172] Unto the Separatists belonged the distinction of having restored the visible Church to its pristine purity, of having re-cast it in that "Apostolicall and primitive mould." As synedoches for God's people in all ages, they stood, as it were, in the vortex of a historical movement

[167]Ibid., 277-78. Cf. *Foxe*, vol. 1, 305-14, and Clapham, *Antidoton*, 24: "Though we were couched here in an vttermost coast, yet it is registered to God his praise and our comfort, that this Prouince was the first of Prouinces in receiuing the Gospell openly . . . the holy fayth planted in our land by Ioseph of Arimathea, who with some others came hither in the yeere of Christ, 60."

[168]*Justification*, 460.

[169]Ibid., 34.

[170]Ibid., 289. (My italics.) Cf. *Works*, vol. 3, 411: "Though you now cry never so loud, 'We have no king but Caesar,' yet is there 'another king, one Jesus,' which shall return and pass a heavy doom upon the rebellious."

[171]*Justification*, 61.

[172]Ibid., 290. Foxe placed the zenith of Antichristian power in 1000 A.D. when Satan was "loosed." The "reforming time of Christes church" began in 1300 A.D. Cf. V. Norskov Olsen, *John Foxe and the Elizabethan Church* (London, 1973), 51-70.

destined to overthrow the powers of darkness, and usher in God's new age.

Robinson warned the Separatists that, as harbingers of divine judgment, their role in the world would be one of conflict and tension. He attributed the opposition they encountered to the intensified efforts of Satan who, in the last days, "doth bend his force most directly against" the restoration of the true visible Church.[173] But, while the conflict is heightened for the Separatists because they live at the very edge of history, affliction and suffering is the *modus vivendi* for all churches in the new dispensation. In contrasting the present situation of the Church with its "established" counterpart in the former dispensation, Robinson describes, in language suggestive of the millennial state though noticeably void of prophetic speculations, the shape of the future age:

> God hath in a peculiar manner entayled afflictions to the sincere profession of the gospel, above that of the law before Christ. The law was given by Moses, whose ministerie began with killing the Egyptian, that oppressed the Israelite; and was prosequuted with leading the people out of Egypt, through the sea, and wildernes with great might, and a strong hand; and lastly, was finished with the bloody victorie over Sihon, and Og the kings of Canaan. But Christs dispensation was all of an other kynde: his birth mean; his life sorrowfull; and his death shamefull. And albeit the love of God towards his people be alwaies the same in it self, yet is the manifestation thereof very divers. Before Christs coming in the flesh . . . God shewed his love more fully in earthly blessings, and peace; and more sparingly in spirituall, and heavenly: But now, on the other side, he dealeth forth temporall blessings more sparingly; and spirituall with a fuller hand. It is not unprobably gathered, that, after the destruction of the dragon, and beast, and recalling of the Iewes after their long divorce from the Lord; the blessings of both kindes shall meet together, and the Church enjoy, for a time, a verie gracefull state upon earth both in regard of spirituall and bodily good things.[174]

Drawing the foregoing considerations together, we may characterize Robinson's resolution of the problem of the two testaments as a *heightened dispensationalism*. When discussing the basic unity of the people of God in terms of their participation in the covenant of grace, Robinson tends to lessen the distance between Old and New covenants. When searching for the scriptural model for the visible Church, however, the distance is increased: the coming of Christ has so altered the form of the visible Church that no unqualified appeal to Old Testament precedent is

---

[173]*Justification*, 268.

[174]*Observations*, 178-79. Stephen Brachlow, "Puritan Theology and Radical Churchmen," 304-11, has shown that Robinson's understanding of history and the future was in line with the "amillennial Augustinian tradition" epitomized by Foxe. Unlike later seventeenth-century sectarians, Robinson was apparently not influenced by the radical eschatological expectations of Brightman, Napier, and Dent, none of whom he quotes.

possible. Placing the Separatist venture at the end of the fourth, and final, age of salvation history, Robinson anticipates the fusion of the "spiritual" and "bodily" dispensations following the imminent overthrow of Antichrist and the instauration of the earthly Paradise.

"TO ALL AND EVERY MEMBER ALIKE": THE CHURCH GATHERED

Discipline: An Essential Mark

The word discipline, as it was used by Puritan polemicists of the sixteenth century, was not always carefully defined and carried at least three distinct meanings. It referred, first of all, to the pattern of personal striving and self-examination by which serious Christians endeavored, in the words of Richard Rogers, "to keepe our lives and hartes in good order." [175] When applied to the concept of the visible Church, however, it was synonymous with the structure or polity by which the Church was organized. Thus Walter Travers, in the most complete statement of presbyterian principles set forth in the Elizabethan period, defined it:

> I call therefore Ecclesiasticall Discipline, the pollicie off the Church off Christe ordeyned and appointed off God for the goode administracion and gouernment off the same. [176]

This definition was also accepted by Bancroft in his *Survay of the Pretended Holy Discipline*, and by Hooker in the Preface to the *Laws*, in their respective counterattacks on the Puritan effort to displace episcopacy with an "eldership." More properly still, the term discipline referred to the exercise of sanctions against recalcitrant members *within* the Church for the purpose of promoting adherence to standards of conduct and doctrinal belief. By insisting upon discipline in this third sense as an *essential* mark of a true visible Church, the Separatists moved beyond the traditional use of the *notae*-concept in the Reformed tradition, and approached the sectarian ecclesiology of continental Anabaptism.

Both the Augsburg Confession of 1530 and the Geneva Confession of 1536, in keeping with the two-mark emphasis of Luther and Calvin, had declared the pure preaching of the Word and the proper administration of the sacraments determinative for the external Church. [177] However,

---

[175] *Two Elizabethan Puritan Diaries*, ed. M. M. Knappen, op. cit., 72.

[176] Walter Travers, *A Full and Plaine Declaration of Ecclesiasticall Discipline* (London, 1574), 6.

[177] On this basis Calvin was willing to extend the title "church" to congregations still in Roman obedience—"to the extent that some marks of the church remain, we do not impugn the existence of churches among them." (*Inst.* 4,2.12).

before the death of Calvin, discipline as a third mark had found its way into two Calvinist symbols, the Scottish (1560) and Belgic (1561) Confessions. A decade earlier the three-mark doctrine had been introduced into England by Bucer's *De Regno Christi* which assigned to the pastoral office "the teaching of Christ, the dispensation of his sacraments, and the administration of his discipline."[178] As James Spaulding has pointed out, toward the end of Edward's reign three symbolic books were promulgated corresponding to the three marks mentioned by Bucer: the *Forty-Two Articles* defining true doctrine; the *Second Prayerbook of Edward VI*, defining correct administration of the sacraments; and the *Reformatio legum ecclesiasticarum*, defining the government and discipline of the Church.[179] The three-mark formulation received further support in the writings of Beza, Knox, and especially Peter Martyr. Therefore, the inclusion of discipline among "the outwarde markes wherby a true christian church is knowne" in the *Admonition* of 1572 followed a well-established precedent.[180]

However, the Cartwright-Whitgift controversy introduced a subtle, but significant modification of the *notae*-concept, one of lasting importance for the Separatist position. In defending the importance of reproducing the "perfect form" of the Church commanded in Scripture, and omitting those features not expressly enjoined, Cartwright was led to equate "matters of discipline and kind of government" with "matters necessary to salvation, and of faith." Whitgift seemed genuinely shocked at this assertion, calling it a strange and unheard of doctrine, and demanded of Cartwright what he meant by "necessary unto salvation":

> whether you mean such things without the which we cannot be saved, or such things only as be necessary or ordinary helps unto salvation: for you know that this word 'necessary' signifieth either that without the which a thing cannot be, or that without the which it cannot so well and conveniently be.[181]

In the *Seconde Reply* Cartwright, obviously perturbed by Whitgift's quotation of Calvin and Bullinger as exponents of the two-mark doctrine,

---

[178] *Melanchthon and Bucer*, ed. Wilhelm Pauck (Philadelphia, 1966), 232.

[179] James C. Spaulding, "The *Reformatio Legum Ecclesiasticarum* and the Furthering of Discipline in England," *Church History* 39 (1970), 162-71.

[180] *Puritan Manifestoes*, 9. See Tadataka Maruyama, "The Reform of True Church: The Ecclesiology of Theodore Beza," unpublished Th.D. thesis, Princeton University (1973), 38-45. On Martyr's possible influence on English congregationalists, see Robert M. Kingdon, "Peter Martyr Vermilgli and the Marks of the True Church," in *Continuity and Discontinuity in Church History: Essays Presented to George Huntston Williams on the Occasion of his 65th Birthday*, eds. F. F. Church and Timothy George (Leiden, 1979), 198-214.

[181] *Works of Whitgift*, vol. 1, 181-84.

claimed that Whitgift had sidetracked their discussion:

> As though the question were, what things the church may want, and *yet* be
> the church of God . . . or how sick the church might be and *yet* live, how
> maimed, and *yet* not slain.[182]

This complaint, however, contained an implicit admission: discipline, for
all its importance, was not an *essential* mark of a true visible Church; the
Church could still be the Church, though only barely, without it. When
faced with the overt separation of Browne and Harrison, Cartwright
described discipline as a thing "necessary to the comely and stable being,"
but not "simplye to the being," of the visible Church. The English
assemblies, he warned his former pupils, should not be given "the blacke-
stone of condemnation" for they remained "the Lordes confederates" so
long as their faith was grounded upon the "foundation christ."[183] This,
retorted Browne, was to make the Lord's discipline or government "an
accident or hangby to the church." But, in fact, it was of the very essence
of the Church; without it there could be no "ioyning, nor coupling
together of the church," no face, sign, or token of the Church at all.[184]

The idea that discipline was the *sine qua non* of the visible Church,
part of its fundamental *credenda* and not merely of its *agenda*, was in fact
a novel concept to the English Reformation. As late as 1585 Bancroft
could write: "In deede of late some haue made ecclesiasticall disciplyne a
third essentiall note of the Church, what theyre meaninge is I knowe not: I
dare affyrme the assertion to be Anabaptisticall." [185] While there is no
evidence that Separatists were influenced in their views on discipline by
contacts with Anabaptists, the two groups both stressed the indispensa-
bility of congregational discipline as a mark of the true Church, and cited
its absence as the basis of their withdrawal from the official state
Church.[186] By the seventeenth century the insistence upon discipline was
generally recognized as one of two distinguishing features of the Separa-

---

[182]Ibid., 186. (My italics.)

[183]*Cartwrightiana*, 52-53.

[184]*An Answere to Master Cartwright*, 462.

[185]*Tracts ascribed to Richard Bancroft*, ed. Albert Peel (Cambridge, 1953), 109.

[186]Jean Runzo, "Communal Discipline in the Early Anabaptist Communities of
Switzerland, South and Central Germany, Austria, and Moravia, 1525-1550," unpub-
lished Ph.D. dissertation, University of Michigan (1977), has shown that a split between
the Swiss Brethren and Hessian Anabaptists centered on the same issue which divided
Puritans and Separatists in England: the role of the ban as an *essential* sign of the true
Church. Hessian Anabaptists, with their less strict view on this issue, were more open to
rapproachement with the state church when faced with sincere efforts, such as those of
Bucer and Landgrave Philipp, to raise its moral standards.

tist position. Thus Hall told Robinson:

> I find you call for a double separation. A first separation in the gathering of
> the Church; a second, in the managing of it: the first, at our entrance into the
> Church; the second, in our continuance: the first, of the Church from pagans
> and worldlings, by an initiatory profession; the second, of lewd men from the
> Church by just censures.[187]

As an essential mark of the true Church, discipline insured that the
integrity of the initial separation would be maintained— by separating
from the Church back to the world those whose lives betrayed their
profession. When couched in the language of edification, discipline corresponded to the elimination of extraneous matter, a necessary function
for every living organism:

> But the Church without this power is as a monstrous body wanting the
> faculties and instruments of evacuation and expulsion of excrements, or
> other noysome things, and therefore is never appointed of God to live, but
> devoted to death and destruction. [188]

"Dic Ecclesiae": The Biblical Mandate

The assumption underlying the elevation of discipline to the status,
almost, of a third "sacrament" was that the New Testament contained a
clearly-defined, universally binding model for such a procedure. The
Lord did not leave

> in the hands of the Church a rude matter to frame after her owne fashion, but
> with the matter he hath also appoynted the manner and form wherein all
> things must be done.[189]

It was therefore natural that those texts in which Christ specifically spoke
of the Church would be the objects of intense scrutiny. There are, in fact,
only two such texts, both in St. Matthew's Gospel, and both now
regarded, ironically, as interpolations of the later Church. The first of
these is the famous passage (16:18-19) in which the Church of Rome
claimed to find the guarantee of continuity in the Pope as the vicar of
Christ. This text presented two problems to those who sought to unravel
its implications for Church polity: what was meant by the power of the
"keys," and in what respect this power was given to Peter and his
successors. Robinson outlined four positions on the latter point, corresponding to four approaches to the government of the Church: first, the

---

[187]Hall, *Works*, vol. 9, 9-10.

[188]*Justification*, 83. Cf. 349.

[189]Ibid., 22.

Papists who affirm the keys were given to Peter as prince of the Apostles and so to the Bishops of Rome as his successors; secondly, the Prelates who point to Peter's role as a chief officer of the Church, and thirdly, those who regard Peter as a minister of the Word, and so assign the keys to all other ministers equally:

> But we for our partes do beleeve and professe that this promise is not made to Peter in any of these forenamed respects, nor to any office, order, estate, dignity, or degree in the Church, or world, but to the confession of faith, which Peter made. . . . So the building of the Church is vpon the rock of Peters confession.[190]

Peter's successors, then, are all of those who share his confession, so that "one faithful man, yea or woman eyther" may as effectively loose and bind as all the ministers in the world, with this qualification, that in matters of discipline the keys may be turned "onely vpon them which are within," that is, only those who are members of a true Church.[191]

Calvin, too, had spoken of Peter's confession as the common foundation of the whole Church, but he found in this passage that Peter is afforded a twofold honor, the first in regard to his own salvation, the second to his apostolic office. As to the former Peter is indeed joined to "all believers who are going to exist in the world," but in the second sense—in binding and loosing—Peter is succeeded by "ministers of the Gospel [who] are like gatekeepers of the Kingdom of heaven, because they bear its keys."[192] According to this reading, then, the exercise of discipline was vested only mediately in the congregation since it was a specifically ministerial function.

More pertinent still for the Separatist rationale of discipline was the other Matthean passage (18:15-17) which contains the word ἐκκλησία:

> If your brother sins against you, go and tell him his fault, between you and him alone. If he listens to you, you have gained your brother. But if he does not listen, take one or two others along with you, that every word may be confirmed by the evidence of two or three witnesses. If he refuses to listen to them, tell it to the church; and if he refuses to listen even to the church, let him be to you as a Gentile and a tax collector (RSV).

Robinson, it will be remembered, was "converted" to the Separatist way while listening to a sermon on this very text. It contained, he later told Ames, the "main ground of our difference from the Church of Eng-

---

[190] Ibid., 149-50.

[191] Ibid.

[192] Calvin's *New Testament Commentaries*, vol. 2, 186-89. "Dicit enim Christus, evangelii ministros regni coelorum esse quasi ianitores, quia claves eius gestent." *Corpus Reformatorum*, vol. 45, 474. Cf. *Inst.* 4,6.11-15.

land."[193] Robinson encountered two contrary interpretations of these verses in his attempt to derive therefrom a uniform pattern of discipline. First, Bernard asserted, the offenses spoken of here are private, secret injuries, not matters pertaining to public admonitions and censures. Consequently, they must not be used as a model for the handling of all matters of church discipline.[194] Bernard put forth five reasons to prove that Christ spoke, in these verses, "according to the tyme." That is, the procedures of admonition and correction were intended to moderate "the Jewes passion for private injuries," with the "church" referring to the Sanhedrin Council from which the only appeal was to "Caesars barr." Robinson responded with ten reasons of his own to prove that the passage applied to the internal discipline of the Church, four of which we may note here. 1) The term "brother" applied to many, such as believing Romans and Samaritans, who could not be brought before the Sanhedrin. 2) The word ἁρμαρτάνω generally refers to sin, not to private injuries. 3) If the offense was a personal injury, then its resolution would not be the gaining of a brother, but the gaining of goods or the regaining of reputation. 4) The binding and loosing are effected in heaven as well as upon earth. By the end of the tenth reason Robinson admitted that the discussion had become a rather "tedious matter," though he declared himself ready to answer, tit for tat, Bernard's "eight fresh reasons" on this text![195] At stake in Robinson's refusal to restrict the offense in question to private, secret misdemeanors was the communal character of the Church itself. No sin was too small or insignificant but that it might not sour or leaven the whole "lump of communion" if not corrected in accordance with the procedures outlined in Matthew 18.

Granted that the offense fell within the bounds of ecclesiastical discipline, it remained to decide what was meant by the "church" to which it should be told. Robinson reviewed three interpretations of this word, corresponding to three distinct systems of discipline, all of which he regards as patently unscriptural.[196] First, there are those who made the

---

[193]*A Manumission to a Manuduction*, 20.

[194]This was precisely Whitgift's argument against Cartwright, citing "the note that is in the margent of the bible printed at Geneva" where the offense is said to be "of secret or particular sins, and not of open or known to others." *Works of Whitgift*, vol. 1, 203.

[195]*Justification*, 177-82.

[196]Stephen Brachlow, in seeking to show that the "ecclesiological distinctions between left-wing puritanism and separatism were fluid and sometimes almost entirely blurred," has criticized Basil Hall for "misquoting" an earlier passage in the *Justification* in which Robinson had sharply distinguished the papist, Protestant (Anglican), and Puritan positions on Matt. 18:15-17 from his own congregationalist interpretation. It is true that

"church" here refer to the civil court of the magistrate, thus vesting disciplinary powers in secular authorities. Robinson had in mind, no doubt, the theory of the Heidelberg physician Thomas Erastus which was attacked with special vehemence by Beza, Zanchi, and others. Closer to home, there were some who understood by the "church" the hierarchical bishop, with his officials, and others, the senate of elders excluding the people. Both of these interpretations, Robinson believed, undermined, in opposite but equally vitiating ways, the clear meaning of the text: the former, the episcopalian option, located the power of discipline in an extra-congregational institution; the latter, presbyterian method delegated it to an "oligarchic" body within the congregation.[197] Calvin was the chief architect of the less inclusive system, claiming that Church order under Christ was based on the synagogical practice of the Jews in which the power of excommunication rested with the elders as representatives of the entire body. Thus the governance of the Church, seen as an "appendage to teaching" (*appendix doctrinae*), is committed to a consistory composed both of the ministers of the Word and certain members from the laity (*ex plebe*) who serve jointly as the collective censor of morals in the congregation.[198] Such a system, Robinson believed, did linguistic as well as theological violence to the text:

> And first the word ἐκκλησία, church, originally Greek, answering to the Hebrew *qahal*, doth primarily and properly signify a convention of citizens called from their houses by the public crier, either to hear some public sentence or charge given: but translated to religious use, denoteth an assembly of persons called out of the state of corrupt nature into that of supernatural grace, by the publishing of the gospel.[199]

Thus, both the Matthew 18 passage, and I Cor. 5, the other *locus biblicus* invariably cited in discussions of Church discipline, assign disciplinary prerogatives "to the whole body together of every christian congregation,

---

Robinson's main purpose in this passage was to refute the charge that Separatist polity excluded "the Elders in the case of government." Brachlow, however, does not point out that Robinson, returning to this passage later in the same treatise, reiterated the same fourfold differentiation with even greater emphasis. Cf. Brachlow, "Puritan Theology and Radical Churchmen," 6-7.

[197]Interestingly, of these two positions Robinson judges the episcopal to come "nearer the truth" in that the bishops nor the commissaries exclude the people from their proceedings, but "offer themselves in their public judgments and censures to the view of all who please to be present thereat." *Works*, vol. 3, 33.

[198]*Calvin's New Testament Commentaries*, vol. 2, 230-31 *Corpus Reformatorum*, vol. 45, 515. This was, in essence, the system of discipline proposed by English Puritans. See Travers, *A Full and Plaine Declaration*, 157-93.

[199]*Works*, vol. 3, 33.

and not to any one member a part, or to more members sequestered from the whole."[200]

The focal point of Church discipline was, of course, the rite of excommunication which, as we have seen, Robinson understood as a distinctive ordinance of the new dispensation. It differed from the Old Testament penalties of expulsion and execution primarily in its *spiritual* character. With respect to the person excommunicated it was remedial in intent, not designed "for the ruyne, and destruction of any, but for the salvation of the party thereby humbled."[201] With respect to the congregation it was a re-affirmation of the covenant by which the community was initially gathered, and a measure of its viability as a "lively Church." Robinson's objections against excommunication as it was practiced in the Church of England fall into two categories. First, there is the usual Puritan complaint that gross offenders are let off with little or no punishment while the machinery of the Church courts is turned against those most zealous for reform. Those guilty of

> treason, witchcraft, incest, buggery, rape, murders, and the like . . . receive condigne punishmet; Where with us if any such enormities arise, those monsters (without their answerable repentance) are by the power of Christ cut of from the body, and do for the most part returne to their proper element the English synagogue.[202]

So corrupt was the Church court system in England that "a good word of a friend or a small bribe" could often stay the excommunication of the worst offender. Moreover, the absolution of excommunicates, especially

---

[200]*Justification*, 124. Robinson's "congregationalist" reading of Matthew 18 was anticipated by developments in the continental Reformation, both in its Radical and Reformed expressions, as well as by earlier Separatists in England. One of the earliest attempts to derive the practice of the ban from this text occurs in Conrad Grebel's famous letter to Thomas Müntzer, dated (Sept. 4, 1524) some five months before the decisive act of rebaptism: "Zuch mit dem wort und mach ein christenlich gmein mit hilf Christi und siner regel, wie wir sy ingestzt findend Mathei im xviii. und gebrucht in den epistlen . . . . Welcher sich nit besseren, nit glouben wil und dem wort und hendlen Gottes widerstrebt und also verhart, den sol man, nach dem im Christus und sin wort, sin regel geprediget, und er ermanet wirt mit den drien zügen und der gmein, den, sprechend wir uss gottes wort bericht, sol man nit totten, sunder ein heiden und zoller achten und sin lassen." *Quellen zur Geschichte der Täufer in der Schweiz*, eds. Leonhard von Muralt and Walter Schmid (Zurich, 1952), vol. 1, 17. A theory of congregational polity was advanced in the French Reformed Church by Jean Morély whose book *Traicté de la discipline and police Chrestienne* was printed in 1562. Unlike Robinson Morély denied women the right to participate in disciplinary decisions, and, in his effort to accommodate his theory to the synodical structure of the French Church, sacrificed somewhat the autonomy of the congregation. See Robert M. Kingdon, *Geneva and the Consolidation of the French Protestant Movement, 1564-1572* (Madison, Wis., 1967), 43-62.

[201]*Justification*, 120.

[202]Ibid., 58.

sexual offenders, involved a lavish display which smacked of popery, and was, in any event, tied to the removal of "civil" penalties often unrelated to the offense.[203]

Far more serious to Robinson's mind than the particular abuses of discipline in the Church of England was the fact that congregations did not retain the right of excommunication at all, but were subject to "forreyners and strangers" in this vital matter.[204] Faced with the charge that Separatist polity would permit one man to excommunicate the whole Church, Robinson replied to Bernard that it is not

> more then your Church allowes to any Bp. in Engl.: for one Bishop with you may excommunicate a thousand Churches: every Diocesan Bishop all the Churches in his Dioces, the two Provincial Bishops their two Provinces, so lively do the reverend fathers the Bishops resemble the holy father the Pope, which may judge all men, but be judged by none.[205]

The minister of every parish, reduced to the status of "the Bishops mans man," is thus expected to read the court official's sentence to the congregation, though even this perfunctory task is made unnecessary by the posting of the bull of excommunication on the church door by the summoner.[206] This procedure grossly violated the relationship of spiritual concern and mutual watchfulness which was essential to the disciplinary process. This was illustrated by the fact that the sentence of excommunication was frequently pronounced "fourty miles off from the body of the congregation," without even the presence or "privity eyther . . . of any one of the body."[207] The intrusion of such "forreyn ayd, and assistance" deprived the congregation of the right to maintain its own life, forcing it to subsist in parasitic relation to an extraneous body. Even when faced

---

[203] Ibid., 57. The procedure Robinson had in mind is illustrated by the case of Elizabeth Stubbyn who was required to make the following penance for fornication in 1611: "That the sayde Elizabeth shall three seuerall Sondayes next and immediately followinge stand penitently in the middle ally of the parishe church of Tacolneston aforesayd nigh unto the minister's seate there from the begyninge of morninge prayer, homely read or sermon preached, untill the whole ende and accomplishinge of these devyne and holy exercises, clothed and haveinge about and uppon her body a white sheete downe to the skirtes of her upper garment, with a white rodd in her hand, and a paper written in capitall letters conteyninge the cause of her offence; and after thr readinge of the Gospel . . . the sayd Elizabeth shall make publique confession of her synne." *The Registrum Vagum of Anthony Harison*, vol. 1, 143-44. An unabsolved excommunicate might be deprived of the assistance of a midwife, or forfeit the right to burial in consecrated ground. See R. A. Marchant, *The Church Under the Law* (London, 1969), 220-26.

[204] *Justification*, 123.

[205] Ibid., 124-25.

[206] Ibid., 244, 123.

[207] Ibid., 158.

with open atheism in its midst, all the congregation could do was call in "Mr. Official." "What remedy hath the church?" asked Robinson.[208]

The Puritans who remained within the Church of England proposed a remedy less severe than formal excommunication, but one intended to safeguard the congregation against the contagion of an obstinate offender: the practice of suspending from Communion those deemed unworthy to participate. The Prayer Book permitted any incumbent to exercise this prerogative, and it was used liberally by the forward preachers as is clear from the "Minute Book" of the Dedham classis.[209] However, Collinson's statement that "the puritans equated suspension from the sacrament with excommunication" is not borne out by the manuals of discipline which treat the former as a preliminary step in the correction process.[210] The Separatists, in any event, repudiated the practice of suspension as a totally inadequate halfway measure based on expediency rather than scriptural precedent. Robinson spoke of the "wooden dagger" of suspension as "a matter of form for the most part, and a remedy as ill as the disease."[211] Suspension, Robinson thought, violated the congregational principle at two points: first, it assigned to a less inclusive institution, the minister according to the Prayer Book, the elders according to presbyterian theory, the discretionary power which belonged only to the whole body; and, it undercut the corporate character of the Lord's Supper which, like the covenant and baptism, pertained to all members not excommunicated as "badges of their association."[212]

Robinson's uncompromising congregationalism may appear as a static legalism or an obsession with external form when divorced from the fundamental Christological context in which he placed it.[213] Drawing

[208]Ibid., 125, 80. *Works*, vol. 3, 68.

[209]Usher, *Presbyterian Movement, op. cit.*, 69-73.

[210]Also, in presbyterian theory, suspension, like excommunication, was the proper function of the local consistory, not the minister alone. Cf. Travers, *A Full and Plaine Declaration*, 164: "Now suspension is a charge geven, by the assembly of the Elders to absteyne a certen tyme from the communication off the supper off Lord," and John Udall, *A Demonstration of Discipline* (London, 1588), 75: "Those that be not reclaimed from their faultes by admonition, are by the Eldership to be suspended from the Lords supper."

[211]*Justification*, 91; *Works*, vol. 3, 68. The issue of suspension had surfaced in Barrow's conference with the Puritan Sperin: "Where finde you in all Christ's Testament that one man may separate anie alone?... Christ never gave anie such censure as this suspencion to his church, or such power to anie one man to seperate anie from the sacraments, which is not pronounced excommunicat." *The Writings of John Greenwood, 1587-1590*, 184.

[212]*Works*, vol. 3, 434.

[213]P. D. L. Avis, for example, regards the Separatist emphasis on discipline as "a legalistic obsession with the Church's circumference," which obscured its proper Christo-

together a series of Biblical images Robinson explained the "near union" between Christ and his Church in terms of the multiple metaphors of vine/branches, head/body, and husband/wife:

> as the branches do receive and draw the sap and juice immediately from the vine, and as the body receiveth sense and motion from the head immediately, and as the wife hath immediate right to, and interest in her husbands both person and goods . . . so hath every true visible Church of Christ direct, and immediate interest in and title to Christ himselfe . . . without any vnnaturall, monstrous, and adulterous interposition by any person whatsoever. [214]

All of these, of course, are organic relationships, and thus complement the imagery of edification discussed earlier. More pervasive than any of these, however, is the theological rubric of the *triplex munus Christi*, the communal embodiment of which Robinson locates in the true visible Church. Robinson described the divine commissioning of Christ by the Father as an anointing with the oil of gladness, an anointing which Christ in turn "communicates" with his body, thus transforming every member severally into "Kings and Priests and all ioyntly a Kingly Priesthood, or communion of Kinges, Preists, and Prophets." So "plenteous" is this anointing that it more than suffices for each individual member, so that "every one is made a King, Preist, and Prophet, not onely to himself, but to every other, yea to the whole." Thus each member is a prophet to teach and exhort, a priest to offer up spiritual sacrifices of prayer and praise, a king to guide and govern. This anointing, moreover, is so equitably distributed throughout the congregation that there is not the "meanest" member of the body but "hath received his drop or dram" of the divine unction.[215] The measure of identity between Christ and the Church is thus expressed in terms of a twofold intercommunication of the triple office: that of Christ to each member of the congregation, and that of the members to each other.

Seen from another perspective the threefold office of Christ corresponded to three vital acts of corporate *worship*, each of them essential to

---

logical center. *Church in the Theology of the Reformers*, 63. This hasty characterization, however, does not take into account the Separatists' own rationale for discipline, which is invariably explained in terms of edification and union with Christ.

[214]*Justification*, 131-32.

[215]Ibid., 133. Significantly, the Separatist *Confession* of 1596 has only one article on the Person of Christ, but devotes nine (Articles 10-18) to the threefold Office. *Creeds and Platforms*, 61-65. In Calvin the *triplex munus* is used primarily to describe the role of Christ in the "objective" procurement of salvation. Cf. *Inst.* 2,15.1-6; J. F. Jansen, *Calvin's Doctrine of the Work of Christ* (Edinburg, 1964). In commenting on I Peter 2:9 Calvin refers to the elect in general, as opposed to a particular congregation, as "associates of His kingdom, and partakers of His priesthood." *Calvin's New Testament Commentaries*, vol. 12, 266.

the furtherance of life within the Church. The Priestly and Prophetical offices are administered in prayer and preaching, and the Kingly office in government. Of the three Robinson placed greatest emphasis on the Kingly aspect because he believed it was the most likely to be neglected: "For the kingdome of the Lord Iesus is as glorious, as his preisthood, or propheticall office: and his throne is to be advanced as high, and made as conspicuous to the eyes of all, as his altar, or pulpit."[216] For this reason he insisted that disciplinary procedures be carried out as a part of the regular service of worship:

> And if the collections for the saynts which concernes they body, be a Lords, or first dayes work, how much more the spirituall ordinances which respect the soule, eyther for humiliation, or comfort?[217]

Following the usual order of service, the offender would be publicly admonished by the officers of the congregation, and upon his impenitence solemnly declared excommunicate "with the people's free consent." The consent could be given by voice, sign, or even silence so long as the liberty to speak, "eyther by way of addition, limitation, or dissent" was preserved.[218] Robinson extended the right to participate in the disciplinary process to all children who had reached the "yeares of discretion" as well as to women, the Pauline injunction to silence notwithstanding. In fact, in rare cases, or when the men are negligent, women may reprove the entire Church rather than allow it to continue in an obvious error. In an apt appeal, no doubt, to the experience of many of his readers, Robinson likened those who would restrict full congregational participation in disciplinary procedures to "the mighty oppressours in the world" who inclose all the commons of their poor neighbors in order to increase their own power: "But if the Lord denounce such heavy judgments against the inclosers of earthly things, Is. 5.8.9. what whilbe the end of those spirituall ingrossers and oppressours, if they repent not?"[219]

For one who placed so much emphasis upon the necessity of excommunication and the procedures to be followed in its execution, Robinson is surprisingly silent about particular sins which might lead to such a

---

[216] *Justification*, 229.

[217] Ibid., 224.

[218] Ibid., 206. *Works*, vol. 3, 435. The order of worship followed by the Leyden congregation was probably similar to that of the Ancient Church as outlined by Clifton: (1) prayer, (2) reading of Scripture, (3) extended exposition of Scripture by pastor or teacher, (4) administration of Sacraments, (5) singing of Psalms, (6) collection. Ibid., 485.

[219] *Justification*, 203. On other elements of social protest embodied in Separatist discipline, see Christopher Hill, *Society and Puritanism in Pre-Revolutionary England,* op. cit., 228-42.

drastic step. In his appendix to Perkins' catechism, he requires that only "scandalous" offences be censured, but the emphasis is upon the obstinancy of the offender, and his refusal to submit to the Lordship of Christ as it is conveyed through the royal assembly of saints. Obviously, of paramount concern was the effect of the Church's witness to those without which would be blunted by retaining a notorious offender in full fellowship.[220] Excommunication was clearly related to the visibility of the Church, to its growth in sanctification. It was not, as Smyth seemed to regard it, a proleptic judgment on the eternal destiny of the person excommunicated; the Church in casting off an offender for some scandalous sin did not thereby reject or deny the faith which he professed nor any virtue or grace which he might retain.[221] Excommunication was to the individual member what "dis-churching" was to the entire body: an ever-present possibility whenever the process of growth and edification had given way to spiritual stupor and decay.

As the Kingly office of Christ manifested itself in the communal acts of censure and excommunication, so the Prophetic office found expression in the distinctive ordinance of prophesying. This too was an aspect of public worship, but it took place after the regular service, that is, after "the ministerial teaching" was ended.[222] It provided an opportunity for ordinary members to exercise whatever gifts of interpretation or exhortation they might have, as well as to raise questions, or voice doubts about

---

[220] *Works*, vol. 3, 434. The right of excommunication was "absolutely necessary to the Church," Robinson held, because the salvation of "them without" would be "most disadvantaged and hindered" by the unholy and prophane life-style of an uncorrected church member. *Justification*, 351. Perhaps this was the motive behind the unusual excommunication by the Gainsborough church of a tailor who took seven shillings for making "a Doublet and Hose" when the going price was five! Bernard, *Plaine Evidences*, op. cit., 117.

[221] *Smyth*, vol. 2, 746: "The seperating of the impenitent . . . is a figure of the eternal reiection and reprobation of them that persist impenitent in sinne." *Justification*, 65. In Robinson's scheme, while the Church was to withdraw all spiritual communion and civil familiarity from the excommunicate, this "shunning" did not extend to every relationship—"the rights of nature, family, and commonwealth ever kept inviolated." *Works*, vol. 3, 41. For comparison with Anabaptist practice, see W. E. Keeney, *The Development of Dutch Anabaptist Thought* (Nieuwkoop, 1968), 162-69.

[222] *Works*, vol. 3, 327. The Reformation phenomenon of prophesying derived from the Biblical seminars attended by ministers and Divinity students in Zürich in the 1520s. As a common feature of Reformed church life, it was primarily a *ministerial* activity, providing a kind of extramural fellowship and continuing theological education. The Separatist adaptation, decisively *lay* in its orientation, was more exactly foreshadowed by the congregational prophesying of the Strangers' Churches under Laski Cf. *Elizabethan Puritan Movement*, 168-76; G. F. Nuttall, *The Holy Spirit in Puritan Faith and Experience* (London, 1946), 75-89.

the formal exposition of Scripture, in other words to "say on," as Robinson put it, quoting Acts 13:15. Robinson's most extensive treatment of prophesying appeared in 1618 as *The Peoples Plea for the Exercise of Prophecy, against Mr. John Yates his Monopolie*.[223] Yates and others were shocked at the practice of lay prophesying which, they alleged, gave to "every mechanical person" the liberty to preach publicly in the church.[224] Yates, an expert in Ramist logic, argued ably against the Separatist use of prophesying, claiming 1) that prophecy in the New Testament was extraordinary and, like the gift of tongues, now defunct; 2) that the ordinary exercise of prophecy was permitted only to those duly installed in office by the imposition of hands; and 3) that the prohibition against women speaking in public worship was later extended to include all laity.[225] Robinson admitted that the gift of extraordinary prophecy had, for the most part, ceased, but he characterized Yates' equation of lay prophecy with this supernatural gift as "extraordinary licentiousness and presumption."[226] Further, the refusal to permit men to prophesy "but by officing them" contradicted the practice not only of the New Testament, but of the Reformed Church as well. Robinson supported this claim by a reference to the Synod of Emden (1571) which had held that "into this fellowship, to wit of prophets, should be addmitted not only the ministers, but also the teachers, and of the elders and deacons, and even of the very common people (*ex ipsa plebe*)."[227]

While edification of the whole body was the aim of lay prophecy, congregational participation was limited in two important respects. First, in accordance with Paul at this point, women were not allowed to participate, unless they were "immediately, and extraordinarily, and miraculously inspired," in which case they might speak without restraint.[228] Also in contrast to the participation of the whole body in the

---

[223]Robinson addressed this treatise to his "Christian Friends in Norwich and thereabouts." Yates was the incumbent at St. Andrew's, where Robinson had ministered in his pre-Separatist days. *Works*, vol. 3, 285. See Keith L. Sprunger, "John Yates of Norfolk: Puritan Preacher and Ramist," *Journal of the History of Ideas* 38 (1976), 697-706.

[224]Ibid., 8.

[225]Ibid., 292. Refuting the argument from ordination Robinson claims that "imposition of hands is no cause at all of prophecy, to speak properly, as Mr. Yates should do, affecting the same of a logician."

[226]Ibid., 319. Robinson takes the prophesying among the Corinthians to be of the ordinary variety, since Paul urges all of them to "covet" it, an inappropriate admonition if the gift were a specialized revelation.

[227]Ibid., 334.

[228]*Justification*, 237.

procedures of censure and excommunication, prophesying required a special "calling" which should be acknowledged to the minister and others before speaking in the public service, although the minister, who presided over the prophesying, had no right to silence any person who was "willing to confer their gift received of God to the common utility of the church."[229] In actual practice the ordinance of prophesying known to Robinson was far from a charismatic free-for-all. Apparently few members were cognizant of the calling—"happily two or three in each of our churches"—and these were apt to be those most able to speak and teach.[230] Indeed, the prophesying seems to have functioned as a training ground for prospective officers, both in providing a forum for the exercise of their gifts, and by permitting the congregation to judge their suitability:

> Mens gifts, and abilities should be known in some measure, before they be once thought on, for officers: and . . . there is none other use, or tryall of those gifts, but in prophesying.[231]

The corporate manifestation of the Priestly office was displayed in the practice of congregational prayer. Robinson defined prayer in general as "the making known our requests to God, according to his will, with fayth in his love, and the feeling of our own wants, in our hearts."[232] As such, true prayer is not an activity common to all, but rather the special ministry of the Holy Spirit by which the promises of God are confirmed to the elect to their comfort and edification. It is thus a "ready means of divine communion" in the most dire of circumstances:

> Not want of fellowship with men, nor solitarines of place, nor depth of dungeon, nor darknes of the night, nor thicknes of wals neyther: but his devout prayers will finde way of ascending unto God.[233]

Prayer is of two sorts: that which is in secret by him that is alone with God, and that which is public in the presence of the entire Church. The former offers certain advantages over the latter. For example, in private prayer a Christian may descend to such particulars, and freely express the "passage of his hearts affection," in a way which would not be appropriate in the company of the whole congregation. However, public prayer is an

---

[229] *Works*, vol. 3, 55.

[230] Ibid.

[231] *Justification*, 238. Cf. 125: "We make no dumb Ministers: neyther dare we admit of any man eyther for a teaching or governing Elder, of whose ability in prayer, a prophecying, and debating of Church matters we have not had good experience before he be so much as nominated to the office of Elder amoast vs."

[232] *Observations*, 248.

[233] Ibid., 252.

essential ingredient in true worship, and must be correctly "performed in the order, and ordinance of the church." This means in the first place that such prayer cannot be read or recited, but must be uttered spontaneously, that is it must not be "set or stinted," but conceived from the inward sighing and groaning of the Spirit, for

> if our prayers be not conceived first in our hearts before they be brought forth in our lips, they are an vnnaturall, bastardly, and prophane byrth.[234]

Like Barrow and Greenwood before him, Robinson did not hesitate to extend the injunction against liturgical prayer even to the Lord's Prayer on the grounds that it was not a prayer at all, properly so called (how could Christ who is sinless pray for forgiveness?), but rather a part of the Sermon on the Mount and thus a discourse on the nature of prayer.[235] Moreover, the reading of prayers detracted from the single-minded engagement of the suppliant: "Let him that prayeth do that which he doth, and not another, not a divers thing. Let the whole man, and all that he is, both in soul and body, be bent upon God, with whom he converseth."[236] Even the proper bodily gesture for public prayer, that of the lifting up of the eyes to heaven, is hindered by the need to focus them upon a book.[237] Written prayers, such as those of Augustine or Calvin, are of course edificatory and can be read with no small benefit by the minister and congregation alike, but only privately, for "better preparation unto prayer," and not instead of, or as a part of, prayer itself.

The performance of public prayer was a conspicuous part of Separatist gatherings, being the first item on their order of worship. The congregation would stand while the pastor or teacher invoked the name of God, and offered thanks and praise, "as the spirit directs their harts to conceive and giveth utterance, and that without the use of any book during that action."[238] Public prayer was thus attached to the pastoral office and

---

[234]*Justification*, 426.

[235]*Works*, vol. 3, 22-23. Robinson found further evidence that we were not "tied to this stint of words alone, and always," in the discrepancy between the Matthean and Lucan accounts both of which preserve the meaning of Christ, but not in the same words.

[236]Ibid., 26.

[237]Ibid. Robinson did not regard the lifting of the eyes as a "simple necessity," but rather as a convenient gesture designed "to express and further the intention of the godly heart" in accordance with the scriptural example (I Tim. 2:8). Robinson's opponents asked whether psalm-singing, a standard part of Separatist worship, did not violate their own rule against set prayers since the whole congregation have their "part for tuneable voice," and follow "a certain and set form, both of words and syllables." In reply, Robinson sharply distinguished singing and praying: in singing we speak to ourselves or to each other, but in praying only to God. Ibid., 20-21.

[238]Clifton, *A Plea for Infants* (Amsterdam, 1610), 10-11.

regarded as "a second part of the ministry." Freedom from liturgical forms permitted the minister to manifest his pastoral gift in conceiving "a prayer according to the church's present occasion, and necessities."[239] At the conclusion of the prayer the people are to add their "Amen" in accordance with the Pauline instruction (I Cor. 14:14-16), thus "by the same voice, banding as it were together," they pour out their prayers as evidence of their full and perfect communion in the holy things of God.[240]

The intimate character of congregational worship envisaged by Robinson presupposed, of course, that no particular Church should consist of more members than could meet together in one place. Thus the Church,

> commonly called visible, is then most truly visible indeed, when it is assembled in one place . . . when all its members inspired, as it were, with the same presence of the Holy Ghost, do from the same pastor, receive the same provocations of grace, at the same time, and in the same place.[241]

When pastors are burdened with "huge and vast flocks," and cannot be acquainted personally with the members committed unto him, then true piety suffers and laxity in discipline follows.[242] To the objection that there is one visible and catholic Church, encompassing all particular churches, as there is one ocean or sea which passes by many shores, Robinson responds, in accordance with nominalist epistemology, that universals or things catholic are in the understanding only, that is, they are mental constructs abstracted of circumstantial accidents, while the "kinds intelligible" have their existence in nature, that is in the individuals.[243] Moreover, each particular assembly of saints, duly covenanted, has the full right to be called "the body of Christ," or "the temple of God" without reference to any extra-congregational authority—"without any either subordination, or co-ordination, or dependency spiritual, save unto Christ alone."[244]

---

[239] *Works*, vol. 3, 27.

[240] Ibid., 13. Cf. Justification, 234: "In prayer one officer vtters the voice, and the rest of the Church say, Amen, & so all communicate."

[241] Ibid.

[242] With reference to the Dutch Reformed churches in Leyden, Robinson proposed that city churches, bloated by the continual accession of members, be divided into different and distinct congregations, with their own pastors and elders. Ibid., 14.

[243] Ibid.

[244] Ibid., 15. Robinson's insistence upon congregational autonomy precluded any subordination to synodical or conciliar structures. He did, however, admit that "messengers" from various churches could meet together to discuss matters of common interest, and that such a meeting could even be called a "Church Synode," provided "they

"Not lords but servaunts of the Church":
The Doctrine of the Ministry

The conception of church government put forth by Robinson seemed to his Puritan critics to subordinate the ministry so completely to the gathered congregation as to deprive it of any independent status. In responding to the "many lowd clamours of Anabaptistry, and Popularity [which] are raysed agaynst our government," Robinson denied that the Separatists lacked an ecclesiastical ministry or proper church order, but he insisted that church-governors be "not lords but servaunts" of the congregation, that in the exercise of their ministry they wield, in the words of Bernard of Clairvaux, not a scepter but a weeding-hook.[245] The issue of the relative balance of power between officers and congregation was a problem of long standing in Separatist polity, and in Robinson's definition of Church and ministry both popular control and executive rule are tempered in the interests of communal edification.[246]

As the community of visible saints must be gathered by covenanting before it can proceed to select leaders from among the members, it follows that the Church is prior, both logically and temporally, to its officers. Thus a company of saints may, and must in the "first planting," be fully a Church without officers, though it never lacks the *right* to this benefit. In other words, officers belong to the *bene esse*, but not to the *esse*, of a true visible Church.[247] Church officers are in no sense an "absolutely necessary appurtenance" unto the congregation, although they are intended to "aedifie the body" and further the faith of the saints over whom they are set. Robinson insisted that the process of selection resided entirely with the congregation in contrast both to the idea that ministerial authority

---

infringe no order of Christ, or liberty of the brethren." *Justification*, 200. On one occasion Robinson and other delegates from the Leyden Church returned to Amsterdam, at the request of the Ancient Church, to help mediate the dispute between Johnson and Ainsworth, an endeavor which met with no success. Cf. Ainsworth, *An Animadversion to Clyfton's Advertisement* (Amsterdam, 1613), 110-17; *Separatist Tradition*, 149-53.

[245] *Of Religious Communion*, 23; *Works*, vol. 3, 61.

[246] Two recent studies of Robinson's doctrine of the ministry have arrived at varying assessments: David D. Hall, *The Faithful Shepherd: A History of the New England Ministry in the Seventeenth Century* (Chapel Hill, N.C., 1972), 36-47; Stephen Brachlow, "Puritan Theology and Radical Churchmen," 322-34. Hall groups Robinson with Smyth whose elevation of the congregation above the ministry robbed the latter of all but "a token sacerdotalism" (p. 41), while Brachlow regards Robinson's attempt to achieve a balance between popular and restrictive tendencies as similar to the larger Puritan quest to formulate a satisfactory polity.

[247] *Justification*, 130. In another context Robinson declares that officers are of, by, in, and for the Church: of it, as members of the body; by it, in respect to their calling; in it, as the accidents or adjuncts in the subject; for it, as aids to its edification. Ibid., 361.

was passed on by succession within a special order, and to the Reformed practice of screening candidates for the ministry through an extra-congregational body, such as the presbytery or company of pastors. To emphasize this point, he gives the hypothetical example of a company of faithful men and women, raised up by the Lord "in America, or the like place," through the instructions of merchants or travellers. How should they come by ministers? Should ministers be sent unto them from Europe? He then asks rhetorically:

> But what to do hath the Pope of Rome, or the Bishops in England, or the Presbytery in Germany, or France to appoynt them in America Ministers?

Such an assembly would be invested with the full power to choose and appoint their own ministers "from within themselves."[248] And, as each congregation retains the inherent right "to braunch out it self" into officers, so it may also "lop, or break off" any officer whose ministry proves unfruitful.[249] A pilot of a ship is to be obeyed by all on board, but if he run upon the sands, he may be lawfully replaced by the passengers with a fitter navigator. Thus in matters of church governance, even "the meanest member" reserves a measure of discretion: he is not bound to obey the determinations of the officers, except as they agree with "order and comliness." And the officer is ever accountable to the congregation for the actions he has taken.

In congregational theory induction to the ministry consists of two steps: election and ordination. By the former the persons chosen have right to their offices, by the latter they are solemnly admitted into the actual possession thereof. In support of the popular election of officers Robinson cited the New Testament example of Paul and Barnabas who ordained elders in various cities only after the suffrage of the churches (Acts 14:23), signified by the lifting up of hands in keeping with the customary mode of voting in the Greek assemblies.[250] In the Leyden congregation two groups, women on account of their sex and children on account of their age, were prohibited from voting in church elections, although they were permitted to be present when the vote was taken.[251] Following the election the duly installed officers, if there be any, would pronounce the person elected to his office and commence the procedure of ordination which consisted of public prayer and the imposition of

---

[248] Ibid., 420.

[249] Ibid., 130.

[250] *Works*, vol. 3, 38.

[251] Ibid., 43.

hands. Ordination was thus "properly the exequution of election."[252] In contrast to the practice of some Reformed churches which had eliminated the imposition of hands from the ordination ceremony, Robinson felt that this was an important part of the induction process. As the mayor at his entrance into office receives the keys of the city at the hands of his predecessor, so it is most appropriate for the newly elected minister to be ordained by the former officers of the congregation. However, in the event that the congregation is bereft of other officers, or the occasion is such that they cannot be present, it is not necessary, nor permitted, to bring in the officers of another Church for the laying on of hands. Rather must the congregation in this exigency "vse other the fittest instruments it hath."[253] Thus, while Robinson criticized the Anglican theory of ordination (in England, he said, ordination is "all in all") which "swallowes vp the peoples liberty," and while he renounced his own ordination received at Cambridge, he nonetheless prescribed a serious and solemn ordinance for ministerial induction in the gathered Church.

Robinson's reason for making the act of ordination an intra-congregational affair is clear enough: the scope of the ministry does not extend beyond the particular Church in which one is elected and ordained. To be sure, a minister, like any other member, may impart whatever spiritual gift he has received to other churches "out of the common bond of charity," but he may do so only as an individual Christian, and not in his capacity as a church officer.[254] As a mayor out of his corporation, or sheriff out of his county, or a constable out of his parish is no mayor, sheriff, or constable,

> so neyther is a Bishop, or Elder, a Church Officer, save in his owne particular Church, and charge, and in relation vnto it, neyther can he without ambitious vsurpation perform any proper work of his Office, or Ministry, save in that Church by, and to which, in his ministration, he is designed.[255]

From this it follows that should a true visible Church cease to be a Church, through apostasy or death or the like, then a minister ceases to be a minister until such time as he may be called and installed by another congregation.

---

[252]*Justification*, 415.

[253]Ibid., 420.

[254]*Works*, vol. 3, 17.

[255]*Justification*, 395. Cf. *Works*, loc. cit.: "It is not lawful for thee, reverend brother, to do the work of a pastor where thou art no pastor. Thou art called, that is elected, and ordained, a pastor of some particular church, and not of all churches."

Robinson, in keeping with Calvin, believed that the extraordinary offices of apostle, prophet, and evangelist, so prominent in the New Testament, were temporary in nature and had ceased at the end of the apostolic age.[256] He accepted in theory the fivefold ministry of pastors, teachers, elders, deacons, and helpers enumerated in the *Confession* of 1596, although two of these offices, that of teacher and helper, were apparently never filled by the Leyden congregation.[257] Robinson sometimes refers to both pastor and "lay" governors as elders, accepting the distinction between a teaching and a ruling eldership. Thus he claims that those elders, that is, pastors and teachers, who labor in the Word and doctrine should have "speciall honour" above those who are employed in ruling.[258] This honor, of course, pertained not to their persons, but to their office by which they stood "in the very stead of Christ, and of God himselfe," and on account of which they were "absolutely and simply to be obeyed" insofar as they faithfully ministered the Word.[259] Moreover, while the congregation could, in the absence of a pastor, perform most of those duties which were vital to its fellowship—it could receive new members by profession of faith, censure and excommunicate offending members, and have the Word expounded through lay prophesying— Robinson drew the line at the administration of the Lord's Supper. The issue came to a head when Robinson was forced to remain in Leyden and the congregation at New Plymouth was left without the use of either sacrament. When an "adversary" of the Church criticized this abstention, Bradford responded:

> the more in our Greiff that our Pastour is Kept from vs by whom wee might Injoy them; for wee vsed to haue the Lords Supper euery sabbath and Baptismee as often as there was occation of Children to Baptise.[260]

Apparently some members felt that Brewster, as ruling elder, should have been able to dispense the sacraments in the absence of the pastor. The question was put to Robinson, and he replied in a famous letter to Brewster:

> I judge it Not lawfull for you being a Ruleing Elder, as Rom 12:7,8: and first of tim: 5:17 opposed to the Elders that teach and exhort and labour in the

---

[256]*Justification*, 146-47. Cf. *Calvin's New Testament Commentaries*, vol. 11, 177-80.

[257]*Creeds and Platforms*, 65.

[258]*Justification*, 364. Cf. the reference to Robinson and Brewster as "ffellow Elders in the same fflock," *Plymouth Church Records*, vol. 1, 53.

[259]*Justification*, 219.

[260]*Plymouth Church Records*, vol. 1, 52.

word and doctrin to which the Sacrament[s] are anexed: to Adminnester them Nor Convenient if it were lawfull.[261]

Robinson's seemingly rigid position on this issue was not so unorthodox as some historians have imagined. The *Confession* of 1596 had declared that sacraments should not be administered "untill the Pastors or Teachers bee chosen and ordeyned into their Office."[262] Robinson's adherence to this policy sprang not from any desire to diminish the importance of the Lord's Supper, but rather from his recognition of the scriptural imperative in the manner as well as the substance of church ordinances.[263]

As for ruling elders, Robinson also accorded them a large measure of responsibility in the life of the congregation. They were charged, among other things, with the important tasks of admitting new members into the fellowship and of seeing that disciplinary procedures, including excommunication, were enforced against members duly corrected by the Church. They also presided at the election and ordination of new officers. These acts were valid, however, only when performed "with the people's privity and consent."[264] Robinson strongly criticized the custom, advocated in certain Puritan circles and practiced in the Dutch Reformed churches, whereby the elders administered church business only in their private consistory, sequestered from the congregation. This "consistorian course," Robinson argued, violates the public nature of the eldership, and prevents the congregation from participating in the deliberation of such matters as concern its welfare. This did not imply that the elders should never meet separately from the larger body to consider matters of church concern; but "it is not sufficient, neither do they indeed fulfil their public and church-office," until such matters are fully discussed openly, "in the face of the congregation."[265] The deacons, though differing in function

---

[261]Ibid., 54. Despite Robinson's unequivocal answer, the issue was shortly revived in Plymouth by John Lyford's attempt to administer the sacraments on the authority of his Anglican orders. Cf. William Hubbard, *A General History of New England* (Cambridge, Mass., 1815), 93-94.

[262]*Creeds and Platforms*, 70.

[263]See the helpful discussions of this issue in Mayor, *The Lord's Supper*, op. cit., 56-67; Nuttall, *The Holy Spirit in Puritan Faith*, op. cit., 90-101. On the question of baptism at the hands of lay members, Robinson has a more nuanced position. He still denies on the basis of I Tim. 5:17 that non-teaching elders may lawfully baptize, but he grudingly allows a Church wanting a pastor to "appoint a member able to teach (though out of office) to baptize." In this way the vital connection between the ministration of the Word and the performance of the sacraments is maintained. Cf. *A Defence of the Doctrine Propounded by the Synode at Dort* (Leyden, 1624), 179 [hereafter *Defence*].

[264]*Works*, vol. 3, 31.

[265]Ibid., 30.

from pastors and elders, were, like the other two officers, elected and
ordained for life. Unlike the "false, and forged office of half priesthood"
in the Church of England, the true diaconate was concerned with the
"bodily welfare" of the congregation. They collected the voluntary contri-
butions at the close of the worship service, and dispersed these funds for
the "common uses of the church," such as relief of the poor and maintenance of the officers.[266]

It is clear that Robinson attempted to strike a balance between the
liberty of the people and the authority of their leaders without sacrificing
the essence of either: the people are to "give their assent to their elders'
holy and lawful administration," but the officers are to remember that
theirs is "an order of service, and not of lordship."[267] In opposition to
Francis Johnson who, in his struggle with Ainsworth, elevated the
presbytery above the congregation and thus made the elders the sole
repository of Christ's regal office within the Church, Robinson returns to
his theme of mutual participation in the *triplex munus*:

> The saints are Christians, and that for, and in respect one of another, as
> members under Christ, one of another, and therefore kings. For to be a
> Christian for another is nothing else but by participation of Christ's anoint-
> ing, to be a priest, prophet, and king for another.[268]

Thus the Church is a "royall assembly" with each saint entitled to an equal
share in the benefits of Christ, with the officers discharging their duties
"not kingly but ministerially."[269] At the same time the officers "in their art
or work of government" are superior to the Church (else why were they
elected?) and thus should be accorded the dignity which becomes their
office. Perhaps Robinson's clearest statement on the relation between
ministerial service and congregational control is his application of the
categories of civil polity to the regiment of the Church. He finds elements
of all three classic polities, monarchy, aristocracy, and democracy, in the
Church order prescribed in the New Testament: in respect to Christ the
Head, it is a monarchy; in respect to the eldership, an aristocracy; in
respect to the whole body, a popular state. The relative balance between
the aristocratic and the democratic principles is further elucidated in
Robinson's response to Robert Parker who, in his book *De Politeia
Ecclesiastica Christi*, had attacked the Separatists' polity as "democracy,"
in the pejorative sense of mob rule:

[266] *Works*, vol. 3, 430; *Justification*, 346.

[267] *Works*, vol. 3, 43, 482.

[268] Ibid., 480-81.

[269] *Justification*, 133-34.

> And first in book one, page 101, he proclaimed our church government to be a democracy, when it is by no means such, but clearly an aristocracy, with respect to the eldership. Indeed, we do believe, the status of the church to be in some respects a democracy, but certainly not the government. On the contrary, with respect to Christ as its Head, it is a monarchy, and by reason of its administration, it is certainly an aristocracy.[270]

By thus distinguishing the *regimen ecclesiae* from the more basic *status ecclesiae* Robinson warded off the charge of having dissolved the ministry as a distinct and vital dimension of Church life while preserving his primary emphasis upon the commonality and equality of all members within the covenanted community. Thus by defining the scope and mandate of ministry exclusively in terms of the congregation, while still retaining a semi-sacerdotal conception of church officers, Robinson bequeathed to later congregationalists a coherent and balanced form of Church government.

"Half way back again" ?: The Limits of Fellowship

Thus far our analysis of Robinson's ecclesiology has revealed an understanding of the Church fully congruent, in its major lineaments, with the earlier Separatist tradition. However, Robinson's place in the Puritan-Separatist spectrum has been the subject of much debate, both in his own century and in ours. Here we touch upon the issue, raised earlier in chapter one, of the relationship between the "mature" Congregationalism of the 1640s and the more suspect "Brownist" variety of the late sixteenth and early seventeenth centuries. Robinson stood, as it were, at the convergence of these two streams, and it is not surprising that his indebtedness to earlier Separatism and his possible influence on later Independency would concern those who saw in him a denominational forbear. However, the attempt to portray Robinson as a somewhat-less-than full-fledged Separatist began shortly after his death with the appearance of John Cotton's *Way of Congregational Churches Cleared* which offered this assessment:

> Mr. Robinson was a man of the most learned, polished, and modest spirit, so piously studious and conscientiously inquisitive after the truth, that it had

---

[270]"Et primo lib. I. pag. 101. statuit, Regimen nostrum Ecclesiasticum Democraticum esse, quum minime sit: sed plane Aristocraticum, & prebyteriale. Statum quidem Ecclesiae nos aliquatenus Democraticum esse credimus, at regimen neutiquam: sed e contra, ut Christi capitis respectu, Monarchicum; sic and administrorum ratione, prorsus Aristocraticum." Robert Parker, *De Politeia Ecclesiastica Christi et Hierarchica Opposita* (Frankfort, 1616), sig. A 2 recto: "Admonitio I. R. ad Lectorem." For a complete transcription of Robinson's prefatory admonition, see Appendix.

been truly a marvel, if such a man as he, has gone on to the end of a rigid Separatist.[271]

Cotton also quoted with approval Robert Baillie's statement that Robinson came back indeed "the one half of the way," adding that "in coming on so far as he did, he came back more than half way of any just distance."[272] By the end of the seventeenth century, when Cotton Mather recounted the "Primordia" of New England's Church history, Robinson's relapse from strict Separatism was accepted as a standard part of an oft-told saga. Robinson is described as having been "in his *younger* time, (as very good Fruit hath sometimes been, before Age hath Ripened it) *Sowred* with the Principles of the most Rigid *Separation*," but afterwards, being enlightened, he embraced the position "which his mistaken *Zeal* had formerly impugned."[273]

It has usually been assumed that Robinson was weaned from his early Separatist convictions under the influence of Henry Jacob or William Ames, or both.[274] No correspondence between Jacob and Robinson is extant, but we know from Bradford's *Dialogue* that he, along with Ames

---

[271]*John Cotton on the Churches of New England*, ed. Larzer Ziff, op. cit., 182.

[272]Ibid., 183.

[273]Cotton Mather, *Magnalia Christi Americana*, ed. Kenneth Murdock, op. cit., 124.

[274]Since first advanced by Burrage in 1912 (*Early English Dissenters*, vol. 1, 33-34, 290-300) this position has been accepted by almost all historians of Congregationalism. It is, however, a revision of the traditional view which can be traced back at least to Neal, *History of the Puritans*, vol. 2, 107, who has Robinson influencing Jacob to embrace "his sentiments of Discipline and Government." Two recent studies of Jacob's relationship to Separatism have arrived at varying conclusions on the well-worn question of "who influenced whom." Walter R. Goehring, "Henry Jacob (1563-1624) and the Separatists," unpublished Ph.D. dissertation, New York University (1975), 247-72, claims that Jacob had "a marked influence" on Robinson's "dramatic" shift from Separatist to Congregationalist Puritan. Tolmie, *Triumph of the Saints,* op. cit., 8-12, 198 note 19, on the other hand, depicts the influence flowing in the other direction, with Jacob moving towards an Independent position as a result of his contacts with Robinson. Slayden A. Yarbrough, "Henry Jacob, A Moderate Separatist, and his Influence on Early English Congregationalism," unpublished Ph.D. dissertation, Baylor University (1972), 93-98, has clarified Jacob's final position by pointing to his distinction between true "churches of England" with which his Southwark congregation was in fellowship and the "false Church of England" from which he remained separated. Brachlow, "Puritan Theology and Radical Churchmen," loc. cit., has provided an excellent review of this question from Robinson's perspective and has concluded that while the Pilgrim pastor became "more flexible and accommodating" with the passing years, he did not abandon his firm commitment to the Separatist position. Also worthy of note are two recent articles on Jacob: John von Rohr, "The Congregationalism of Henry Jacob," *Transactions*, Congregational Historical Society 19 (1962) 106-17; Robert S. Paul, "Henry Jacob and Seventeenth-Century Puritanism," *Hartford Quarterly* 7 (1967), 92-113.

and Parker, were frequent visitors to Leyden, and on occasion lodged
with certain of the Pilgrims:

> Some of vs knew mr Parker doctor Ames and mr Jacob in holland when they
> sojourned for a time in Leyden and all three for a time boarded together and
> had theire victualls dressed by some of our acquaintance.[275]

All of these were men of keen intellect and strong personality, and each
pursued his own distinctive course of religious dissent: Ames was the chief
architect of non-separating congregationalism among the brethren of the
Puritan diaspora; Parker at first held to this position as well, but subsequently embraced presbyterian polity and joined the Dutch classis in
Amsterdam; Jacob passed from Puritan conformity to congregational
Independency before returning to England in 1616 to found at Southwark a non-parochial church with a voluntary membership. According to
the church record of the Southwark congregation, known as the Jessey
memorandum, Jacob's decision to organize the gathered Church in England occurred *after* "in the low Countries he had converse and discoursed
much with Mr Jn Robinson late Pastor to the Church in Leyden and with
others about them."[276] It is on the basis of this document that historians
from Neal to Tolmie have attributed to Robinson a significant measure of
influence in Jacob's developed ecclesiology. Robinson evidently considered Jacob's congregation to be a true visible Church, and accordingly
he welcomed Sabine Staresmore and his wife into the fellowship of the
Leyden Church on the basis of their covenant-taking at Southwark.[277]
However, in one important respect Jacob's congregation fell short of the
Separatist pattern: it permitted its members to practice intercommunion
with the parish churches without penalty of censure, thus acknowledging
them in some degree as true churches. It was, in other words, *separate* but
not *Separatist* in its stance toward the Church of England. Robinson too
was forced to come to grips with the issue of intercommunion, and while
he may have come "nearer to Henry Jacob than did the other Separatists," his position is clearly distinguishable and fully within the bounds of
the Separatist tradition.[278]

Robinson's thinking on the touchy subject of "secondary" separation,
that is, separation from "godly" persons who were not themselves

---

[275] *Plymouth Church Records*, vol. 1, 131.

[276] Regent's Park College, Oxford University, MS. Stinton, f. 1. The Jessey memorandum is one of several documents collected in 1712 by Benjamin Stinton in "A Repository
of Divers Historical Matters relating to the English Antipedobaptists." Cf. *Early English
Dissenters*. vol. 1, 336-56.

[277] *Works*, vol. 3, 384-85; Burgess, *Robinson*, 290-97.

[278] White, *Separatist Tradition*, 159.

members of a true visible Church, seems to have passed through several
stages, and his position does not admit of ready classification. The issue
came to the fore in a series of three letters between Ames and Robinson
written in 1611 when Ames was minister of the English Church at The
Hague. Ames described what he called "the very bitterness of Separation"
and argued for full fellowship among like-minded believers: "Whom-
soever I can rightly discern to have communion with Jesus Christ, with
him may I have visible communion." In reply, Robinson stressed the
priority of church order over private fellowship by giving two extreme
examples: if an innocent person be excommunicated from the Church, I
must forbear communion with him, until I can persuade the Church of his
innocency; and, if a brother in covenant commit some great wickedness
which he denies, and I cannot prove, I must keep communion with him
"for order's sake, till God discover him."[279] Clearly, at this stage private
fellowship outside of correct church order was not a viable option for
Robinson.

The controversy was accelerated when, in 1612, these letters were
published, with Ames' connivancy Robinson believed, but without his
"consent, privity, or least suspition of such dealing."[280] Two years later
Robinson responded with a major treatise, *Of Religious Communion,
Private and Publique*, in which he significantly modified his earlier
position by distinguishing personal from church actions, and by permitting private fellowship in the former while still prohibiting public communion in the latter. By personal actions Robinson meant private prayer,
thanksgiving, psalm singing, Scripture reading, acts which might be
performed "in the family, or els where, without any Church power, or
ministery comeing between."[281] Church actions, on the other hand,
included those aspects of worship and ministry which required the free
consent and corporate participation of the whole congregation, such as
reception of members, election of officers, administration of the sacraments, and the like.[282] Such practice, as Robinson now saw it, did not
imply approval of a false church structure since "we do not communicate

---

[279] *Works*, vol. 3, 85-87. The Ames-Robinson correspondence was printed surrepti-
tiously as a part of Christopher Lawne's blistering attack on the Separatists: *The Prophane Schisme of the Brownists* (n.p., 1612), 47-54.

[280] *Of Religious Communion*, The Preface.

[281] Ibid., 1.

[282] Ibid., 10: "Neyther yet may we admit them into communio of the publique ordinances with vs, till they be actually members of a true and lawfull publique body ecclesiasticall, or visible Church."

with them, as members of the Ch: but merely as Christians."[283] The basis for this private intercommunion Robinson located, significantly, in the doctrine of election:

> And if God wilbe known, and honoured in all his creatures, yea even in the sillyest worm that crawleth vppon the earth, how much more in the holy graces of his spirit vouchsafed to his elect; notwithstanding theyr faylings of infirmity, especially in outward ordinances.[284]

Those who were truly faithful and sanctified, "though never so weakly" because of their continuance in a false church, could be known, like a tree, by their fruits—"haveing in them the heavenly sap, and iuyce of his spirit though growing for the present out of the Lords walled Orchard, the true visible Church, and in the wilde wildernes of the prophane assemblyes."[285] Robinson himself, after all, had been in this very category before joining the Separatist movement. He now recognized that as he had once been accepted as a true believer by others who had already seen the light, in fairness he could only extend the same charity to those in the like situation.

Robinson's acceptance of limited fellowship with "the better sorte in the assemblyes" was certainly a mollification of the "extream streytnes" expressed in his initial correspondence with Ames.[286] However, it was neither a totally new discovery nor a retreat from the essential principles of his earlier Separatism. In fact, it seems to have been a return to the position originally held by the Scrooby congregation before their migration to Holland. Robinson says as much in the preface where he explains how he had at first argued for private intercommunion against Smyth, but afterwards, in the interest of preserving peace among the various Separatist churches, remitted and lost his "former resolution."[287] This is further borne out by the instance of his preaching in the parish assemblies even after he had formally united with the Scrooby group, an act incompatible with the strict policy of non-fellowship.[288] Moreover, Robinson declared that even during the interval when he wavered in his original conviction about private fellowship, and on occasion argued against it, he never held to *that* position with the "certaynty of perswasion, which I had

---

[283]Ibid.

[284]Ibid., 5.

[285]Ibid., 4.

[286]Ibid., The Preface.

[287]Ibid. Cf. *Separatist Tradition*, 156-57.

[288]See *supra*, 85-86.

and *have* of the common grounds of our separation."[289]

Ames, pleased with Robinson's espousal of private communion, and perhaps over-estimating his own influence on this decision, issued in the same year "A manudiction [sic] for Mr Robinson and Such as consent with him in privat communion to lead them on to publick."[290] Robinson came back with his own *A Manumission to a Manuduction* (1615) to which Ames, not to be outdone, replied with *A Second Manuduction for Mr. Robinson, Or a confirmation of the former, in an answer to his manumission* (1615).[291] In these tracts Ames urged Robinson on to public communion arguing that godly members within the national Church, by virtue of an implicit covenant, constituted true visible Churches. This Robinson could not accept. He remarked that "this manducent or hand-leader," would have done better to "guide men by the plain and open way of the Scriptures and not by subtle quaeries and doubtful suppositions." As for the concept of an implicit covenant, it was a mere "exercise of wit" on the part of "Dr. Amisse," comparable to the popish doctrine of *fides implicita.* Only by means of a covenant entered into by the free and deliberate consent of visible saints could a true visible Church arise.

Robinson's views on the limits of permissible fellowship underwent one further modification in the direction if intercommunion following the exchanges with Ames. In consonance with the teaching of Barrow and Greenwood, Robinson had earlier denounced the church buildings of the parish assemblies as "idol houses" into which gathered saints were not so much as to enter. But Brewster, on his occasional business trips back to England, attended preaching services in certain of the parish churches, and his experience apparently led Robinson to rethink this principle of earlier Separatism. We are able to reconstruct the approximate date of this important shift in Robinson's thought from the following comment by John Paget:

> Mr Robinson though he have written in such high words against these temples . . . yet hath he for this long time tolerated Mr. B to hear the word of God in such places and now of late this last month [that is, July, 1617] as is witnessed unto me, he begins openly in the midst of his congregation to plead for the lawful use of these temples.[292]

---

[289] *Of Religious Communion,* The Preface. (My italics.)

[290] Ames' "Manudiction" was published jointly with William Bradshaw's *Vnreasonableness of the Separation* (Dort, 1614).

[291] Robinson's *Manumission* is not included in the Ashton edition of his collected works, but is printed in *Collections,* Massachusetts Historical Society, ser. 4, vol. 1, 165-94.

[292] Paget, *Arrow against the Separation,* op. cit., 28-29; cf. Burgess, *Robinson,* 131.

Robinson's new position represented a significant advance over his earlier advocacy of private fellowship, for "the lawful use" for which he now contended referred to an aspect of *public* worship sanctioned by the Church of England. Thus one might not only have personal communion with individual members of parish churches but might also attend sermons preached by godly ministers of those parishes.

Robinson's final position on intercommunion was spelled out in his last major work, *A treatise of the lawfulness of hearing the ministers of the Church of England.* This writing, composed shortly before his death, was "found in his studie after his decase [sic]," and published in 1634 along with a letter from the Leyden congregation to the Southwark Church concerning the Staresmore affair and other matters relating to inter-church fellowship. He begins by expressing his affection for "my Christian countrymen, to whom God hath tied me in so many inviolable bonds," and whose "holy graces" he had never questioned, "even when I seemed furthest drawn from them."[293] He then states the purpose of the work: to prove the hearing of the Word of God preached by ministers of the Church of England lawful for "all sects and sorts of Christians." The heart of the treatise consists of sixteen objections against this policy which Robinson takes up and answers one by one. His primary justification of attending sermons in parish churches lies in his distinction between "hearing" and "having spiritual communion with" the parish ministers. To merely hear a sermon is not necessarily to approve or support the office of the preacher for, unlike participation in the sacraments which implies union in the same faith and church order, hearing the Word of God is "not so inclosed by any hedge, or ditch . . . but lies in common for all, for the good of all."[294] While the act of sermon-hearing does not imply an active spiritual communion between the preacher and listener, yet great profit can come thereby. In the same way that "a standerby" might benefit from hearing a discussion not intended for him at all, so might a duly-covenanted Christian be edified by overhearing, as it were, the sermons of a godly minister with whom he was not joined in church order.[295] But, in this same treatise, Robinson still required members of gathered churches to maintain their Separatist stance against the national Church even in the passive act of hearing sermons— "sequestering themselves from all communion with the hierarchical order

[293] *Works*, vol. 3, 353.

[294] Ibid., 363.

[295] Ibid., 367-68.

there established."[296] In addition, recognizing perhaps that regular attendance at other ministers' sermons might weaken allegiance to one's own Church, he insisted that this practice not become a regular habit:

> It is lawful to use it upon occasion, as it is to borrow of other men; but to make it our course, is to live by borrowing, which no honest man that can do otherwise possibly, would do.[297]

From the foregoing it is clear that Robinson's writings do reveal a progressive widening of the horizon of fellowship from no communion, to private communion, to a limited, "passive" public communion with godly ministers of the Church of England. It is reasonable to suppose, though there is no conclusive evidence to prove, that Robinson's development was furthered by his contacts with non-separating congregationalists such as Jacob and Ames, but his influence on them is not to be gainsaid either. Finally, Cotton's claim that Robinson "came back indeed one half of the way" must be balanced against his persistent refusal to acknowledge any parish in England as a true visible Church. Until his death the demands of congregational integrity and the impulse toward intercommunion were held together in uneasy equipoise.

ASSESSMENT

The concept of the Church which emerges from this survey of Robinson's ecclesiology represents a distinctive quest for a new sense of Christian community at odds, on crucial points, with both Anglican and Puritan models. In keeping with Calvin's emphasis on sanctification as corporately manifested in the visible Church, but redefining the visible Church *exclusively* in terms of a covenanted congregation, Robinson frees the Church from any allegiance to civil authority which would hinder its growth in edification. Essential to the life of the Church thus conceived is the constant maintenance of discipline, applied according to the method prescribed by Christ, which both reinforces the mutual interdependence of the members within and demonstrates the quality of discipleship to the world without. As the imperatives of obedience and edification provide the motivation for separation, so communal participation is the basis for internal order and organization. No external authority may impose any religious practice or decision upon the congre-

---

[296]Ibid., 354.

[297]Ibid., 375.

gation, nor do the officers, freely elected and fully answerable to the Church, have an independent ministerial status outside of their particular calling.

Robinson's understanding of the Church clearly falls within the bounds of the earlier Separatist tradition. This connection is evident from his frequent citation of Separatist writings and his adoption of the *Confession* of 1596. Unlike the Amsterdam hard-liners, however, Robinson was willing to extend private communion to those worthy Christians outside the Separatist fold, and eventually even allowed a measure of public communion with godly ministers of the parish churches. However, this gesture, though not to be minimized, did not imply an abandonment of the basic principles of Separatism set forth with cogency in the *Justification* of 1610.

Along with Robinson's analysis of the form and content of "visible Christianity" there is a parallel concern with the invisible Church—"that one mystical body of Christ scattered far and wide throughout the world."[298] The foundation of the invisible, supramundane Church, unlike its earthly counterpart, is not discernible to the human eye but resides solely in the eternal decision of God, in the mystery of the doctrine of election. We must now turn to Robinson's exposition of this important doctrine.

---

[298]Ibid., 377-78.

CHAPTER 5

THE MYSTERY OF ELECTION

"The secresie of God does drive men to much trouble. It is like an unbeaten way to the Seamen, they must sound every part of it."[1]

The previous chapter examined the shape of Separatist ecclesiology as it was recast by Robinson who drew upon an already well-established tradition of English Dissent. Without making claims for genetic connections, or even direct influence, it might be argued that Separatism in its rejection of magisterial initiative in matters religious, and in its elevation of congregational discipline to the status of an essential mark of the visible Church, approached the Anabaptist concept of the Church as a radical, spiritual community, local in scope, committed in membership, vigorous in the maintenance of internal order. There was, nonetheless, a wide area of agreement between the Separatists and their Puritan foes, the more legitimate representatives of the Reformed tradition in England.[2] On two points of commonality, the retention of infant baptism and adherence to predestinarian theology, Robinson was drawn into dispute with some of his fellow Separatists whose application of the principle of voluntarism had led them to abandon these twin pillars of orthodox Calvinism. This development within the ranks of Separatism coincided with a major modification of Calvin's doctrine of predestination in the Dutch Reformed Church, inspired by Arminius, which was decisively rejected at the Synod of Dort. The decisions of Dort thus provided the

---

[1]Thomas Hooker, quoted, Perry Miller, *The New England Mind: The Seventeenth Century* (London, 1939), 374.

[2]The difficulty of constructing an adequate typology for Separatism was felt even by Troeltsch who claimed that the early Congregationalists "stood midway between the Calvinistic church-type and the sect-type." He attributes their rise to "Anabaptist influence" but claims that they were also "influenced by a type of spirituality which differed greatly from Anabaptist ideals." *Social Teaching of the Christian Churches,* op. cit., vol. 2, 664.

occasion for Robinson's most extensive treatment of the mystery of election.

ELECTION AS A PRIMARY POLEMICAL AND THEOLOGICAL CONCERN

The two lines of Separatist ecclesiology, one centered in the definition of the visible Church as a collection of "lively" stones willingly united into the Lord's "house," and the other in the emphasis upon the sovereignty of God in election, converged in the ritual of covenant-taking, by which the community was "inchurched" at its inception, and by re-enactment of which new recruits were admitted into fellowship. This covenant was, as we have seen, conditioned upon the obedience of the covenant-takers; it could be breached by an individual member who persisted in obstinate sin, or by the whole body if it failed to discipline offending members. Bredwell was quick to see in this premise the Achilles' heel of the whole Separatist position. Arguing against Browne he reasoned that if breaking the covenant disanulled the Church, then it followed necessarily that the covenant was "holden and kept by workes." And he further pointed out that at least one of Browne's disciples had pursued this theme to its logical conclusion: "From this maner iustifying or condemning the Churche by workes, Glouer turned it to the iustification of particular Christians by woorkes."[3] Here indeed was a cogent accusation. If it were true, what was Separatism but the perhaps endemic British heresy of Pelagius in a new guise? While both Browne and Barrow, in their sparse statements on predestination, remained formally faithful to Calvin, and while the *Confession* of 1596 affirmed the double pre-ordination of men and angels to salvation or condemnation, it was left for Robinson to place the Separatist concept of the visible Church within an overarching context of predestinarian theology.[4]

Robinson's first line of defense against the charge of crypto-Pelagianism was to insist that the "voluntary yeelding" which was requisite in the formation of a visible Church was itself an act of the divine Spirit in cementing together "lively stones." Unlike the national coven-

---

[3] *The Rasing*, 72.

[4] Article 3 of the *Confession* of 1596 states that God "from everlasting . . . ordeyned som men and Angells, to eternal lyfe to bee accomplished through Iesus Christ, to the prayse of the glorie of his grace . . . and other both Angels and men, to eternall condemnation, to bee accomplished through their own corruption to the prayse of his iustice." *Creeds and Platforms*, 60. Cf. the comparable wording of the Lambeth Articles of the previous year.

ant, to which submission was supposedly made by the entire land at the beginning of Elizabeth's reign, the Church covenant could not be ratified by nominal assent. To constitute a reformed Church there must first be a reformed people who are "first fitted for" and "made capable of" the act of covenant-taking:

> The gospel is a supernaturall thing, and cannot possibly be yeelded vnto voluntarily by a naturall man, or perswaded, but by a supernaturall motive, which is onely it self: and that by the operation of the spirit.[5]

To suppose that the Church could be gathered simply by the concurrence of like-minded individuals, each an autonomous agent, would be to make the Word of God "a very charm," and the covenant, an *ex opere operato* contract. While the furtherance of life within the community depended upon its ethical élan, and could be forfeited through moral laxity, its very existence as a "body" presupposed the priority of divine grace.

Far from admitting that Separatism was doctrinally deficient in the question of election, Robinson returned this very charge against the Church from which he had withdrawn. We have earlier noted his claim, addressed to Hall, that the "error of universal grace, and consequently of freewill, groweth on apace amongst you." Hall, himself a predestinarian, was obviously miffed at such a charge: "What hath our Church to do with errors of universal grace of freewill? errors which her Articles do flatly oppose?" Yet his concession that "some few private judgments" were amiss on the point of predestination lent at least some credence to Robinson's accusation.[6] So pervasive was this error within the Church of England, Robinson believed, that most parishes were filled with "swarmes of graceless persons" who imagined their salvation to depend upon works-righteousness. In support of this claim he cited a work by Mr. Nichols, "a Minister of good note amongst your selves," who, having preached for a good while in his parish and having conferred personally with his constituents, reported that

---

[5]*Justification*, 303, 300.

[6]Hall, *Works*, vol. 9, 67-68. In the light of Robinson's position the statement of Nicholas Tyacke that "doctrinal Calvinism does not explain why Elizabethan Protestants became nonconformists, and sometimes separatists," must be modified somewhat. "Puritanism, Arminianism, and Counter-Revolution," in *The Origins of the English Civil War*, ed. Conrad Russell (New York, 1973), 121. Tyacke rightly emphasizes the *prevailing* Calvinist consensus in the Church of England during the Jacobean period, but his claim that "conformists and nonconformists, episcopalians and presbyterians all had in common Calvinist predestinarian ideas" during the first two decades of the seventeenth century underrates the significance of the nascent Arminian party whose roots went back to the Cambridge disputes of the 1590s, and whose representatives included Bishops Overall, Andrewes, and Richard Neile.

> of 400 comunicants be scarce found one, but that thought, and professed, a
> man might be saved by his own well doing, and that he trusted he did so live,
> that by Gods grace he should obteyn everlasting life, by serving God, and
> good prayers.[7]

Here was evidence that, no matter what the doctrine officially promulgated, the Reformation tenet of *sola gratia* had not penetrated to the people in the parish.

But Robinson did not rest his case on this one statistic alone. He claimed that, quite apart from the doctrine established by law, certain traditional rites of the Church of England carried with them an implicit denial of predestination. Just as the act of kneeling at Communion implied the doctrine of transubstantiation, so the two *rites de passage* which bounded the earthly existence of every Englishman, infant baptism and the funeral ceremony, concealed a latent doctrine of universal grace as they were practiced in the Church of England. Concerning the former, Robinson's objection centered on the indiscriminate baptism of all infants within the parish. Baptism, as a seal of the covenant of grace, pertained only to the elect and their seed, and further *only* to those of the elect who were members of a covenanted congregation: baptism is not without, but within the visible Church.[8] Yet the ministers in England are sent out to baptize all that are born within their parishes, "whether their parents be taught or vntaught, the disciples of Christ or of antichrist."[9] Such a system converted baptism into a "lying sign," and made an unwarranted presumption against the grace of God.

> Surely the grace of Christ must needs be universal, and wherein all have
> interest, if the seal thereof appertain unto all. Neither should the church,
> amongst whose sacred furniture baptism is, by this rule be any more the
> house of God, peculiar to his children and servants; but more like a common
> inn, whose door stands wide open to all that pass by the highway.[10]

Equally presumptious to Robinson's mind was the elaborate funeral rite which smacked of purgatory and prayers for the dead: "your Christian burial in holy ground; your ringing of hallowed bells for the soul; your singing the corpse to the grave from the church stile; your praying

---

[7]*Justification*, 274.

[8]Ibid., 77. Cf. *Works*, vol. 3, 434: "Q. 35. May all the faithful partake in the sacraments? A. No. except they be added also to some particular congregation, unto which the public ordinances and ministry doth appertain."

[9]*Justification*, 91.

[10]*Works*, vol. 3, 18.

over, or for the dead."[11] That the act of burial should be imbued with
religious trappings at all was itself an abuse of the ministerial office since
funerals, like marriages, were not ecclesiastical but civil functions.[12]
Objections to the Anglican burial rite were a standard element of Puritan-
Separatist rhetoric against the trappings of popery, but Robinson focussed especially on one part of the service, namely that rubric which
directed the priest to cast dirt upon the corpse while commending the soul
of the deceased to God and committing his body to the ground "in sure
and certayne hope of resurrection to eternall lyfe."[13] Thus everyone in the
parish (even excommunicates, if their family could meet the charge!) was
buried as a "deare brother" regardless of his profession in life.[14] Hall
defended this practice as "an harmless over-weening and over-hoping of
charity," far preferable to the "proud and censorious uncharitableness" of
the Separatists.[15] Robinson's point was that the extension of such charity
was the prerogative of God alone, and that to institutionalize it and apply
it indiscriminately was to make the Church again a "common inn" and the
grace of God, the rightful possession of all.

However compromised the Church of England may have been in its
theology of grace, it was within the Dutch Reformed Church that the first
serious attempt to modify formally the doctrine of predestination
occurred. Shortly after Robinson and the Pilgrims arrived in Leyden a
major public disputation was held on July 25, 1609. The principal speaker

---

[11]Ibid., 414. Richard Greaves has described the Separatist critique of contemporary funeral ceremonies as a "root and branch attack, with serious implications for the social order." Separatist objections to contemporary burial customs went beyond the less radical protests of the Puritans. *Society and Religion in Elizabethan England*, 695-706, 729-36.

[12]Separatist funerals were stark affairs lacking even the comfort of prayers or sermon: "The Nonconformists will have the dead to be buried in this sort, (holding no other way lawful,) namely, that it be conveyed to the place of burial, with some honest company of the church, without either singing or reading, yea, without all kinds of ceremony hereto-fore used, other than that the dead be committed to the grave, with such gravity and sobriety as those that be present may seem to fear the judgments of God, and to hate sin, which is the cause of death." John Canne, *A Necessitie of Separation from the Church of England* [London, 1634] (London, 1849), 113. Also see James Hitchcock. "Early Separatist Burial Practice," *Transactions*, Congregational Historical Society 20 (1966), 105-06; Keith Thomas, *Religion and the Decline of Magic* (New York, 1971), 58-59, 66, 106; David E. Stannard, *The Puritan Way of Death* (New York, 1977), 96-110.

[13]Cf. *Puritan Manifestoes*, 28; *The Writings of Henry Barrow, 1590-1591*, 82-83. *The First and Second Prayer Books of Edward VI* (London, 1910), 269-70. In 1661 the words "sure and certain" were stricken from the prescribed committal service. Cf. *Documents Relating to the Settlement of the Church of England* (London, 1862), 143.

[14]*Justification*, 105. Cf., 78.

[15]Hall, *Works*, vol. 9, 85.

was Arminius, professor at the university since 1603, who defended his
thesis, "On the Vocation of Men to Salvation." Arminius defined vocation as partly external, partly internal: externally it was contained in the
proclamation of the Word, internally it was effected by the operation of
the Spirit. But this calling, Arminius made a point of saying, was not
irresistible; it could be rejected, and the divine counsel contemned,
through the "hardness of the human heart."[16] Arminius was answered by
his two appointed disputants and a Jesuit priest, but his real opponent
was his arch-rival and adversary at the university, Franciscus Gomarus,
who at the conclusion of the performance exclaimed, "The reins have
been given up to the Papists in fine style today!"[17] This disputation was to
be Arminius' swan song at the university. He suffered a sudden attack the
same evening and died several months later on October 19. Less than a
year after the death of Arminius, forty-six Dutch Reformed ministers met
at Gouda and prepared a Remonstrance against certain Calvinist doctrines, and then formulated their own position in five articles: 1) God in
Christ had decreed to elect those who believed. 2) Christ died for all, but
only those who believe may obtain forgiveness; 3) fallen man needs God's
grace in order to obtain justifying faith and a renewed will; 4) the Holy
Spirit imposes no necessity on man—grace is resistible; 5) it is uncertain
whether a true believer can lose grace.[18] The publication of these articles
initiated a series of conferences and debates which found resolution only
in the triumph of the Contra-Remonstrants at the Synod of Dort and the
consequent expulsion of the vanquished Arminians.

It is not known whether Robinson attended Arminius' last disputation at the university, and it is unlikely that he and the ailing professor had
further personal contacts during the few months in which their paths
intersected.[19] However, as a registered *theologus* at the university he was
drawn into the thick of the dispute which intensified with each passing
year. The mantle of Arminius fell upon Simon Episcopius, one of the
principal signers of the Remonstrance of 1610 and second in succession to

---

[16] *The Writings of Jacobus Arminius*, tr. James Nichols (Buffalo, 1853), vol. 1, 574. On
this disputation see Gerard Brandt, *History of the Reformation in the Low Countries*
(London, 1722), vol. 2, 55ff. and Carl Bangs, *Arminius: A Study in the Dutch Reformation* (Nashville, 1971), 323-25.

[17] Ibid., 325.

[18] The "Articuli Arminiani sive Remonstrantia" are printed in *Creeds of Christendom*,
vol. 3, 545-49.

[19] Robinson was well acquainted with Arminius' writings, however, and on one occasion quoted one of them in support of his Sabbatarian views. Cf. *Works*, vol. 3, 52.

Arminius as lecturer in theology at Leyden.[20] It was he who would represent, almost single-handedly, the Remonstrant cause at the Synod of Dort and who would emerge as the most successful apologist and re-organizer of Arminianism in the 1620s. His chief antagonist at the university was, expectedly, Gomarus' protégé, Johannes Polyander. These two developed an intense personal rivalry, the students of one refusing to attend the lectures of the other. Robinson, however, attended the lectures of both professors and participated in the discussions that followed. In Bradford's words, "He began to be terrible to the Arminians."[21] This challenge aroused Episcopius to more vigorous assaults so that he "put forth his best strength and set forth sundry theses which by public dispute he would defend against all men."[22]

It was at this point that Polyander began to urge Robinson to enter the lists against Episcopius in a public disputation. Ordinarily this would have been the prerogative of Polyander himself being a colleague of Episcopius with similar academic standing. At first Robinson refused the request because of his foreign status and perhaps because of his age. But at last he acquiesced and began to prepare himself for the confrontation. Unfortunately, we have no record of the content of the disputation which lasted for three days. Bradford, obviously a biased witness, gives the following account:

> And then the day came, the Lord did so help him, to defend the truth and foil the adversary, as he put him to an apparent nonplus in this great and public audience. And the like he did a second or third time upon such like occasions. The which as it caused many to praise God that the truth had so famous victory, so it procured him much honor and respect from those learned men and others which loved the truth.[23]

Edward Winslow, later governor of Plymouth Colony, provides the only other (presumably) eyewitness report of this event:

> Our pastor Mr. Robinson in the time when Arminianism prevailed so much, at the request of the most Orthodox divines, as Poliander, Festus Homlius,

---

[20]The immediate successor of Arminius was Konrad Vorstius whose appointment was cut short due to the stern opposition of King James who discerned in Vorstius' writings a number of heterodox opinions and had his books burned at St. Paul's churchyard. On King James' role in the Vorstius affair, and on his repeated interventions in the Arminian dispute, see Christopher Grayson, "James I and the Religious Crisis in the United Provinces, 1613-19," in *Reform and Reformation: England and the Continent*, ed. Derek Baker (Oxford, 1979), 195-219. On Episcopius see Frederick Calder, *Memoirs of Simon Episcopius* (London, 1838) and A. H. Haentjens, *Simon Episcopius als Apologeet van het Remonstratisme* (Leyden, 1899).

[21]*Of Plymouth Plantation*, 21.

[22]Ibid.

[23]Ibid.

and so forth, disputed daily against Episcopius (in the Academy at Leyden) and others the grand champions of that error, and had as good respect amongst them, as any of their own Divines. [24]

Bradford intimates that Robinson's performance was so well received that he would have been offered some outstanding preferment, perhaps a lectureship at the university, had it not been for fear of English reprisal.[25]

The dispute with Episcopius is important, despite our meager information about it, because it provides the only evidence of Robinson's complicity in anti-Arminian activities outside of his own writings. It should also give pause to those who would too hastily attribute to Robinson "a broad view of Christian doctrine," and thus make "the Robinson philosophy of religion" an important element in the development of religious liberalism.[26] Robinson himself felt that while religious controversy was always dangerous, given the human proclivity to distortion and derogation, it was nonetheless "sometimes necessarie."[27] One of the dangers in public disputations, especially in a place such as Holland where one was free to profess any religion or none at all without fear of recrimination, was that opposing arguments, openly aired, would tend to confuse those who are "lightly turned about, like weather-cocks, with everie puffe of new Doctrine."[28] It was all the more important, then, that the matter in dispute be worthy of such a risk, and that the disputant be motivated only by a passion for the truth:

He that strives for errours, strives for Satan against God: He that strives for victorie, strives for himself against other men: But he that strives for truth

---

[24]*Hypocrisie Vnmasked,* op. cit., 95. The Dutch ecclesiastical historian, Jan Hoornbeck, sometime professor at Leyden, also gives a brief account of Robinson as disputant: "Vir ille (Johannes Robinsonus) gratus nostris, dum vixit, fuit et theologis Leidensibus familiaris ac honoratus. Scripsit praeterea varia contra Arminianos: frequens quippe et acer erat Episcopii in Academia adversarius et opponens." *Summa Controversarium Religionis,* op. cit., 378.

[25]In view of the controversy surrounding the proposed appointment of Ames, this fear was certainly well founded. See Keith L. Sprunger, *The Learned Doctor William Ames* (Chicago, 1972), 65-70.

[26]Bartlett, op. cit., 337-38. Bartlett sees Robinson as a "major influence in the development of the liberal Congregationalism of the nineteenth and twentieth centuries." Ibid., 336. An earlier representative of this perspective, E. C. Towne, described Robinson as a "theological reasoner profoundly grounded in new democratic ideas" who overcame his Arminian disputant "not because his reasonings told so heavily against Arminian reasonings, but because of the gentleness of his demeanor, the fine charity of his spirit, the tolerant tone and temper of his position. . . ." *Studies in Pilgrim Story* (Boston, 1905), 11.

[27]*Observations,* 44.

[28]Ibid., 46.

against errour helps the Lord against Gods, and his own enemie Satan, The Father of Lyes, and this specially, if withall he handle Gods cause according unto God.[29]

Obviously, then, Robinson must have felt that the issues at stake in the exchange with Episcopius were of foundational significance for the Christian faith.

The Arminian controversy, of course, was defined by the interplay of political and ecclesiastical issues other than the five points set forth in the Remonstrance. In the intervening decade between the signing of the Twelve Years Truce (April 9, 1609) and the concluding session of the Synod of Dort (April 24, 1619) a number of centrifugal forces within the United Provinces, held in check heretofore by the common opposition to Spain, brought the country to the brink of civil war and left the Church permanently divided.[30] Calvinism had been introduced under the aegis of the House of Orange, and the consolidation of the Reformed faith was identical in the popular imagination with the national struggle for independence from Spain. Though the Union of Utrecht (1579) had prescribed religious autonomy for each province, the integrist party, headed by Maurice of Orange, son of William the Silent, called for a national synod with power to impose confessional uniformity on all churches and disciplinary sanctions against all ministers. Early in the controversy the Remonstrants alligned themselves with the republican party, led by Jan van Oldenbarnevelt, the Advocate of Holland, whose strength derived from the merchant and burgher classes in the maritime provinces, with its political base in the States of Holland. This alliance, and Oldenbarnevelt's policy of peace with Spain, left the Remonstrants even more open to the charge of crypto-Catholicism, seen already in Gomarus' jibe at Arminius.

The two parties were also sharply divided on two fundamental issues which antedated the predestinarian controversy proper: the confessional basis of the Church, and the relation of Church and state. The former problem arose because the two documents which constituted the confessional writings of the Dutch Church, the Belgic Confession and the Heidelberg Catechism, had never been approved by a national council, and the extent to which they were binding upon ministers and churches

[29]Ibid., 45.

[30]On the crisis which led to the Synod of Dort see Pieter Geyl, *The Netherlands in the Seventeenth Century: Part One, 1609-1648* (London, 1961), 58-63; Harrison, *Arminianism,* op. cit., 190-299; Jan den Tex, *Oldenbarnevelt, 1606-1619* (London, 1973), *passim.*

within the Dutch Reformed communion was hotly debated.[31] The Arminian theory of Church and state approached that of Erastus in disallow-
ing any ecclesiastical sovereignty separate from that of the state. As
formulated by Jan Uytenbogaert, the magistrate was invested with a
number of responsibilities which usually fell within the prerogative of a
Church body in a Reformed system of polity.[32] These included the
appointment and discipline of ministers, the convening and presiding
over Church councils, and the enforcement of dogmatic decisions. The
Contra-Remonstrants advocated what Uytenbogaert called the "collater-
ality" of Church and state, theoretically a system of dual sovereignty, but
in practice one which required the magistrate to ratify and enforce
conciliar decisions on the pain of censure.

At first glance it might seem that Robinson, as a radical congregationalist, would be impervious both to the claims of Calvinist confessionalism
and to the definition of magisterial authority in a territorial Church. On
both of these issues, however, Robinson was measurably closer to the
position of the Contra-Remonstrants than to that of the Arminians. *A
Just and Necessary Apology* was written to explain the differences
between the Separatists and their Dutch Reformed neighbors, but also to
demonstrate points of contact. Robinson professed himself ready to sign
the Belgic Confession, with one small reservation, and he designated the
Dutch congregations as "true churches of Jesus Christ," an honor he
never accorded to the Church of England.[33] In fact, so close were the
affinities between Robinson and the Dutch churches that intercommunion was openly practiced:

> their sermons such of ours frequent, as understood the Dutch tongue; the
> sacraments we do administer unto their known members, if by occasion any
> of them be present with us.[34]

---

[31]The Belgic Confession, written by Guy de Brès, and the Heidelberg Catechism,
originating in the Palatinate, were both characterized as "foreign" symbols by those who
advocated their revision. Cf. Bangs, op. cit., 225. They had received synodical sanction at
Emden (1571) and at the first Synod of Dort (1574), but not all the provinces were
represented at these gatherings. Arminius strongly objected to the attempt to require all
officers of Dutch churches to affirm allegiance annually to these documents: "how could
one state more clearly that they were determined to canonize these two human writings,
and to set them up as the two idolatrous calves at Dan and Beersheba?" *Writings of
Arminius*, vol. 1, 265; Harrison, op. cit., 35.

[32]The fullest exposition of Uytenbogaert's church-state theory is Douglas Nobbs,
Theocracy and Toleration: A Study of the Disputes in Dutch Calvinism from 1600 to 1650
(London, 1938), 25-49.

[33]*Works*, vol. 3, 11.

[34]Ibid. Further evidence of Robinson's close ties with the Dutch churches is found in a
letter of Antonius Walaeus, dated May 25, 1628, three years after Robinson's death, in

While Robinson's understanding of magistracy prevented him from accepting the Calvinist theory that a ruler was to ratify and implement the disciplinary decisions of the Church, he would have sympathized with the Contra-Remonstrant protest against the attempt of the States to settle doctrinal disputes (in 1614 the Arminian interpretation of predestination was declared sufficient for salvation and further speculation about it by ministers forbidden), or to appoint and dismiss ministers. With these confessional and Church "politial" affinities in mind it is easier to understand why Robinson would throw himself so wholeheartedly into the theological fray in support of the Calvinist coalition which triumphed at the Synod of Dort.

The Synod of Dort, though properly a national assembly, took on the character of an ecumenical Reformed Council due to the presence of twenty-six foreign delegates, including five from England.[35] The precipitous military action of Prince Maurice insured the Calvinists a solid majority at the Synod, and the fate of the Remonstrants was sealed before they arrived. Pierre du Moulin, the head of the French delegation which Louis XIII did not permit to attend, wrote to congratulate the Dort deputies on the condemnation of the Arminian "*heretiques, sectaires, monstres, hardis blasphemateurs*" before the discussions had even begun![36] In the early sessions the Synod addressed itself to questions of preaching and catechizing, commissioned a new translation of the Bible in Dutch, and established criteria for the training and discipline of ministers, acts intended to implement the predetermined doctrinal deliverances. The tensions underlying the Synod came into dramatic focus with the appearance of Episcopius, Robinson's erstwhile opponent, who

---

which he recalls the Pilgrim pastor's stated intention to have his son trained for the ministry in a Dutch Reformed Church rather than one of the English Puritan congregations in Holland. Young Robinson eventually graduated from Leyden in 1633. Cf. Burgess, 282-84; A. C. Carter, "John Robinson and the Dutch Reformed Church," in *Studies in Church History*, ed. G. J. Cuming (Leiden, 1966) 232-41.

[35]Four of these had been fellow students of Robinson at Cambridge in the 1590s: Samuel Ward, Joseph Hall, Thomas Goad, and John Davenant. Oldenbarnevelt had requested that James, one of the chief promoters of the Synod, send the pro-Arminian bishops, Overall and Andrewes. Cf. T. M. Parker, "Arminianism and Laudianism in Seventeenth-Century England," in *Studies in Church History*, ed. C. W. Dugmore (Leiden, 1964), 20-34, and John Platt, "Eirenical Anglicans at the Synod of Dort," in *Reform and Reformation: England and the Continent*, ed. Derek Baker (Oxford, 1979), 221-43.

[36]*La France protestante*, ed. Henry Bordier (Paris, 1877), vol. 5, 814. The Canons of Dort were made binding on the French Reformed clergy at the Synod of Alais in 1620. In part Amyraldianism, the second major modification of predestination within the Reformed tradition, was a reaction to this imposition of Calvinist orthodoxy. See Brian G. Armstrong, *Calvinism and the Amyraut Heresy* (Madison, Wis., 1969).

delivered an eloquent, if somewhat self-righteous, oration on behalf of the Remonstrants. He protested that the calumny and abuse heaped upon his party by the high predestinarians had made them the objects of common scorn—"as every mechanic and vagabond of the *canaille* can testify."[37] The prevailing theology of the Synod he characterized as the "peculiar and obnoxious opinions" of private men which should not be allowed to pass as the acknowledged doctrine of the Dutch churches.[38] Knowing full well that he was addressing a hostile audience, Episcopius urged, as a practical compromise, a policy of mutual toleration, arguing that the attempt to secure uniformity of religious opinion would be "as Herculean and hopeless a task, as was that of Nero to cut a passage through the Isthmus of Corinth."[39] The orthodox party interpreted Episcopius' speech as an attack on the authority of the Synod itself, an attempt to turn it into a mere *collatio* where the Remonstrants and their opponents might debate as equal parties. In fact he was told that the purpose of the Synod was to judge, and not to confer. For the Arminians the judgment was swift in coming. Hardly a month after Episcopius' speech, they were summarily dismissed by the *praeses* of the Synod:

> You are full of fraud and double-dealing. You are not worthy that the synod should treat with you further, *dimitto, Exite.* You began with a lie, with a lie you ended. Go![40]

The delegates then proceeded to answer, point by point, the five articles of the Remonstrance. Out of their deliberations emerged the Canons of Dort, promulgated in May, 1619, which redefined the boundaries of Calvinist orthodoxy in terms of the five controverted heads of doctrine.[41] The immediate impact of the Synod was the repression of the Arminians: politically the republican party was dealt a severe blow by the execution of Oldenbarnevelt; as a viable force in the Church the Remonstrants were rendered ineffective by the sanctions imposed on their clergy. Eventually, in Holland alone, some 200 Remonstrant ministers were deposed from their offices, eighty of whom were sent into exile from which they

---

[37]*Memoirs of Simon Episcopius,* op. cit., 292.

[38]Ibid., 289.

[39]Ibid., 303.

[40]*Golden Remains of the Ever Memorable Mr. John Hales* (London, 1673), 77. The letters of Hales, who is famous for having bidden John Calvin "good night" at the Synod of Dort, provde a running commentary on the proceedings. Cf. James E. Elson, *John Hales of Eton* (New York, 1948), 65-84.

[41]The Canons of Dort are printed in *Creeds of Christendom,* vol. 3, 550-80. For a collection of essays commemorating the Synod of Dort from a contemporary Reformed perspective, see *Crisis in the Reformed Churches,* ed. Peter Y. De Jong (Grand Rapids, 1968).

returned only at the death of Maurice in 1625.

The Synod of Dort generated a vast amount of controversial literature which is yet to be carefully catalogued and analyzed.[42] The dispersed
Remonstrants lashed back at the Canons of Dort with a flurry of polemical tracts giving their own version of what had happened, the most
notable of which was Episcopius' *Acta et Scripta Synodalia*. John Quick
later described the effect of this public relations campaign: "Although ye
Synod of Dort had condemned ye Remonstrants, yet ye Remonstrants by
their writeings had atchieved a most noble tryumph over that Synod."[43]
On the other hand, those who supported the decisions of Dort came to its
defense with learned treatises of their own. Among these we may include
Robinson's *A Defence of the Doctrine Propounded by the Synode at
Dort*, published in 1624. It is likely that Robinson himself attended some
of the sessions at Dort which was only a brief journey from Leyden.
During this period he was also in close contact with Ames who served as
private secretary to the *praeses* of the Synod. At any rate we may be sure
that Robinson followed the proceedings at Dort with keen interest and
heartedly concurred with the doctrinal expressions there formulated, if
not so heartedly with the summary dismissal and subsequent harassment
of the Arminians.

Robinson's *Defence* was written in response to a book published in
1620 entitled *A Discription of What God Hath Predestined Concerning
Man, in His Creation, Transgressions, Regeneration, and so forth.*[44] The
book was written in the form of a dialogue between Ereunetes, "a
Searcher," and his guide Odegos who leads his inquisitive friend through
the labyrinth of predestinarian theology touching, in due course, upon all
of the five points affirmed at Dort. At the beginning of the dialogue an
echo of the anti-confessional argument is heard when Ereunetes is made
to ask whether the "Counsell of Dort was subiect to erre?"[45] Odegos
replies that true Protestants had always held conciliar pronouncements to
be fallible, and that the Calvinists' elevation of the Canons of Dort to the
status of a binding confession was akin to the popish exaltation of the
Council of Trent.

---

[42]For example, Richard Montague's charge that the position of Dort on the parity of
ministers was incompatible with episcopacy elicited a lengthy response from George
Carleton, one of the English delegates: *A Joynt Attestation Avowing that the Discipline
of the Church of England was not Impeached at the Synod of Dort* (London, 1626).
Another apology for Dort was William Ames' *Animadversiones in Synodalia Scripta
Remonstrantium* (Amsterdam, 1629).

[43]Quoted, Sprunger, op. cit., 77-78.

[44](London, 1620). Hereafter *Disciption*. Only two copies of this book are known to be
extant. Citations are from the copy in the Bodleian.

[45]Ibid., 1.

A Discription claimed to be written by "Iohn Murton and His Associates." Intensive research by the historians of Separatism has yielded little information about Murton or his career.[46] Originally a furrier of Gainsborough, Murton seems to have followed Smyth to Amsterdam and to have witnessed the famous se-baptism in the winter of 1608/09.[47] This event, as momentous if not quite as datable as the re-baptisms of the Grebel group more than three-quarters of a century earlier, created a stir among Anglicans, Puritans, and Separatists alike. Less dramatic but no less important for future denominational developments was Smyth's subsequent abandonment of the Calvinist interpretation of predestination. The first indication that Smyth had become "taynted with the errors of general redemption and free wil" appears in Clyfton's *The Plea for Infants*, published in 1610. Clyfton related two theses which Smyth had circulated along with "his reasons in defence thereof": "1. Christs redemption stretcheth to all men. 2. Man hath not lost the faculty of willing any good thing that is shewed him."[48] Both in the replacement of the covenant with adult baptism as the means of church-gathering, and in the renunciation of the received predestinarian theology, Smyth's church was in one accord. However, as their protean pastor ("whose course is as changeable as the Moone," quipped Bernard)[49] came to doubt the validity of his precipitate self-baptism and to adopt other obviously Anabaptist tenets,

---

[46]Dexter, *Congregationalism*, 321-23; Burrage, *Early English Dissenters*, vol. 1, 241, 250-69; White, *Separatist Tradition*, 140.

[47]Bernard, who had known Smyth in England, apparently coined the sobriquet "Se-Baptist" to needle his erstwhile friend: "Vpon so extraordinarie an act, I will be somewhat exorbitant with my self, to cal him Mr. Iohn Smith, the Anabaptisticall Se-baptist." *Plain Evidences*, 17.

[48]*The Plea for Infants* (Amsterdam, 1610), "An answer to Mr. Smyth's Epistle to the Reader." There are at least three possible sources of influence on Smyth's break with orthodox Calvinism: (1) the complex of ideas put forth in the 1590s by Baro and Overall at Cambridge where Smyth had been a Fellow at Christ's; (2) the public excitement generated by the Arminian disputes which was at a high pitch during the last years of Smyth's life; (3) the Dutch (Waterlander) Anabaptists in Amsterdam from whom Smyth later sought membership. Though all of these may have been contributing factors in Smyth's doctrinal metamorphosis, there is good reason for accepting Tolmie's recent conclusion that "Waterlander influence was decisive in converting Smyth's church from the orthodox predestinarian doctrine of the puritans to . . . the doctrine of general redemption." *Triumph of the Saints,* op. cit., 70. This is supported both by the timing of the new insight (i.e. a full year after the settlement in Amsterdam) and by the known contacts of Smyth (his church met in the bakehouse of Jan Munter, a leading Amsterdam Mennonite). For an opposing view on this much discussed subject, see L. D. Kliever, "General Baptist Origins," *Mennonite Quarterly Review* 36 (1962), 316-24. The case for Anabaptist influence is ably argued by E. A. Payne, "Contacts Between Mennonites and Baptists," *Foundations* 4 (1961), 39-55.

[49]*Plain Evidences,* 18.

a minority of the congregation, led by Helwys and Murton, refused to go along. These two, along with eight other members, excommunicated Smyth and the majority when they applied for membership in the Waterlander church. Smyth eventually came to accept the Anabaptist position on magistracy, oaths, and the celestial flesh of Christ. Before his death in 1612 he signed the *Confession* of Hans de Ries thus paving the way for the organic union of the two groups. Meanwhile the Helwys-Murton band had become convinced that their initial flight from England had been an act of irreligious cowardice. After having "thoroughly considered what the cost and danger may be," they resolved to "lay downe their lives in their owne Countrie" rather than remain in disobedience in Holland.[50] In the same year, 1612, that Edward Wightman, the last Anabaptist to be executed in England, was burned at the stake, this splinter group from Smyth's congregation founded at Spitalfield, near London, the first Baptist church, properly so called, on English soil. By 1616 Helwys was dead, a victim of harsh imprisonment. Murton too was in and out of prison but lived until 1626 when the tiny sect of "General" Baptists had grown into a fledgling denomination of six congregations.[51]

Shortly before his death Helwys wrote *A Short and Plaine Proofe by the Word and workes off God that Gods decree is not the cause off anye Mans sinne or Condemnation and that All Men are redeamed by Christ.*[52] It is the most elaborate published statement of his revised interpretation of election. As a layman he shows no reticence in plunging into so deep a mystery: "it concerns us as much as anie."[53] He writes with contempt of "that Faire glorious deceaving opinion off perticuler Election and perticuler reprobation, and so off perticuler Redemption," and hopes for the "conversion" of those who pry into the secret counsels of God.[54] The

---

[50] Helwys, *The Mistery of Iniquity* (London, 1612), 212. The issue of flight in persecution, prominent in the early Church (cf. Tertullian's *De fuga in persecutione*), was revived in Separatism by Helwys' return to England. Robinson, branded by Helwys as one of the "deceitfull harted leaders" who had fled to save their lives when they should have stayed to face martyrdom, responded to this criticism with a brief tract. In it he put together a catena of Scriptural precedents for flight, from Jacob's escape from "his Churlish uncle Laban" to St. Paul's unorthodox departure from Damascus in a basket. He argued that neither "flying" nor "abydeing" was absolutely commanded, that there are "tymes & occasions seasonable for both," and that we must choose the one that will be "most for Gods glory." *Of Religious Communion*, 39-45.

[51] R. G. Torbet, *A History of the Baptists* (Valley Forge, 1965), 38-40.

[52] (Amsterdam ?, 1611).

[53] Ibid., 3.

[54] Ibid., sig. D 3 verso. The doctrine of general redemption, rather than believer's baptism, was the fundamental tenet of the early General Baptists. Thus they re-opened

opinion that God had "foredecreed" some to be damned, apart from
having no basis in Scripture, carried with it two positive dangers: it
prompted some to despair utterly, believing themselves non-elect; it made
others desperately careless of their salvation, relegating all responsibility
for their souls to God's unknown decree. Moved by pastoral and evangelistic concerns, Helwys' objection to high predestinarian theology was,
like that of Wesley a century later, a protest against the imposition of
human restraints on the love of God.

In *A Discription* Murton maintained this emphasis of Helwys and
applied it specifically to the Canons of Dort. Murton too was a layman—
without the "advantages of knowledge of Tongues, and Arts,"
Cambridge-trained Robinson reminded his readers. Yet he and his company presumed to judge anyone who received not their "new Gospell of
Anabaptistry and Free-Will" as "perishing without remedie"![55] The tone
of Robinson's treatise is condescending throughout ("they know not what
they speak") and, at points, contemptuous ("you poore seduced
soules").[56] Robinson nowhere called his opponents Arminians, although
he evidently thought their arguments were cut from the same cloth, and
referred to the Arminians as "these mens Masters."[57] Murton, for his
part, denied any direct connection with the Remonstrant party: "And for
the Armenions (as they are called) wee are not truely enformed of their
opinions."[58] There were in fact important nuances of difference between
the position adopted by the Helwys-Murton band and the Arminian
criticism of predestination.[59] It is altogether possible, even likely, that the
General Baptist modification of predestination was derived via Smyth
from the Waterlanders without specific Arminian influence. On the other
hand, Arminians had long been suspected of conniving with the Anabaptists. Before coming to Leyden Arminius himself had been asked to write
a treatise against the Anabaptist view of free will, but had postponed this

---

negotiations with Hans de Ries and the Dutch Mennonites in the 1620s, but refused to
accept the Calvinist Baptists as fellow Christians, calling them instead "the gates of Hell,
their common enemy." Tolmie, op. cit., 72.

[55] *Defence*, sig. A 2 recto.

[56] Ibid., 12, 7.

[57] Ibid., 100.

[58] *Discription*, 3.

[59] For example, Article 4 of "A Declaration of Faith of English People Remaining at
Amsterdam in Holland" describes the condition of fallen man as "haveing all disposition
vnto evill, and no disposition or will vnto anie good," a statement which suggests the
Calvinist concept of depravity. *Baptist Confessions of Faith*, ed. W. L. Lumpkin (Chicago, 1959), 118.

task indefinitely preferring instead to challenge his fellow Reformed theologians on this point.[60] In the aftermath of the Synod of Dort "Murton and his associates" clearly stood in theological sympathy with the Arminians over against Robinson and the Contra-Remonstrants on the other side of the predestinarian divide.

Robinson's role in the Arminian Controversy and his defense of the Synod of Dort represented a natural progression of the predestinarian theology he had learned at Cambridge. The issues of the 1610s were not unlike those of the 1590s though the focus had changed as the debate had widened. The intraconfessional as well as the international dimensions of the controversy are illustrated by the fact that the Church of England, whose doctrine of grace Robinson had attacked, was prominently represented at the Synod, while Robinson's *Defence* was a reaction to some of his fellow Dissenters who still accepted his Separatism but not his Calvinism.

In the *Defence* Robinson follows his usual procedure of pursuing his opponent in "all the out-leaps and turnings which he makes."[61] This results in a tedious and untidy method of presentation. Therefore, our analysis will attempt to draw out the systematic implications of his doctrine of election while keeping in mind the polemical thrust of the treatise itself.

ROBINSON'S THEOLOGY OF GRACE

Sin and Fallen Man

Among Smyth's most significant departures from Calvinist orthodoxy was his repudiation of the traditional doctrine of original sin:

> Original sin does not exist, for every sin is either actual or voluntary. That is to say, it is something actually done or desired against the law of God. Therefore, infants are without sin. As all fell in Adam, all were restored by God. Hence on account of this restoration no one from the fall of Adam is born in sin or guilt.[62]

---

[60]Cf. Bangs, op. cit., 166-71. Bangs points out that Anabaptists frequently attended Arminius' sermons.

[61]*Defence*, 3.

[62]*Smyth*, vol. 2, 682, 685. "Nullum esse peccatum originis, verum omne peccatum esse actuale et voluntarium viz: dictum factum aut concupitum contra legem dei: ideoque infantes esse sine peccato. . . . Omnes in Adamo lapsi, restaurati sunt a deo, adeo ut é posteris Adae nemo, ob hanc restaurationem, in peccato aut reatu natus sit."

Moreover, even if Adam's sin could have been transmitted to his posterity, the death of Christ, which was effectual before the birth of Cain and Abel, would have "stopped the issue and passage therof." Original sin, then, is an "idle terme" with no referent in reality: "ther is no such thing as men intend by the word."[63] Faced with Smyth's outright denial, and Arminius' less sweeping modification, of original sin, Robinson set forth in some detail the nature of original sin with special emphasis on its extent and its transmission.

The Reformers were the inheritors of two classic definitions of original sin, one associated with Augustine, the other with Anselm. Beginning with the concept of the human as appetitive, Augustine located the essence of original sin in the *amor sui*: the fundamental redirection of the will which placed the self at the center of all human desiring. While this self-love, or concupiscence, was most vividly displayed in the carnal passion associated with the act of procreation, it permeated the entire self, perverting all of the affections. In the Middle Ages this understanding was restated by Peter Lombard who defined original sin as a *qualitas morbida anime, vitium scilicet concupiscentie*, and by radical Augustinians such as Gregory of Rimini.[64] A competing interpretion, put forth by Anselm and supported by Scotus and Ockham, redefined original sin as the absence or loss of original righteousness. This view could also be traced to Augustine's notion that sin had no positive subsistence of its own, that it was defect or debility, privation of the good (*privatio boni*). It lacked, however, the other Augustinian connotation of sin as an active, corrosive power.

Robinson employs both Augustinian and Anselmian terminology in describing the nature of original sin. As we shall see, he finds the latter especially useful in answering the charge that God is the author of sin. However, when describing the effect of sin on fallen man, Robinson, like Calvin and Perkins, views sin as a positive inclination to evil.[65] So decided is this propensity in fallen man that it has a progressively corrupting effect

---

[63]Ibid., 735.

[64]Oberman, *Harvest*, 120-23. Cf. Lombard, *Libri quatuor sententiarum*, vol. 2, d. 30 c. 10: "Ex his datur intelligi, quid sit originale peccatum, scilicet vitium concupiscentiae, quod in omnes concupiscentialiter nators, per Adam intravit, eosque vitiavit."

[65]*Inst.* 2,1.8: "Thus those who have defined original sin as 'the lack of the original righteousness, which ought to reside in us,' although they comprehend in this definition the whole meaning of the term, have still not expressed effectively enough its power and energy. For our nature is not only destitute and empty of good, but so fertile and fruitful of every evil that it cannot be idle." *Calvini Opera*, vol. 3, 238. Cf. *Workes of William Perkins*, vol. 1, 165.

on all human faculties. Original sin issues in actual sins, and one sin often brings on another, for example, rash anger leads to strife, and Peter's denial of Christ was preceded by his forswearing him:

> So also by those degrees of iniquitie do men proceed in one and the same particular enormitie: in which, as in a chayn drawing from heaven to hell, each link moveth his next, from the one, and smaller end, to the other greater.[66]

This chain reaction, ignited by those pre-cognitive urges aroused by concupiscence, what Lombard called the "tinder of sin" (*fomes peccati*), leads unavoidably, without the interposition of grace, to ultimate estrangement from God:

> There is in a man concupiscence by which he is drawn away from God, unto whom he ought to cleave with the whole heart . . . . He that begins to do evill, or to forsake that which is good, in the affection of his heart, is like him that puts his feet into a pit, and lets the hold of his hands go: and without Gods gratious hand catching hold of him, can never stay, till he come to the bottom of the pit of perdition.[67]

Robinson also follows Calvin by describing the effect of the Fall in language which suggests a concept of total depravity. Smyth had claimed that while Adam's sin involved a loss of innocence, it did not abrogate any natural power or faculty with which God originally endowed him.[68] Robinson is willing to grant that Adam had free will as much after as before the Fall insofar as human nature itself is defined as volitional. However, human willing after the Fall was "corrupted, disordered and clean contrarily disposed," to the extent that it tended—"willingly" but necessarily—only toward evil.[69] This corruption, of course, affects not only the will proper, but also the mind where it is defined variously as ignorance, error, doubtings, and unbelief, as well as the body which is subject to debility and death on account of sin.[70] The impact of this

---

[66]*Observations*, 266.

[67]Ibid., 266-67. Cf. Lombard, *Sent.*, vol. 2, d. 30 c. 6.

[68]*Smyth*, vol. 2, 735: "That Adam being fallen did not loose anie naturall power or facultie which god created in his soul. For the worke of the devill, which is sine, cannot abolish gods works or creatures: and therfor being fallen he still retained freedome of will."

[69]*Of Religious Communion*, 106.

[70]Ibid. Against Smyth's acceptance of the Pelagian view that mortality was the natural destiny of man apart from his sin, Robinson reasserts the Augustinian position which attributes physical decay and death to the Fall. Though both body and soul are, as finite creatures, naturally mortal, they would have been sustained "by the continuall influence of the Divine power" had Adam not sinned. Robinson speculates that an unfallen Adam would not have continued forever in his natural estate of tilling the garden, procreating

corruption is to render man totally incapable of spiritual things. In this
sense it is not too much to say that sin indeed abolished "Gods works or
creatures." For what was Adam's spiritual death but an abolition and
destruction of his spiritual life, innocence, created graces, and so forth, all
of which were the works of God? The same may be said of "the whole
Image of God."[71]

As a presupposition of the doctrine of gratuitous election, the concept
of original sin underscores the equal and collective involvement of all
persons in the fallen condition of humanity. This implies the seminal
identity of the human race in Adam: his sin was a radical and total
determination of all his successors who share both the guilt and the
punishment of the original disobedience. Sin is incident only to reasonable creatures. God as Creator is above sin while the unreasonable creatures are beneath it, the "disorders in bruit beasts" being the punishment
of man's sin against God.[72] But what of infants or very young children
who are not capable of committing actual sins? How can the burden of
original sin be justly attributed to them? This issue was at the heart of
Smyth's disavowal of original sin, and of his refusal to extend baptism to
infants.[73] In response to this challenge Robinson marshals four arguments in support of the universal application of original sin. First, while
infants, no less than the rest of humanity, had no distinct life or being at
the Fall, they did have both "after a sort, and as branches in the root."[74]
The idea of a descendant being both present and implicated in the act of a
progenitor is elucidated by the Biblical statement that Levi paid tithes to
Melchizadek insofar as he was in the loins of Abraham when Melchi-

---

children, etc., but in time would have undergone a "change of all those earthly imperfec-
tions, as there shal be in the bodies of all the faythfull, who shalbe alive at Christes second
comeing: but the same without all greif, & payn. . . and without the bodies corrupting, &
rotting in the grave: which are the proper fruits of sin." Ibid., 104-105.

[71]Ibid., 106. Cf. Calvin's description of fallen man in *Sermon on Job* 2:1: "Car il y a
plus de valeur en toutes les vermines due monde, qu'il n y a pas en l'homme: car c'est une
creature où l'image de Dieu est effacée." Quoted, T. F. Torrance, *Calvin's Doctrine of
Man* (Grand Rapids, 1957), 85.

[72]*Observations*, 265.

[73]Smyth put his objection to infant baptism in the form of a syllogism: "Qui peccato
vacui in innocentia sua permanent, non sunt baptisandi. Infantes peccato vacui in
innocentia sua permanent. Ergo Infantes non sunt baptisandi," and supported the minor
premise with this argument: "Omne peccatum voluntarium est. Infantes autem neque
mentis neque voluntatis actus ullos persentiunt, neque a peccato tentantur Sathanae motu
et instigatione, neque ullos concupiscentiae motus persentiunt, quibus assentiantur."
Smyth, vol. 2, 714.

[74]*Defence*, 136.

zadek met him (Heb. 7:9). Levi was in Abraham as in a particular root; mankind was in Adam, as in a general root. Secondly, the federal headship of Adam is shown in the fact that the punishment for his sin was extended to all of his prosterity:

> All Adams naturall posterity were souls sinning in him: whom in that his sin, we must not consider as a private person, but as the common father of mankinde, communicateing with the nature, the sin (which was not merely personall, but naturall) with his naturall posteritie: both which are also their own. . . . And hence was it, that in the punishment of his sin, the earth was cursed, not to him alone, but to his ensueing posterity: neyther was Eve alone to suffer the sorrowes of conception, and childbirth, but all her daughters after her: neyther were the Cherubims set to keep them two alone, but all their after posterity out of the garden of Eden: and so it is for death itself, and all the passages which lead vnto it.[75]

Thirdly, infants, as reasonable creatures, have already within them the faculties of understanding and will, though they lack the actual use of these endowments. It is impossible, Robinson asserts, for understanding or will to be instilled neutrally in infants. To illustrate this he borrows an example from the animal world: "As the yong whelps and cups, of Lyons, Beares, and Foxes, haue in their naturall and sensitiue faculties, a pronenesse and inclination to raven," so infants in their reasonable faculties are bent from their cradles toward evil.[76] Thus they are prone to lie, even if brought up to hear no lie told; they pride themselves in "any gay, or gorgeous thing" while begrudging the same to others, and so on. The perversity of infant nature is as evident to common sense and experience as "that the fyre is warme, and a stone heavy."[77] Finally, the hereditary character of original sin is confirmed by the clear witness of Scripture (Robinson follows Augustine's interpretation of the two *loci classici*: Ps. 51:5, Rom. 5:12) and by the example of Christ's death. If sin were passed on by imitation rather than propagation, as Pelagius had thought, then we might be justified merely by imitation of Christ's righteousness, and not by his performing righteousness for us as our "spirituall root" into which we are grafted by faith.[78]

In this response to Smyth, Robinson touched upon the classic question of how original sin is transmitted from one generation to the next. Two major theories of the soul's origin, and hence of the transmission of original sin, derived from the Patristic period. Tertullian, and for a brief

---

[75] *Of Religious Communion*, 107.

[76] *Defence*, 137.

[77] *Of Religious Communion*, 109.

[78] *Defence*, 138.

period Augustine, claimed that the whole person, soul and body, was generated *ex traduce* from the substance of his progenitors, and that original sin was received along with the soul as a part of the biological inheritance. The alternative theory, advanced by Jerome and Pelagius, and accepted by Catholics and classical Protestants alike (except for Luther who revived traducianism), regarded the soul of each person as created by the immediate agency of God, and joined to the body either at conception, or birth, or at some point in between.[79] Robinson refused to concede that either of these views necessitates the repudiation or original sin, as Smyth's defense of creationism implied. Most of those who hold the direct creation theory are at pains to prove that their hypothesis is compatible with original sin. For himself, though he elsewhere refers to traducianism as "a Philosophicall doubt," Robinson tends to favor the view that soul and body are simultaneously generated and thus inherit the corruption which was theirs in Adam.[80] He finds the creationist view open to several objections. First, he fails to see how a "dead body" before its union with the soul can be the proper subject of sin, or indeed any way sinful, any more than after it is separated from the soul. More problematic still is that part of the theory which requires the material body to infect the soul, a spiritual substance, with the contagion of sin. More in accord with Scripture is the view that our immaterial as well as our material being is derived from Adam by the laws of natural propagation. Otherwise Adam could not be said to have begotten a son after his own image (Gen. 5:3), that is, corrupt and sinful as opposed to God's image, had he begotten only the body and not the soul as well. Also, God's command to "increase and multiply" must have pertained to the whole person, and "not onely a dead carkas, and livelesse body," else human kind, the crown of Creation, would have been assigned a method of procreation inferior to that of the bruit beasts who reproduce both body and soul, or life, after their kind.[81] Robinson does not deal with the principal objection to the traducianist theory, namely that it assumes the

---

[79]Despite the Formula of Concord's affirmation of creationism (*Creeds of Christendom*, vol. 3, 98), later Lutheran dogmatics returned to Luther's own traducianist view, while the Reformed tradition generally, following Calvin, was creationist. Cf. Heppe, *Reformed Dogmatics*, 227-38. The only other Separatist to broach the topic, also in the context of arguing for original sin, was Ainsworth who maintained the creationist view: "For though the soule is created of God, and is not materially from the parents as the body, yet the parents giue occasion to infuse the soule (for without corporall generation no soule is created), and so the soule may in some sort be said to haue the beginning from Adam, though not of any matter from him." *A Censure upon a Dialogue* (n.p., 1623), 39.

[80]*Observations*, 87.

[81]*Of Religious Communion*, 108; *Defence*, 139-40.

divisibility of the soul which is universally acknowledged to be simple in its essence (though a reference to this problem may be veiled in his admission of "Philosophicall doubt"). Robinson, like Augustine, seems to have been attracted to traducianism because it afforded a more plausible theory of the transmission or original sin.[82]

Robinson's defense of the doctrine of original sin is directed more toward Smyth's outright denial of it than toward the more subtle modification of Arminius.[83] We may summarize his position as strongly Augustinian in his emphasis upon the essence of sin as concupiscence, though original sin has both a positive (*amor sui*) and a negative (*nihil*) aspect. His description of the effect of sin as all-pervasive corresponds to Calvin's doctrine of total perversity, though he deviates from the Reformed tradition in accepting the traducianist theory of the transmission of original sin.

Prescience and Providence

When the fallen condition of human nature is placed within the context of God's overarching purpose in Creation, then the problem of God's authorship of sin becomes acute. This problem may be stated succinctly in two propositions: 1) God cannot by His very nature be the primary or proper cause of sin; 2) yet nothing in the world, including sin, occurs apart from God's will and providence. Stated otherwise, how, if at all, can God's holiness be reconciled with His omnipotence in the light of the fall of Adam and the consequent reality of human sin? Robinson devotes more attention to this question than to any other single issue in his defense of the Canons of Dort.

Closely related to the question of God's rule in the fall of man is the order or sequence of the divine decrees, and Robinson begins his discus-

---

[82]Augustine, originally a creationist, accepted traducianism provisionally in his struggle with Pelagius. The following passages in Augustine are supportive of the traducianist theory: *De Genesi ad litteram*, 10, 23; *De peccatorum meritis et remissione*, 3, 7; *De Civitate Dei*, bk. 13, 14. His final position is one of studied equivocation: *Retractationes*, 1, 1. 3. Cf. J. N. D. Kelly, *Early Christian Doctrines* (New York, 1959), 344-46.

[83]While Arminius admitted the seminal identity of the human race in Adam, the consequence of that inbeing he described more in terms of punishment suffered than of guilt imputed. Consequently, original sin is defined exclusively as deprivation, the absence of original righteousness, rather than as concupiscence or depravity. On the question of whether infants who die without having committed actual sins are condemned, Arminius equivocates, insinuating however that condemnation would be unfair having a different basis from that of those who reject the gospel. Cf. *The Writings of Arminius*, vol. 1, 252-54, 317-24, 575-83; vol. 2, 78-79; Bangs, op. cit., 337-40.

sion with a defense of the infralapsarian position adopted by the Synod of Dort. The Synod itself did not specify a precise arrangement of the decrees, but merely decided that the object of predestination was *homo creatus et lapsus* as opposed to *homo creabilis et labilis*, the supralapsarian alternative advanced by Gomarus.[84] In the infralapsarian scheme the decrees are usually formulated in the following order: 1) the decree of the creation of man; 2) the decree of the permission of the Fall; 3) the decree to elect certain ones out of those fallen and to reject (or pass by) the others; 4) the decree to send Christ to redeem; 5) the decree to send the Holy Spirit to apply this redemption to the elect. By contrast the supralapsarian formulation, in its most rigid expression, places the decree of election not only prior to the decree to permit the Fall, but even before the decree to create, speaking of election in respect to man as "creatable."[85] It is important to note that *both* of these views permit (though neither requires) a doctrine of absolute, double predestination and a definition of the atonement as limited in scope and intention. However, the order in which the decrees are placed does bear directly on the relation between God's sovereignty and the reality of human sin. By assigning logical priority to the decree of predestination, supralapsarianism subordinates everything else to the execution of that decree. Thus even sin and the Fall become the means by which God effects His purpose in election and reprobation. To avoid this dire conclusion, infralapsarianism places the decrees of creation and allowance of the Fall before that of predestination, more closely connecting sin and reprobation. This was clearly the intention of the Canons of Dort in declaring that the decree of reprobation "by no means makes God the author of sin . . . but the awful,

---

[84]The supra-infralapsarian controversy was not contemporary with Calvin, and he can be quoted in favor of either position. Supralapsarianism, clearly the more logically satisfying of the two, was advanced by more systematic theologians such as Beza and Perkins. On the other hand, the infra-motif was adopted by all of the Reformed confessions. The issue was hotly debated at Dort with a sizable minority favoring no synodical determination of the question. In the end the infralapsarian position was embraced, election being defined as God's immutable decision to choose certain persons "ex universo genere humano, ex primaeva integritate in peccatum et exitium sua culpa prolapso." *Creeds of Christendom*, vol. 3, 553. On the debate at Dort, see Hales, *Golden Remains, op. cit*, 127-33 and the article on "Supralapsarianism" by James Orr in *Encyclopedia of Religion and Ethics*, ed. James Hastings (New York, 1922), vol. 12, 123.

[85]Thus James Nichols, the translator of Arminius, characterized Beza's position as "the Creabilitarian opinion." Writings of *Arminius*, vol. 1, 241. Cf. Perkins' statement of supralapsarianism in *The Works of William Perkins*, ed. Ian Breward (Cambridge, 1970), 80-99, 183-86.

irreprehensible, and righteous judge and avenger of it." [86] With this in mind Robinson asserts that since his opponents' criticism is aimed at the supralapsarian position, he might well "forebeare to meddle about Adams sin, in the case of predestination" considering that Dort had applied the decree of predestination to man as fallen, referring the decrees of creation and permission of the Fall "to a more general work of divine providence."[87] But this is too facile an answer. Robinson recognizes that infralapsarianism must also face at a deeper level the problem of God's acquiescence to evil. For if the decree to permit the Fall is antecedent to the decree of election/reprobation, then the question still arises why permission of sin is included in God's counsel at all. To get a handle on this problem Robinson turns to the categories of God's foreknowledge and providence.

Robinson boldly sets forth his position in two interrelated affirmations. He first claims that all events, and hence Adam's fall, come to pass necessarily after a sort, that is in respect to God's providence. Further, God not only permits or suffers these events to happen, but in some sense wills them and remains active in their performance. He is quick to add that the *manner* of God's working, especially in regard to sin, is a mystery: how God who hates and forbids sin could so order persons and things by His providence that the same can not but be, is inconceivable. Yet whoever will not confess that God can (and did in Adam's sin) thus order and dispose of things, so as to preserve inviolate both His own holiness and the creatures will, is himself "guilty of that pride, which was Adams ruine, by which he desired to be as God in knowledge."[88]

But the question remains: If the Fall came to pass by God willing it, through His inviolable decree, does not this make God the author of sin? As we have seen, the Canons of Dort already anticipated this criticism, and Robinson sought to bolster their arguments by a series of distinctions worthy of his mentor Perkins. To begin with, Robinson thinks this charge is spurious arising from the failure of the Arminians to distinguish between God's working of the sin as its author and His appointing and ordering, both of sin and sinner, to His own holy ends. To illustrate this point he recalls Peter's ascription of the death of Christ, which occurred at the hands of wicked men, to God's determinate counsel (Acts 2:22, 23). Certainly God neither commanded nor approved "the covetousnesse of

---

[86] *Creeds of Christendom*, vol. 3, 555: "Deum neutiquam peccati authorem . . . sed tremendum, irreprehensibilem, et justum ac vindicem constituit."

[87] *Defence*, 2-3.

[88] Ibid., 4.

Iudas, the envy of the Priests, and injustice of Pilate," but He used and ordered all of these evil deeds to effect the death of Christ to His own glory and to our profit. In response to the question of whether Christ might have been slain without the involvement of sinful acts, Robinson replies that what was possible by God's absolute power (*de potentia absoluta*) is beyond our ken; that it was necessary in terms of God's ordained power (*de potentia ordinata*) for Christ to die as he did is evident both from Scripture and the event itself.[89]

The Arminians also granted that God had decreed the death of Christ, but they drew back from affirming that the means and manner thereof were similarly ordained. Robinson felt that this position made God into an idle looker-on, "letting men alone without medling with them":

> Surely the Art of Chimists is nothing to these mens, in evaporeating; who can reduce those most just and powerfull works of God to a very nothing; for no more is a bare suffering then a not doing.[90]

To further illustrate divine concurrence in human actions Robinson uses two "similitudes." First he give the example of a farmer who by "his artificall ditches and trenches" is able to irrigate a field by directing the water which of itself is prone to flow to and fro, wherever he chooses.[91] The other example is that of a military captain who is in charge of a motley company of soldiers. Some have joined his army in hope of booty and prey, others to avoid prison, still others who are weary of wife or friends, and so on. Yet the captain is able to order them all in spite of their corrupt motives to his lawful ends, in offensive or defensive wars. If one frail man can thus make lawful use of the sinful lusts of other men, should we quarrel with God's infinite power and wisdom?

> Or will they (vain men) conjure him herein within the narrow circle of their understanding? Denying him at all to haue any hand in working, where they (blinde molles) cannot discern how he works?[92]

Thus God's providence is seen to be active as "a hand steady" in all acts, even sinful ones.[93] Robinson quotes in support of this conception Augus-

---

[89]Ibid., 7. Cf. 6: "For howsoever it bee not for them, nor me, to determine what was possible to God's absolute power; yet we know . . . that in regard to Gods decree, it was necessary that Christ should dye, as he did."

[90]Ibid., 32-33.

[91]Ibid., 7-8.

[92]Ibid., 34-35.

[93]Ibid., 4. Robinson cites the "sinfull commixture" of Judah and Tamar, being on his part whoredom and on hers incest. Yet this union was blessed with a child from whom Christ descended. Ibid., 26.

tine's famous statement that the things which are done against God's will are not done without His will.[94] Though Robinson has no extensive discussion of providence, he does reject two popular notions which distort this important doctrine. The first is the idea advanced by "the Ethnicks" that all things are determined by blind chance or fortune. Such a system of fatalism, with its presupposition of an inviolate chain of cause and effect, disallows both the personal character of God's activity and the voluntary nature of human sin.[95] Also at odds with the Christian view is the concept, later characteristic of Deism, of God as "the skilfull Artificer" who constructs "his Clock, or other work of like curious deuise" so as to function independently, with only an occasional repair from its maker. Rather we are to understand that God "by continuall influx preserves, and orders both the being, and motions of all Creatures."[96] Calvin referred to this "continuall influx" as a *creatio continua*, de-emphasizing, though not eliminating, the role of secondary causation: God is not the creator of a moment, but the perpetual governor of the world.[97] Thus on one level providence is linked to Creation as the means by which God maintains and perpetuates all that He had made; on the other it belongs to the eternal decrees as God's unfailing determination effectually to direct all creatures to their appointed ends. In this latter connection God's providential activity is directly related to His prescience.

Robinson takes it as axiomatic that the certainty of God's decree follows from the infallibility of His foreknowledge. He argues, however, that God's foreknowledge is of two sorts. There is God's foreknowledge natural and indefinite by which God knows all possible things, and there is God's foreknowledge definite and determinate by which of things possible He knows what shall and shall not be. Here Robinson transposes the Nominalist metaphysical distinction of *potentia absoluta/potentia ordinata* into an equally rigid epistemological dualism: *praescientia absoluta/praescientia definita*. Of course, the foreknowledge is one in God; but in our conception the former of those acts of God's foreknowledge goes before the decree, the latter presupposes it. In other words, God's

[94]Ibid., 39-40.

[95]Ibid., 26.

[96]*Observations*, 17-18.

[97]Cf. *Inst.* 1, 16-18. For a similar statement in Robinson, see *Defence*, 6-7. On the place of providence within Calvin's theological system, see Charles Partee, *Calvin and Classical Philosophy* (Leiden, 1977), 126-45; E. De Peyer, "Calvin's doctrine of Divine Providence." *Evangelical Quarterly* 10 (1938), 30-44.

decree occupies a middle position between His unlimited knowledge of all possibilities and His knowledge of particular, preordained events. Therefore

> God certainly and infallibly forsees a thing shall be, because he unchangeably decrees it shall be in and according to its kind.[98]

The incest of Absolam is a case in point. Murton claimed that God foresaw this event simply because Absolam would certainly practice it in time. But Robinson points out that there was no "absolute necessitie" that Absolam would even be born, or being born that he would survive till that time, or surviving that he would have either natural ability or opportunity to perform an act. Whence then arises the certainty of Absolam's sin? Either

> Gods decree from eternitie (and so his work in time) must be acknowledged for the disposing and ordering of all events unavoydably, or his knowledge be denied in forseeing them infallibly.[99]

However, Robinson is not quite willing to say flatly that God willed the sin of Adam. It is true that the decree to permit the Fall was such that the same could not but follow thereupon. But it followed as a consequent upon an antecedent, not as an effect upon a cause.[100] Here Robinson introduces the distinction between God's revealed and His hidden or secret will. This distinction corresponds to the bifurcation in divine prescience described above and may be illustrated with respect to the decree to permit the Fall as follows:

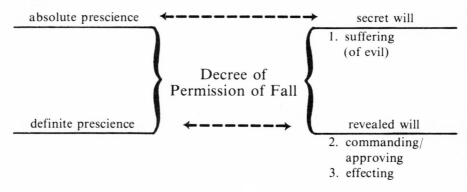

---

[98] *Defence*, 8.

[99] Ibid., 9.

[100] In Scholastic thought this distinction is usually discussed in connection with God's knowledge of future contingents (e.g. Thomas, *Summa Theologica* I, 1. 14, a. 13) and expressed as the difference between *necessitas consequentis* and *necessitas consequentiae*.

Robinson is careful to note that God's will, like His prescience, is "simple, and one in its nature," yet it exercises itself diversely in regard to God's works *ad extra*. Thus God's will is manifested in three progressively powerful degrees: suffering, commanding, effecting. This means that God's concurrence works differently with respect to good and evil actions. God did not will the Fall immediately, that is by His revealed will, but by His secret will as a means of illustrating His glory. The Jews' unwillingness to be gathered into Christ was, like Adam's fall, against God's commanding (revealed) will, but not against His "willing, which sets his almightie power awork."[101] Adam's sin, then, was of necessity (*necessitas consequentiae*), but not by compulsion. Robinson sees no logical inconsistency in the two. The elect angels, for example, serve God voluntarily yet of necessity; the demons, on the other hand, work evil necessarily yet most willingly.

There is a further question still which must be raised concerning God's causality of the first human sin: could not God have made Adam in such a way that he would have been impervious to temptation and so to sin? Arminius had decided this question by declaring that God "neither denied nor withdrew any thing that was necessary for avoiding this sin."[102] Robinson can only accept this in a highly qualified sense. It is quite true, he says, that Adam was given "grace sufficient and necessarie" to withstand the temptation, and that his fall came about "through his owne

---

The former is a simple or absolute necessity which may be predicated of things whose opposites are impossible because of the nature of the cause or subject, such as the attributes of God. Necessity of consequence, also called *necessitas ex hypothesi*, follows inevitably from a prior condition, but allows for contingency. Thus we may say that it necessarily follows that Adam would sin if God willed this to happen by His eternal decree, but it does not follow that he sinned necessarily, since his own will was also involved in the act.

[101]Ibid., 22. It might be well to distinguish Robinson's understanding of the twofold will in God, which he called "the received distinction," from two other interpretations: 1) the Scholastic distinction between *voluntas antecedens* and *voluntas consequens* where the latter is understood to limit the former in terms of predestination by taking into account human merits and free will, cf. H. A. Oberman, *Archbishop Thomas Bradwardine* (Utrecht, 1958), 95-99; 2) the Amyraldian juxtaposition of the secret and revealed wills so as to distinguish predestination to salvation from predestination to faith within a framework of hypothetical universalism, cf. Armstrong, op. cit., 192-96. Robinson's use is more in line with that of Luther in *De Servo Arbitrio* where the revealed or "preached" will corresponds to election and the hidden will to reprobation. On this formulation in Calvin see *New Testament Commentaries*, vol. 8, 259-61; *Concerning the Eternal Predestination of God*, tr. J. K. S. Reid (London, 1961), 64-68, 105-09; in Perkins, *op. cit*, 178-86, 250.

[102]*Writings of Arminius*, vol. 1, 482.

default, in not depending upon God as he ought."[103] Yet God could have prevented Adam from sinning altogether by granting him "irresistable grace" or by placing some impediment which would have hindered his sin. But in fact God sustained the natural motions and faculties and even provided the occasions (the forbidden fruit, the subtle serpent) by which the sin was wrought. Why He chose to leave Adam subject to temptation is a "deep mystery" which resides in God's secret will.

Finally, it is improper to speak of God as willing Adam's sin in so far as sin is the "absence and want of that conformity and agreeablenesse which ought to be in the thought, word, or work of the reasonable creature to the Law of God."[104] As we saw earlier, Robinson generally stresses the nature of sin as concupiscence, but here he latches onto the other element of the Augustinian definition: sin is the privation of the good. Sin in no way refers to the natural acts of motions, but to their abuse or misapplication. In this sense sin is a "nothing"—not negatively, but privatively. Hence sin cannot be seen to be the destinated end of Creation. Rather it came in by accident (*per accidens*), though God by His infinite wisdom and power, without violating His holiness or the creature's will, so ordered and disposed it as to effect what He had purposed in His eternal decree.

Obviously, the definition of sin as non-being alleviates the problem of explaining God's authorship of evil. Yet it is not a completely satisfying answer. For if God did not will the Fall properly, that is by commanding, approving, or compelling it, He did do so proximately, by permitting it, and that, not as a "bare sufferer" but as an infallible Foreseer. Ultimately Robinson, in company with all theological determinists who posit the contingency of human willing on the one hand and the inviolability of the eternal decree on the other, has recourse only to the unfathomable resolution expressed in the *O altitudo* of the Pauline doxology (Rom. 11:33).

Predestination and Perseverance

In the preceding section divine prescience was treated in connection with providence as it bears upon the second (in the infralapsarian scheme) decree, that of permission of the Fall. More commonly in the history of

---

[103] *Defence*, 13.

[104] Ibid., 24.

the doctrine of election, however, God's foreknowledge has been seen to be decisive in the subsequent decree of predestination/reprobation. In the context of protesting against Bernard's attempt to make Church government "as vncertayne as an Almanack" by presenting contrary opinions concerning it, Robinson makes the following parenthetical comment:

> Now if other men should take this course Mr. B. doth, in other points of religion, and one lay down the differences that are about predestination and the points depending vpon it, some vtterly denying it, others affirming it, and of these some grounding it vpon Gods mere grace, others vpo mans faith or workes foreseen . . . there could not be a course devised by the Divell more pregnant to perswade the multitude, that there were no certaynty, nor soundnes in the scriptures.[105]

Leaving aside those who completely deny predestination, Robinson refers here to three competing approaches to predestination: one which denies that God's decision in election is informed in any way by variability within the human condition, two others which subordinate God's decision to His foreknowledge of human response.

No one in the tradition denied, given Paul's clear statement to the contrary, that those are predestined whom God foreknew (Rom. 8:29). Rather the issue is whether the *object* of God's knowledge is the faith or works which will reside in the elect, or God's own determination to choose certain members of the human family irrespective of their activity. In other words, is predestination primarily an act of the divine will or an act of the divine intellect? Those who opted for the latter position were generally motivated by a dual concern. First, they felt that the impartiality of God would be threatened by a doctrine of radical gratuity. As a demonstration of His basic fairness, they claimed, God's initial disposition toward the human race was one of equanimity: God related on an equal basis to all (*se aequaliter habet ad omnes*). Only after the divine intellect had ascertained whether man's free will would make proper use of the gift of grace did the divine will decide to apportion such grace to this or that individual.[106] Another motive for the subordination of predestination to prescience can be traced to the original "Semi-Pelagian" reaction to Augustine's exposition of prevenient grace. Under the leadership of John Cassian the monks of southern Gaul protested that Augus-

---

[105]*Justification*, 172.

[106]Alexander of Hales, an early Franciscan scholastic, may be cited as representative of this position: "praescientia se habet aequaliter ad omnes, voluntas similiter uno modo se habet ad omnes; sed voluntas cum praescientia non se habet aequaliter ad omnes . . . . unde praedestinatio non solum dicit voluntatem Dei, sed voluntatem cum praescientia quod bene usuri sunt dono suo." *Summa Theologica*, vol. 1 (Quaracchi, 1924), 320.

tine's emphasis on inevitability would have a paralyzing effect on the attempt to implement the counsels of perfection, and thus undermine the moral effort of the *militia Christiana*.[107] When applied to the doctrine of predestination this concern for human responsibility, combined with the urgency of moral exhortation, found expression in the concept of election *post previsa merita*. Predestination in this scheme is not so much an act of divine sovereignty as it is a reaction to human activity.[108]

The Canons of Dort can be seen as the culmination of a theological voluntarism which springs from the writings of the *Doctor Gratiae* and winds its way, not without many turns and stops, through the points of Gottschalk, the systems of Scotus, Bradwardine, and Gregory of Rimini, to the numerous Reformation debates over predestination of which the Arminian Controversy was a delayed echo. Though he was frequently accused of Pelagianism, Arminius—a student if not a disciple of Beza— saw himself as a Reformed theologian whose departure from Calvin was, as Carl Bangs has rightly noted, a development within Reformed theology, not an intrusion from without.[109] His doctrine of predestination cannot, then, be simply equated with the "Neo-Semi-Pelagianism" of the late Middle Ages against which Luther and Calvin lodged such strong objections. Indeed, Arminius' primary concern was to reassert the fundamental Christological basis of election which he felt was threatened by the orthodox Calvinist formulation of predestination in its reduction of Christ to the mere means by which God executed His prior decree.[110] Nonetheless, Arminius posed a serious threat to radical voluntarism in one particular—he reintroduced the category of prescience as a limiting factor to God's general purpose of salvation. This feature of his doctrine of predestination is clearly seen in his peculiar arrangement of the divine decrees. According to Arminius God has determined: 1) to appoint Jesus Christ to obtain salvation for all mankind; 2) to save all those who repent

---

[107]The essential elements of the Semi-Pelagian reaction may be summarized in two propositions: (1) the first impulse or beginning of faith (*initium fidei*) is not through the gift of grace, but is in us by nature; (2) God predestinates no one to evil (*ad malum*). The latter of these was incorporated in the canons of the second Council of Orange (529). Cf. *Documents of the Christian Church,* ed. Henry Bettenson (London, 1963), 61-62 Jaroslav Pelikan. *The Emergence of the Catholic Tradition* (Chicago, 1971), 318-31.

[108]Indicative of this position, and of the corollary understanding of justification as process rather than as imputation is Gabriel Biel's claim: *Deus non prius est ultor quam aliquis sit peccator.* For a discussion of Biel's doctrine of election and reprobation, see Oberman, *Harvest,* 185-248.

[109]Bangs, *Arminius,* 349.

[110]Cf. *Works of Arminius,* vol. 1, 211-22. This is, of course, also the focus of Karl Barth's reinterpretation of the doctrine of election. Cf. *Church Dogmatics* II/2 (Edinburg, 1957).

and believe, while leaving in sin all impenitent and unbelieving persons; 3) to administer sufficient means necessary for repentance and faith to all; 4) to elect or damn those persons whom God from eternity foreknew would believe or not believe.[111] Arminius' doctrine of predestination can be called *absolute* only in respect to the first decree, that predestination which has at its object Jesus Christ. A further problem from the orthodox Calvinist perspective arises from the fact that Arminius disallows predestination of individuals qua individuals; there is only predestination of classes of individuals (believers) who possess a certain quality (faith). Predestination on the basis of foreseen faith is not the same as predestination *post previsa merita* for faith is understood in an evangelical, that is, Protestant sense as the mode by which one apprehends Christ's imputed righteousness.[112] Still, faith is not inalienable: it can be resisted when offered and forfeited after obtained. Predestination for Arminius was effectual only after the divine will had been furnished through prescience with information concerning the grasp of faith.

This amounted to a significant revision of the Reformed doctrine of predestination, and the delegates of Dort responded with a definition which represented the consensus of strict Calvinism:

> Election is the unchangeable purpose of God, whereby, before the foundation of the world, he hath, out of mere grace, according to the sovereign good pleasure of his own will, chosen, from the whole human race, which had fallen through their own fault, from their primitive state of rectitude, into sin and destruction, a certain number of persons to redemption in Christ, whom he from eternity appointed the Mediator and head of the elect, and the foundation of salvation.[113]

They also explicitly rejected, as having a "strong tang of Pegagius," the

---

[111] *Writings of Arminius*, vol. 2, 247-48. This ordering of the divine decrees is properly neither supra nor infralapsarian. By excluding the Fall from the decrees Arminius is spared the difficulty of accounting for God's authorship of sin. He is open, however, to the charge of making the plan of redemption appear as an *ad hoc* decision of God, an act designed to counter the unexpected consequences of Adam's fall.

[112] Ibid., 355-64. Arminius denied that he ever said that faith is not "the pure gift of God, but depends partly on the grace of God, and partly on the powers of Free Will." Ibid., 365.

[113] *Creeds of Christendom*, vol. 3, 552-53. "Est autem electio immutabile Dei propositum, quo ante jacta mundi fundamenta ex universo genere humano, ex primaeva integritate in peccatum et exitium sua culpa prolapso, secundum liberrimum voluntatis suae beneplacitum, ex mera gratia, certam quorundum hominum multitudinem, aliis nec meliorum, nec digniorum, sed in communi miseria cum aliis jacentium, ad salutem elegit in Christo, quem etiam ab aeterno Mediatorem et omnium electorum caput, salutisque fundamentum constituit."

Arminian formulation of election *ex praevisa fide*.[114] The election of God cannot be tied to the fulfillment of any indeterminate condition. It is prior to, not dependent upon, repentance and faith whether considered as foreseen or actual.

Robinson does not pursue the theological problem posed by the Canon's affirmation (in contrast to the Heidelberg Catechism [Q. 36] but in keeping with Calvin and Beza) of the *eternal* Mediatorship of Christ, namely the resultant inferiority of the Second to the First Person of the Trinity.[115] Significantly, on one occasion Robinson was accused by an unknown opponent of Trinitarian heterodoxy, but he deemed the charge so spurious as to warrant no more than a formulary response.[116] Like Article 2 of the *Confession* of 1596, Robinson remained fully within the limits of the orthodox doctrine of the Trinity, but the unresolved problem of Mediatorship concealed a weakness in Reformed Triadology which would eventually manifest itself in the appearance of Unitarianism among Robinson's spiritual descendants at Plymouth and elsewhere.

Robinson's opponents paraphrased the Synod's definition of election in their criticism of it. Robinson quotes it verbatim to avoid "the partiall and perverse relations" of his adversaries, and focusses his defense of predestination on three elements alluded to in the definition: unconditionality, particularity, and duality.[117]

Unconditionality. Robinson begins his treatment of predestination with a discussion of the meaning of the term and its proper use. He protests the way his adversaries have framed their objection. It is not sensible to say, as they have, that "God predestinated to make the world and man." To predestinate is to predetermine or ordain beforehand a thing to its ends. Thus, it is correct to say that God purposed to make the world and man; He predestinated them to their ends, that is, to redound to the glory of God. Predestination, then, may be properly predicated of things in both the created and uncreated orders. Christ, though uncreated, was predestined "before the foundation of the world" to the end that he might bring many sons to glory. On the other hand, the glory of God's grace in man's salvation, while a created thing, is not "preor-

---

[114]*The Judgement of the Synode Holden at Dort* (London, 1619), 13. This was the first English translation of the Canons of Dort.

[115]On Calvin's struggle with the problem of the Mediator, see Jill Raitt, "The Person of the Mediator: Calvin's Christology and Beza's Fidelity," *Occasional Papers of the American Society for Reformation Research*, ed. R. C. Walton, vol. 1, (1977), 53-80.

[116]*Works*, vol. 3, 8.

[117]*Defence*, 41.

dained to any end, being it selfe the utmost end of all things."[118]

The *ab aeterno* character of absolute predestination, so prominent in the definition of Dort, seemed to the Arminians to require a degree of arbitrariness which was inconsistent with the universal mission of the Church. Murton's caricature of the Calvinist view was that of a physician who, upon entering a house of sick men, cures some for no reason who are then bound to thank him, while ignoring others equally sick who cannot complain because they have nothing coming to them in any event. Rather, he went on, is Christ to be likened to a "Phisition truely mercifull" who proclaims that he will heal all who will take a medicine. Some, taking it, are cured while others, refusing because it is bitter, remain uncured. This example, Robinson responds, underestimates both the gravity of the human condition and the efficacy of God's grace. It assumes that there is an equal disposition to respond in all who hear the offer of salvation. Yet the ability to respond is itself the result of God's special prevening grace:

> So that not onely the medecine it selfe, and offer of it, but also the hand to receiv it with (which is faith, and a beleeving heart) is Gods gift.[119]

This faith, then, is not the "fore found conditions for which God chuseth a man," but the actual conferring and confirming of that which God had purposed in eternity past.[120] The doctrine of foreseen faith, on the other hand, posits a reason for predestination which is extrinsic to God Himself. Robinson believes that this is the root error of the Arminian system for it compromises the sovereignty of God in two respects. First, by interposing faith as a qualifying factor into the decree of election, God's deliberation is robbed of its decisiveness and God Himself is made

> like a weak man, contriving his purposes with its etc. ands; as though he stood in a mammering, and unresolved, what to doe, till hee found by experience what men would doe first.[121]

At the same time, if faith as a human possibility antedates (via foreknowledge) the decision of predestination, then God is inexorably *bound* to save all who believe. But this contradicts the character of the gospel as "meer grace" by turning it into a debt which is owed by God to man upon

---

[118]Ibid., 1-2. Election and predestination are often used interchangeably. Robinson holds that they are the same in substance, but that predestination denotes the supernatural ends purposed by God whereas election is used in respect to others from whom God selects His own. Ibid., 51.

[119]Ibid., 44.

[120]Ibid., 52.

[121]Ibid., 56.

the fulfillment of a condition. Both of these objections are designed to protect the nature of God from anthropomorphic encroachments, and to underscore the wholly gratuitous character of predestination.

Particularity. Murton had urged in connection with the example of Christ as a merciful physician the Dominical words of Matt. 11:28: "Come unto me, all ye who labor and are heavy laden." It is on this basis that the promise of the gospel, that is, God's will to save all who believe, is extended universally. In reply, Robinson claims that God indeed desires the conversion of all to whom the gospel is preached so as to command and approve the same. But a closer analysis of the proclamation event is required. First it is clear that not all are exposed to this preaching, and of those who are, some are illumined while others remain in spiritual darkness. To account for this differentiation Robinson distinguishes various degrees of God's calling. This point is illustrated by the parable of the marriage banquet and the oft-quoted saying of Jesus: "Many are called, but few are chosen" (Matt. 22:14). In this story there are three levels of response to the gospel: the first, when those who hear the invitation simply refuse to come; the second, when some are persuaded to come after a manner, but without true faith and repentance, as those who lacked the proper garment; the third, those who come in true faith, as those guests who were permitted to stay. Only to this last group can the Pauline statement be applied: "Whom be predestinated them also he called" (Rom. 8:30). Thus there is a disjunction between the offer of salvation and its actual appropriation. God can be said to will the conversion of all insofar as He directs that the gospel be preached promiscuously, but He wills the conversion of the elect "with another and further intention of will."[122] This "further work" is described as an inward work of the Holy Spirit by which the outward means of salvation are made effectual.[123] As we shall see, this emphasis upon particularity has direct implications for the understanding of the work of Christ. The gift of saving faith does not merely presuppose a prior satisfaction of God's justice. It presupposes as well the limited design of Christ's atonement by linking it directly to that part of the decree of predestination which applies only to the elect.

The insertion of foreseen faith into the divine decrees was intended by the Arminians to have a widening effect on the doctrine of predestination.

---

[122]Ibid., 44.

[123]Ibid., 45: "It is then Gods holy Spirit, which he giues to one that hears the Gospell, and not to another; which makes one hearer spirituall, and not another: thereby changing both the will, and the whole man of him to whom he giues it."

To Robinson it seemed to abrogate predestination altogether since the object of God's decision was transferred from individual members of the human race to classes or groups (believers), or in some formulations to the quality of faith itself.[124] The Scriptures, he insists, never mention election of qualities, but always of persons. Moreover, apart from predestination, God foresees nothing in fallen man that is not worthy of destruction: "What quality but of sin, and misery, sees the Lord in them whom he calleth?"[125] The doctrine of particular predestination was also defended on another front. Murton had claimed that actual or particular election as taught by the Calvinists was a logical impossibility since individual persons "could not be actually chosen before they had any being."[126] Robinson acknowledges that predestination derives from a pretemporal decree, but denies that election of individuals is thereby precluded:

> Nothing in God is potentiall, but all actuall. Otherwise there should be imperfection in God, as all potentialls are being to be perfected by their actualities.[127]

Here, as in his defense of unconditionality, Robinson's focus is more directly theological (that is, relating to the doctrine of God) than soteriological. At no point may God's role as supreme Actor in the salvation of His creatures be limited by the imputation of a passive waiting on God's part till man has acted.

Duality. The negative side of predestination is expressed in the doctrine of preterition, the belief that God out of the good pleasure of His will has resolved not only to ordain certain persons to eternal life but to reprobate others to eternal death. Since, in its strictest form, both aspects of this determination are seen to derive equally from God's apriori sovereignty, this doctrine is often called double, or "twin" predestination (*gemina praedestinatio*).[128] The relationship of predestination and repro-

---

[124]This concern was also expressed in the Canons of Dort (I.x): "Caussa vero hujus gratuitae electionis, est solum Dei beneplacitum, non in eo consistens, quod certas qualitates seu actiones humanas, ex omnibus possibilibus, in salutis conditionem elegit; sed in eo, quod certas quasdam personas ex communi peccatorum multitudine sibi in peculium adscivit." *Creeds of Christendom*, vol. 3, 554.

[125]*Defence*, 55.

[126]*Discription*, 42.

[127]*Defence*, 48.

[128]Though sometimes attributed to Augustine, double predestination is found in his works only by implication. The first positive statement of this doctrine comes from Isidore of Seville: "There is a double predestination, whether of the elect to rest or of the damned to death. Both are caused by divine judgment." *Sentences* 2, 6; cf. Jaroslav Pelikan, *The Growth of Medieval Theology* (Chicago, 1978), 88. This formulation was repeated and

bation was at the heart of the predestination-*streite* of the sixteenth century, and it was here that the Arminians found the implications of the Calvinist schema most invidious.[129]

Robinson's discussion of the *decretum horribile* (*Inst.* 3,23.7) flows in two, not exactly parallel, directions. Much of what he says about the dark side of predestination suggests that he accepted the equal ultimacy and parity of election and rejection. There are not, properly speaking, two separate decrees, one of election, the other of reprobation, but a single decree with two aspects.[130] The two-sidedness of this decree is held together in the intention of God, that is to manifest diversely several facets of God's nature. In this view election and reprobation are seen as the means by which, alternately, the divine attributes of mercy and justice are displayed:

> Why God should thus chuse some, and passe by others, in the generall, we see reason, both by the light of nature, and the Scriptures; namely, that the glory of his power, and justice might be seen in the one, and of the riches of his mercy in the other.[131]

Robinson further explains that the "reason" for election/rejection here discerned refers only to the general purpose of predestination; why this particular man or woman is chosen, and another not, is imperceptible even to the eye of faith. Lest one presume to call God to account for His non-granting of salvation to some, Robinson reiterates the wholly gratuitous character of His saving any. Nothing would have been lost to His justice had He left all in the state of misery and sin!

---

defended by several medieval theologians, notably Gottschalk, Bradwardine, and Gregory of Rimini, and re-emerged as a distinctive feature of the doctrine of election in both Luther and Calvin. On Luther see Wolfhart Pannenberg, "Der Einfluss der Anfechtungserfahrung auf den Prädestinationsbegriff Luthers," *Kergyma und Dogma,* vol. 3 (1957), 109-39. Perhaps the clearest statement of double predestination in Calvin is *Inst.* 3,22.11: "Ergo si non possumus rationem assignare cur suos misericordia dignetur, nisi quoniam ita illi placet: neque etiam in aliis reprobandis aliud habebimus quam eius voluntatem." And a few lines later: "Ipsa electio nisi reprobationi opposita non staret." *Calvini Opera,* vol. 4, 393-94.

[129]In attempting to mediate the double predestinarianism of Nikolaus von Amsdorf and the synergism of Johannes Pfeffinger, the Formula of Concord makes the cause of damnation entirely man's doing, without reference to the decree of election. see *Creeds of Christensom,* vol. 3, 165-73. Cf. Robert Kolb, "Nikolaus von Amsdorf on Vessels of Wrath and Vessels of Mercy: A Lutheran Doctrine of Double Predestination," *Harvard Theological Review* 66 (1976), 325-43. On double predestination in the Reformed tradition after Calvin, see Heppe, op. cit., 178-89.

[130]Cf. Barth's comment that Calvin's doctrine of predestination is double in that election and rejection may be considered as "two species within the one genus designated by the term predestination." *Church Dogmatics,* II/2, 17.

[131]*Defence,* 58.

The parity of predestination to life and reprobation to death is further suggested by the contrasting examples of Ishmael-Esau and Isaac-Jacob in Paul's disquisition on election in Romans 9. The Arminian exegesis of this obviously crucial passage was based on the premise that it should be interpreted in the light of Paul's earlier discourse on justification in chapters three and four. The issue in Romans 9 was precisely the same which concerned Paul before: whether righteousness is derived by obedience to the works of the Law, or simply by faith in Christ. Isaac-Jacob are thus interpreted as types of those who seek righteousness by faith, while Ishmael-Esau typify the "children of the flesh" who seek righteousness by works. In both cases the individuals in question are removed from the grip of particularity by being made the representatives of two groups or classes, that is, believers or unbelievers, who are (as classes) the proper objects of predestination.[132]

Against this reading Robinson registers two general objections. First, it does violence to the clear order of the epistle which begins with an analysis of the sinful condition of humanity under God's wrath (chs. 1-2), then treats of justification (chs. 3-5), sanctification (chs. 6-7), perseverance (ch. 8), and finally election (chs. 9-11). Second, it ignores the real question posed in chapter nine: how to account for the fact that not all members of the elect nation are chosen ("They are not all Israel, which are of Israel" [9:6b]). Nor is the attempt to interpret Jacob and Esau typologically allowed: "It is the high way to heresie, to be bold and in framing typical expositions."[133] Still less can God's prior love or hate in respect to these brothers (9:13) be grounded upon some future disposition in each to receive or repudiate grace. The dual decision of God was not subject to such a subsequent ratification because, as the Apostle says, it was made before they were yet born, or had done any good or evil (even in God's foreknowledge), in order that "the purpose of God according to election might stand" (9:11). To permit foreseen unbelief to function as the determining cause of reprobation would be to place it on the same footing with grace; for as grace occasioned the salvation of some, so unbelief would occasion the loss of others.[134] The contrast in God's attitude toward Jacob and Esau is simply a reminder that no one is predestined casually or fortuitously, but each is ordained with specific ends in mind.

God's role in reprobation is made even more explicit by Paul's citation of another Old Testament example, that of Pharaoh whose heart was

---

[132]Cf. Arminius' exegesis of this controverted passage: *Writings of Arminius*, vol. 3, 527-58.

[133]*Defence*, 84.

[134]On Calvin's use of this argument against Albert Pighius, see Reid, op. cit., 105-09.

hardened by God (9:17-18). The Arminians again extracted from this example a general principle: "God wills to harden only those sinners who persevere in their sins against the long-suffering of God."[135] They thus assigned to God a completely passive or reactive role in rejection. But, Robinson insists, the text imports a further activity of God. In the hardening of Pharaoh God was not a sufferer only, that is, in giving Pharaoh up to his own sins, but a doer as well in that He "raised him up" in order to manifest His glory and power thereby. Robinson comments:

> Every end must have an efficient or working cause. The glory of God was not the end of Satans work, nor of Pharaohs work; and therefore of Gods work in it.[136]

Had it not been for the "powerfull, and unerring hand of God" Pharaoh's heart might indeed have been softened by the miracles in which case God's will would have been contravened, and His word, which before had foretold the hardening, would have been made of no effect.[137]

Thus far our analysis of Robinson's discussion of reprobation has shown him to be a thoroughgoing double predestinatian, laying equal stress on the negative and positive aspects of God's all-embracing decree. This is, however, not a completely accurate portrayal of his position for, in addition to emphasizing the equal ultimacy of election and rejection, Robinson also recognized—at least in one respect—the nonparity of predestination to life and its antithesis. The inequality of the two may be described as a fundamental difference in their respective *modi operandi*. The Synod of Dort had already anticipated this reservation when, in the conclusion of the Canons, it rejected the position, foisted upon it by the Remonstrants, that

> in the same manner in which election is the fountain and cause of faith and good works, reprobation is the cause of unbelief and impiety.[138]

This hesitation to consider—"in the same manner"—election and reprobation springs from the same motive raised earlier in connection with prescience, namely the need to exculpate God from the *blame* of human sin. In the counsel of God, therefore, salvation and damnation are corollaries but not co-ordinates. Both are ultimately grounded in God's sovereign will, but the latter also has a proximate cause—human wickedness—which the former lacks. God's hardening of the non-elect,

---

[135] *Writings of Arminius*, vol. 3, 548-49.

[136] *Defence*, 90.

[137] Ibid., 91.

[138] *Creeds of Christendom*, vol. 3, 576: "eodem modo, quo electio est fons et caussa fidei ac bonorum operum, reprobationem esse caussam infidelitatis et impietatis."

then, while not based on their foreseen sins, is nonetheless not effected without respect to them. Robinson uses a rather inelegant metaphor to explain:

> As the Sun puts no ill favour into the dunghill, though the stink therof be increased by its shining: so neither doth God add any hardnesse, or impenitency to any, but onely leaves unrestrained, occasions, stirs up, and orders the corruption which he finds in men to this event.[139]

We have come upon a curious twist in Robinson's doctrine of election: while the elect are chosen with no reference to their faith, the reprobates are chosen, not because of but nonetheless in view of, their foreseen sins. So God "predestinates none to condemnation; or which is all one purpose, to condemne none, but for sin freely by them to be practised, as the fore-going condition, and onely deserving cause of condemnation."[140] But does not this linkage of reprobation and prescience admit the Arminian thesis that variability within the human condition decisively informs the counsel of God? Robinson anticipates the question and responds— expectedly!—with a distinction. Within the realm of God's secret will reprobation has for its object sin permitted by God and the sinner preordained by God to redound to His own glory. Here God's apriori sovereignty is unconditional and impregnable. The other aspect of reprobation, the *praedamnatio* itself, refers to the actual appointment of punishment due, and in this respect God decrees it toward none, "but for their sin, by him infallibly foreseen, and by them freely to be committed and continued in without repentance."[141] Robinson is able to make this distinction because he is defending the infralapsarian sequence of the decrees. Only when the decree of election presupposes the Fall can reprobation in any sense be conditioned by foreseen actualities.

In summary, we may characterize Robinson's understanding of the relation between election and rejection as asymmetrical: salvation finds its sole origin in God's gracious decision, but reprobation, while also ultimately traceable to the secret will of God, carries with it a proximate as well as a remote cause, namely, man's own sinfulness.

Predestination refers to God's sovereign purpose, embodied in the eternal decree, to bring to glory certain members of the human family while assigning others to their deserved condemnation. The actual effecting of this decree, as concerns the elect, is expressed in the doctrine of the

---

[139] *Defence*, 94.

[140] Ibid., 80.

[141] Ibid., 92.

perseverance of the saints.[142] By this doctrine, which declares that God's decision will be finally confirmed in all of the elect despite all obstacles, however serious, the abstractness of the eternal decree is brought within the purview of historical vicissitudes and related directly to the earthly pilgrimage of the elect.

Despite the heat generated by the debate over this doctrine, there is on first sight a striking similarity between the Arminian position on perseverance and that adopted at the Synod of Dort. (In this connection it is well to remember that the Remonstrance of 1610 had taken an equivocal stand on this point, reflecting the ambivalence of Arminius himself.)[143] Both parties hold that only true believers will persevere to the end, both agree that it is possible for believers to fall, and that once fallen they may be restored by grace. However, these are only surface similarities which disguise a more deep-seated difference. The issue may be said to turn on the question of the indefectibility of faith, on whether, in the words of the Westminster Confession, one "whom God hath accepted in his Beloved, effectually called and sanctified by his Spirit" can totally or finally fall away from the state of grace.[144] The Arminians thought that they could and backed up their contention with a battery of scriptural examples. The Calvinists denied any such ultimate frustration of God's purpose in election and so based perseverance upon the faithfulness of God rather

---

[142]This aspect of the doctrine of election derives its name from the title of one of Augustine's anti-Pelagian works, *De dono perseverantiae*, where perseverance is included with obedience and chastity, as a special gift which adheres to the elect unto death. Augustine's clearest statement on perseverance is found, however, in an earlier work, *De corruptione et gratia* 9, 22: "Quia ergo non habuerunt perseverantiam sicut non vere discipuli Christi, ita nec vere filii Dei fuerunt, etiam quando esse videbantur et ita vocabantur. Qui autem cadunt et pereunt, in praedestinatorum numero non fuerunt." ML 44, 929. This thesis was reasserted by a number of medieval theologians, including Thomas, who denied that one who is predestined could die in mortal sin and be eternally lost (*Summa theologica* 1, q. 24, a. 3). As formulated at the Synod of Dort, though, the perseverance of the saints is a distinctively Reformed doctrine which reflects Calvin's twofold alteration of the Augustinian view: 1) by linking perseverance with faith and salvation-assurance Calvin allows believers to be "certainly persuaded" that they are among the elect (*Inst.* 3,2.15-21), a proposition which Augustine explicitly denies (*De dono perseverantiae*, 1,1); 2) Calvin asserts that once true faith is engendered, it can never be totally lost—the scope of perseverance is thus widened to include not only the final end of the elect, but also the entire life of faith (*Inst.* 3,2.12). Among Reformed theologians Peter Martyr seems to have been unique in not following Calvin on the second point. Cf. John P. Donelly, *Calvinism and Scholasticism in Vermigli's Doctrine of Man and Grace* (Leiden, 1976), 154. On this doctrine in Reformation theology generally see Jürgen Moltmann, *Prädestination und Perseveranz* (Neukirchen, 1961), esp., with reference to the Arminian Controversy, 127-37.

[143]*Creeds of Christendom*, vol. 3, 548-49. Cf. *Writings of Arminius,* 458-70.

[144]*Creeds of Christendom*, vol. 3, 636.

than the steadfastness of the believer. Robinson takes up in succession three arguments levelled against this construction of the doctrine of perseverance: that it is incompatible with the teaching of Scripture concerning apostasy, admonition, and temptation.

Perseverance and Apostasy. The doctrine of perseverance set forth in the Canons of Dort (V. viii) affirmed that, as a consequence of God's free mercy, the elect were never in jeopardy of falling *totaliter* nor *finaliter*. It is with the former of these qualifying adverbs that the issue of apostasy is concerned. Apostasy is defined as a fall so grievous as to provoke the total desertion and complete withdrawal of the Holy Spirit. The difficulty for the Calvinist position is that there are a number of Scriptural passages which suggest that believers are indeed liable to such a lapse. Robinson devotes considerable attention to the perusal of these texts and finds that they fall into two general categories. First there are those conditional statements which do not imply an actual state of apostasy. Such are the oft-cited verses in the Epistle to the Hebrews: "If they shall fall away, it is impossible to renew them again to repentance" (6:4-6); "If we sin wilfully after we receive the truth, there remaineth no more sacrifice for sins" (10:26). Robinson anticipates an objection: If these are only hypothetical suppositions why do they contain such dire consequences, and why are they addressed to the Church? Three answers come to mind: 1) they keep the truly faithful from falling into gross sin; 2) they guard against a false security; 3) they depict the fearful state of the incurable hypocrites and apostates.[145] As for other texts which seem to allow for apostasy among the elect, such as the lurid examples of the sow returning to wallow in its mire and the dog in its vomit (2 Pet. 2:20-22), the fall described therein is from an outward profession only, and is spoken of those who were never truly and effectually sanctified, except in their own and other men's opinion. Moreover, the passages which speak of such apostasy often make it clear that the referent is not one of the elect. For example, Judas is said to be not among those given to Christ, but a son of perdition (John 17:12), and they that fall are such as *think* they stand, rather than they who do so in fact (I Cor. 10:12).[146]

Closely connected with the phenomenon of apostasy is the sin against the Holy Spirit, declared by Christ to be irremissible (Luke 12:10). The Canons (V. vi) explicitly state that the elect, as a part of their perseverance, are prevented from committing this particular sin. It can be committed only by the reprobate, but it is not committed by all of the

---

[145] *Defence*, 105-06.

[146] Ibid., 124.

reprobate. Some theologians had understood this sin as the final impenitence of the wicked, the antithesis of the perseverance of the saints.[147]
Robinson sees it as a persistent and malicious attitude toward the work of
the Holy Spirit which manifests itself in three progressively insidious acts:
hatred, blasphemy, and persecution. This sin presupposes some degree of
enlightenment, and is usually committed after "some singular profession
made, and forsaken." It is more commonly incurred, Robinson believes,
than is ordinarily thought, especially by those "malitiously hateing and
persequuting true, and conscionable gospellers."[148] The sin is irremissible
not because it is more heinous than God's mercy is gracious, but because
God has determined never to vouchsafe faith and repentance to one who
so despises the work of His Spirit.

   Perseverance and Admonition. Perhaps the most telling argument
against perseverance, as formulated at Dort, is that it rendered men, as
the Remonstrants were made to say in the Conclusion to the Canons,

> carnally secure, since they are persuaded by it that nothing can hinder the
> salvation of the elect, let them live as they please; and, therefore, that they
> may safely perpetrate every species of the most atrocious crimes.[149]

In short, it is prejudicial to piety and undermines morality. Against this
peril the Arminians brought a host of Scriptural texts which abound in
admonitions and warnings about the tensions and dangers of the life of
faith. But if perseverance is guaranteed by an apriori decree, what are
these warnings but empty words? Robinson answers that these admonitions are real, not contrived, because the hazards faced by the believer are
real. Since no one in this life is immune from indwelling sin, and since
spots adhere to the best works of the saints, it is imperative for the elect to
be on guard lest he be drawn into enormous sins by Satan, the world, and
the flesh, and so grieve the Holy Spirit and forfeit the sense of God's
favor. Thus a true understanding of perseverance is not contradicted but
reinforced by the moral exhortations and admonitions of Scripture: they
are the very means by which God has determined to keep the elect from
utter defection. It is not more strange that God should infallibly obtain
His own end by His own means than it is that a skilled water worker
should transport water from the spring-head to the conduit by the careful

---

[147]Cf. Calvin's interpretation: "Certum enim est reprobationis signum in spiritum
blasphemia. Unde sequitur, quicunque in eam prolapsi fuerint, in reprobum sensum datos
esse." *Corpus Reformatorum*, vol. 45, 341.

[148]*Observations*, 269.

[149]*Creeds of Christendom*, vol. 3, 576: "carnaliter securos, quippe ex ea persuasos
electorum saluti, quomodocunque vivant, non obesse, ideoque eos secure atrocissima
quaeque scelera posse perpetrare."

laying of pipes. Therefore, the truly faithful cannot ultimately fall away because they are armed by manifold admonitions against the evil of apostasy.[150]

Perseverance and Temptation. Just as the doctrine of perseverance is not negated but rather confirmed by the Biblical warnings, so it does not exclude but rather encompasses the various temptations which constantly beset the elect. The Canons (V. xi) attempt to give full weight to this element in the Christian pilgrimage by admitting that "under grevious temptations" (*in gravi tentatione*) believers often lose the full assurance of their faith and the certitude of perseverance. Believers are subject to temptation from three directions. First, there is "the heavy clog of our own corruption, which we draw after us": the depravity of our fallen nature fueled by the ever-active principle of concupiscence.[151] Thus every person has his own unique vulnerability to temptation, related to his temper of body, or sex, or age, or education, or custom, or company, and so forth, against which he must be on guard.[152] Second, temptation often originates with Satan who, though he cannot compel the mind to assent nor the will to consent, is able, being a spirit, "to unite himself in his suggestions with our spirits, after an unknown manner; and the same also very persuasive."[153] Third, there are also temptations of a sort from God though these are not provocations to sin, against which Jesus taught the disciples to pray, but "moderate tryals of fayth."[154] God's rule in the temptation process at once recalls the central affirmation of the doctrine of perseverance: all of our lives, including the testing and temptation, falls within the scope of God's ultimate intention. Even when the immediate agent of temptation is Satan, or our own self-love, God is active in His direction and permission. He is, therefore, the ultimate *limiting* factor in all temptations faced by the elect (I Cor. 10:13) and thus the ground of their perseverance. Believers are not immunized from temptation but neither are they ultimately jeopardized by it. Robinson gives the following example to illustrate both of these aspects of temptation, its reality and its limit, as they relate to perseverance:

> A Rebell lurking in a Kingdom, may, by some advantage watched, and taken prevail against the lawfull King, in a conflict, or two; and yet for all that, not

[150]*Defence*, 101-02.

[151]*Observations*, 32.

[152]Ibid., 241.

[153]Ibid., 239. Robinson discounts the idea that it is wiser to confess secret sins silently lest Satan overhear and take better advantage of our weaknesses for he is already "well acquainted with his own work in men." Ibid., 242.

[154]Ibid.

raign in the Kingdom: so may the trecherous flesh, lurking in a Spirituall
man, get the masterie in some combat; and yet not therefore drive the Lord
quite out of his Kingdom there.[155]

The life of faith is thus conceived as struggle, and, because perfection is
eschewed, possible defection. Yet the elect are assured, in the face of the
most contradictory circumstances, of the gift of final perseverance.

Limited Atonement and Irresistible Grace

If the process of salvation is represented as a linear development
originating in the decree of election and culminating in the final perseverance of the saints, all of which depends on God's apriori sovereignty, then
the essentiality of the work of Christ seems to be threatened. The Canons
of Dort anticipated this objection and sought to meet it in its affirmation
of the doctrine of limited atonement: Christ died only for those who in the
end will be saved, that is, the elect.[156] All of the antagonists of Dort—the
Remonstrants, Smyth and the Waterlanders, Helwys and the General
Baptists—were united in opposition to this doctrine. "God would have all
men saved," wrote Helwys.[157] Nor was the final position of the Synod
achieved without considerable debate among the delegates themselves.[158]
It was necessary, therefore, for Robinson to review with care the most
controversial of the five heads of doctrine decided at Dort.

Ostensibly the debate over the work of Christ centered on its extent
rather than its nature. The Remonstrance of 1610 says nothing explicitly
about the "how" of atonement, but simply affirms that Christ "died for all
men and for every man, so that he obtained for them all, by his death on
the cross, redemption and the forgiveness of sins."[159] Yet the second
chapter of the Canons (II. i-vii) proceeds to define the necessity for
atonement before locating its design in the sovereign counsel of God (II.

---

[155]Ibid., 31.

[156]The term "limited atonement" (neither word is used in the Canons) has been
criticized by Roger Nicole who prefers to speak of definite atonement which more clearly
conveys the element of intentionality. Cf. "The Doctrine of the Definite Atonement in the
Heidelberg Catechism," *The Gordon Review* 7 (1964), 138-45.

[157]Lumpkin, *Baptist Confessions of Faith*, 118.

[158]At the Synod the position that Christ died for "all particular men" was advanced by
Martinus of Bremen and supported by two of the English delegates, Davenant and Ward.
The Hessian delegates reported that there was greater dissension on this point than on any
other article. Hales, *Golden Remains*, 101. Cf. Herbert Darling Foster, "Liberal Calvinism: The Remonstrants at the Synod of Dort in 1618," *Harvard Theological Review* 16
(1923) 1-37.

[159]*Creeds of Christendom*, vol. 3, 546.

viii-ix). The view of atonement here presented is a variant of the "Latin" theory as formulated by Anselm in *Cur deus homo*? The necessity for atonement derives from the requirement that God's justice be satisfied because of the offense incurred through the committal of sin. Such offense, because it violates the infinite majesty of God, cannot simply be absolved on the basis of an equitable *quid pro quo*, but requires a satisfaction of infinite worth and value. The fact of the atonement, therefore, derives from the mercy of God who was pleased to give His Son in our stead that he might make satisfaction to divine justice on our behalf. The death of Christ, who in his self-offering was at once real man and co-essential with the Father and the Holy Spirit, in fact procured such a satisfaction in that it placated the wrath of God and removed the curse of sin.[160] This understanding of the atonement is *objective* in that God is both the reconciled and the reconciler in the work of Christ; it is *vicarious* in that Christ suffered as a proxy for those who were unable to make satisfaction in their own persons. Arminius had also spoken of the death of Christ as a satisfaction but he drew back from the Anselmian theory on one crucial point: he denied the infinitude of the guilt to be atoned. Thus the atonement is all the more a demonstration of God's mercy. Though Arminius did not write extensively on the nature of the work of Christ, his restriction of the magnitude of sin contains *in nuce* the idea which Hugo Grotius more fully elaborated, namely that Christ's death was not necessitated by anything intrinsic to the nature of God.[161]

---

[160]Calvin's principal modification of the Anselmian theory was his recognition of the saving efficacy of Christ's whole course of obedience, i.e. by dying, was Christ able to make satisfaction for others since by no other act could he forfeit what he was not going to lose (his life) or pay what he did not owe (the debt for sin). Cf. *A Scholastic Miscellany: Anselm to Ockham*, ed. E. R. Fairweather (New York, 1970), 176-79. His life, however exemplary, was not meritorious since he too was obliged—as man—to obey the law for himself. Calvin emphasized the unity of Christ's obedience—"the one obedience which embraced his entire life" (*Inst.* 2,16.5; 3,14.12)—thus including his active obedience to the law as a part of his reconciling task. The doctrine of a twofold obedience, *obedientia vitae* and *obedientia mortis*, was revived by Johann Piscator, and aroused a heated controversy in the Reformed churches. The Synod of Dort rejected Piscator's distinction and reaffirmed Calvin's emphasis on the unity of the work of Christ in obedience. Cf. G. C. Berkouwer, *The Work of Christ* (Grand Rapids, 1965), 325 n. 123; F. L. Box, *Johann Piscator* (Kampen, 1932).

[161]Grotius' famous rectoral theory of the atonement is based on a subtle inversion of the concept of substitution. Christ's death is taken to be a substitute for the penalty of sin (*acceptilatio*), on the basis of which God as the supreme sovereign (*summus princeps*) relaxes the penalty of eternal death demanded by the law. In the Anselmian view Christ bears the precise penalty of the law, and his death is thus an equivalent substituted penalty. Cf. Robert S. Franks, *The Work of Christ* (Edinburgh, 1962), 389-409; *The Writings of Arminius*, vol. 2, 2-51, 301-306.

The primary purpose of the atonement, then, is not the reconciliation of God to Himself, but the exhibition of His love for fallen man (Arminius), or the proper governance of the created order (Grotius).

Robinson assumes but does not enlarge upon the definition of atonement provided in the Canons. In his clearest statement on the nature of the work of Christ he reiterates its objective quality:

> The chief, and first work of our redemption by Christ is the freeing of vs from the guilt of sin, and most fearefull wrath of God, by paying the price of his pretious blood for a ransom to the iustice of his father, thereby procuring him of a most severe, and fearefull Iudg to become vnto vs a gracious father, and to love vs vnto life.[162]

Robinson is here responding to one of the propositions set forth in the confession published by the remainder of Smyth's company before they were absorbed by the Waterlanders. They had affirmed that although the sacrifice of Christ's body and blood which was offered unto the Father on the cross "be a sacrifice of a sweet smelling savour, yet it doth not reconcile God unto us, which never did hate us, nor was our enemy, but reconciled us to God."[163] Robinson replies that if the death of Christ were a sweet smelling savour to the Father, "is it not evident that we did formerly stinck in Gods nostrils by reason of our sins? Where he gave himself a sacrifice for vs, was it not to appease the fathers wrath toward vs?"[164] The description of Christ's death as a propitiation, derived from the ancient Jewish ritual of the mercy seat, entails an appeasement or conciliation intended to regain the favor of another. The focus of atonement, therefore, is not the laying aside of our hatred and enmity against God, though that should follow as an effect upon the other, but rather the taking away of God's hatred and enmity toward us.

Though the redeeming scope of Christ's death is limited by its subordination to the decree of election, this in no way implies that the work of Christ is intrinsically deficient. To underscore the significance of this claim Robinson employs a distinction which was first observed by Lombard and repeated in subsequent discussions of the work of Christ.

---

[162] *Of Religious Communion*, 120. Though Robinson here uses the word "ransom" there is no hint of the classic theory of the atonement since it is the justice of the Father which must be compensated, not the usurped rights of Satan.

[163] *Baptist Confessions of Faith*, 129.

[164] *Of Religious Communion*, loc. cit. The Victorian Calvinist theologian, Augustus H. Strong, gave the following illustration of God's wrath in relation to sin: "A pure woman needs to meet an infamous proposition with something more than a mild refusal. She must flame up and be angry. So it belongs to the holiness of God not to let sin go unchallenged. It is the wrath of God which sin must meet." *Systematic Theology* (Old Tappan, N.J., 1907), 743.

Lombard had asserted that the death of Christ was a sufficient sacrifice for the whole world (*pro omnibus*), but that it was *efficacious* only for those who were predestined to salvation.[165] This distinction might smack of scholastic hairsplitting, but in the later Reformation it was a matter of lively debate both within Reformed circles and in Reformed-Lutheran exchanges.[166] The universal sufficiency of the death of Christ, absolutely considered, is an affirmation of the infinite worth of Christ's sufferings and thus of the divine nature of his person. We might express the import of this statement thus: Had God elected all to salvation, no greater suffering would have been imposed on Christ than what he endured; and, conversely, had the number of the elect been fewer than what it is, Christ would have suffered no less than what he did. Robinson thus admits that Christ's death "might have been an effectual price for all if it had pleased the Father, and him so to have ordained."[167] The idea of the all-sufficiency of the death of Christ undergirds the doctrine of predestination in two ways. First, it safeguards the deity of Christ by recognizing that he who fulfilled by his death the eternal decree is none other than he who, as the second person of the Trinity, participated in its issuance, and that as God his sacrifice of himself can sustain no inherent limitation. Second, by admitting the hypothetical salvation of all, it highlights the actual salvation of only those selected by God. In other words, if there was no deficiency in the death of Christ, then God was not restrained from providing salvation to everyone by any factor other than His own will.

That God has not in fact decreed everyone to be saved is taken for granted by Robinson. Both he and his opponents agree that some will be ultimately lost, but Robinson proceeds from this fact to the limited design of Christ's death. This argument he puts in the form of a syllogism:

> All for whom Christ shall be saved.
> Yet all are not saved.
> Ergo, Christ died not for all.[168]

---

[165] *Sent.* bk. 3, d. 20: "Christus ergo est sacerdos, idemque et hostia pretium nostrae reconciliationis; qui se in ara crucis non diabolo, sed Trinitati obtulit pro omnibus, quantum ad pretii sufficientiam; sed pro electis tantum quantum ad efficaciam, quia praedestinatis tantum salutem effecit."

[166] The absolute sufficiency of Christ's death was one of the points on which Beza and Jacob Andreae could not agree at the Colloquy of Montbéliard in 1586. Beza rejected the sufficient/efficient distinction as a weakening of the particularism of election. W. Robert Godfrey has traced the development of Reformed thought on the extent of the atonement in his unpublished Ph.D. dissertation, "Tensions Within International Calvinism: The Debate on the Atonement and the Synod of Dort, 1618-1619," Stanford University (1974), chapter two.

[167] *Defence*, 59.

The minor premise is based upon the *ex post facto* observation that when the gospel is preached some respond and others do not. The source of this differentiation Robinson locates in the secret will of God, although the blame, as we have seen, he imputes to individual fallen men. For the Arminians man (through unbelief) is altogether responsible for his lost condition in his refusal to accept the removal of original sin which Christ has effected for him. On the major premise there is no agreement at all, the Arminians positing a decisive disjunction between the satisfaction rendered on behalf of all and the appropriation conditioned upon faith, the Calvinists insisting upon the necessary interrelation of these two aspects of Christ's work. Those who would extend the scope of the atonement in a universalistic direction advanced three lines of argument in favor of their position, and Robinson had to come to grip with each of these points.

In the first place, Murton cited as evidence of his contention that Christ was offered for all the universal revelation of God in nature and the sacrifices of the Gentiles which he believed were primordial remembrances of Christ. Robinson admits that God as creator, though not Christ as mediator, is reflected in the works of nature. This is evident both from the law of conscience within—"this naturall manuscript, or writing of Gods hand"—with which even infants are endowed, and from the display of divine power and majesty in the celestial bodies—"the Sun and Moon teaching God, as well before, as since Christ."[169] But, even so, man only dimly perceives this natural revelation "as he that lying in a dungeon, sees some little glimpse of light, and groaps after it, by the wall, hoping to come in time to some dore or window."[170] As for the Gentile sacrifices, they are by no means proof that salvation has been offered to all:

> The Apostle maketh the sacrifices of the Gentiles, means of fellowship with devils; these men make them means of fellowship with God . . . . Thus transforming God into the devill; the true Christ into a false, the Gospell into a heynous Idolatry; and the means of salvation into the highway, and most effectual cause of utter perdition.[171]

It is therefore vain to argue on the basis of a universal proffer of salvation that Christ died indiscriminately for all. Indeed, how many "1000 thou-

---

[168]Ibid., 61.

[169]Ibid., 70, 74.

[170]Ibid., 75.

[171]Ibid., 72-73.

sands are there at this day," who have never heard of Christ, at least in his role as "Redeemer of mankind by his death?"[172] Yet God cannot on this account be charged with injustice for all is of mercy: He no more owes the offering of Christ to all than He did the giving of him for any.

Those who believed that Christ died for the salvation of all had in their arsenal a battery of universalistic Biblical statements which the strict Calvinists could not merely gainsay. For example, there are Paul's clear statements that Christ "died for all" (II Cor. 5:15) and that he "gave himself a ransom for all" (I Tim. 2:6). Robinson qualifies this theology of "all" by adding an explanatory phrase which he claims the texts warrant: "all" means either "all of the elect" or all groups in a certain class. By this facile exegetical (eisegetical?) technique he is able to blunt the force of numerous passages which seem to contradict his position. From this general rule Robinson descends to the particular verses. The "all" of I Tim. 2:6 refers not to all individuals in the world, but to all sorts of people: that Christ was a ransom for all means that God's election ranges through all levels of society. It includes kings as well as commoners, and so all classes are represented in the work of atonement.[173] The note of universality which is found in many texts is often not to be understood absolutely, but as a form of hyperbolic discourse. Thus when Paul says "All things are lawful for me" (I Cor. 6:12), we are not to assume that he includes murder or adultery, and when it is said (Acts 2:5) that devout men from every nation under heaven were dwelling in Jerusalem, need we imagine that "English and Irish and Iappanians were there?"[174] But if, in those verses which state Christ died for all, "all" means invariably the elect, is it not redundant to include this word at all? Robinson answers that the "all" indicates an evenness in the death of Christ as applied to the elect:

> Those for whom Christ died, he died alike for: and therefore not specially for any, above others, but alike for all, for whom he dyed.[175]

---

[172]Ibid., 72,

[173]Ibid., 62. If this reading seems strained it should be noted that it was the standard Reformed interpretation. Cf. Calvin's *New Testament Commentaries*, vol. 10, 208-09: "The apostle's meaning here is simply that no nation of the earth and no rank of society is excluded from salvation, since God wills to offer the gospel to all without exception. He is speaking of classes and not of individuals and his only concern is to include princes and foreign nations in this number." R. T. Kendall, *Calvin and English Calvinism to 1649* (Oxford, 1979), 14-28, has claimed that Calvin did not teach a doctrine of limited atonement, but see my critique of Kendall's argument in *Review and Expositor* 78 (1981), 434-36.

[174]*Defence*, 61, 67.

[175]Ibid., 62.

A third argument for the universal scope of the atonement is drawn by inference from the Dominical mandate to preach the gospel to all the world (Matt. 28:19-20). The Canons (II. v) assert that the gospel should be proclaimed to all persons promiscuously and without distinction (*promiscue et indiscriminatim*). But if the death of Christ is limited in the intention of God, is it not useless to preach the gospel? Put otherwise, how can the gospel be unfeigningly offered to all when God has not in fact provided salvation for all? Robinson's answer to this is twofold. In the first place God has ordained all things, the means as well as the ends. And the ordinary means He has ordained to bring the elect to faith is the preaching of the Word (I Cor. 1:18). Furthermore, since God's decrees are inscrutable, no one can tell who is really elect and who is not. Outward, visible signs of grace may be misleading, and no one save the individual himself can have "certain knowledge" of his election. Therefore, it behooves the faithful minister to proclaim the gospel to everyone:

> Now the Apostles not knowing which in particular were elect, and redeemed in the secret purpose of God, and Christ were to sow the seed of grace upon all grounds, and to preach to all indifferently, as they had occasion; hoping in charity that this, and that, and any one particular, might be of the elect vessels, and good ground in Gods destination.[176]

As Christ when offered on the cross was sufficient to save all, so "Christ offered in the gospel" (IV. ix) must be proclaimed to all, though such promiscuous preaching must ever recognize the mysterious freedom of divine mercy.[177]

After defending his own interpretation against the various biblical statements which seemed to imply universalism, Robinson turns to the doctrine of his opponents. He likens their efforts to extend the scope of Christ's work in a universalistic direction to the erection of a new tower of Babel, "by which they would, as it were, scale heaven, and deprive God of divers his most glorious Attributes."[178] In particular, he sees three of the

---

[176]Ibid., 65.

[177]The tension between election and preaching was of special concern to the General Baptists who were among the most aggressively evangelistic sects in pre-Revolutionary England. Cf. Tolmie, op. cit., 69-84. Robinson's brand of Separatism was much more conservative in its promulgation of the missionary mandate. Robinson regarded the conversion of the heathen to have been the proper work of the apostles, whereas pastors were to "feed them that are already begotten, converted, & prepared." *Justification,* 383. However, he did not for this reason preclude the direct presentation of the gospel to outsiders as the occasion allowed. Cf. his response to the report that certain Indians had been killed by the Plymouth colonists: "Oh, how happy a thing had it been, if you had converted some before you had killed any"! *Of Plymouth Plantation,* 374-75.

[178]*Defence,* 64.

divine attributes, wisdom, omnipotence, and justice, threatened by the doctrine of indefinite atonement. First, God's wisdom is curtailed by the supposition that God would purchase, with so precious a price as the blood of His Son, the justification, sanctification, and salvation of those whom by His prescience He knew would never possess these benefits. Second, God's almighty power is called into question in that He is portrayed as unable to save any more than He does in fact save, though He desire it ever so much. For surely He who gave the greatest thing He possibly could, that is, His only Son, to save all will spare no effort in doing whatever else He can to convert and seal with His Spirit those for whom Christ died. Third, God's justice is controverted for God is made to take a full price for all men's sins at the hands of their surety Christ, and yet to exact again the debt of their sins at their own hands by assigning (many of) them to eternal punishment. By the same token, the unique and infinite (*unica et perfectissima*, II, iii) character of Christ's death is reduced if a subsequent payment for sin is required. Here, as in other aspects of his doctrines of election and atonement, the primary concern of Robinson is to buttress the doctrine of God against all encroachment from human autonomy. At no point may divine sovereignty be compromised in the accomplishment of God's eternal purpose.

There is another angle from which Robinson views the work of Christ in its relation to the decree of election: the continuing efficacy of the atonement is based upon the ministry of Christ's session at the right hand of the Father. Arminius had sharply distinguished the death of Christ from his heavenly intercession: by the former Christ had procured salvation for all; by the latter he applied it only to those who believed.[179] Such a distinction, however, does violence to the unity of the work of Christ by severing it, on the one hand, from God's prior intention in election and, on the other, from its appropriation through faith. To counter this disjunction Robinson appeals to I John 2:1-2 where Christ's death is integrally related to his role as an advocate with the Father. So close is the connection between Christ's *satisfactio* and his *sessio* that he is said to make continual propitiation for our sins "by pacifying the father's anger toward us in procuring actually the forgiveness of our sinnes, and acceptance with him."[180] The intercession of Christ with the Father on behalf of the elect in no way implies a deficiency in his earthly self-offering, but is

---

[179] *Writings of Arminius*, vol. 3, 326: "For the sacrificing is prior to the intercession; the sacrificing belongs to the merit, the intercession to the application of the merit . . . . He acquired merit by sacrifice; for the application He intercedes."

[180] *Defence*, 62.

rather a continuation of the same with this difference, that now it is performed in the state of exaltation. The harmony between these two aspects of Christ's work is expressed thus: the subjects of his intercession are precisely those for whom he has made satisfaction. Thus both Christ's death on the cross and his being in heaven derive their salvific import from God's absolute determination to redeem certain members out of fallen humanity.

In summary, while Robinson, in accord with the traditional distinction, accepted the universal sufficiency of Christ's death, he agreed with the Canons that the atonement was from eternity limited in its scope and intention. The sufficiency/efficiency distinction also points to an interesting reversal of the concept of particularity. For the Calvinists the decree of election/ reprobation is particular in that it determines the destiny of each individual, whereas for the Arminians predestination is of classes, not of individuals. Concerning the work of Christ, however, the Arminians are particularists, including all individuals within its saving compass, while the Calvinists restrict its efficacy to the elect (a class!). The Calvinists can thus allow no disjunction between the accomplishment of atonement in Christ's death and the application of the merit of atonement by Christ's session in heaven which is infallibly applied to the elect by the ministry of the Holy Spirit.

The universal sufficiency of the atonement corresponds to the general, or external, calling of God which is indiscriminately extended through the promiscuous preaching of the gospel, whereas the definite design of the atonement is applied through the special, efficacious calling of the Holy Spirit to the elect. Robinson describes the effect of this special calling in terms of God's exclusive role in the saving process:

> The effectual calling of a Christian is that by which the Lord first differenceth actually, and in the person himself, the elect from the reprobate: and by which the called approacheth, and draweth nigh unto God that calleth him: and that takes away his sin, which separated betweene the Lord, and him; both by justifying and sanctifying him.[181]

The question arose whether such a calling could be resisted, and if it could not, whether the imposition of God's grace did not constitute an improper constraint upon the human will. Though the Canons do not contain the term "irresistable grace," in the "Rejection of Errors" appended to the fourth chapter, the Synod rejects those who teach that, when all of the works of grace which God employs in conversion have been used, man still

---

[181] *Observation*, 147. Arminius denied the distinction between a universal and a special call. Cf. *Writings of Arminius*. vo. 2, 497.

can so resist, and by the same act often resist, as to prevent his own regeneration. Indeed, to such an extent does this remain in one's own power, as to be regenerated or not regenerated.[182]

According to this formulation the advances of the Holy Spirit can be ultimately rejected; the human will is the final arbiter in the matter of salvation. Robinson devoted one chapter of the *Defence* to a refutation of this thesis.

Robinson begins by denying that the Calvinists teach that the human will is somehow forced to respond to the proffer of grace. He employs a distinction he earlier introduced in connection with the fall of Adam, that between necessity and compulsion. It is perfectly correct to say that the elect are regenerated necessarily, in the sense that God has preordained it, and by His providence so ordered that it could not but be. But from this it does not follow that in the act of conversion God so overwhelms the will that it cannot respond spontaneously, without the necessity of coaction. The will, by its very nature, can do nothing unwillingly or by coercion. Thus whatever good or evil a man does, he does it not by violence or compulsion, but "from the inward principles of his mind; the understanding, directing, and the will consenting."[183] God's activity in relation to the elect, then, is not an external force or violent pressure which takes away the spontaneity or inherent freedom of the will, as when a man is struck with such a force that he is compelled to stagger or fall. Rather God's working is of a different sort:

> Not that God drawes men, as horses draw a cart, or by any violence, or compulsion against, or without their will; but that he makes them by the inward work of his Spirit (joyned with the outward word) of unwilling, willing, effectually driveing away ignorance and rebellion; and so enlightening the minde, as to assent, and the will, to consent.[184]

Robinson elsewhere refers to the drawing of God as an "inclination" which consists of two moments: first, the removal of the former naturally corrupt inclination by which the will was bound as with a cord; then, the giving of a new inclination contrary to the former which is accompanied

---

[182] *Creeds of Christendom*, vol. 3, 570: "ita posse resistere, et actu ipso saepe resistere, ut sui regenerationem prorsus impediat, atque adeo in ipsius manere potestate, ut regeneretur vel non regeneretur."

[183] *Defence*, 126. "It is true, that men whether receiving or refusing grace, doe it freely, and without compulsion: but the latter freely of themselves, being left of God to themselves; the former freely, by Gods speciall grace, and spirit, giving them, and effectually drawing them to Christ." Ibid., 130.

[184] Ibid., 45-46.

by an interior reshaping of the will and strength of grace.[185] These two aspects of conversion correspond to the gifts of repentance and faith, and are comprised in the act of regeneration.

Having exonerated the Calvinist understanding of the operation of grace from the false charges of necessitarianism, Robinson next turns to the question of whether a man can do anything to help or hinder in the work of his regeneration. The difference between the defenders and the detractors of Dort on this issue stemmed from their varying assessments of the extent of human fallenness. While the Canons insist that men after the Fall are not to be considered "senseless stocks and blocks" (*truncis et stipitibus*), the effect of the Fall is so devastating and pervasive that man is totally unable to contribute anything toward his salvation. The Remonstrance also confessed that man could not "by the energy of his free will" (*ex liberi arbitrii sui viribus*) effect his own salvation apart from prevenient grace, but it also affirmed that the will was not so vitiated by sin but that it retained its mode of acting (*modus agendi*), even to the extent of co-operating with divine grace in regeneration.[186] Robinson levelled two objections against this synergistic understanding of the relation of grace and human will in salvation: first, he insisted upon the inviolate linkage between the outward means and the inward work of the Spirit in the conversion process; and he challenged the Arminian ordering of faith, repentance, and regeneration in the *ordo salutis*. By the general call of the word promiscuously preached God calls all men, but this call inevitably falls on deaf ears unless God by His Spirit joins with it an additional call which cannot fail. Robinson does not claim that the Spirit acts independently of the outward word, but he also refuses to limit the Spirit's activity to external means: "Will they deny any inward work of Gods spirit at all, above the words work, through it, and by it?"[187] Thus, salvation is not effected by "the outward teaching of heavenly doctrine" alone, nor by moral suasion of the human will, but by the supernatural operation of the Spirit in the impartation of spiritual life. Against this interpretation of the

---

[185]Ibid., 126-27.

[186]The position that the human will concurs with divine grace in the act of conversion is known as synergism. On this point Arminian theology corresponds most closely to the Melanchthonian modification of Luther. Melanchthon's belief that the human will constituted a third factor in conversion, as it was acted upon by the Spirit through the Word, provoked the famous Synergistic Controversy within Lutheranism. On the history of this controversy and its resolution in the Formula of Concord, see Robert D. Preus and Wilbert H. Rosin, eds., *A Contemporary Look at the Formula of Concord* (St. Louis, 1978), 29-33, 122-36.

[187]*Defence*, 127.

divine-human encounter Murton again raises the charge of partiality in
God. Robinson responds with two examples: it is not my fault that a
drunkard falls and lies in the street, though he cannot but so do except I
hold him up, unless I be bound to so help him; nor is it my fault if a
prodigal spendthrift is cast into the debtors' prison, and cannot escape
except I pay his debts, unless I be bound to pay them:

> So neither is it Gods fault that men remain and perish in that impenitency,
> out of which they neither will, nor can come without Gods speciall gift of
> repentance, except it be Gods bounden duty (as these men seem to make it) to
> bestow that grace upon them.[188]

The Arminians also allowed a greater role to the human will in
salvation than was warranted by equating regeneration with the gifts of
faith and repentance. Robinson argues that this statement betrays theological imprecision and can be easily turned into a *reductio ad absurdum*,
for if faith and repentance be regeneration, then God believes and
repents, seeing that it is God who regenerates. To avoid this pitfall it is
important to recognize that regeneration *precedes* faith and repentance:

> He thereby regenerates them, or gives them faith and repentance, which they
> must have before they can beleev or repent: as the childe must have life before
> it can liue, or doe acts of life, and must be generated or begotten, before it
> haue life, or being.[189]

The enlightenment of the understanding and the redirection of the will so
that it is "holily bent" presuppose a prior regeneration, and follow as
fruits or effects of the same, not as the cause thereof. If this regeneration is
the special work of the Spirit in bringing into existence that which was
not, that is, a spiritual creature, then it cannot be resisted any more than
the initial act of creation. This does not mean that there is an immediate
or facile acquiescence to the drawing of the Spirit, for indeed the unregen-
erate can do nothing else but withstand the call of God. But in time God
so overcomes whatever impediments to grace the unregenerate-elect may
interpose and so "works in them, not to resist, but willingly to follow him,
that calleth them."[190] Thus that which God purposed in eternity, and
Christ by his death definitely accomplished, is infallibly applied by the
Spirit.

Because Robinson emphasizes so strongly that faith and repentance
are the fruits of regeneration and thus, in this respect, belong to the

---

[188]Ibid., 127-28.

[189]Ibid., 133.

[190]Ibid., 134.

process of sanctification, it is necessary to ask how they are related to the recognition of election, or the assurance of salvation. The Canons twice affirm (I. xii; V. x) that the elect may be sure of their calling, "not by prying inquisitively into the secret and deep things of God, but by observing in themselves (*in sese . . . observando*)" the fruits of their election.[191] Though Robinson, unlike Puritan casuists such as Perkins, Richard Sibbes, and Thomas Hooker, has no elaborate analysis of the interior life in respect to the morphology of grace, he does recognize both the need for, and the possibility of, salvation certitude. Robinson reflects upon the significance of assurance: "He whom God loves though he know it not, is an happy man: He that knows it, knows himself to be happy." By this knowledge the believer is able to face with equanimity and hope all of the vicissitudes of life:

> By it our afflictions work together with our election, redemption, vocation, and so forth, for our good. By reason of it the stones of the Field are at league with us, and the beasts of the Field at peace with us: yea even the very Sword that killeth us, the Fire that burneth us, and the Water that drowneth us, is a kinde of Spirituall, and invisible league with us, to do us good.[192]

Moreover, from our assurance of salvation spring all the good works and charitable deeds which we return again unto God: "By this our cold and frozen hearts are not onely thawed, but inflamed also with love again to him, and to men for him."[193]

---

[191] The pronouncements on assurance made at the Synod of Dort reflect both a modification of Calvin's doctrine within the Reformed tradition and a reaction against the Tridentine formulation. In its decree on justification the Council of Trent denied that anyone, apart from special revelation, could know that he is assuredly in the number of the predestined (*Creeds of Christendom*, vol. 2, 103). Calvin grounded assurance upon Christ as the only true *speculum electionis*: "Christ, then, is the mirror wherein we must, and without self-deception may, contemplate our own election" (*Inst.* 3, 24. 5). He did allow, however, "another means" for the confirmation of assurance, namely the evidence of good works in the believer's life. Cf. *Calvin's New Testament Commentaries,* vol. 5, 244-50. Though Calvin insisted that good works were only a relative and subordinate indicator of salvation, in later Reformed theology—especially in Beza—the empirical basis for assurance assumed a primary importance in the so-called *syllogismus practicus*. The Canons reflect this development when they place the *propria filiorum Dei signa*, i.e. assurance via self-observation, before the *constantissimes Dei promissiones* ("Rejection of Errors" V.v). For recent discussions of the *syllogismus practicus* see Barth, *Church Dogmatics* II/2, 333-40; Wilhelm Niesel, "Syllogismus practicus?" *Festgabe für E. F. K. Müller* (Neukirchen, 1933), 158-79; John S. Bray, *Theodore Beza's Doctrine of Predestination* (Nieuwkoop, 1975), 57-60, 107-11. Arminius advocated a doctrine of provisional assurance: one may be presently sure of his current status as a believer, but not presently sure of final salvation since in this life the possibility of irredmedial lapse is never totally removed. Cf. *The Writings of Arminius,* vol. 2, 503; vol. 3, 540.

[192] *Observations*, 6-7.

[193] Ibid., 7.

The first fruit of regeneration which issues in salvation assurance is repentance. Robinson reviews a number of definitions of repentance and rejects them all as inadequate. Repentance is neither a mere knowledge of sin by the law, nor a confessing of sin, nor a sorrow for sin, nor a promise to forsake sin, not yet an endeavor to forsake it. He then proposes his own definition:

> Repentance is properly, a growing wise afterwards, and changing of the minde from sin to God, in the purpose of the heart, having an effectuall endeavour to forsake sin accompanying it, as the effect thereof.[194]

The work of true repentance affords a "certain and infallible" token of election which is self-evident to the believer:

> As we may certainly know, that the Sun shines, by the beams, and heat thereof below, though we climbe not into Heaven to see: so may we haue certain knowledg of Gods gracious love towards us, without searching further then our own hearts, and waies; and by finding them truly, and effectually turned from sin to God.[195]

Likewise, faith by which the believer is justified is necessarily joined with a certain "affiance," a certitude as sure as either extraordinary revelation or particular nomination of person. Faith in this sense is, of course, not a human possibility but a supernatural gift, and Robinson stresses again its irresistible quality: being by the Spirit and the Word persuaded of God's love in Christ, we cannot but trust ourselves unto Him, rest and repose ourselves in Him, and expect accordingly all good things from Him. This act of fiducial trust, of "laying hold" of God's promises, precedes full assurance and is the basis thereof:

> As we must lay hold of the stay or prop before we can rest upon it; So must Faith go before affiance in order of causes: and we lay hold of Gods love before we can repose ourselves upon it.[196]

Thus by observing in one's life the presence and effects of true repentance and saving faith, it is possible to acquire a firm confidence of one's election. Yet Robinson is aware of the subtle dangers of over-scrupulosity which can lead either to despair or, more often, to that presumptious security which precipitates a sudden and certain destruction. He therefore recalls his readers to the ultimate foundation of assurance: "We must therefore in this scrutiny neither trust our selves, nor any other creature,

---

[194]*Defence*, 152.

[195]*Observations*, 8.

[196]Ibid., 7.

but God alone in the testimony of his Word."[197] Especially is it important not to equate the temporal distribution of rewards and punishments with God's eternal intention in election. So when God displays some signs of his anger toward us, we are not to imagine ourselves hated of Him and cast away from grace; and conversely, when we enjoy a measure of God's benificence we are not to grow careless in our faith, or imagine that there is anything in us which He desires, except that which He Himself has given.

Robinson has followed the Canons of Dort in rejecting the Arminian disjuction between salvation purchased (atonement) and salvation applied (regeneration). Both of these steps in the salvation process derive their soteric significance from the decree of election and so they are inseparably linked in the intention of God. In like manner, salvation assurance is imparted through the exercise of faith and repentance, and so cannot be finally frustrated in any of the elect. Nonetheless, since the actual enjoyment of this assurance depends upon one's growth in grace and consistency in obedience—"our living to God"—the admonition of introspection is not extended in vain.[198]

BAPTISM AND ELECTION

In the last and longest chapter of the *Defence* Robinson addresses himself to an issue which does not belong to the Arminian Controversy proper, and which was not even discussed at the Synod of Dort, but which nonetheless became for all Separatists who also remained Calvinists an increasingly acute problem in the 1610s, namely the theory and practice of baptism. As we have seen already, Robinson protested against the

---

[197]Ibid. Stephen Brachlow, "Robinson and the Lure of Separatism," 295-96, has argued that for Robinson soteriological assurance depended on the observance of correct church polity. It is true that adherence to proper, i.e. Separatist congregational, church order was essential to the process of sanctification/edification. Thus Robinson called upon those still within the Church of England to follow him in the way of separation in order to make "theyr election more sure to themselves . . . provideing for themselves the Prophets assurance, which was that he should not be ashamed, when he had respect to all Gods commandments." Nonetheless, even in this context, Robinson does not strictly equate salvation assurance with correct church membership. He admits that there are thousands of "the better sorte in the assemblyes" who are "faythfull persons, & vnder the assurance of salvation." *Of Religious Communion*, 13.

[198]*Defence*, loc. cit. Cf. Ames' famous definition of theology as "the doctrine of living to God," *The Marrow of Sacred Divinity* (London, 1643), 1. R. T. Kendall, *Calvin and English Calvinism to 1649*, 151-64, discusses Ames' doctrine of assurance, but curiously he does not cite Ames' specifically anti-Arminian writings.

wholesale application of infant baptism as practiced in the Church of England because he felt that it prostituted the grace of God by making the Church a "common inn" for all passers-by rather than the true household of faith. However, Smyth's self-baptism and the subsequent merger of his church with the Waterlanders, together with the new Baptist ecclesiology forged by Helwys and Murton, signalled a new crisis over baptism among the Separatists themselves.[199] Two distinct but related aspects of Smyth's challenge to Separatist baptismal theology, both with important ramifications for the doctrine of election, came to the fore in the ensuing debate: the validity of baptism received in the Church of England, and the basis for the Separatist retention of infant baptism. Robinson defended the received Separatist baptismal practice on both of these points, and in so doing further clarified the implications of the doctrine of sovereign predestination for his concept of the true visible Church as a covenanted community of elect saints.

"Belshazzars quaffing bowles": The Seals in Captivity

In spite of its shocking impact on his contemporaries Smyth's dramatic rebaptism merely brought to the surface an ambiguity inherent in Separatist sacramental practice. Barrow, like Browne and Harrison before him, argued that baptism received in the Church of England was false, but that it need not be repeated by those who had withdrawn from the parish assemblies.[200] Some Separatists, it seems, withheld their children from baptism indefinitely rather than submit them to Anglican ministers, while others, anticipating Smyth, rejected their baptism

---

[199]The fact of Smyth's self-baptism was long denied by Baptist historians, but Smyth admitted it himself (*Smyth*, vol. 2, 660), and his testimony was corroborated by a number of contemporaries including Robinson who gave this account: "Mr Smith, Mr Helw & the rest, haveing vtterly dissolved, & disclaymed their former Ch: state, & ministery, came together to erect a new Ch: by baptism: vnto which they also ascribed so great vertue, as that they would not so much as pray together, before they had it. And after some streyning of courtesy, who should begin, & that of Iohn Baptist, Math: 3.14. misalledged, Mr Smith baptized first himself, & next Mr Helwis, & so the rest, makeing their particular confessions." *Of Religious Communion*, 48. It seems that Smyth's act was not without precedent among earlier Separatists. In 1600 Clapham claimed to have known one who "baptizeth himselfe . . . and then he baptizeth other." *Antidoton*, 33.

[200]Powicke, *Barrow*, 112, attributes Barrow's "confused" view of baptism to his desire to dissociate himself at all costs from the "wicked Anabaptistt." This was no doubt an important motive in his baptismal theology, but he does attempt a more positive solution in his distinction between adulterate and false sacraments, a point which Robinson develops at greater length. Cf. White, *Separatist Tradition*, 79-81.

received in infancy for believers' baptism at the hands of Dutch Mennonites.[201] Smyth's self-baptism followed his exegetical discovery that the
"character," that is, the mark or stamp, of the beast received in the
forehead (Rev. 13:16) was nothing other than the baptism applied to
infants in false churches such as England and Rome! Thus Smyth and his
group "disannulled" their former church estate and proceeded to rebaptism and recovenanting. Nor was Smyth alone in his conviction that the
logic of Separatist ecclesiology demanded such a procedure. From the
Anglican side Hall challenged Robinson: "Either you must go forward to
Anabaptism or come back to us. All your Rabbins cannot answer that
charge of your re-baptized brother: if we be a True Church you must
return, if we be not (as a False Church is no Church of God) you must
re-baptize."[202]

Robinson defied the dilemma of Hall's alternative by making a fundamental distinction between outward baptism, administered by men, and
an "inward, and greater Baptism" of the Holy Spirit. The latter is applied
infallibly to all of the elect in the act of regeneration, whereas the former is
properly a seal of the visible Church, a "lively signe" to the covenanted
elect of their union with Christ and an "effectuall means" of applying the
same unto them.[203] Outward baptism then is a measure of the visibility of
the Church, a communal seal *subsequent* to the covenant and not, as
Smyth would have it, the very basis for Church-gathering.

But what of baptism in a false Church? Outward baptism, Robinson
argues, is to be considered in two respects: nakedly, in its essential parts,
that is, washing with water in the name of the Trinity; and according to its
application, that is, the minister by, the person upon, the communion
wherein it is administered. As concerns the former, baptism retains its
character as a seal of the covenant of grace even when administered in a
false Church. It is therefore not to be repeated, contrary to a baptism
performed by a Turk or a child in sport which is no baptism at all,
although its "spiritual uses" cannot be had without repentance, "by which
repentance and the after baptism of the spirit it is sanctified, and not to be
repeated."[204] The presence of true baptism in a false Church is analogous

[201]Cf. the celebrated case of Widow Unwen's child who had reached the age of twelve
without being baptized though, reportedly, "the pore infant desyred the mother often that
it might be baptized." *Early English Dissenters*, vol. 2, 30-31.

[202]Hall, *Works*, vol. 9, 25.

[203]*Defence*, 149; *Of Religious Communion*, 47.

[204]Ibid., 60-61.

to the vessels of the temple carried, along with the Children of Israel, into captivity where

> they remayned still, both in nature, and right, the vessels of the Lords house: though in respect to their vse, or rather abuse, they became Belshazzars quaffing bowles. So is it in the destruction of the spirituall house of the Lord, the Church, by the spirituall Babylonians, and in the vsurpation, and abuse of the holy vessels, and in special of this holy vessel of baptism.[205]

The insistence on the sacramental objectivity of baptism in the Church of England—"the stolen waters of Babilon"—is related to the belief that God's purpose will prevail despite the ecclesiastical aberrations of man. Outward baptism, however, is not a "charme" which perforce invests the baptizand with "saynt-ship" or cleanses him from sin; its benefits pertain only to those who are within the covenant of grace.[206] In other words, election is the determinant of baptismal efficacy. When applied to the non-elect, outward baptism is a false and lying sign, "and like a seal set to a blank."[207] Yet to those who are elect, though not visibly so in respect to correct church order, the seal retains its validity. Just as the apostates of Israel were excluded from the covenant, and the circumcision of their children was "as if they had cut the foreskin of their dogs," and yet the outward cutting was not to be repeated afterwards, if God gave repentance, so:

> neyther is the outward washing in the name of the trinity now, though merely vsurped by them, who are forbidden to medle with it.[208]

Therefore it is plainly heretical to attempt the "vn-baptizing" of a baptized individual: "a man once baptized is alwayes baptized."[209] Even in manifestly false churches such as those of England and Rome, "the Lord hath his people, and for their sakes, many his truthes, and ordinances, which he so far blesseth vnto his elect, as by them (notwithstanding all the confusion there) he doth communicate, and confirm his saving grace vnto them." Thus when God's people are called to manifest their election by coming out of Babylon, and are given the task of rebuilding the temple anew, they are to acknowledge the seal of God's promise made to them in

---

[205] *Justification*, 285.

[206] Ibid., 110. Cf. Sibbes' comment: "If the baptized have no other relation to God, they may go to hell, as Judas and others did." Quoted, E. B. Holifield, *The Covenant Sealed* (New Haven, 1974), 47.

[207] *Of Religious Communion*, 56.

[208] Ibid.

[209] *Justification*, 395.

captivity, and through the act of covenantal cleansing, restore it to its rightly place in the "house" of God.

"Children are of the Church": The Baptism of Infants

Smyth's scruples about retaining baptism received in a false Church might have been resolved by simply reinstituting a new order of baptism, administered to adults in the first instance, but afterwards to the children of duly separated and covenanted members, thus preserving intact the normal pattern of infant baptism.[210] However, Smyth's baptismal innovation constituted an even more radical departure from Anglican practice in its restriction of baptism only to believers who were able to make profession of their own faith. Against this new procedure Robinson defended the doctrine of infant baptism with extensive but largely traditional arguments based upon covenantal continuity and the analogy of circumcision.

The argument from circumcision was anticipated by Smyth and subsequent Baptists who challenged the equation of an Old Testament ritual with the ordinance of baptism instituted by Christ. In response, Robinson insists that circumcision as the seal of the covenant of grace made with Abraham is not to be considered an appendage to the Law (which was in any event given to Moses several centuries later), but rather as a token or pledge of His gracious will toward him and his seed. Thus circumcision in the Old Testament stands in direct anagogic relation to baptism in the New.[211] The Baptists level three objections to this claim to which Robinson responds. First, it is claimed that no specific commandment or instance of infant baptism can be adduced from the New Testament. Robinson grants that the Scriptures nowhere say "Baptize infants" or "Infants were baptized," but argues that it does imply as much by true consequence. Christ's own coming as a child and his subsequent embrace and blessing of little children indicate that he did not exclude "our childehood" from his salvific mission. Moreover, in commanding the children to be brought unto him, and including them in the kingdom, he required, by consequence, that they be baptized, for how else can they

---

[210]In the 1630s a strict Separatist offshoot of the Jacob Church seems to have adopted this practice. See Tolmie, op. cit., 21-29.

[211]"The Scriptures do most playnly & plentifully teach, that the Covenant with Abraham, & his seed, the Israelitish Church, was the same with ours in nature (though diversely dispensed) & therefore the Covenant of the Gospell." *Of Religious Communion*, 79.

now be brought to him save by baptism? "And if Infants be to pertake of Christes blood, and spirit, there must be some ordinary means to apply them, God workeing ordinarily by ordinary means, and the same none but baptism, that lavacher of the new birth, as the Apostle calleth it" (Tit. 3:5).[212] In addition, the baptism of whole households must have included infants for Peter expressly extends the promise of baptism to the children of the faithful (Acts 2:38). The parity of circumcision and baptism is further illustrated by the fact that Christ himself submitted to both, "thereby sanctifying Baptism to us, as circumcision to the Fathers."[213] In the light of these examples, Robinson feels, it rather behooves his opponents to show where infants are cut off from the covenant of grace and from its sacramental seal, before they exclude them from its benefits. The second and third objections concern the fact that circumcision, unlike baptism, was for males only and performed only on the eighth day. Robinson dispenses with these points in an almost cavalier manner: ministers are successors to the Levites, yet they are not tied to a single tribe; the Lord's Supper is equivalent to the Passover, but is not restricted to a certain day or month. Such "Legall differences of daies and sexes" are minor details of little moment.[214]

Robinson regards infant baptism as the irrevocable seal of election applicable only to the children of the faithful as a sign or "ratification" of their inclusion in the covenant of grace.[215] The Baptist claim that infants were to be excluded from the rite on the grounds that they could not manifest the requisite faith and repentance contradicted the fundamental character of baptism as a gift received rather than a work performed:

> The Gospell aymes not at the exacting upon man obedience due . . . neither yet servs it, and its Ordinances, primarily to declare and manifest, what man in right owes, and performs to God, But what God in mercy, purposeth and doth, and will perform to man: being Εὐαγγέλιον a joyfull message, or glad tydings of salvation by Christ.[216]

Robinson dismisses the objection, based on Mk. 16:16, that infants are not to be baptized because they believe not. May we not as reasonably conclude, he asks, that infants are not to eat because they work not, based

---

[212] Ibid., 83.

[213] Defence, 157-58.

[214] Ibid., 163.

[215] Robinson required at least one parent of the baptizand to be a Church member in good standing. Later discussions at Plymouth centered on whether a bastard or the child of a member under censure might be baptized. Cf. Plymouth Church Records, vol. 1. 212-13, 280-81.

[216] Defence, 151.

on Paul's dictum in 2 Th. 3:10? Further, he does not agree that infants are completely void of faith. To be sure, the actual manifestation of faith is indiscernible in infants, but in the elect infants it is truly there—"in disposition."[217] Likewise they are to be considered holy and regenerate, in regard to that "foederall holinesse, and the spirit of regeneration" in which they, as the seed of the godly, share.[218] Consequently, their parents are

> even from their cradle to bring them up in instruction, and information of the Lord: and so to prepare them for the publique ministery.[219]

The children of the faithful are thus presumed to be elect. But their generation of godly parents and their reception of the baptismal seal do not, *ex opere operato*, effect or guarantee their election. God remains sovereign even in respect to the visible signs He has given. Yet when administered to elect infants in the context of a true visible Church baptism carries with it a proleptic obligation: God declares His gracious intention to cleanse them with the blood and Spirit of His Son, but they also are "bound, in their times, to reciprocall duties." If, for example, in their "riper years" they demonstrate their obedience by participating in the common life of the congregation, then they are to be continued in the Church; but if not, they are in due time, "as vnprofitable branches to be lopped off."[220]

Robinson's doctrine of baptism thus reflects the dual emphasis we have observed throughout this study. On the one hand baptism is a communal seal, subsequent to the Church covenant, and belonging in its administration only to a true visible Church. On the other hand, in its "naked" aspect, baptism as the means by which God both declares and effects his goodness toward elect infants is valid even when performed in a false Church. Both of these aspects are brought together in Robinson's attempt to define the fourfold function of baptism in the order of descending importance. In the first place, God's taking both of us and our infants to be His people and His sealing the same with baptism is an act of unmerited favor, and so baptism "in the mayn end performed, is not on mans behalfe towards God, but on Gods behalfe towards man."[221] In a

---

[217]Ibid., 149.

[218]Ibid., 157. "Even litle ones born in the Church, may in their order, and after their manner, he sayd to be converted, or turned to the Lord, or borne agayne, which are all one." *Justification*, 384.

[219]Ibid.

[220]Ibid.

[221]*Of Religious Communion*, 72.

second and inferior respect, it is a work of man unto God in the exercise of faith and repentance and in the attitude of thankfulness which it evokes. Thirdly, baptism is a sign of union among the members of the Church and the basis of their joint participation in the other ordinances of the congregation, such as the Lord's Supper and excommunication. And, finally, baptism is a "badg of Christianity," and a mark which distinguishes the true visible Church from all false Churches.

In keeping with his predestinarian theology over against the early Baptists with their Arminian leanings, Robinson believed that baptism was *primarily* neither ecclesiologically constitutive nor individually testimonial. It was rather the means by which God communicated to the elect the benefits of His grace. The other functions, though important, were secondary and derivative. The fact that the "double washers" were also "free willers" insured their twofold indictment at the hands of Calvinistic Separatists such as Robinson who sought to place as much distance as possible between themselves and their erstwhile associates in separation.

ASSESSMENT

Having studied in detail Robinson's treatment of the doctrine of election we are now in a position to draw out certain of its implications by way of an overview. First, it is clear that election was a primary theological concern for Robinson. He was thoroughly grounded at Cambridge in the high Calvinism of Perkins and, unlike Smyth, carried this theological orientation with him into Separation. His perception of the doctrinal deficiency of the Church of England surfaced in his early exchanges with Hall and Bernard, and, as a *theologus* at the University of Leyden, he participated in public disputations with the leading exponent of Arminianism. When the predestinarian pronouncements of the Synod of Dort were challenged by fellow Separatists who had abandoned their originally Calvinist understanding of election for a view approaching that of the Arminians, Robinson issued an elaborate and spirited defense of the decisions at Dort. To be sure, the picture which emerges does not comport well with the traditional portrayal of a doctrinally indifferent Robinson who was drawn reluctantly into a squabble over theological niceties about which he was only slightly concerned. Rather we are confronted with a major intellectual spokesman of a still suspect sect determined to demonstrate his orthodoxy on what he doubtless considered to be a crucial point of Christian doctrine.

No responsible theologian can treat the doctrine of election in isolation from the whole complex of ideas concerning the nature of God, the condition of the human, and ultimate purpose in salvation. Robinson does not hesitate to spell out the implications of sovereign predestination for these related issues, although the *ad hoc* character of his writings does not lend itself to ready systematization. Robinson's conception of the *ordo salutis* may be depicted as a continuum with four distinct but interrelated moments which derive both their unity and their uniqueness from the counsel of God. If, for the sake of clarity, we call these moments metahistorical, historical, existential, and eschatological, then the continuum may be illustrated as follows:

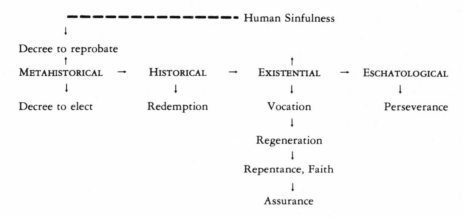

Throughout his doctrine of election Robinson has striven to protect the sovereignty of God against the unwarranted encroachments of human autonomy. This primarily *theological* rather than *soteriological* focus has led to a preoccupation with the ordering of the decrees and the relationship of prescience to predestination. No variability within the human condition is allowed to compromise the ultimacy and unconditionality of the metahistorical moment. However, because Robinson is defending the *infralapsarian* sequence of the decrees, election and reprobation are not (as in Perkins' *Golden Chaine*) symetrically related. Though the determinative cause of reprobation lies in God's secret will, it also, unlike election, has a proximate cause, that is, human sinfulness, in view of which the decree is pronounced. Therefore God is exculpated from the *blame* of human sin.

The historical radius of salvation centers in the work of Christ which Robinson describes in terms of the Anselmian theory of atonement. This historical act of Christ is limited in scope and intention because of its subordination to the decree of election, though it is intrinsically sufficient to save all mankind. While Robinson usually refers to the sacrifice of Christ's death as "redemption," there is no disjunction (contra Arminius) between Christ's *satisfactio* and his *sessio* since the objects of both, that is, the elect, are the same. Thus Robinson tends to amplify the work of Christ in such a way that the very term redemption gets disassociated from the unique event and becomes the generic term for experiential salvation leading to personal and congregational holiness in the present.

Robinson describes the calling of the elect in terms of irresistible grace, but claims that the human will is "holily bent" in such a way that its spontaneity is preserved. The growth in grace which manifests itself in repentance, faith, assurance, and good works belongs to the process of sanctification which is never perfected in this life, but which cannot be ultimately frustrated since the elect are kept from falling totally or finally from the state of grace. The proper locus of sanctification is the congregation of gathered saints to which pertain the seals of the covenant of grace. However, in his attempt to base sacramental benefits on the inscrutable decrees, Robinson consistently refuses to bind God even to the visible signs He has given. Thus the true visible Church and the sacraments therein dispensed are not so much vehicles of grace as *witnesses* to God's grace which derives from the mystery of the divine decision.

CHAPTER 6

CONCLUSION:
YET MORE TRUTH AND LIGHT

"I knew a witty physician who found the creed in the bilary duct and used to affirm that if there was a disease in the liver, the man became a Calvinist, and if that organ was sound, he became a Unitarian."[1]

John Robinson died on March 1, 1625, in his fiftieth year. "If either prayers teares or meanes would haue saued his life hee had not Gon hence," wrote his brother-in-law Roger White to the Plymouth Church. Upon hearing of his death someone at Plymouth—"a frind"—penned the following verses which, if void of poetic merit, resound with genuine affection and esteem:

Blessed Robinson hath Run his Race
from earth to heauen is Gon
to be with Christ in heauenly place
the blessed saints amonge

A burning and a shining Light
was hee whiles hee was heer
a preacher of the Gospell Bright
whom wee did loue most deare

What tho hee dead his workes aliue
and liue will to all Age
The Comfort of them pleasant is
To liueing saints each day

Oh Blessed holy Sauiour
the fountaine of all Grace
from whom such blessed Instruments
are sent and Run theire Race

To lead vs and Guid vs in
the way to happines

---

[1] Ralph Waldo Emerson, "Experience," *Essays* (1844).

That doe oh Lord wee may alwaies
for euermore Confesse

That whosoeuer Gospell preacher be
or waterer of the same
Wee may alwayes most Constantly
Giue Glory to thy Name.[2]

The legacy of Robinson was preserved at Plymouth so long as those with personal memories of him, especially Brewster and Bradford, survived. However, the Separatist ideal, born in persecution and nurtured in exile, did not easily accommodate itself to the demands of a well-ordered, all-embracing society. At the end of the century when Cotton Mather set out to record the "History of New-England Israel" Plymouth had been swallowed up by Massachusetts and the Separatist tradition, though not extinguished, had been sufficiently assimilated into the larger religious community so that Robinson could easily be detached from the sectarian context and treated as a patriarch of the new civilization. In keeping with this perspective one of the leading Church historians of the twentieth century has found echoes of Robinson in the Declaration of Independence and the speeches of Franklin D. Roosevelt![3] With only slightly more historical credibility, Christopher Hill has found in Robinson's farewell sermon a presentiment of the belief in continuous revelation which characterized such diverse radical groups as the Levellers, Ranters, Seekers, and Quakers.[4]

In a similar way Robinson's significance as a theologian of stature has been overshadowed by religious innovators of all sorts from Unitarians to Mormons to modern Congregationalists and Baptists who have seized upon the "more truth and light" quotation as a prophecy of their own special insights. Thus in 1907 when Frank Hugh Foster opened his classic study, *A Genetic History of the New England Theology*, with a brief sketch of Robinson's thought, noting its affinity with "the common Calvinism of the day," he was not stating a truism but issuing a challenge. But Foster, who had taken the pains to read Robinson, was right, and no assessment of Robinson as theologian can ignore his conclusion.

In an age of ecumenical emphasis the ecclesiology of Separatism seems far removed from current concerns. Few Christians today are

---

[2]*Plymouth Church Records*, vol. 1, 62-63.

[3]Ernest A. Payne, *The Free Church Tradition in the Life of England* (London, 1951), 48.

[4]Christopher Hill, *The World Turned Upside Down: Radical Ideas during the English Revolution* (London, 1972), 366-67.

capable of being as exercised about the minutia of Church order or the perplexities of predestination as the Separatists of the seventeenth century. But if F. M. Powicke's dictum, "A vision or an idea is not to be judged by its value for us, but by its value to the man who had it"[5] is not the whole truth, it at least reminds us that we cannot begin to evaluate the significance of earlier Christians, including Robinson, until we have asked ourselves their questions and listened well to their answers.

Hence, it has been necessary to detach Robinson from the tradition of Pilgrim hagiography which has colored most modern interpretations of him. When judged against the temper of his own times, he emerges not only as a wise and exemplary pastor, but also as a significant theologian and interpreter of the Separatist experience. Our examination of his life and writings has yielded the following general conclusions.

First, it is clear that Robinson belonged to the Separatist tradition which took its rise in the pre- and early Elizabethan conventicles, became articulate in the writings of Browne and Barrow, and found systematic expression in the *Confession* of 1596. Robinson and his congregation adopted this confession as their own, and he frequently acknowledged his debt to the earlier Separatists. Though he subsequently modified his position on the principle of fellowship with non-separating Christians, he remained a staunch advocate of Separatist ecclesiology in all of its essentials, and consistently refused to recognize any parish in England as a true visible Church.

Second, Robinson defined the true visible Church as a covenanted company of gathered saints, *separated from* the world in its organization and autonomy, and *separating back to* the world through congregational discipline those members whose lives betrayed their profession. The community of faith is thus sustained in outward covenant by mutual interdependence and common participation of the members, each of whom is at once a prophet, priest, and king under Christ and unto one another.

The compelling motivation for separation, moreover, was related to what G. F. Nuttall has called "a passionate desire to recover the inner life of New Testament Christianity."[6] The Separatists themselves resorted to the Pauline language of edification to describe the contour and purpose of their distinctive brand of churchmanship. Far from being merely "hasty Puritans," too impatient to "tarry" for a magisterially-enacted reformation, the Separatists' decision to withdraw from the Church of

---

[5]Quoted, G. F. Nuttall, *The Holy Spirit in Puritan Faith,* op. cit, 168.

[6]G. F. Nuttall, *Visible Saints* (Oxford, 1957), 3.

England was based on their adherence to the imperative principles of Christian liberty and edification.[7]

The inner dynamic of Separatist ecclesiology thus implied a radical rejection of the basic premise of the Elizabethan Settlement, defended by apologists from John Foxe to Richard Hooker: the coextension of church and commonwealth. Robinson claimed that quite apart from its proximity to Rome in the corruption of worship, which might be reformed, the Church of England, as a national church, was not, nor ever had been, truly the Church at all. For the Separatists' opponents, Anglican and Puritan alike, the controlling metaphor for church reform was not the apostolic model but ancient Israel. Had not Josiah and Manasseh initiated reform in the elect nation? "What have Queen Elizabeth or King James done more?" asked Joseph Hall. Robinson insisted, however, that the Separatist quest for a true visible Church, with saints for its matter and a covenant for its form, was "cast in the apostolical and primitive mold, and not one day or hour younger, than the first church of the New Testament." The Separatists, no less than their radical counterparts on the Continent, were fundamentally concerned with *restitution* rather than *reformation*. In other words, they were about nothing less than the complete recovery of pristine Christianity.

Unlike the Anabaptists, however, who identified the base line between restitution and re-formation within Scripture itself in terms of Old and New Testaments, Robinson held to the essential unity of the Church through all ages. This led him to a more strictly dispensational interpretation of the "church of the Jews," a concept which permitted him to appropriate much of the Old Testament typologically, while claiming as normative for church practice only New Testament directives. This was worked out within the framework of the Calvinist distinction of visible/invisible Church, a distinction Robinson carefully maintained as in his exposition of the parables of the tares and the draw-net.

---

[7]White, *Separatist Tradition*, xiv. White has asserted (ibid., xii), and Brachlow argued at length ("Puritan Theology and Radical Churchmen," *passim*), for the basic congruity of Separatist and radical Puritan ideals. It is not doubted that Separatism derived historically from Puritanism, nor that the Separatists, especially Robinson, retained a large measure of sympathy and agreement with their less forward brethren who remained connected, however loosely, with the Church of England. However, in an age of uniformity and royal supremacy, the act of separation itself implied a radical repudiation of the prevailing religio-political mythos. If Collinson's claim that the Separatists advocated "a totally alien, select Christian society" (*Elizabethan Puritan Movement*, 12) is a bit of an overstatement, the Separatists are nonetheless clearly enough distinguished in their theology and churchmanship "to deserve a category of their own." Cf. the perceptive essay by Paul Christianson, "Reformers and the Church of England under Elizabeth I and the Early Stuarts," *Journal of Ecclesiastical History* 31 (1980), 463-82.

Robinson's view of the magistracy was also more equivocal than that of the Anabaptists. He admitted that a Christian might serve as a magistrate, and even become a "nursing father" unto the Church, but within the Church he was to have no coercive power to fashion doctrine, worship, or polity. In fact, the magistrate within the Church was to be subject to the same disciplinary procedures, including, if needs be, excommunication, as the lowliest member of the particular congregation to which he belonged!

All of the Separatists agreed that congregational discipline, applied according to the Dominical injunction in Matthew 18, was a *conditio sine qua non* of a true visible Church. Early on Robert Browne had pointed out the inadequacy of the two-*notae* theory: "neither the word in the preacher's mouth, nor the Sacraments can make an outward Church, except they have the power of Christ to separate the unworthy."[8] Robinson likewise argued that the Church of England was false not because of the abuses therein, but because it lacked "the power of Christ" to remove those abuses. None of the Puritans, for all of their criticism of Anglican discipline, had drawn the radical conclusion of the Separatists—that a Church which lacked the "power of Christ" also lacked his presence, and was therefore no Church at all.

Perry Miller has argued that the function of discipline in Separatist polity was related to the doctrine of election. Only persons who could prove that they were redeemed could be admitted to church membership, and the rigorous application of congregational discipline insured that those who had taken the church covenant had also been received into the covenant of grace. As John Coolidge has shown, this argument, though widely accepted, is misleading at several points. The Separatists never attempted to correlate the visible Church with the invisible, nor to base church membership on the secret counsel of God. Robinson, like Calvin, was willing to accept in the judgment of charity one who embraced the covenant, realizing that there were hypocrites within the visible Church and elect saints without. Edmund Morgan has further shown that the test for election is a later development, applied neither by the Separatist churches in Holland nor by the Plymouth church in the 1620s. While most of the Separatists, and certainly Robinson, were high predestinarians, their insistence upon discipline was not related so directly to the doctrines of election and justification as it was to the Reformed emphasis on sanctification, and to their understanding of the visible Church as a unique kind of communal order sustained by the Spirit of life, issuing in mutual fellowship and edification.

---

[8] *An Answere to Master Cartwright*, 443.

Robinson was, nonetheless, deeply concerned with the doctrine of predestination. If his depiction of the visible Church—gathered, planted, disciplined—was an extension of the principle of discernibility, already evident in Calvin, then his emphasis on the invisible, supramundane Church derived from his equally insistent view of divine sovereignty in election.

While the principle of voluntarism led some Separatists, notably John Smyth and Thomas Helwys, to abandon both the received predestinarian theology and infant baptism, Robinson strongly defended these twin pillars of orthodox Calvinism. During the Leyden years the doctrine of election was Robinson's primary theological and polemical concern. He opposed not only the doctrinal innovations of his fellow Separatists but also the universalistic implications of two practices in the Church of England: the *indiscriminate* baptism of infants and the committal rubric of the funeral rite. As a registered *theologus* of the University of Leyden he was also drawn into the thick of the Arminian Controversy and disputed publicly with the leading Arminian theologian, Simon Episcopius.

The analysis of Robinson's doctrine of predestination is derived from his treatise, *A Defence of the Doctrine Propounded by the Synode at Dort* (1624). For the sake of clarity the discussion is divided into four sections: sin and fallen man, prescience and providence, predestination and perseverance, limited atonement and irresistible grace. In due course Robinson touches upon each of the five controverted points decided at Dort. While advocating a doctrine of absolute, double predestination, he is at pains to exculpate God from the responsibility for human sin. For example, he accepts the infralapsarian sequence of the divine decrees which permits the sentence of reprobation to be pronounced in view of sinful acts. Thus his doctrine of election has a more directly theological (that is, relating to the doctrine of God) than soteriological focus. The work of Christ is defined in terms of the Anselmian theory of atonement, but it is limited in scope and intention by subordination to the eternal decision. There is no disjunction between the *satisfactio* and the *sessio* of Christ since both the procurement of salvation and its application pertain only to the elect. The picture which emerges from this survey is that of a major intellectual spokesman of a still suspect sect determined to demonstrate his orthodoxy on what he doubtless considered a crucial point of Christian doctrine.

The concern of Robinson for the visible Church did not attenuate his interest in the invisible. The tension between a sectarian ecclesiology on the one hand and a high predestinarian theology on the other is the controlling dynamic in Robinson's thought and the resolution of it, his chief contribution to the English Separatist tradition.

Most modern historians of English Puritanism have interpreted the Separatists primarily in terms of the negatives of dis-sent and non-conformity. In this book, through the figure of Robinson, we have tried to examine Separatism in its own terms, from within as it were. We have discovered that beyond the incessant wrangling over liturgical trifles and nuances of church government lay very real concerns about the nature of authority, the meaning of community, and the extent of mutual responsibility. In an age of innovation the Separatists were—to appropriate a phrase from an eminent opponent of all sectaries, Francis Bacon—"pioneers in the mine of truth." Like all pioneers they have left behind a mixed legacy of accomplishment and failure. Few would wish to transpose their precise model of church reform into the late twentieth century. Yet in an age of increasing diversity, perplexity and shifting values, when the aging institutions of both church and state seem out of touch with the deeper quests of the human spirit, perhaps the Separatist experiment to realize authentic Christian community over against the environing culture may yet have value for the corporate life of the Church. Indeed, may there yet be still more truth and light to break forth from God's Word!

APPENDIX

Robinson's "Admonitio ad Lectorem" appeared in 1616 as the preface to Robert Parker's *magnum opus, De Politeia Ecclesiastica Christi et Hierarchica Opposita*, published posthumously at Frankfort "apud Godefridum Basson." the following is a transcription from the copy on deposit in the British Museum. In subsequent editions of this volume the "Admonitio" was omitted, and it is not included in Ashton's edition of Robinson's collected works. Robinson's authorship is strongly suggested not only by the content, but also by a comment of the contemporary Puritan polemicist Thomas Drakes who quotes from the admonition and refers to its author as "one of the princiall Separatists" (*Early English Dissenters*, vol. 2, 143). Parker, a non-separatist and a frequent interlocutor of Robinson, is often held to have influenced his developing moderation on the question of inter-communion. In the admonition Robinson defends the Separatist position against certain characterizations of Parker, but admits that there are many pious and holy men in the parish churches, "both of the Reformist and Conformist parties, as they are called, whom we also regard as brothers in Christ."

ADMONITIO I. R. AD LECTOREM S V O SUORUMQUE NOMINE

Habes (pie Lector) in hisce *D. Parkeri* scriptis saepiùs factam mentionem *Brownistarum and Separatistarum* quorundam: quos & tanquam reos iniqui schismatis ab Ecclesia Anglicana satis acriter insectatur. Eorum ille sententiam, & praxin non plenè videtur assequutus: sed easdem aessimasse, plus aequo, ex vulgi fama: quae ut saepiùs ficti nuncia, ita nunquam non iniquia miseris hominibus, & temporum injurijs (quas illi sentiunt) expositis.

Et primò lib. I. pag. 101. statuit, Regimen nostrum Ecclesiasticum *Democraticum* esse, quum minimè sit: sed planè Aristocraticum, & presbyteriale. Statum quidem Ecclesiae nos aliquatenus Democraticum esse credimus, at regimen neutiquam: sed e contrà, ut Christi capitis respectu, Monarchicum; sic & administrorum ratione, prorsùs Aristocraticum: ita tamen administrandum à presbyteris (Christi, & suis servis) ut sarta tecta sibi maneat libertas in electionibus, censuris Ecclesiasticis, & reliquis suis privilegijs quibus à Christo capite donata est. Ad secessionem, & separationem nostram ab Ecclesia Anglicana quod attinet; nec ea tam absoluta est, quàm ab Authore innuitur, nec eis praecipuè, quae ponit, innixa fundamentis. Verum quidem est nos separationem instituere ab Ecclesiarum (uti appellant) Provincialium, Diocaesanatum, cathedralium, & parrochialium formali statu; utpote quae & conflatae sunt ex omnibus, & singulis regni subditis sine ullo discrimine, uipaenarum legalium in easdem coactis (quas and ipse *Whitgiftus* (nuper Archiepiscopus Cantuariensis) non tam fatetur, quàm, in rem suam, sedulò inculcat, *Papistis, Atheis, Hypocritis, Ebriosis, Adulteris,* and ejusmodi malè feriatis hominibus oppletas esse:) & insuper Hierarchico Dominico, & libidini proscriptae, and prostitutae. In qua tamen & rerum, & personarum confusione, Dei gratiam, per Evangelium, (quoad capita summa vere fidei Christianae à nonnullis fideliter annunciatum) ita exuberare, & firmiter credimus, & libenter profitemur, ut plurimi in istis caetibus pij, & sancti viri existant, cum reformistae, tum conformistae, (uti vocant,) quos and pro fratribus in Christo habemus, & quibuscum communionem in omnibus licitis (nostro saltem judicio) piè colimus.

Denique non nos propriè, aut praecipuè nosmet sejungimus, propter *Christi disciplinam repudiatum*, aut *corruptam*, (sicuti illi videtur, lib: I cap. 13 and 14.) sed propter disciplinam, and regimen Antichristi receptum, & sancitum statutis regijs, & canonibus Ecclesiasticis: cui nos nosmet ullo modo subijcere religio est. Et quandoquidem Regimen hoc Hierarchicum in hisce Ecclesijs obtinens (ut alibi alij) *Parkerus* ipse, vel in hoc suo doctissimo scripto, & multis verbis asserat, & doceat argumentis, illegitimum, papale, & Antichristianum esse; quae nostra eidem subjectio legitima, & Christiana; aut quae communio in institutis Ecclesiasticis (in quae omnita, & singula, Regimen Ecclesiae se necessariò diffundit) sine hac illicita submissione esse poterit? Nobis certè videre non est, licet maximè velimus, quomodo posterius priori conveniat: ab alijs audire cupimus, qui (quod facilè fieri potest) plus vident: semper parati meliora docentibus, (per Dei gratiam) submissè cedere. Vale.

BIBLIOGRAPHY

PRIMARY SOURCES

Manuscripts

Angus Library, Regent's Park College, Oxford University: Stinton MSS.

British Museum:
  Additional MSS.
  Harleian MSS.
  Lansdowne MSS.

Cambridge University Library:
  Baker MSS.
  Registry Guard Books

Coleman and Rye Library of Local History, Norwich:
  Beechens MS., "History of St. Andrew's Parish"

Norwich and Norfolk Record Office:
  Parish registers of the Diocese of Norwich
  "Great Hospital Account Rolls"

Robinson's Works

"Admonitio ad Lectorem." Preface to Robert Parker, *De Politeia Ecclesiastica Christi et hierarcnica Opposita*, Frankfort, 1616. See Appendix.

"An Answer to a Censorious Epistle." Printed in Joseph Hall, *A common Apologie of the Church of England, against the unjust challenges of the over-just sect commonly called Brownists . . . occasioned by a late Pamphlet, published under the name of "An Answer to a Censorious Epistle," which the reader shall finde in the margent.* London, 1610.

An Answer to John Robinson of Leyden by a Puritan Friend, ed. Champlain Burrage. Harvard Theological Studies, Vol. 9. Cambridge, Mass.: Harvard University, 1920. A transcription of Jones MS. 30, Bodleian Library, Oxford.

Apologia Justa et Necessaria quorundam Christianorum, aeque contumeliose ac communiter dictorum Brownistarum sive Barrowistarum. Leyden, 1619. English translation by Robinson: *A Just and Necessary Apology of certain Christians . . . .* Leyden, 1625.

An Appeal on truths behalfe. Leyden, 1624.

"A Brief Answer to the Exceptions of Francis Johnson." Printed in Ainsworth, *An animadversion to Mr Clyftons advertisement.* London, 1613.

A Briefe Catechism concerning Church Government, an appendix to Mr Perkins Six Principles of the Christian Religion. Leyden, 1623.

A Defence of the doctrine propounded by the Synode at Dort, against I. Murton. Leyden, 1624.

A Justification of Separation from the Church of England. Amsterdam, 1610.

Letter to William Ames. Printed with a reply in Christopher Lawne, *The Prophane Schism of the Brownists.* London, 1612.

Letters to Edwin Sandys, Sir John Worsingham, John Carver, the Church at Plymouth, William Brewster, William Bradford. *Plymouth Church Records,* 1, 32-54.

A manumission to a manuduction. Leyden, 1615. Reprinted in *Collections,* Massachusetts Historical Society, ser. 4, vol. 1, 165-94.

Observations divine and morall for the furthering of knowledg, and virtue. Leyden, 1625.

Of religious communion private, and publique. Leyden, 1614.

The Peoples Plea for the Exercise of Prophecy against Mr John Yates his Monopolie. Leyden, 1618.

Seven Articles to the Privy Council of England. Printed in *Creeds and Platforms,* 81-92.

A treatise on the lawfulness of hearing the ministers of the Church of England. Leyden, 1634.

The Works of John Robinson, ed. Robert Ashton. 3 vols. London: John Snow, 1851.

Sixteenth and Seventeenth Century Printed Books

Ainsworth, Henry. *A Censure upon a dialogue.* N.p., 1623.

_____. *Counterpoyson.* Amsterdam, 1608.

_____. *A reply to a pretended Christian plea.* N.p., 1620.

Baillie, Robert. *A Dissuasive from the Errours of the Time.* London, 1645.

Bernard, Richard. *Christian advertisements and counsels of peace.* London, 1608.

_____. *Plaine evidences: the Church of England is apostolicall.* London, 1610.

Bredwell, Stephen. *The Rasing of the Foundations of Brownisme.* London, 1588.

Edwards, Thomas. *Gangraena.* London, 1646.

Fairlambe, Peter. *The Recantation of a Brownist.* London, 1606.

Golden Remains of the Ever Memorable Mr. John Hales. London, 1673.

Goodwin, Thomas, et al. *An Apologeticall Narration.* London, 1643.

Helwys, Thomas. *A Short and Plaine Proofe by the Word and workes of God that Gods decree is not the cause off anye Mans sinne or Condemnation and that All Men are redeamed by Christ.* Amsterdam, 1612.

Hoornbeek, Jan. *Summa Controversarium Religionis.* Rheims, 1658.

Johnson, Francis. *A Brief Treatise . . . against two errours of the Anabaptists.* Amsterdam, 1609.

_____. *A short Treatise Concerning the exposition of those words of Christ, Tell the Church, etc.* Amsterdam, 1611.

Johnson, George. *A discours of some troubles in the banished English Church at Amsterdam.* Amsterdam, 1603.

Murton, John. *A Discription of What God Hath Predestined Concerning Man, in His Creation, Transgressions, Regeneration, etc.* London, 1620.

Paget, John. *An Arrow against the Separation of the Brownists.* Amsterdam, 1618.

A parte of a register, contayinge sundrie memorable matters, written by divers godly and learned in our time, which stand for, and desire the reformation of our Church. Middelburgh, 1593.

Travers, Walter. *A Full and Plaine Declaration of Ecclesiasticall Discipline.* London, 1574.

Winslow, Edward. *Hypocrisie Vnmasked.* London, 1646.

Printed Primary Sources

Ayre, John, ed. *The Works of John Whitgift.* 3 vols. Cambridge University, 1851-1853.

Bradford, William. "A Diologue or 3rd Conference," *Proceedings of the Massachusetts Historical Society.* Vol. 11. Boston, 1870.

————. *Of Plymouth Plantation,* ed. Samuel Eliot Morison. New York: Knopf, 1952.

Bruce, J. and T. T. Perowne, eds. *The Correspondence of Matthew Parker.* Cambridge: Cambridge University, 1853.

Burrage, Champlain. *The Early English Dissenters in the Light of Recent Research.* 2 vols. New York: Russell and Russell, 1912.

Carlson, Leland H., ed. *The Writings of Henry Barrow, 1587-1590.* London: Allen and Unwin, 1962.

————. *The Writings of Henry Barrow, 1590-1591.* London: Allen and Unwin, 1966.

————. *The Writings of John Greenwood, 1587-1590.* London: Allen and Unwin, 1962.

————. *The Writings of John Greenwood and Henry Barrow, 1591-1593.* London: Allen and Unwin, 1970.

Eekhof, A. *Three Unknown Documents concerning the Pilgrim Fathers in Holland.* The Hague: Martinus Nijhoff, 1920.

Foxe, John. *Actes and Monuments of the English Martyrs,* ed. George Townsend. 8 vols. London: Clarke, 1837-1841.

Frere, W. H. and C. E. Douglas, eds. *Puritan Manifestoes: A Study of the Origin of the Puritan Revolt.* London: S.P.C.K., 1954.

Lumpkin, W. L., ed. *Baptist Confessions of Faith.* Chicago: Judson, 1959.

Murdock, Kenneth, ed. *Cotton Mather: Magnalia Christi Americana.* Cambridge, Mass.: Harvard University, 1977.

Nicholas, James, ed. *The Writings of Arminius.* 3 vols. Buffalo, N.Y.: Derby, Miller and Orton, 1853.

Nicholson, William, ed. *The Remains of Edmund Grindal.* Cambridge: Cambridge University, 1843.

Peel, Albert, ed. *The Seconde Parte of a Register being a Calendar of Manuscripts under that title intended for publication by the Puritans about 1593, and now in Dr Williams's Library,* London. 2 vols. Cambridge: Cambridge University, 1915.

————, and Leland H. Carlson, eds. *Cartwrightiana.* London: Allen and Unwin, 1951.

————. *The Writings of Robert Harrison and Robert Browne.* London: Allen and Unwin, 1953.

Plymouth Church Records, 1620-1859. Vol. 1. New York: Wilson, 1920.

Porter, H. C., ed. *Puritanism in Tudor England.* Colombia, S.C.: University of South Carolina, 1971.

Robinson, Hastings. *Original Letters relative to the English Reformation.* 2 vols. Cambridge: Cambridge University, 1846-1847.

_____. *The Zürich Letters.* 2 vols. Cambridge: Cambridge University, 1842.

Schaff, Philip. *The Creeds of Christendom.* 3 vols. New York: Harper and Brothers, 1877.

Walker, Williston, ed. *The Creeds and Platforms of Congregationalism.* Boston: Scribner's, 1893.

Whitley, W. T. *The Works of John Smyth.* 2 vols. Cambridge: Cambridge University, 1915.

Wynter, Philip, ed. *The Works of Joseph Hall.* Oxford: Clarendon, 1863.

Young, Alexander, ed. *Chronicles of the Pilgrim Fathers of the Colony of Plymouth.* Boston: Little and Brown, 1841.

Ziff, Larzar, ed. *John Cotton on the Churches of New England.* Cambridge, Mass.: Harvard University, 1968.

SECONDARY SOURCES

Books

Arber, Edward. *The Story of the Pilgrim Fathers, 1606-1623 A.D.* London: Ward and Downey, 1897.

Avis, Paul D. L. *The Church in the Theology of the Reformers.* Atlanta: John Knox, 1981.

Babbage, Stuart B. *Puritanism and Richard Bancroft.* London: S.P.C.K., 1962.

Bangs, Carl. *Arminius: A Study in the Dutch Reformation.* Nashville: Abingdon, 1971.

Bartlett, Robert M. *The Pilgrim Way.* Philadelphia: Pilgrim, 1971.

Brown, John. *The Pilgrim Fathers of New England.* New York: Revell, 1896.

Burgess, Walter H. *John Robinson: The Pastor of the Pilgrims.* New York: Harcourt, Brace, and Howe, 1920.

_____. *John Smith the Se-Baptist, Thomas Helwys and the First Baptist Church in England.* London: Clarke, 1911.

Brook, Benjamin. *The Lives of the Puritans.* 3 vols. London: Black, 1813.

Burrage, Champlain. *The Church Covenant Idea.* Philadelphia: American Baptist Publication Society, 1904.

_____. *The True Story of Robert Browne.* London: Frowde, 1906.

Carlson, Leland H. *Martin Marprelate, Gentleman.* San Marino, Calif.: Huntington Library, 1981.

Carter, Alice C. *The English Reformed Church in Amsterdam.* Amsterdam: Scheltma and Holkema, 1964.

Christianson, Paul. *Reformers and Babylon: English apocalyptic visions from the reformation to the eve of the civil war.* Toronto: University of Toronto, 1978.

Collinson, Patrick. *Archbishop Grindal, 1519-1583: The Struggle for a Reformed Church.* Berkeley: University of California Press, 1979.

_____. *The Elizabethan Puritan Movement.* Berkeley: University of California, 1967.

Coolidge, John S. *The Pauline Renaissance in England: Puritanism and the Bible.* Oxford: Clarendon, 1970.

Cragg, Gerald R. *Freedom and Authority: A Study of English Thought in the Early Seventeenth Century.* Philadelphia: Westminster, 1975.

Dale, R. W. *History of English Congregationalism.* London: Hodder and Stoughton, 1907.

Davies, Horton. *The Worship of the English Puritans.* Glasgow: Glasgow University, 1948.

Davis, Ozora S. *John Robinson: The Pilgrim Pastor.* Boston: Pilgrim, 1903.

Dexter, Henry Martyn. *The Congregationalism of the Last Three Hundred Years as Seen in Its Literature.* New York: Harper and Brothers, 1880.

————, and Morton Dexter. *The England and Holland of the Pilgrims.* Boston: Houghton, Mifflin and Co., 1905.

Dillon, Francis. *A Place for Habitation: The Pilgrim Fathers and Their Quest.* London: Hutchinson, 1973.

Eekhof, A. and Edgar F. Romig. *John Robinson.* The Hague: Martinus Nijhoff, 1928.

Geller, Lawrence and Peter Gomes. *The Books of the Pilgrims.* New York: Gardland Publishing Inc., 1975.

George, Charles and Katherine. *The Protestant Mind of the English Reformation, 1570-1640.* Princeton, N.J.: Princeton University, 1961.

Greaves, Richard L. *Society and Religion in Elizabethan England.* Minneapolis: University of Minnesota Press, 1981.

Hall, David D. *The Faithful Shepherd: A History of the New England Ministry in the Seventeenth Century.* Chapel Hill, N.C.: University of North Carolina, 1972.

Hanbury, Benjamin. *Historical Memorials Relating to the Independents or Congregationalists.* 2 vols. London: Fischer, 1839.

Horst, Irvin B. *The Radical Brethren: Anabaptism and the English Reformation to 1558.* Nieuwkoop: De Graaf, 1972.

Jordan. W. K. *The Development of Religious Toleration in England.* 2 vols. London: Allen and Unwin, 1932.

————. *Edward VI: The Young King.* Cambridge, Mass.: Harvard University, 1968.

Kendall, R. T. *Calvin and English Calvinism to 1649.* London: Oxford University, 1979.

Knappen, M. M. *Tudor Puritanism: A Chapter in the History of Idealism.* Chicago: University of Chicago, 1939.

Langdon, George D. *Pilgrim Colony: A History of New Plymouth.* New Haven: Yale University, 1966.

Marchant, Ronald A. *The Puritans and the Church Courts in the Diocese of York, 1560-1642.* Cambridge: Cambridge University, 1960.

Marsden, J. B. *The History of the Early Puritans.* London: Hamilton, Adams, and Co., 1853.

Marshall, George N., ed. *The Church of the Pilgrim Fathers.* Boston: Beacon, 1950.

Martin, Raymond G. *John Robinson (1575-1625).* London: Independent, 1961.

Mayor, Stephen. *The Lord's Supper in Early English Dissent.* London: Epworth, 1972.

Miller, Perry. *Orthodoxy in Massachusetts.* Cambridge, Mass.: Harvard University, 1933.

Milward, Peter. *Religious Controversies of the Elizabethan Age: A Survey of Printed Sources.* Lincoln, Neb.: University of Nebraska, 1977.

Morgan, Edmund. *Visible Saints: The History of a Puritan Idea.* Ithaca, N.Y.: Cornell University, 1963.

Neal, Daniel. *The History of the Puritans, or Protestant Non-Conformists,* 5 vols. Boston: Ewer, 1817. Original edition, 1731.

Neale, J. E. *Elizabeth I and her Parliaments, 1584-1601.* New York: Norton, 1958.

Nuttall, G. F. *The Holy Spirit in Puritan Faith and Experience.* Oxford: Blackwell, 1946.

———. *Visible Saints: the Congregational Way, 1640-1660.* Oxford: Blackwell, 1957.

Peel, Albert. *The First Congregational Churches: New Light on Separatist Congregations in London, 1567-81.* Cambridge: Cambridge University, 1920.

———. *The Noble Army of Congregational Martyrs.* London: Independent Press, 1948.

Plooij, Daniel. *The Pilgrim Fathers from a Dutch Point of View.* New York: New York University, 1932.

Porter, H. C. *Reformation and Reaction in Tudor Cambridge.* Cambridge: Cambridge University, 1958.

Powicke, F. J. *Henry Barrow, Separatist and the Exiled Church of Amsterdam.* London: Clarke, 1900.

———. *John Robinson, 1575-1625.* London: Hodder and Stoughton, 1920.

Punchard, George. *History of Congregationalism from about A.D. 250 to 1616.* Salem, Mass.: Jewett, 1841.

Scheffler, J. de Hoop. *History of the Free Churchmen called the Brownists, Pilgrim Fathers and Baptists in the Dutch Republic, 1581-1701.* Ithaca, N.Y.: Andrus and Church, 1922.

Sprunger, Keith L. *The Learned Dr. William Ames.* Chicago: University of Illinois, 1972.

Strype, John. *Annals of the Reformation.* 4 vols. Oxford: Clarendon, 1824-1828.

———. *Ecclesiastical Memorials.* 3 vols. Oxford: Clarendon, 1820-1840.

Tolmie, Murray. *The Triumph of the Saints: The Separate Churches of London, 1616-1649.* Cambridge: Cambridge University, 1977.

Toon, Peter. *The Pilgrims' Faith.* Reading, England: Bradley and Son, 1970.

Usher, Roland G. *The Reconstruction of the English Church.* 2 vols. New York: Appelton, 1910.

Verburgt, J. W. *Leyden and the Pilgrim Fathers.* Leyden: Pilgrim Fathers Document Center, 1970.

Watts, Michael R. *The Dissenters from the Reformation to the French Revolution.* Oxford: Clarendon, 1978.

White, B. R. *The English Separatist Tradition.* London: Oxford University, 1971.

Williams, George H. *The Radical Reformation.* Philadelphia: Westminster, 1962.

Willison, George F. *Saints and Strangers.* New York: Reynal and Hitchcock, 1945.

Articles

Atkinson, David W. "A Brief Discoverie of the False Church: Henry Barrow's Last Spiritual Statement," *Historical Magazine of the Protestant Episcopal Church* 48 (1979),   265-78.

Avis, P. D. L. " 'The True Church' in Reformation Theology," *Scottish Journal of Theology* 30 (1977), 319-45.

Biggs, Wilfred W. "The Controversy concerning Kneeling in the Lord's Supper—after 1604," *Transactions*, Congregational Historical Society 17 (1952), 51-62.

Booty, John. "Tumult in Cheapside: The Hacket Conspiracy," *Historical Magazine of the Protestant Episcopal Church* 42 (1973), 293-317.

Brachlow, Stephen. "John Robinson and the Lure of Separatism in Pre-Revolutionary England," *Church History* 50 (1981), 288-301.

―――. "More Light on John Robinson and the Separatist Tradition," *Fides et Historia* 13 (1980), 6-22.

Carlson, Leland H. "A Corpus of Elizabethan Nonconformist Writings," in *Studies in Church History*, ed. G. J. Cuming, vol. 2, 297-309. London: Nelson, 1965.

Carter, Alice C. "John Robinson and the Dutch Reformed Church," in *Studies in Church History*, ed. G. J. Cuming, vol. 3, 232-41. Leiden: Brill, 1966.

Christianson, Paul. "Reformers and the Church of England under Elizabeth I and the Early Stuarts," *Journal of Ecclesiastical History* 31 (1980), 463-82.

Collinson, Patrick, "Towards a Broader Understanding of the Early Dissenting Tradition," in C. Robert Cole and Michael E. Moody, eds., *The Dissenting Tradition: Essays for Leland H. Carlson*. Athen, Ohio: Ohio University, 1975, 3-38.

Cowell, Henry J. "The French-Walloon Church at Glastonbury, 1550-1553," *The Proceedings of the Huguenot Society of London* 13 (1928), 483-515.

Crippen, T. G. "Early Nonconformist Bibliography," *Transactions*, Congregational Historical Society 1 (1901-04), 106-07.

Fenn, William Wallace. "John Robinson's Farewell Address," *Harvard Theological Review* 13 (1920), 236-51.

Forman, Charles C. "John Robinson: Exponent of the Middle Way," *Proceedings of the Unitarian Historical Society* 17 (1973-75), 22-29.

Foster, Herbert Darling. "Liberal Calvinism: The Remonstrants at the Synod of Dort in 1618," *Harvard Theological Review* 16 (1923), 1-37.

Grayson, Christopher. "James I and the Religious Crisis in the United Provinces, 1613-19," in Derek Baker, ed., *Reform and Reformation: England and the Continent, c 1500-c 1750*. Oxford: Blackwell, 1979, 195-219.

Greaves, Richard L. "The Origins and Early Development of English Covenant Thought," *The Historian* 31 (1968), 21-35.

Hargrave, O. T. "The Freewillers in the English Reformation," *Church History* 37 (1968), 271-80.

Hitchcock, James. "Early Separatist Burial Practice," *Transactions*, Congregational Historical Society 20 (1966), 105-06.

Huxtable, J. "The Spirituality of John Robinson," *The Month*, no. 236 (1975), 152-54.

Kingdon, Robert M. "Peter Martyr Vermigli and the Marks of the True Church," in F. F. Church and Timothy George, eds., *Continuity and Discontinuity in Church History: Essays Presented to George Huntston Williams on the Occasion of his 65th Birthday*. Leiden: Brill, 1979, 198-214.

Lake, Peter. "The Dilemma of the Establishment Puritan: the Cambridge Heads and the case of Francis Johnson and Cuthbert Bainbrigg," *Journal of Ecclesiastical History* 29 (1978), 23-25.

Matthews, Albert. "The Term Pilgrim Fathers," *Publications*, Colonial Society of Massachusetts 17 (1915), 380-92.

Muller, Richard A. "Perkins' *A Golden Chaine*: Predestinarian System or Schematized Ordo Salutis?" *Sixteenth Century Journal* 9 (1978), 69-81.

Nicole, Roger. "The Doctrine of the Definite Atonement in the Heidelberg Catechism," *The Gordon Review* 7 (1964), 138-45.

Owen, H. Gareth. "A Nursery of Elizabethan Nonconformity, 1567-1572," *Journal of Ecclesiastical History* 17 (1966), 65-76.

Packard, A. Appleton. "A Reformer of the Reformed." *Congregational Quarterly* 30 (1952), 154-68.

Parker, T. M. "Arminianism and Laudianism in Seventeenth-Century England," in *Studies in Church History*, ed. C. W. Dugmore, vol. 4, 20-34. Leiden: Brill, 1964.

Paul, Robert S. "Henry Jacob and Seventeenth-Century Puritanism," *The Hartford Quarterly* 7 (1967), 92-113.

Payne, E. A. "Contacts between Mennonites and Baptists," *Foundations* 4 (1961), 39-55.

Peters, Robert. "John Hales and the Synod of Dort," in *Studies in Church History*, eds. C. J. Cuming and L. G. D. Baker, vol. 7, 277-88. Cambridge: Cambridge University, 1971.

Platt, John. "Eirenical Anglicans at the Synod of Dort," in Derek Baker, ed., *Reform and Reformation: England and the Continent*, c. 1500-c. 1750. Oxford: Blackwell, 1979, 221-43.

Powicke, F. J. "John Robinson and the Beginnings of the Pilgrim Movement," *Harvard Theological Review* 13 (1920), 252-89.

————. "Lists of the Early Separatists," *Transactions*, Congregational Historical Society 1 (1901-04), 141-43.

Reinitz, Richard. "The Separatist Background of Roger Williams' Argument for Religious Toleration," in *Typology and Early American Literature*, ed. Sacvan Bercovitch (Amherst, Mass.: University of Massachusetts, 1972, 107-37.

Russell, Conrad. "Arguments for Religious Unity in England, 1530-1650," *Journal of Ecclesiastical History* 18 (1967), 201-26.

Selement, George. "The Covenant Theology of English Separatism and the Separation of Church and State," *Journal of the American Academy of Religion* 41 (1973), 66-74.

Smith, D. C. "Robert Browne, Independent," *Church History* 6 (1937), 289-349.

Spalding, James C. "Restitution as a Normative Factor for Puritan Dissent," *Journal of the American Academy of Religion* 44 (1976), 47-62.

Sprunger, Keith L. "Other Pilgrims in Leiden: Hugh Goodyear and the English Reformed Church," *Church History* 41 (1972), 46-60.

Von Rohr, John. "The Congregationalism of Henry Jacob," *Transactions*, Congregational Historical Society 19 (1962), 107-17.

————. "*Extra Ecclesiam Nulla Salus*: An Early Congregational Version," *Church History* 36 (1967), 107-21.

White, B. R. "A Puritan Work by Robert Browne," *Baptist Quarterly* 18 (1959-60), 109-17.

Williams, George H. " 'Congregationalist' Luther and the Free Churches," *Lutheran Quarterly* 18 (1967), 283-95.

Dissertations

Ashmall, Donald. "John Smyth, John Robinson and the Church." Unpublished M.Div. thesis, Andover Newton Theological School. 1969.

Brachlow, Stephen. "Puritan Theology and Radical Churchmen in Pre-Revolutionary England, with Special Reference to Henry Jacob and John Robinson." Unpublished Ph.D. dissertation, Oxford University, 1978.

Collinson, Patrick. "The Puritan Classical Movement in the Reign of Elizabeth I." Unpublished Ph.D. dissertation, University of London, 1957.

Davis, Thomas M. "The Traditions of Puritan Typology." Unpublished Ph.D. dissertation, University of Missouri, 1968.

Fraser, Alwyn Ray. "The Magistrate and the Church in the thought of the Elizabethan Separatists." Unpublished M.Litt. thesis, Cambridge University, 1971.

Godfrey, W. Robert. "Tensions Within International Calvinism: The Debate on the Atonement at the Synod of Dort, 1618-1619." Unpublished Ph.D. dissertation, Stanford University, 1974.

Goehring, Walter R. "Henry Jacob (1563-1624) and the Separatists." Unpublished Ph.D. dissertation, New York University, 1975.

Hargrave, O. T. "The Doctrine of Predestination in the English Reformation." Unpublished Ph.D. dissertation, Vanderbilt University, 1966.

Hobson, P. A. "The Pilgrim Pastor: A Compilation of the Teachings of John Robinson on Reformed Churchmanship." Unpublished M.A. thesis, University of Durham, 1958.

Maruyama, Tadataka. "The Reform of the True Church: The Ecclesiology of Theodore Beza." Unpublished Th.D. dissertation, Princeton University, 1973.

Morey, Verne D. "The Brownist Churches: A Study in English Separatism, 1553-1630." Unpublished Ph.D. dissertation, Harvard University, 1954.

Pamp, Frederic E. "Studies in the Origins of English Arminianism." Unpublished Ph.D. dissertation, Harvard University, 1950.

Rickwood, D. L. "The Origin and Decline of the Stranger Community of Norwich (with Special Reference to the Dutch Congregation), 1565-1700." Unpublished M.A. thesis, University of East Anglia, 1967.

Runzo, Jean. "Communal Discipline in the Early Anabaptist Communities of Switzerland, South and Central Germany, Austria, and Moravia, 1525-1550." Unpublished Ph.D. dissertation, University of Michigan, 1977.

White, B. R. "The Development of the Doctrine of the Church among the English Separatists with especial reference to Robert Browne and John Smyth." Unpublished Ph.D. dissertation, Oxford University, 1960.

Worthley, Harold. "The Lay Offices of the Particular Churches of Massachusetts, 1620-1755." Unpublished Ph.D. dissertation, Harvard University, 1970.

Yarbrough, Slayden A. "Henry Jacob, a Moderate Separatist and His Influence on Early English Congregationalism." Unpublished Ph.D. dissertation, Baylor University, 1972.

INDEX OF SUBJECTS

INDEX OF PERSONS